ช

D0274464

WOMEN IN MEDIEVAL ENGLISH SOCIETY

Edited by
P.J.P. GOLDBERG

SUTTON PUBLISHING

First published in the United Kingdom in 1992 as *Woman is a Worthy Wight: Women in English Medieval Society c. 1200–1500* by
Alan Sutton Publishing Limited, an imprint of
Sutton Publishing Limited · Phoenix Mill · Stroud
Gloucestershire · GL5 2BU

First published in this edition in 1997

British Library Cataloguing in Publication Data
A catalogue record for this book is available from the British Library

ISBN 0-7509-1640-0 (case)
ISBN 0-7509-1477-7 (paper)

Cover illustration: detail from MS. Bodl. 764, f. 41v (The Bodleian Library, Oxford)

 ALAN SUTTON™ and SUTTON™ are the
trade marks of Sutton Publishing Limited

Typeset in 10/11 Goudy.
Typesetting and origination by
Sutton Publishing Limited.
Printed in Great Britain by
WBC Limited, Bridgend.

Contents

List of Tables

List of Figures

Preface

This is a new edition of a collection of essays that were first published under the title *Woman is a Worthy Wight: Women in English Society c. 1200–1500.*[1] It is a great delight to me that the collection is now being reissued and may thus reach a wider audience. The essays have not been changed, but there has been no need for revision. Individual authors would probably elaborate on some of their ideas, and in some cases have been able to elsewhere, but the arguments as articulated here have not been superseded.[2] Despite the continued outpouring of books and articles on topics related to the study of medieval women over the past few years, there remains a paucity of scholarship that is rooted in archival research. Biller's work on the questions asked of women by priests at confession, Cullum's study of patterns of charitable giving by and for women, and Gilchrist's spatial analysis of nunneries remain exciting pioneering approaches. No one has yet challenged in print Graham's imaginative re-reading of manor court evidence relating to women's brewing and baking activities, and the case for a distinctive north-west European pattern of servanthood and marriage, reflected in chapters by Biller, Smith, and myself, though yet to be universally accepted, seems increasingly to be regarded as the orthodox perspective.[3]

This is not to imply that scholarship has stood still.[4] An important collection of biographical essays on London widows has illuminated the lives of some individual aristocratic widows, but also tanners' widows.[5] Jennifer Ward has likewise presented a general survey of noblewomen and, even more recently, a collection of documents in translation relating to aristocratic and gentry women.[6] Aristocratic widows again feature prominently in a collection of essays edited by Susan Walker which also contains an important essay by Richard Helmholz on married women's testamentary rights.[7] Other collections of translated source material are Alcuin Blamire's edition of anti-feminist and misogynist literature, Shannon McSheffrey's translation of selected marriage cases from later fifteenth-century London, and my own edition of material relating to the lives of women below the level of the aristocracy.[8]

Little new work has appeared on peasant, artisan, or labouring women, though we should note Ruth Karras's study of prostitution, Caroline Barron's article on women's education in London, and Felicity

Riddy's work on the Middle English didactic text, 'How the Goodwife taught her Daughter'.[9] Perhaps the liveliest area of research remains the field of piety and devotion. Although not specifically concerned with England and focused primarily on the experience of women mystics rather than the experience of women more generally, Caroline Walker Bynum's volume of essays, *Fragmentation and Redemption*, is of particular importance.[10] Patricia Cullum and Mary Erler have both drawn attention to those mercantile and gentry widows who took vows of chastity.[11] Valuable work has also been done on women's reading and there is now a growing appreciation that aristocratic and mercantile women had access to a vernacular literary devotional culture.[12] Katherine Lewis's important study of the cult of St Katherine should also be noted.[13] The picture that emerges from this scholarship is one that allows women, particularly from the middling and upper echelons of society, rather fuller and more satisfying devotional roles within the parameters of late medieval catholicism than has hitherto been supposed. Indeed Shannon McSheffrey's account of the participation of women in Lollardy, the only heretical movement to have had any real following in medieval England, cogently argues against the view that heresy appealed to women because alienated from Catholicism. She suggests rather that Lollardy attacked precisely those aspects of popular devotion, such as eucharistic devotion and the cult of saints, that appealed to women.[14]

It may finally be noted that although recent scholarship has done little to take further some of the social history themes of the present collection, some exciting new questions are being posed. This is especially true in respect of gender. The work of Joan Cadden on sex difference provides an important insight into contemporary learned discourses on this subject.[15] Caroline Bynum's work has already been cited and we should note the collection of essays edited by Sarah Kay and Miri Rubin.[16] Kim Phillips is currently completing a study of maidenhood which grapples with the question of femininity.[17] At the same time work is beginning on medieval concepts of masculinity and this will no doubt help clarify our understanding of gender relations. But as always, new scholarship generates new questions. The study of medieval women is very much alive and very lively. It is within this spirit that this new edition of these essays is presented.

P.J.P.G. 1997

1   The original title, used for a conference held in Cambridge in 1988 at which versions of several of the present chapters were first given, is a quotation from an early sixteenth-century lyric 'Women are Worthy', one of only a handful that is neither ironic nor misogynistic in tone. The lyric praises women as hard working and caring, but laments

that they have only 'care and woe'. I am grateful to the Nuffield Foundation for funding the Cambridge conference.

2   Roberta Gilchrist has elaborated her ideas in her *Gender and Material Culture: 'the Archaeology of Religious Women* (London, 1993) and I likewise in *Women, Work, and Life Cycle: Women and Work in York and Yorkshire c. 1300–1520* (Oxford, 1992). P.H. Cullum's *Hospitals and Charity in Medieval England* (Manchester, forthcoming) will place her work on women and charity within the wider context of welfare and charitable provision.

3   Kathy Troop of the University of Waikiko has challenged Graham's interpretation in a conference paper, but her work has not yet been published.

4   The following discussion does not claim to be an exhaustive bibliographical survey, but rather a selection of the more important writings that are rooted in primary research and which, in most instances, draw upon English case studies.

5   C.M. Barron and A.F. Sutton, eds., *Medieval London Widows 1300–1500* (London, 1994).

6   J.C. Ward, *English Noblewomen in the Later Middle Ages* (Harlow, 1992); ead., ed., *Women of the English Nobility and Gentry, 1066–1500* (Manchester, 1995).

7   S.S. Walker, ed., *Wife and Widow in Medieval England* (Ann Arbor, 1993).

8   A. Blamires, ed., *Woman Defamed and Woman Defended* (Oxford, 1992); S. McSheffrey, *Love and Marriage in Late Medieval London* (Kalamazoo, 1995); P.J.P. Goldberg, ed., *Women in England c. 1275–1525: Documentary Sources* (Manchester , 1995).

9   R.M. Karras, *Common Women: Prostitution and Sexuality in Medieval England* (New York, 1995); C.M. Barron, 'The Education and Training of Girls in Fifteenth-Century London', in D.E.S. Dunn, ed., *Courts, Counties and the Capital in the Later Middle Ages* (Stroud, 1996), pp. 139–53; F.J. Riddy, 'Mother Knows Best: Reading Social Change in a Courtesy Text', *Speculum* 71 (1996), pp. 68–96. Research in these areas has not dried up however. Mavis Mate is currently working on English peasant women and Cordelia Beattie is at an early stage of research into the single woman in late medieval England.

10   C.W. Bynum, *Fragmentation and Redemption* (New York, 1992). See especially 'The Female Body and Religious Practice in the Late Middle Ages', pp. 181–238.

11   M.C. Erler, 'English Vowed Women at the end of the Middle Ages', *Medieval Studies* 57 (1995), pp. 155–203; P.H. Cullum, 'Vowesses and Female Lay Piety in the Province of York, 1350–1530', *Northern History* 32 (1996), pp. 21–41.

12   Of particular importance are the essays by Julia Boffey, Carol Meale, and Felicity Riddy in C. Meale, ed., *Women and Literature in Britain* (Cambridge, 1993). See also Anne Dutton, 'Women's Use of Religious Literature in Late Medieval England' (unpublished University of York D.Phil. thesis, 1996).

13   K. Lewis, 'The Cult of St Katherine of Alexandria in Late Medieval England' (unpublished University of York D.Phil., 1997). This argues that St Katherine served as a role model for a variety of groups, not least young women.

14   S. McSheffrey, *Gender and Heresy: Men and Women in Lollard Communities 1420–1530* (Philadelphia, 1995).

15   J. Cadden, *Meanings of Sex Difference in the Middle Ages: Medicine, Science, and Culture* (Cambridge, 1993).

16   S. Kay and M. Rubin, eds., *Framing Medieval Bodies* (Manchester, 1994).

17   K.M. Phillips, 'The Medieval Maiden: Young Womanhood in Late Medieval England' (unpublished University of York D.Phil. thesis, forthcoming 1997). Noël James, Katherine Lewis, and Kim Phillips are at present compiling a collection of essays on the subject of young womanhood.

Abbreviations

Annales: ESC	*Annales: Economies Sociétés Civilisations*
BIHR	Borthwick Institute of Historical Research, York
BL	British Library, London
CAD	*Calendar of Ancient Deeds*
CCR	*Calendar of Close Rolls*
CFR	*Calendar of Fine Rolls*
CPR	*Calendar of Patent Rolls*
CROS	Staffordshire County Record Office, Stafford
EETS	Early English Text Society
PRO	Public Record Office
ser.	series
SRS	*Staffordshire Record Society, Collections for a History of Staffordshire*
YML	York Minster Library

Place of publication is London unless stated otherwise.

Introduction

Until comparatively recently most history was written in terms of the activities of a (predominantly male) élite. In part this was a product of the view that history was about Great Events and Great Men. It was also a consequence of the particular range of sources that were known to scholars. The growth of interest in social history and, more recently the revival of interest in women's history have prompted scholars to ask new questions of well-known source material, but also to search for new or neglected sources. There has indeed followed a flowering of scholarly studies devoted to aspects of medieval womens' history drawing upon a wide range of records, be they saints' lives, coroners' rolls, town ordinances, manor court rolls, wills or tax returns. In this respect this present collection of essays will be viewed by some as just another product of a growing and fashionable trend. Such a reaction would be to see scholarship on the lives of medieval women as at best an interesting sidelight on the past. It is the contention here, however, that it is not possible to understand the structure and working of medieval society without exploring the lives of both women and men, a point made forcefully by both Archer and Smith in their chapters. Most recent books on medieval women have, moreover, tended either to focus on relatively narrow subject areas or to range very widely across both space and time. The result is that we now have several book-length studies of medieval women religious and mystics of the High Middle Ages, a few monographs on women in medieval town society, and still less on peasant women.[1] This is perhaps insufficient basis for any more general synthesis and works that make such claims must necessarily deliver less than they claim. This collection focuses specifically on later medieval England, but still brings together essays spanning a consciously wide spectrum of society and social issues.

Over the past decade or more the study of English social history has been transformed by the work of demographic historians. They have been able to throw new light on such issues as the structure of the family and of households, age at marriage, and patterns of migration. Much of this work has been dependent upon the survival of parish listings and of parish registers and is thus confined to the period after 1538. As Smith remarks in his chapter, the medievalist is not so fortunate in respect of the sources available and there is nothing directly compatible to the Tuscan *catasto* or tax survey of 1427. He has, however, elsewhere drawn upon a range of sources, not least poll tax evidence, to suggest a greater degree of continuity in terms of household and marriage regimes from the late Middle Ages into the era of parish registration than has often been supposed.[2] More substantive evidence for such a distinctive marriage regime characterised by late, companionate (i.e. at like ages) marriage from at least the second half of the fourteenth century is provided by my study of data relating to persons making depositions within the York Consistory, mostly in respect of matrimonial litigation. The evidence further suggests that many young people spent some of their teens or early adulthood prior to marriage working as servants in the households of others.

Smith draws upon this evidence for adolescent 'life-cycle' service among females in late medieval England to demonstrate and further elucidate the distinctiveness of this northwest European pattern from that apparent in Northern Italy at the same period, and to comment on the demographic implications of these contrasting household systems. In Tuscany and perhaps more widely, he argues, service was not a state preparatory to marriage and the responsibilities of householding, but something of a 'last resort' for women who were unable to find marriage partners. Female service thus did not underpin a late marriage regime, as in England, but merely accommodated the losers within, what was for women, an early marriage regime. This, however, represents but one aspect of broader cultural differences that, despite the attraction for some medievalists of the idea of Europe as a coherent and culturally homogeneous unit, distinguished northwestern from Mediterranean Europe. Biller takes this theme as the starting point for his own chapter. This last makes striking use of pastoral manuals to suggest differing regional concerns and emphases, themselves reinforced or even partly shaped by the use of such manuals for the purpose of instructing the laity, regarding matters such as marriage formation, maternal care, sexual double standards, prostitution or even dress.

The northwestern manuals, for example, deriving from a culture associated with late, companionate marriage, appear to show much more interest in marital affection. The southern manuals, associated with a culture of early and arranged marriages for women, place more emphasis on the question of the canonical minimum age of marriage and the role of marriage-brokers. Given, moreover, that women were absorbed into their husbands' families and often lived with their in-laws, questions directed at wives concerning their relations with their husbands' parents and wider kin are less surprising in this regional context. Interesting also is the northwestern concern with the care of infants and emphasis on the importance of maternal breast-feeding. This contrasts with the comparative silence in manuals from a culture that appears to have accepted as normal the practice of farming infants out to wet-nurses and the abandonment of infants to hospitals. The comparatively sympathetic treatment of prostitutes in northwestern manuals also deserves comment. Evidence relating prostitution from later medieval England suggests that it was much less institutional than was true of regions of southern Europe. There, in the context of sexual double standards, but a high premium on female 'honour', prostitution was regarded almost as a public service. 'Public' women were ideally confined to duly regulated brothels and little allowance was made for their reintegration into respectable society.[3] In England women appear to have engaged in prostitution out of economic need on a freer and more informal basis.[4] The corollary may have been a greater interest in persuading such women to penance and back into society.

Another theme noted by Biller from northwestern manuals concerns the abuse of canon law in respect of marriage litigation. The records of litigation in the church court have been used by historians of canon law both to explore the influence of the Church on society through the judicial enforcement of canonical teaching and to determine how the canons were interpreted in practice. The law on marriage has attracted particular attention recently.[5] The Church had jurisdiction over marriage and what constituted a valid marriage was defined by canon law. Consent by the couple alone was the essential element. This might be by words of present consent or by words of future consent, which last was made immediately binding if the contract was subsequently consummated. Such contracts were canonically valid so long as there were no lawful impediments, e.g. the couple were related within forbidden degrees or one or both parties were under age, and could be enforced within the Church courts if a minimum of two witnesses could be found. The ability of couples to form valid marriages even without parental consent, with the minimum of witnesses, and wherever was convenient helps explain the Church's concern to enforce publicity through the reading of banns in a region where arranged marriages were perhaps not the norm, but also left considerable scope for valid contracts subsequently to be broken by mutual consent or alternatively to give rise to argument.

Any dispute as to the validity of a contract, any attempt by a jilted lover to enforce a contract of marriage, or any attempt to dissolve a marriage on the grounds that it contravened canon law was liable to result in litigation within the Church courts.[6] The relationship between the tiny minority of marriages that came before the scrutiny of the courts and have left evidence in the form of depositions and the majority of marriages that were never the subject of litigation must, however, be a matter for conjecture. It could be argued that disputed marriages by their nature are atypical and can tell us little about the ordinary pattern of marriage and marriage formation. On the other hand it can be argued that problems inherent in disputed marriages are extreme manifestations of the tensions inherent in the formation of most marriages given the necessarily conflicting interests of parents, children, and the wider community.

Using matrimonial litigation within the consistory of York, it is possible to explore some of these tensions. The case argued in this collection is that the degree of initiative allowed to young women in terms of courtship and choice of marriage partner was influenced by the availability of what may be termed economic niches within the local economy. In town society during the comparatively buoyant decades of the later fourteenth and earlier fifteenth centuries many adolescents, female and male alike, found employment away from their natal homes as servants. Still other young women found independent employment as spinsters, carders, seamstresses, and petty retailers, or as wage labour in a wide variety of crafts.[7] Such young people were comparatively unconstrained either by parents or employers in their courtship. Numbers of couples appear indeed to have first met whilst in service and were married with their employers' blessings. The greater focus of agrarian society on the economy of the family holding meant, however, that the opportunities for daughters of landholding peasants to find niches away from the natal family were much more limited. Daughters of prosperous peasant farmers were particularly likely to remain at home until they married and, like their aristocratic cousins, were under much more pressure to accommodate parental priorities centred around social standing and the descent of property than their poorer neighbours or their urban sisters.[8] It may also be that young women in arable economies were more constrained than those in pastoral where there existed a greater range of paid employment open to women.

Although English towns may have appeared unusually attractive to young women in the prosperous times at the end of the fourteenth and early years of the fifteenth century, it remains true that the majority of women and men in the preindustrial era lived in the countryside and made their living from working the land. As can be shown from manorial account and Peace Session rolls, women participated in most aspects of agrarian life whether as family labour or paid employees. Only ploughing and mowing seem to have been closed to women.[9] One of the sources most frequently used by medievalists for life in the countryside, however, are the records of the customary or manorial court. Over the past thirty years both the Birmingham and the Toronto schools have been especially active in developing methodologies to exploit these as a source for social history.[10] It is, however, only recently that they have been used to study peasant women. Bennett, a representative of the Toronto school, has analysed the court rolls of the ancient demesne manor of Brigstock in

Northamptonshire for her important study of women and work before the Black Death.[11] For the Birmingham school, Hilton devoted one of his Ford lectures to the subject and has since written about female rural migrants in small town society.[12] Questions relating to marriage, fertility, and illegitimacy have been explored by Razi from the remarkably full series of court rolls from Halesowen in Worcestershire, and Penn has used Peace Session evidence to explore patterns of female paid employment in the English countryside in the later fourteenth century.[13] Graham, in this present collection, has employed the court rolls from Alrewas in Staffordshire to focus specifically on women's work and on brewing in particular.

What begins to emerge from these studies is that manor court rolls are a far more enigmatic source than may once have appeared.[14] The record of the customary court is by its nature primarily concerned with the affairs of the customary tenants and the enforcement of customary law. Adult male landholders are especially conspicuous, but many other groups within village society, notably the young, the landless or near landless, and women who did not brew, are only indifferently recorded in the court rolls and some not at all. The manor court is thus a distorting lens, throwing some individuals, notably the upper echelons of peasant society, and certain activities, such as the transfer of land or the brewing of ale for sale, into sharp focus, but completely obscuring other individuals and perhaps the greater part of village life. It follows that to understand better what is recorded, it is necessary to ask why it is recorded and what is not recorded. The court roll itself can only record the procedure of the court. The relationship between the procedure of the court and the society out of which the business of the court is generated is not directly recorded.[15]

Graham's study of Alrewas demonstrates this observation in relation to fines recorded in the court rolls for brewing ale contrary to the Assize, which is usually understood to mean brewing for gain. Bennett attempted to use the record of persons fined to establish gender-specific patterns of commercial brewing within differing agrarian economies. Her thesis was that women would be most involved in brewing where men were most fully occupied in other agricultural tasks, but men would be more active as brewers in a less labour-intensive pastoral economy. Graham has now shown that the court record need not reflect the person who was actually responsible for brewing since the court was more concerned to record who was responsible for paying the fine. At Alrewas both male and female names are recorded. The males so recorded can be shown to have been tenants who owed suit of court and were thus present in the court when fines under the Assize of Ale were enforced. The females, however, are shown to have been married to men who were not tenants of the lord and who were thus exempt from owing suit and who would not have been present in the court when the fines were levied. Graham's thesis is that married women and widows constituted the great majority of brewers on the manor, but where the husbands were present in the court when the fines were made then they would have paid and their names been recorded. Elsewhere the clerk of the court may have recorded the names of married men as being responsible for brewing fines since in law a married man was responsible for his wife's debts. Thus the norm may have been that brewing was primarily a woman's activity, but this may be partly or wholly concealed according to the particular recording conventions used by the court or even the individual clerk.

That the court rolls were written in the name of the lord, or even, as for a time at Alrewas, the lady, reminds us of another level of manorial society, that of the landed aristocracy. Much has been written about individual representatives of the aristocracy or aristocratic families, about aspects of aristocratic culture, and about the political aspirations of the aristocracy.[16] Surprisingly little has so far been written about aristocratic women as a class. In this respect Archer's chapter is a useful contribution to the literature. She shows how the supervision of landed estates was often exercised by females, whether as spouses during the periodic absences of their husbands or as dowagers. Indeed, during the fifteenth century an estimated '76 per cent of noble households were reduced by at least one third for, on average, a period of seventeen years'. Administrative competence was expected of these women and indeed can regularly be observed. This finding is perhaps less remarkable in the broader context of a society that valued the contribution of women to the economic partnership of matrimony and saw nothing remarkable in widows taking control of their late husbands' affairs. In this context more emphasis was placed on practical experience, often gained initially through adolescent service in the households of others, than on formal education about which, in the case of women, we know all too little.[17]

Biller comments that it was a common theme in priests' manuals that women were expected to be charitable. Cullum's chapter attempts to show that this normative ideal, integral to the construction of femininity, was also reflected in social practice. She argues that married women were often expected by their husbands to give alms in the form of food and drink and even to provide shelter to the poor. Such was an extension of their responsibilities as the providers of food, warmth, and care for their spouses and households. This is further reflected in the provision by women of fuel for the use of their poor neighbours. Cullum's analysis further stresses female agency by producing evidence that women were often the initiators of charitable projects undertaken jointly with their husbands. She thus challenges the assumption that married women were merely passive partners, a fiction created by the legal convention that effectively prevented married women acting on their own. Cullum further considers patterns of charity directed towards women. Her analysis suggests a growth in such provision by the later fifteenth century. This she relates to a feminisation of poverty in a period of economic recession.

The role played by women as dispensers of charity, so central to late medieval devotional practice, provides a useful counterbalance to the current interest in female mystics and visionaries. Together with recent or forthcoming studies of nuns, sisters of hospitals, anchoresses, and vowesses, there is beginning to emerge a fuller picture of the nature and range of female piety in the late Middle Ages.[18] As so often, scholarship has been furthered not so much by discovering new sources, but by asking new questions. The study of English medieval nunneries, for example, had until recently made little advance on Power's still monumental study of 1922. Since 1988, however, three important new studies have appeared.[19] Within this collection, Gilchrist's chapter opens up fertile new ground by asking questions about gender in relation to the spatial planning of female religious houses. She points to the significantly higher proportion of nunneries compared with male religious houses whose cloisters were located to the north rather than the more conventional south. This she explains in terms of a 'web of meanings' linking the north side of the church with, following Passion iconography, the Virgin Mary and with the female sex more generally. This is further reflected in the location of many chapels dedicated to the Virgin, as the Lady chapels at Ely or (now destroyed) Peterborough, to the north of the main body of the church. Aston has independently argued for a degree of north–south spatial segration between the sexes within medieval churches more generally, but only for southern Europe is this evidence relatively unambiguous.[20] This again may reflect contrasting cultural concerns with sexual honour and reputation.

P.J.P.G. 1992

Notes

1   E.g. C.W. Bynum, *Holy Feast, Holy Fast: The Religious Significance of Food to Medieval Women* (Berkeley, 1987); B. Newman, *Sister of Wisdom: St. Hildegard's Theology of the Feminine* (Berkeley, 1987); S.K. Elkins, *Holy Women of Twelfth-Century England* (Chapel Hill, NC, 1988). For urban women: C. Klapisch-Zuber, *Women, Family, and Ritual in Renaissance Italy* (Chicago, 1985); M.C. Howell, *Women, Production, and Patriarchy in Late Medieval Cities* (Chicago, 1986); E. Uitz, *Women in the Medieval Town* (1990). J.M. Bennett, *Women in the Medieval English Countryside* (New York, 1987) is still the only English monograph on medieval peasant women.

2   See in particular R.M. Smith, 'Hypothèses sur la Nuptialitié en Angleterre aux XIIIe–XIVe siècles', *Annales: ESC* 38 (1983), pp. 107–36.

3 The two most influential recent studies are L.L. Otis, *Prostitution in Medieval Society: The History of an Urban Institution in Languedoc* (Chicago, 1985) and J. Rossiaud, *Medieval Prostitution* (Oxford, 1988).

4 P.J.P. Goldberg, 'Women in Fifteenth-Century Town Life', in *Towns and Townspeople in the Fifteenth Century*, ed. J.A.F. Thomson (Gloucester, 1988), pp. 118–21.

5 See for example the works cited in Smith, below ns. 7, 8, 26–8 and C.N.L. Brooke, *The Medieval Idea of Marriage* (Oxford, 1989).

6 The most useful introduction is R.H. Helmholz, *Marriage Litigation in Medieval England* (Cambridge, 1974).

7 For a brief introduction to the role of women in the urban labour market see P.J.P. Goldberg, 'Female Labour, Service and Marriage in the Late Medieval Urban North', *Northern History* 22 (1986), pp. 18–38.

8 For studies of marriage within the peasant élite and the gentry respectively see J.M. Bennett, 'The Tie That Binds: Peasant Marriages and Families in Late Medieval England', *Journal of Interdisciplinary History* 15 (1984), pp. 111–29 and K. Dockray, 'Why Did Fifteenth-Century English Gentry Marry?', in *Gentry and Lesser Nobility in Late Medieval Europe*, ed. M. Jones (Gloucester, 1986), pp. 61–80.

9 S.A.C. Penn, 'Female Wage-earners in Late Fourteenth-century England', *Agricultural History Review* 35 (1987), pp. 1–14; R.H. Hilton, *The English Peasantry in the Later Middle Ages* (Oxford, 1975), ch. 6.

10 A good example of the Toronto methodology is A. DeWindt, 'Peasant Power Structures in Fourteenth-Century King's Ripton', *Mediaeval Studies* 38 (1976), pp. 236–67. For a Birmingham school critique of the Toronto school see Z. Razi, 'The Toronto School's Reconstitution of Medieval Peasant Society: A Critical View', *Past and Present* 85 (1979), pp. 141–57. The Birmingham school has no distinctive methodology, but is influenced by Marxist ideology. A good example is C. Dyer, 'The Social and Economic Background to the Rural Revolt of 1381', in *The English Rising of 1381*, ed. R.H. Hilton and T.H. Aston (Cambridge, 1984) pp. 9–42.

11 Bennett, *Women in the Medieval English Countryside*.

12 Hilton, *The English Peasantry*, ch. 6; R.H. Hilton, 'Lords, Burgesses and Hucksters', *Past and Present* 97 (1982), pp. 3–15.

13 Z. Razi, *Life, Marriage and Death in a Medieval Parish* (Cambridge, 1980); Penn, 'Female Wage-earners'.

14 Cf. the debate between Poos and Smith on the one hand and Razi on the other in the pages of *Law and History Review*. See Smith, below n. 45.

15 For example, Hilton's observation that women migrants greatly outnumbered men in pre-plague Halesowen appears to be based on the simple observation that women were more numerous than men in the surviving court rolls and that many of these women were clearly migrants. However, these women were recorded for the most part because they fell foul of the borough's trading regulations, notably with regard to the trade in victuals. Those whose trade activities did not fall the wrong side of borough law are as a consequence unlikely to be recorded. It may thus be that men were generally better able to find legitimate employment, whereas some women, particularly migrant women were unable to secure work other than on the margins of legality. Women would consequently outnumber men in the court record, but not necessarily in the society out of which the record is generated: Hilton, 'Lords, Burgesses and Hucksters', p. 10; P.J.P. Goldberg, 'The Public and the Private: Women in the Pre-Plague Economy', in *Thirteenth Century England III*, ed. P.R. Coss and S.D. Lloyd (Woodbridge, 1991), pp. 83–6.

16 Recent studies include N. Saul, *Scenes from Provincial Life: Knightly Families in Sussex, 1280–1400* (Oxford, 1986); K. Mertes, *The English Noble Household 1250–1600* (Oxford, 1988); S. Walker, *The Lancastrian Affinity 1361–1399* (Oxford, 1990).

17 Mertes, *English Noble Household*, pp. 53–4, 173–4.
18 Elkins, *Holy Women of Twelfth-Century England*; S. Thompson, *Women Religious: The Founding of English Nunneries after the Norman Conquest* (Oxford, 1991); P.H. Cullum, *Hospitals and Charity in Medieval England* (Manchester, forthcoming); A.K. Warren, *Anchorites and Their Patrons in Medieval England* (Berkeley, 1985); A.E. Goodman, 'The Piety of John of Brunham's Daughter, of Lynn', in *Medieval Women*, ed. D. Baker (Oxford, 1978), pp. 347–58; M.A. Hicks, 'The Piety of Margaret, Lady Hungerford (d. 1478), *Journal of Ecclesiastical History* 38 (1987), pp. 19–38; M.G. Underwood, 'Politics and Piety in the Household of Lady Margaret Beaufort', ibid., pp. 39–52; P.H. Cullum, 'Vowesses and Female Lay Piety in the Province of York, 1350–1530', *Northern History* 32 (1996), pp. 21–41.
19 E. Power, *English Medieval Nunneries* (Cambridge, 1922). In addition to Elkins and Thompson cited in n.18 above, R. Gilchrist, *Gender and Material Culture: The Archaeology of Religious Women* (London, 1994).
20 M. Aston, 'Segregation in Church', in *Women in the Church*, ed. W.J. Sheils and D. Wood, Studies in Church History, 27 (1990), pp. 237–94.
21 P.J.P. Goldberg, 'Marriage, Migration, Servanthood and Life-cycle in Yorkshire Towns of the Later Middle Ages: Some York Cause Paper Evidence', *Continuity and Change* 1 (1986), pp. 141–69.

1

Marriage, Migration, and Servanthood: The York Cause Paper Evidence

P.J.P. Goldberg
University of York

The past, we are warned, is a foreign country. This is certainly true in respect of the medieval family as an institution. We may suspect that things were done differently, but how they differed and why they differed remains an open question. The medievalist cannot hope to reclaim *mentalités* in the absence of private letters or journals. The relationship between husbands and wives, parents and children, employers and servants, kin and non-kin can only be glimpsed occasionally. Usually it is judicial records that allow this privileged view, but these are not unproblematic sources.[1] The woman who sought legal separation from her husband on grounds of cruelty may or may not have hidden a hundred similar battered wives.[2] The woman dragged lifeless from the well or the baby incinerated in her cradle may or may not have been the victims of accident.[3] These are not problems the historian can hope to resolve in any dogmatic way. It may be, however, that a knowledge of the basic demography of the family will provide some framework from which hypotheses may be developed. Marital relations between a teenage bride and a mature groom would, for example, not be the same as those between a couple marrying at much the same age. Similarly a society in which daughters left home in their early teens must have had values different from one that kept its daughters in the natal home until marriage. We need to know whether the structure of English family life that prevailed in this 'feudal' age differed from that which has been described from the 'capitalist' early modern era.

The survival of the very full and detailed tax survey or *catasto* from Tuscany in 1427 has allowed historians a rare opportunity to reconstruct the demographic structure of a particular region within the medieval era.[4] This suggests a pattern of early marriage for women, but late marriage for men, and a paucity of widow as opposed to widower remarriage that echoes the world of the Pyrenean village of Montaillou about a hundred years earlier.[5] Herlihy argues that this is not a specific Tuscan or even

Mediterranean phenomenon, but part of a general 'medieval' pattern. This view does not, however, seem to be supported by other studies. Though the evidence for more northerly regions is less substantial, it tends to suggest a divergent pattern or patterns.[6] Razi is attracted to the notion of a distinctive 'medieval' marriage regime, but his painstaking attempt to reconstruct peasant genealogies from the remarkably full series of manor court rolls surviving from the later thirteenth century for Halesowen in Worcestershire suggests a relatively early age at marriage, i.e. in the late 'teens or very early twenties, for women and for men alike'.[7] Howell's study of Leiden and Cologne at the close of the Middle Ages, in contrast, argues for a pattern of delayed marriage for both sexes, although this rests upon rather scanty material.[8] Slightly more substantial evidence, notably from the poll tax of 1377, is assembled by Smith in respect of England in the thirteenth and fourteenth centuries. His hypothesis of a late marriage regime suggests continuity into the early modern era, but conflicts with Razi's interpretation.[9]

Perhaps the most interesting evidence for regional diversity relates, however, not to marriage patterns *per se*, but to servanthood. Servants, in the specific sense of live-in employees, are found in Mediterranean society of the later Middle Ages, but not in great numbers. They tend to be of low social status, predominantly female, and were, like the servant-saint Zita of Lucca, sometimes so employed throughout their lives.[10] The same does not appear to be true of parts of Northern and Western Europe. Tax evidence indicates that servants of both sexes were numerous in such major towns as Nuremberg, Ypres, Reims, Coventry, and York.[11] Probate evidence shows that employers regularly remembered their servants and even former servants. Women servants in particular were often bequeathed household utensils and bedding, an indication perhaps that these were invariably young people who would eventually marry and set up households of their own.[12] Rural servants are also found in number from the poll tax of 1377, although few historians of medieval English rural society have recognised this.[13] The reasons for this are twofold. Whereas on the one hand the poll tax records servants as household dependents, manor court rolls, concerned as they are primarily with landholders, are more ambiguous. Relatively few servants are named and it is seldom clear whether these are actual members of the household or merely employees or labourers. On the other hand the concept of a pattern of servanthood parallel to that which is known to have existed in early modern England is anathema to those who see late medieval English society as distinctively 'feudal'.

In the absence of more substantive qualitative and statistical evidence relating to servanthood and marriage regimes there would be little hope of clarifying or even resolving this debate. Some such evidence does, however, exist in the form of written depositions made by witnesses in response to set questions in the Church court. Such depositions and related material survive in some quantity from the consistory of York and have come to be known as cause papers. These relate to litigation concerning such matters as tithes, appropriation of churches, testamentary disputes, breach of faith, defamation, and matrimonial disputes. It is these last that are especially valuable since women and servants feature regularly both as witnesses and as litigants. Deponents were invariably identified by name, place of residence, status, relationship, if any, to the parties in dispute, and, by the later fourteenth century, age. In total, data were extracted from some 1,094 depositions, mostly relating to matrimonial causes, for the period 1303–1520.[14] The marital status of female deponents is often implicit in the way they are named, viz. Alice, wife of Thomas Etardby or Isabel, daughter of Alan de Belyngham.[15] Servants are likewise identified in relation to their employer, e.g. Katherine Lorymer, servant to Agnes Schibotill.[16] In addition, former servants can sometimes be recognised from statements made in their depositions. Thus Joan Fleschawer deposed that she had been present in Robert Lonesdale's home eighteen months earlier because she was then employed as his servant.[17]

Closer analysis shows that these data are imperfect and represent only a limited cross-section of society. Evidence concerning the ages of deponents is especially problematic. For deponents in their teens or twenties, ages are regularly recorded with apparent precision, but for older deponents they are frequently rounded to the nearest multiple of ten. Such ages are often qualified by the phrases 'about' (*circiter*) or 'or more' (*et amplius*). The impression here is that this last could imply an age several years beyond the number actually stated. It thus appears that only for young adults can absolute ages as recorded be regarded with some degree of confidence, although the relative ages of older married couples may still be of value. A variety of age groups are represented, but not the very young. Those below canonical age, twelve in the case of girls and fourteen for boys, were forbidden to testify, but deponents are found from around their mid teens. Poor deponents are common enough, but the courts were suspicious of the very poor as being especially vulnerable to bribery. The landed aristocracy and the mercantile élite are represented, but not to a disproportionate degree. The majority of deponents are, to use early modern parlance, drawn from the 'middling sort', viz. artisans, peasant farmers, their wives, children, and servants. It would appear, however, that there was some bias against admitting young adolescents as deponents and that this became more pronounced by the later fifteenth century. More importantly there appears also to have been some prejudice against women deponents. Only a quarter of all deponents in matrimonial causes prior to 1500 were female. This imbalance is more marked for rural causes than for those associated with the larger towns. It is also progressively more pronounced from the later fourteenth century; by the earlier sixteenth century some causes contained no depositions made by women.

The deposition evidence allows for twenty-three female and twenty-four male servants to be identified by age and a further thirteen female and sixteen male former servants to be likewise identified retrospectively from their testimonies. In a few instances these two groups overlap. Rather more of these servants were resident in urban than rural households. Since these deponents were invariably adolescents or young adults, some confidence can be placed in the ages recorded. A fairly good picture of the sort of ages at which both females and males might be found in service is thus possible, although the precise ages at which persons first entered or finally left service cannot be known. It is further possible that the bias against younger deponents has resulted in more youthful servants being comparatively under-represented, although some younger servants can be identified retrospectively. Thus Agnes de Polles, who was twenty-six at the time of her deposition, stated that she had entered service with Robert de Rouclif fourteen years earlier, i.e. when she would have been about

Table 1.1
AGE DISTRIBUTION OF FEMALE SERVANTS OVER TIME

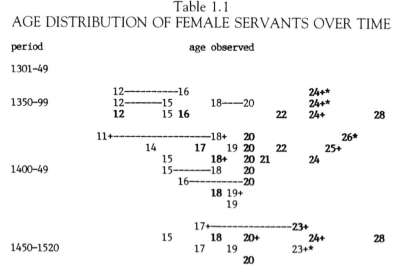

```
period                              age observed

1301-49

                    12----------16                  24+*
1350-99             12--------15      18----20       24+*
                    12      15 16              22    24+         28

            11+-------------------18+  20                26*
                 14        17   19 20   22      25+
                 15       18+   20 21          24
1400-49          15------18     20
               16----------20
                 18 19+
                    19

                    17+---------------23+
            15         18   20+        24+          28
1450-1520        17     19           23+*
                            20
```

Notes: Figures in regular type represent age of service at deposition, figures in **bold type** represent age at service calculated retrospectively. Where ages are described as 'or more' this is indicated by a plus sign.
* Status as servant uncertain.

Table 1.2

AGE DISTRIBUTION OF MALE SERVANTS OVER TIME

period   age observed

1301–49

```
          13----------------19 20   22
1350–99          16+             20 21-------24 25+           29

                18 19+                24    26
1400–49   14+------17+   19+          24         27+
                    19+   21-------24   26
                18+    20

                17    19 20        24 25+
1450–1520           18+   20+  22  24
          8+---------------------20+              27+
```

Notes: Figures in regular type represent age of service at deposition, figures in **bold type** represent age at service calculated retrospectively. Where ages are described as 'or more' this is indicated by a plus sign.

twelve. These age data are tabulated in Tables 1.1 and 1.2. Twelve would indeed seem to have been the minimum age at which girls first became servants. It may be more than coincidental that this was also the age at which girls were deemed to have achieved their canonical majority. The evidence for boys is less satisfactory, but suggests that they entered no earlier and perhaps a little later than their sisters.

Considerable numbers of young people are observed as servants from the mid teens until the mid twenties. Few males and still fewer females are found in service after their twenty-fifth year. No woman servant is noticed aged more than twenty-eight and much the same is true of men. The consistency of this pattern over the period for which age data are recorded adds to our confidence in the representativeness of the observed pattern. There seems little marked difference between urban and rural patterns, though very few rural female servants are found in their twenties. Servanthood in late medieval Yorkshire thus appears to have been an institution associated with teenagers and young single adults. In this respect it differs from the pattern of service associated with Southern Europe. In late medieval Florence or Barcelona, for example, servants, usually female, often entered service as early as eight years of age, but left still in their teens to marry.[18]

The cause papers thus provide telling evidence for the existence of what may be described as life-cycle servanthood in later medieval England; it is evident from their depositions that servants were invariably young, unmarried, and living with their employers. Only apprentices, themselves but one element among male servants, regularly stayed with their employers for several years at a time.[19] Servants generally were an especially mobile group, often moving every year or two at customary hiring dates, though a few did stay longer.[20] Martinmas was the most common of these, being noted in seventeen cases. This remained the customary hiring date within this northern region into the present century, whereas Michaelmas was probably more common in the English Midlands.[21] Pentecost would also appear to have had some importance as a counterpart to Martinmas; one women was hired at Pentecost and another left her position at the same time.[22] It is unclear, however, how far hiring fairs had established themselves at this early date. A Good Friday fair 'be which people were lette for service' is noted at Coventry in 1452, but more informal means of matching those seeking service to those

Table 1.3
AGE DISTRIBUTION OF SINGLE FEMALES, OTHER THAN SERVANTS

period		age observed				
1338–49		20+	22*			30*
1350–99	14+	20 21+		24	26	
		20	22			
1400–49		20+				30+*
						30+*
1450–1520		20+				30

Notes: Where ages are described as 'or more' this is indicated by a plus sign.
* Status uncertain.

Table 1.4
AGE DISTRIBUTION OF SINGLE MALES, OTHER THAN SERVANTS

period			age observed			
1301–49						
1350–99	15+		20 21 22			
1400–49			20+	24+		
1450–1520		18	20	24+		
				23+		26+
				24+		
				23+		

Note: Where ages are described as 'or more' this is indicated by a plus sign.

seeking servants seem to have been normal. Servants were, for example, not infrequently kin to their employers. Thus Joan Fleschawer was the goddaughter of her mistress and Alice, her fellow servant, was a relative (*cognata*) of her master.[23]

Not all young people were servants and it is likely that even those who did spend time in service spent only part of their adolescence and early adult years so employed. Alice Dalton, who was probably a native of Poppleton, went back to Poppleton for a year between periods of service with different employers in York. Robert, her husband-to-be, likewise returned to his father's home in Poppleton after three years in the service of a York baker. He lived with his father for five months, and seven months after that married Alice.[24] A number of other young, single persons of known age, but not in service are to be found among our sample of deponents. Their ages are shown in Tables 1.3 and 1.4. Very few teenagers are noticed, but a number of women and men in their early twenties are found. A few older women are also noticed, but in three of these instances their status as never married is uncertain. These observations accord well with those already made in respect of servanthood, i.e. that the young appear frequently to have remained unmarried up until their early twenties. There is slight evidence here that males may have remained single slightly longer than their sisters and that young people in towns remained unmarried longer than their rural siblings.

It was not just the unmarried that made depositions, but although many deponents of known age can be identified as currently married, it is rarely the case that the evidence allows us to know at what age individuals were first married. For townsfolk this is known in only one instance, viz. William Gascone of York who was only fourteen when he married in 1502, although Alice de Stodlay of St Saviourgate in York can be calculated to have been already married and pregnant at eighteen or more.[25] The former is atypical since it is derived from the only urban matrimonial cause prior to 1520 alleging marriage under canonical age, but the latter may be no more representative. Persons in their twenties, let alone teenagers, are only occasionally found among the currently married deponents resident in York or other larger towns. Only four such female deponents are noticed, viz. a nineteen-year-old, two other women said to be twenty or more, and one aged twenty-four. Similarly a nineteen-year-old and a man of twenty-six are the only such male deponents.[26] All other currently married deponents were aged thirty or more, an observation that would appear improbable if marriages in the late teens or early twenties were commonplace, but which accords well with the evidence already presented that many young adults remained unwed until around their middle twenties.

For rural deponents, age at marriage is known or may be calculated retrospectively for twenty individuals. Nine of these concern parties to litigation alleging marriage under canonical age, a phenomenon much more common in the countryside, notably among the landed gentry, than was true of urban society.[27] Such cases appear, moreover, to have been rare between the later fourteenth and early sixteenth centuries. It is unlikely that they have much to say about the modal (i.e. most common) age at first marriage that may more generally have been found in peasant society. The remaining twelve instances are suggestive of a rather earlier pattern of marriage than the evidence just discussed for urban society. The age at marriage for women is known in only three instances, viz. at fourteen years, between sixteen and eighteen years, and at eighteen years. These are taken from causes dated 1499, 1370, and 1430 respectively.[28] Discounting one doubtful case, the mean male age at first marriage is in excess of twenty-two years (N=8). It should be noted that this rests on imperfect age data, makes no allowance for six instances where the age recorded is stated to be a minimum, and is almost entirely dependent on causes dating between 1430 and 1466. This slight, but suggestive evidence may be augmented from a further sixteen individuals known to be married by a certain age below thirty years. Of five females known to have been married before thirty years, one was married by nineteen or more, one by twenty or more, two by twenty-six, and one by twenty-nine.[29] This appears consistent with a pattern of marriage in the late teens or early twenties, but this cannot be more than a hypothesis for the sample is much too small to inspire real confidence. Two males were married by age twenty or more, a further four, by age twenty-four, and four more by age twenty-six or more. This is again indicative of an age at first marriage in the early rather than the mid-twenties.

These findings may be set against the data pertaining to the ages of the unmarried discussed before. The ages of six unmarried rural females and ten equivalent males other than servants are known from our sample. Five of the women were aged twenty or more, and two were aged thirty. It cannot be claimed, however, that this sample is entirely representative; none of the female deponents are drawn from causes dating to the fifteenth century and only two are drawn from later fourteenth-century causes. The male sample is more satisfactory. It is enhanced by five men drawn from a cause of 1450. This relates to events at the Summer Game in Wistow which only the unmarried were eligible to attend.[30] Although all the men in the sample were aged twenty or more, only one, aged twenty-six (or more), was older than twenty-four (or more). Such a pattern seems in line with the earlier suggestion that the modal male age at first marriage was a couple of years short of twenty-five. The ages of rural servants, at deposition or calculated retrospectively, are known in twenty-four cases, of which eleven are women. Unfortunately this female sample is again deficient for the fifteenth century. With the exception of one woman servant aged twenty-eight found in a cause dated 1398, women are not apparently found in rural service much beyond their early twenties. Most male servants are found in their late teens or early twenties; three men were still in service at twenty-four years, one at twenty-five or more, and one at twenty-seven or more. Males may thus have stayed in service a little longer than their sisters, but rarely beyond their mid twenties.[31]

The cause paper evidence indicates that early marriage was not the norm in late medieval Yorkshire. In the larger towns, where the institution of service was especially common, a distinctive late marriage regime appears to have prevailed. In peasant society marriages seem often to have been a little earlier, but they still deviate from the sort of early marriage regime described by Razi for the manor of Halesowen. The evidence does, however, accord with Razi's model in one important respect. Couples tended to marry one another at similar ages; in demographic terms, marriages were companionate. In a number of instances, moreover, the wife was the senior of her spouse. This is apparent from an analysis of the age differences between couples whose ages are recorded. This is shown in Table 1.5. The age data, it has already been remarked, are imperfect. Where ages are only given as multiples of ten, the resulting age difference is invariably either zero or ten, but more

Table 1.5

AGE DIFFERENCES BETWEEN SPOUSES FROM CAUSE PAPER SAMPLE

wife senior				husband senior			
10	6-9	1-5	=	1-5	6-9	10	>10
10	6-	2+	+ 0	+ 2 4 5	6+	10- 10	10+ 14 18 20+
		2	+ 0	+ 4 5	**6** 7	10	**10+** 14+ 18
			0	+ **4** **5**	7	10	
			0			10	
			0			10	
			0			10	
			0			**10**	
			0			**10**	
			0				
			0				
			0				

Notes: Where husband and wife were of like age (=) the age difference is indicated as zero. Where ages are described as 'or more' this is indicated by a plus sign. Figures in **bold type** indicate rural couples.

Table 1.6
MIGRANTS FROM DEPOSITION EVIDENCE

BIHR CP.	date	sex m/f	moved from / to	then aged	current location	age	distance moved
E.76	1357	m	?Reedness	[8]	'Elsyn'		
E.89	1366	m	Shipton		?Hutton		
		m	?		Rawcliffe		
		f	Rawcliffe		'Slaykston'		
		f	?		Rawcliffe		
		f	Skelton		Clifton		3 miles
		f	Rawcliffe		Clifton		1½ miles
		f	i Rawcliffe				2½ miles
			ii Bootham		York		½ mile
E.102	1367	f	Aike		Beverley		4 miles
E.111	1372	f	Uncleby	[19]	York	23	14 miles
		f	?	[15+]	York	30+	
		m	?	[14]	York	20	
		m	?	[10+]	York	20+	
E.126	1382	f	Newcastle		York	21+	73 miles
		f	Newcastle		York	20	73 miles
		f	Newcastle		York		73 miles
E.153	1389	f	?		London		
E.155	1374	m	?	[15+]	Althorpe	40+	
E.159	1394	m	Crayke		York	20+	12 miles
E.193	1392	f	Wakefield		Beverley		46 miles
E.221	1396	m	i ?	[14]			
			ii York	[19]	Ouseburn	20	12 miles
E.248	1346	f	Richmond		York		41 miles
E.255	1384	m	Skinningrove	[33]	Scarborough	40	28 miles
		f	Skinningrove	[28]	Scarborough	35	28 miles
E.257	1349	m	nr. ?Leicester		Newcastle		?160+ miles
		m	Benwell		Newcastle		2 miles
		m	i Middleton in Teesdale				
			ii Newland, nr. Newcastle		Newcastle		?30 miles
F.46	1422	f	?	[18+]	Hull	20+	
F.59	1410	f	Bilsdale		York		16 miles
		m	Wharram		Bilsdale		22 miles
F.61	1411	f	?		York		
F.64	1412	m	Linton on Ouse	[14+]	York	16+	9 miles
F.79	1418	f	Knaresborough		York	40	16 miles
		f	Preston		York	40	68 miles
		f	Stockeld	[29]	York	30	15 miles
		m	Stockeld	[39]	York	40	15 miles
F.81	1418	f	?Aughton*		Pontefract		20 / 22 miles
F.113	1434	m	Snape	[17]	Well	40	2 miles
F.129	early C15	f	Westmorland		Ayton		70+ miles
		f	Westmorland		Ayton		70+ miles
F.177	1433	m	Meltonby		North Burton		14 miles
		f	Meltonby		North Burton		14 miles
		m	i Meltonby	[19+]			24 miles
			ii Barton on Humber		Barmby	20+	22 miles
		m	Meltonby	[19+]	Wilberfoss	20+	4 miles
F.179	1438	m	Carnaby		Full Sutton		26 miles
F.185	1450	m	Kildwick		York	18	38 miles
		m	Marton		York	17	13 miles
		m	Marton		York	20	13 miles
F.201	1430	m	i ?Poppleton	[14+]			4 miles
			ii York	[17+]	Poppleton	36+	4 miles
		f	i ?Poppleton	[15]			4 miles
			ii York	[17]			4 miles

BIHR CP.	date	sex m/f	moved from / to	then aged	current location	age	distance moved
			iiiPoppleton	[17½]			4 miles
			iv York	[18]	Poppleton	36	4 miles
F.202	1462	f	Appletreewick		Denton	80	9 miles
		m	?	[24]	Appletreewick	74+	
F.240	1466	m	?	[24+]	Burn	40+	
F.241	1447	m	?	[10+]	Burton Agnes	30+	
		m	i Driffield				12 miles
			ii Beverley		Driffield	26+	12 miles
		m	?	[17+]	Burton Agnes	25+	
		m	?	[20+]	Beverley	32+	
		m	i Hedon				
			ii 'Moretown'		Beverley		
F.257	1477	f	Samlesbury		Ribchester		5 miles
F.284	1494	f	Leconfield		London		165 miles
F.336	1465	f	i York	[17+]			20 miles
			ii Methley	[22+]	York	23+	20 miles
G.26	1507	m	Pickering		?[the South]		
G.35†	1409	f	?Rolston		York		?38 miles

Notes

All distances are as the crow flies. Ages in square brackets have been calculated retrospectively and are thus only approximate. Where ages are described as 'or more' this is indicated by a plus sign.

* Identity ambiguous. Two vills similarly distant share the name 'Aughton'. One is to the south, below Rotherham, the other to the north-east, beyond Selby. Text records 'Aghton' or 'Haghton'.

† Cause paper at present misclassified. Should be class 'F'.

precise ages are recorded in a sufficient number of cases to permit a fuller picture to emerge. Where very substantial differences in age are recorded, it is always the husband that is the senior. These can be shown in several instances to relate to the remarriage of widowers, presumably to women marrying for the first time.[32] Excluding these suspected remarriages, the mean age difference for urban couples is only 2.9 years (N = 31). For rural couples the age difference is about a year greater, viz. 3.8 years (N = 9), an observation that coincides with that suggested from the ages of unmarried deponents.

There remains one further issue, that of migration, for which the deposition data are able to provide statistical evidence. Thirty-one female and thirty-two male migrants are more or less well recorded. Only occasionally can the actual age of persons when they migrated be calculated with any confidence, nor is the place of origin of migrants always known. The evidence is shown in Table 1.6. Despite the limitations of the source, certain observations are possible. Firstly, the majority of migrants appear to have been adolescents or young adults. In the context of the findings just described, most would have been single and would only have married after settling in their new abode. Secondly, most journeys made were comparatively short. Discarding two atypically lengthy journeys, the mean distance travelled was under twenty-two miles, i.e. no more than a day's walk. Much of this movement was of people into town from the surrounding rural hinterland. Towns may have exercised a particular pull over migrant labour in the labour-starved decades of the later fourteenth and earlier fifteenth century and it is noticeable that women migrants are most numerous over this period. Some of these journeys were very short. Thus Joan del Hill moved to Beverley from her native Aike four miles away. Some young people were drawn to town by reason of service. This would appear to have been true, for example, of Isabel Foxhole of Aughton who was employed by her uncle in Pontefract or Alice Dalton of Poppleton who found work in York.[33]

Two observations follow. Although migrational information is often only recorded by chance and it is thus not possible to know what proportion of the adult population had not been born in their place of abode, it is apparent that late medieval Yorkshire folk did not necessarily spend all their days in their natal village. Besides the regular movement of people to and from market or to their place of work, some moved permanently in the process of finding employment. Much of this movement was localised, i.e. over comparatively short distances, though some moved much further.[34] Migration can also be seen as an integral part of the prevailing demographic regime. By and large it was the young and unwed that moved permanently from their natal homes only to marry and settle down subsequently. This is also reflected in a comparatively high level of peasant women marrying outside the manor suggested from the evidence of merchet payments.[35] For some at least the lengthy interval between sexual maturity and marriage was marked by a physical separation from the natal family as young people sought work or places as servants and sometimes this process took them some distance from their place of birth. This was at least as true of young women as it was of men.

To return to our original observations, late medieval Yorkshire seems to have little in common with Mediterranean Europe in respect of the prevailing marriage regime. There was no large age difference between spouses. Marriage for women as well as men was relatively late, i.e. well beyond the pattern of teenage marriage normal for Tuscan brides. This late, companionate marriage regime seems to have been strengthened by an institution of 'life-cycle' service, a stage between childhood and independent adulthood that is well documented from the early modern period and which differed from the pattern of servanthood found in Southern Europe. The transition from the late medieval to early modern era seems, in Yorkshire at least, to have been marked more by continuity than change. There is, moreover, little to suggest that this regional evidence is not more generally representative of wider English patterns.[36] The question that arises is not so much how a modern 'European' marriage regime evolved from a 'medieval' regime, for such labels only disguise a more subtle evolutionary pattern that has yet to be unravelled. Nor is the question how the structure of family life changed from feudalism to capitalism, for these ideological concepts seem to impose too great a strain on the evidence. A more useful approach seems to be to ask instead what were the structures of a variety of regional marriage regimes and how did these evolve over time. This last must be explored in relation to the nature of and changes in the agrarian economy, urbanisation and industrial growth, demographic change and the gender-specific demand for labour. This is an exciting and challenging agenda and one that has implications far beyond the medieval era.

Notes

1   B.A. Hanawalt, *Crime and Conflict in English Communities, 1300–1348* (Cambridge, Mass., 1979); J.B. Given, *Society and Homicide in Thirteenth-Century England* (Palo Alto, 1977); J.M. Carter, *Rape in Medieval England* (Lanham, 1985).

2   E.g. BIHR, CP.E.221.

3   P.J.P. Goldberg, 'The Public and the Private: Women in the Pre-Plague Economy', in *Thirteenth Century England III* ed. P.R. Coss and S.D. Lloyd (Woodbridge, 1991), pp. 78–9.

4   D. Herlihy and C. Klapisch-Zuber, *Tuscans and Their Families* (New Haven, 1985).

5   E. Le Roy Ladurie, *Montaillou* (Harmondsworth, 1980).

6   D. Herlihy, *Medieval Households* (Cambridge, Mass., 1985), pp. 110–11.

7   Z. Razi, *Life, Marriage and Death in a Medieval Parish* (Cambridge, 1980), pp. 61–3.

8   M. Howell, *Women, Production, and Patriarchy in Late Medieval Cities* (Chicago, 1986), pp. 12–13, 43–4.

9   R.M. Smith, 'Hypothèses sur la Nuptialité en Angleterre au XXIIIe–XIVe siècle', *Annales: ESC* 38 (1983), pp. 107–24.

10 C. Klapisch-Zuber, 'Female Celibacy and Service in Florence in the Fifteenth Century', in *Women, Family, and Ritual Renaissance Italy* (Chicago, 1985), pp. 165–77; Klapisch-Zuber, 'Women Servants in Florence during the Fourteenth and Fifteenth Centuries, in *Women and Work in Preindustrial Europe*, ed. B.A. Hanawalt (Bloomington, 1986), pp. 56–80; M. Goodich, '*Ancilla Dei*: The Servant as Saint in the Late Middle Ages', in

Women of the Medieval World, ed. J. Kirshner and S.F. Wemple (Oxford, 1985), pp. 119–36. See Smith, below.

11   K. Bücher, 'Zur mittelalterlichen Bevölkerungsstatistik mit besondere Rücksicht auf Frankfurt a.M.', *Zeitschrift für die gesammte Staatswissenschaft* 37 (1881), table 1, p. 566; H. Pirenne, 'Les Dénombrements de la Population d'Ypres au XVe siècle (1412–1506)', *Vierteljahrschrift für Social- und Wirtschaftegeschichte* 1 (1903), pp. 15, 19–20; P. Desportes, 'La Population de Reims au XVe siècle', *Moyen Age* 72 (1966), pp. 486–90; C. Phythian-Adams, *Desolation of a City: Coventry and the Urban Crisis of the Late Middle Ages* (Cambridge, 1979), pp. 205–11; P.J.P. Goldberg, 'Urban Identity and the Poll Taxes of 1377, 1379, and 1381', *Economic History Review* 2nd ser. 43 (1990), pp. 198–202, 212.

12   P.J.P. Goldberg, 'Female Labour, Service and Marriage in the Late Medieval Urban North', *Northern History* 22 (1986), pp. 23–4.

13   Smith, 'Hypothèses sur la Nuptialité', pp. 129–31.

14   This sample was made up of 469 deponents drawn from urban litigation and 625 from rural litigation.

15   BIHR, CP.E.126, 213.

16   BIHR, CP.F.113.

17   BIHR, CP.G.35. This cause is dated 1409, but is at present misclassified among the sixteenth-century cause papers.

18   Klapisch-Zuber, 'Female Celibacy and Service', pp. 173–4; T. M. Vinyoles, *Les Barcelonines a les darreries de l'edat mitjana* (Barcelona, 1976), pp. 33–66.

19   Female apprentices, though found, would appear to be rare outside London and are in any case confined to the crafts of the silkwoman and seamstress. The period of contract for apprentices was often stipulated in guild ordinances.

20   A small number of servants can be identified from their depositions to have remained with their employers for periods between two and seven years. Four others remained for only six months. A year was the minimum customary term of contract permitted under the Statute of Labourers (1351).

21   A. Kussmaul, *Servants in Husbandry in Early Modern England* (Cambridge, 1981), p. 50; F. Kitchen, *Brother to the Ox* (1940).

22   BIHR, CP.E.155; CP.F.201.

23   *Coventry Leet Book*, ed. M.D. Harris, EETS 134–5, 138, 146 (1907–13), p. 272; BIHR, CP.G.35.

24   BIHR, CP.F.201.

25   BIHR, CP.E.198, CP.G.32.

26   BIHR, CP.E.121; CP.F.46, 75, 116; D/C CP.1417/2.

27   BIHR, CP.E.259 is an action for annulment of marriage on grounds of impotence, but relates to the youthful marriage of a knight's daughter.

28   BIHR, CP.E.105; CP.F.201, 308.

29   BIHR, CP.E.89; CP.F.201; CP.G.55, 56.

30   BIHR, CP.F.246.

31   Compare Tables 1.1 and 1.2.

32   E.g. BIHR, CP.F.36 and Prob. Reg. 2 fo. 539 (Laxton); CP.F.114 and Prob. Reg. 3 fo. 575 (Bolton); D/C CP.1417/2 and Prob. Reg. 2 fos. 45, 308 (del Close).

33   E.g. BIHR, CP.E.102; CP.F.81, 201.

34   Cf. S.A.C. Penn and C. Dyer, 'Wages and Earnings in Late Medieval England: Evidence from the Enforcement of the Labour Laws', *Economic History Review* 2nd ser. 43 (1990), p. 363; P. McClure, 'Patterns of Migration in the Late Middle Ages: The Evidence of English Place-Name Surnames', *Economic History Review* 2nd ser. 32 (1979), pp. 167–82.

35   J.M. Bennett, 'Medieval Peasant Marriage: An Examination of Marriage Licence Fines in the *Liber Gersumarum*', in *Pathways to Medieval Peasants*, ed. J.A. Raftis

(Toronto, 1981), p. 197. It is also reflected in the paucity of suits for annulment of marriage on grounds of consanguinity or affinity.

36   There is good evidence that the institution of life-cycle servanthood was comparatively widespread in the later fourteenth century, cf. Smith, 'Hypothèses sur la Nuptialité', pp. 129–31.

2

Geographical Diversity in the Resort to Marriage in Late Medieval Europe: Work, Reputation, and Unmarried Females in the Household Formation Systems of Northern and Southern Europe

Richard M. Smith
Downing College, Cambridge

Interpretations of demographic patterns, processes and their related family forms in medieval Europe have tended to stress changes which are regarded as having been *common* to most of the continent. In particular, the period of demographic flux associated with the great migrations of the fourth and fifth centuries, the colonisation of, and settlement expansion into, land of increasingly marginal quality reaching its zenith in the early fourteenth century, followed by demographic decline and settlement retreat in an era of frequent epidemic outbreaks that has been termed by one historian 'the Golden Age of Bacteria'. The generalised, indeed pan-European, character of all of these long secular demographic waves has now achieved the status of an orthodoxy, although the impact of these oscillations on the societies experiencing them continues to form the subject of lively debate.[1]

A distinctive feature of much of the discussion of these demographic phases has been the tendency to treat the population dynamic working throughout Europe as largely deriving from variations in the level of mortality, either in the guise of Malthus' endogenously determined 'positive check' or operating largely through autonomously driven disease cycles.[2] The demographic evidence employed in such accounts is unfortunately of a fairly rudimentary kind. Certainly with the arrival of the 'parish register' era in the sixteenth century the range of hypotheses relating to the determinants of European demographic processes and the sophistication of the tests used in their evaluation increases exponentially when compared with evidence available to demographic students of the earlier centuries. However, the great change which has occurred in our understanding of early modern European demography in recent years does not lie ultimately with the yield of empirical information or in the proliferation of developments in technique, but rather in its logical status.

As long as the demographic history of the Middle Ages was a catalogue of fact, for example, the 'lure of aggregates' as Postan once referred to a preoccupation on the part of English medieval historians for deriving population totals for England from such sources as the Domesday Book of 1086 or the Poll Tax of 1377, a history of cataclysms which could be viewed as acts of God (outbreaks of disease on the scale of the Black Death), or a feature of medieval society, the characteristics of which were believed to be readily determinable from a knowledge of some other aspect of the society in question (i.e. agricultural prices, the charting of settlement expansion or the study of village desertions), it was likely to prove a matter of peripheral significance to the investigation of larger historical 'problems'.

Wrigley has suggested that the single most important publication tending to create a new logical status for demographic history is Hajnal's article on European marriage patterns.[3] In that essay Hajnal showed that both the late timing and low incidence of marriage for women in western Europe were radically different from patterns found anywhere else in the world and that this pattern can be demonstrated unambiguously to be visible from the sixteenth century onwards over England, Northern France, the Low Countries, and much of Germany west of the Elbe.[4] Other things being equal, this marriage pattern implies a lower level of fertility than elsewhere and makes possible a different balance of population and resources – a 'low pressure' rather than 'high pressure' equilibrium. It suggests different relations between the generations, frequently different patterns of co-residence within the household, different life-time patterns of production, saving, and expenditure, and, especially relevant to the discussion which follows in this chapter, a distinctive status attaching to females, particularly those who, substantial in number, although sexually mature, are unmarried. Indeed in some discussions it is even implicated within that long-standing theme in European historical writing which attempts to provide an explanation of the nature of the difference between western civilisation and other great civilisations and to account for the greater dynamism of western civilisation in the recent past – the 'European miracle' as Ernst Gellner has termed it.[5]

What was striking about Hajnal's essay was the evidence he presented bearing upon marked geographical variations in the matter of matrimonial behaviour in early modern Europe. The 'European marriage pattern' was essentially to be found in an area west of a line stretching from Trieste to Leningrad (St. Petersburg) although possibly absent south of the Alps and Pyrenees. Hajnal believed that this pattern had not always been in place in western Europe, for he had reason, based on the evidence of English tax documents of the fourteenth century and the marriage ages displayed by the English medieval aristocracy, to assert that West Europeans in the medieval centuries behaved in ways that still characterised the Slavs and the Serbs of the later nineteenth century or most contemporary societies in Asia and North Africa.[6] In so doing, Hajnal's interpretation gave rise to a view of medieval Europe possessing a social structure or ethnography that was *not* greatly differentiated across space and unrecognisable as markedly different from most other moderately heavily populated parts of the world with respect to the marital behaviour of its female inhabitants.[7]

The remainder of this essay falls into two parts. The first part reviews certain of the repercussions which follow from Hajnal's attempt both to identify a 'European marriage pattern' and to specify its origins. It is particularly concerned to discuss some of the identifiable preferences that continue to distinguish recent writings which form a loosely structured corpus associated with a school of historians who are inclined to argue for the existence of a homogeneous medieval European social structure regarding marriage and female status, especially a homogeneity that owes a great deal to the influence of the Christian Church. The second part of the chapter is more narrowly focused and considers an issue concerning the circumstances of females in the age-groups from 10 to 30 years in two late medieval societies located respectively on the northern and the southern edges of Europe. It will be argued that those female circumstances were in the two locations so different that they led to fundamentally different demographic responses to the stimuli deriving from the operation of disease cycles in the two centuries after 1348.

.   .   .

In 1983 there appeared a provocative study which had been greatly influenced by Hajnal's findings bearing upon the demographic attributes of the Europeans in the matter of their marriages after 1600, although rather than seeing European society diverging from much of the remainder of the world at that epoch, wishing to push the break-away point back to the beginning of the fourth century.[8] Goody is the author of this work which one favourable reviewer, Duby, has characterised as being 'concerned with chronology' and not with geographical variation.[9] It should, furthermore, be stressed that Goody's study is not focused solely on the narrowly demographic aspects of marriage but on its strategically central role in Europe's social and economic comportment. It is an argument concerned with how, in Goody's view, there came about a 'shattering of the unity of the circum-Mediterranean patterns towards the end of the Roman Empire'.[10] It is indeed an argument that the historical demographer and family historian of both medieval and early modern Europe cannot ignore and will ultimately stand or fall on its capacity to accord well with demographic data from the circum-Mediterranean world and from those areas north of the Alps and Pyrenees in the period from c.500 to c.1500.

Goody in an intriguing discussion takes issue with certain characteristics that are drawn by the medievalist Guichard, in the contrast the latter makes between the social structures of Christian ('Western') and Islamic ('Eastern') Spain.[11] In relation to the pattern of family organisation Guichard emphasises the opposition between the West and the East. He treats the 'West' as distinguished by bilaterality of kin alliances, the functional and authoritative predominance of the restricted family unit, well developed traditions of exogamy and monogamy, the less oppressed position of women, and a concept of honour which is attached less to persons, particularly women, than to material possessions.

Goody's critique attempts to show that the contrast is much less clear-cut with regard to certain characteristics that Guichard believes are indigenous to Andalusia and derive from Christian culture and those introduced subsequently by the conquerors from North Africa.[12] So far as the criteria of differentiation are concerned, Goody argues that the contrasts are less in respect of polygyny and the structure of the kin groups. Polygyny, Goody regards as rare on the North African shore, especially when contrasted with its far higher incidence in sub-Saharan Africa. When polygyny is detectable in the North African context it is confined to higher status groups. Goody views monogamy as characteristic of both sides of the Mediterranean and regards it as predating both Christian and Islamic influences. Indeed it is, he argues, a fundamental Eurasian trait which owes much to a feature of the kinship system that derived from the property inheriting rights of women throughout the wider Eurasian continents (including North Africa and the Middle East). On either side of the Mediterranean women acquired property from males as well as females, both through marriage and through inheritance. Goody in his earlier work, has labelled this trait 'diverging devolution' and argues that because of this system, whereby wives required and obtained from their parents or kin (or even husbands) an endowment in property, severe restrictions would be placed on their accumulation in marriage by males.[13] Goody believes that, above all other features of these societies, this latter feature, which relates to a specific mode of property devolution and its impact on the position of women, linked the peoples of Europe north of the Alps and the Mediterranean northern and southern shores together, whether they were in Anglo-Saxon England, Roman Egypt or Moorish Spain. It is a feature, Goody asserts, that overrides 'the fact that from the earliest historical periods some . . . European societies had patrilineal clans while others were organised on the basis of bi-lateral kindreds'.[14] Likewise Goody believes that Guichard overdraws the distinction he makes between a concept of honour in 'oriental' structures which is a question of being and is active and passive among males and females respectively, as opposed to an 'occidental' concept where honour is a matter of having.[15] Goody is emphatic in arguing that this distinction is universal in its occurrence and in a short passage banishes from the discussion an issue that for many years has preoccupied anthropologists in their descriptions of southern European and North African cultures. Honour is an issue to which we will return in the second half of this essay, particularly when we come to consider certain themes to do with sexuality and reputation in southern and northern European medieval societies.

In the final analysis, Goody believes, the major opposition between eastern and western or 'north-shore' and 'south-shore' structures occurs in the plane of matrimonial strategy, between *endogamy* and *exogamy*, in-marriage on the Muslim side and out-marriage on the Christian.[16] Goody believes that there was a simple economic explanation for the prevalence of in-marriage in the earlier circum-Mediterranean world which can be readily linked to the existence throughout the area of 'diverging devolution'. As Goody remarks in quoting Guichard, 'by marrying their sons with their cousins German, the members of the elementary kinship group prevented part of the patrimony – the inheritance of the female – from leaving the clan'.[17] The prohibition on close marriage is therefore central to the key difference between the Islamic and Christian shores, for today 'close marriage continues to distinguish the Asiatic and African shores of the Mediterranean, running from the Bosphorous to the Maghreb, from the European one running from Turkey to Spain'.[18]

The break in continuity around the Mediterranean came, in Goody's opinion, with Christianisation. More specifically, it started in the fourth century, at the time when a sect was transformed into a Church, into an organisation whose 'interests' required that it build up and defend a patrimony of landed wealth. The Church then constructed, in Goody's opinion, in almost conspiratorial fashion, a system of rules which, without displacing the pre-existing terminology of kinship, proceeded to condemn existing practices that he believes were directed to the restriction of inheritance of family goods to the direct male line. Goody therefore sees the Church proscribing a set of actions that, for want of a better term, were, or had been, primarily directed towards 'patriline repair'; these were, adoption, polygyny and/or remarriage, divorce, concubinage and especially endogamy.[19]

The need for constant vigilance in the matter of heir-provision, Goody believes, had much to do with the ease with which land might have drifted away from the patriline when women because of 'diverging devolution' could inherit property. Goody makes much of the fact that these proscribed practices would have been vital, for he argues that in a stationary demographic situation in approximately 20 per cent of instances a man would have no direct heirs of either sex alive to succeed him, and in a further 20 per cent of cases he would have only daughters and no sons.[20]

What is interesting, Goody emphasises, is in contrast to the indigenous customs, the proscriptions generated by the Church in no way derived from Roman law, nor from the Old or New Testament.[21] Like all sects, Goody argues, the Christians had begun by destroying family ties, detaching individuals from their kinsfolk so that they could merge into the new community: 'the despair of the parents is the joy of the revolution'.[22] While the Church placed an emphasis on family stability, it did so within a new framework which safeguarded the individual's liberty to dispose of his and especially *her* goods, thus favouring the mobility of land and its alienation, and hence its eventual devolution on the Church and the accumulation of capital in the Church's hands.[23]

Goody seems therefore to be suggesting that the Church set out in particular to confer on priests control over strategies of heirship and, especially, control over close marriages. Marriage by mutual consent and freedom of testation Goody writes 'are surely intrinsic to the whole process whereby the Church established its position as a power in the land, a spiritual power certainly, but also a worldly one, the owner of property, the largest landowner, a position it obtained by gaining control over the system of marriage, gift and inheritance'.[24] In moving to buttress the conjugal unit Goody believes an association was established between the emergence of the new Christian sect and its subsequent transformation into a Church by means of a vast accumulation of property alienated from the lands of kin groups.

In developing this avowedly materialist thesis of how he believes the Church came to endow Christian Europe with a distinctive pattern of marriage and family forms, Goody is aware that the process was not instantaneous but marked by periods of intensified activity such as during the so-called Gregorian reform of the eleventh and twelfth centuries and the Counter-Reformation centring upon the Council of Trent in 1563.[25] In his overall approach, although certainly not one which imputes the same motive to the actions of the Church, Goody appears to have support from a highly active body of canon law and ecclesiastical historians who in the last twenty years have, through their investigations of the Church's actions in the realm of ideas and moral guidance, documented what they believe in the eleventh and twelfth centuries was the crystallisation of a common set of ideas that concerned marriage.[26] Sheehan writing of the late eleventh and twelfth century reforms in marriage doctrine notes that 'whilst it *was* [my emphasis] characteristic of Europe to consist of many areas with different family customs and different marriage usages, matrimony came to an ever greater extent under the religion that was common to Europe . . . there was to appear a common set of ideas that concerned an essential mode of family recruitment, and that, we may theorize, was an important influence on the family itself'.[27]

In broad terms, the resulting view of marriage that emerged, as is argued by what can be termed, the 'triumphalist' school of Christian influence was as follows: 1) The matrimonial bond was created by consent; neither consummation nor formality of any kind was required for validity. 2) It was the consent of the couple that created the marriage bond. Whatever the role of the kin group or the politically powerful, it was secondary and dispensable. 3) It was preferred that the marriage bond be created in a public setting but, in as much as external formalities were developed and imposed, they were located within neither familial nor seignorial struc-tures, but in the local community considered in its religious or parochial capacity. 4) There was a desire to internalise the marriage relationship; theologians emphasised the bond of charity between spouses and the possibility of its growth as a reason for their choice of each other. 5) Throughout the discussion by both eleventh and twelfth century canonists and theologians their concern was to focus upon the couple: by and large, lordship was ignored; the wider family circle and even the children born to the couple received little attention.[28]

A similar preference for perceiving a unified Europe with regard to marital practice in the Middle Ages is to be found in Herlihy's pioneering attempt to provide an interpretation of household and family patterns extending from the Classical World to the late fifteenth century. Indeed this study stands at present as the only attempt that can be situated alongside the work of Goody. Herlihy is also inclined to allocate to the Church a key role in inducing change although, like the 'triumphalist' canon law historians, he disputes the motives that Goody attributes to the ecclesiastical reformers.[29]

Herlihy's argument is founded upon an account of late Classical Antiquity in which girls are considered to have been very young at first marriage, whereas their husbands were quite mature – a pattern he believes compatible with what he identifies as a contemporary inflation of dowries. In such an interpretation males whose marriages are delayed are believed to become in increasingly short supply relative to the abundance of potential, but much younger, brides. Consequently, their fathers were obliged to make them more attractive prospects in marriage which served still further to inflate dowries which they would take into marriage. One outcome of this problem created by the female 'burden', Herlihy suggests, was a widespread practice of exposing or abandoning unwanted female infants.[30]

In contrast to the Classical Mediterranean societies, the northern barbarians, Herlihy asserts, practised polygyny imbalancing the sexes in society as a consequence of concentrating women in households of the rich.[31] However, like Goody, he believes that the ethical teachings of the Christian Church had a powerful impact upon marriage through its insistence both on monogamy and exogamy for 'no other society is known to have applied the incest taboo with such extreme vigour'.[32] The Church through its insistence upon exogamy, Herlihy suggests, fostered the emergence of commensurable and comparable household units, based in part upon marriage rules that forced a circulation of women through society that was fundamentally viri- or patrivirilocal in so far as women almost invariably moved into their husband's or husband's father's co-resident group. Poor males, as a result of these reforms, had improved chances of attracting a mate, and women came to be more evenly distributed over the whole of the social spectrum. Herlihy advances the thesis that the 'new similarity of marriages and households, fairer access to women, and reduced levels of violence helped lay the foundations for a stable social order in the early medieval West'.[33]

Herlihy builds upon his argument concerning the more even distribution of women in society resulting from rules against incest and concubinage to suggest that, as a consequence, it became easier for men to marry earlier. Herlihy argues, although heavily dependent upon Tacitus for his evidence, that females came to differ little in age from males when first entering into marriage which they did in their early twenties.[34] Such a pattern, he believes, was geographically widespread throughout Europe in the tenth and eleventh centuries and was accompanied by the increasing resort to bridewealth or reversed dowry.[35]

However, this pattern lacked durability since Herlihy is prepared to view the emergence of the patrilineage as the dominant model of family organisation from the twelfth century.[36] He cites Duby in developing the view that in such familial structures great efforts were made to place all daughters into marriage, but only the first-born or eldest surviving son.[37] The increased competition in the marriage market, exacerbated by an improvement in female life expectancy once again led to the chief burden of matrimony falling on the bride and her family.[38] In such conditions the worsening 'terms of trade' faced by women when contemplating marriage supposedly prompted them to seek a mate at younger ages, while favourable terms enjoyed by males encouraged them to marry later. Consequently, Herlihy believes that across Europe both in its northern and southern regions, a pattern of marriage became established in which brides in their late teens took husbands in their late twenties. Indeed this is the pattern that he and Klapisch-Zuber encountered in their massive statistical analysis of the Florentine *catasto* of 1427 and which he believes is ubiquitous in later medieval Europe.[39]

While Herlihy was adventurous in proceeding to attribute specific demographic outcomes to the processes that ultimately derived from measures taken by the Church to reform the rules surrounding marriage, Goody was somewhat reticent in making such explicit connections.[40] In fact demographic historians have been generally disinclined to ponder the explicit and implicit links that Goody made between his treatment of ideology, canon law, and practices, largely documented with respect to the uppermost echelons of society and the demographic qualities and consequences of popular marriage in medieval Europe. Goody, however, is quite explicit in arguing that any changes in behaviour that led to the social structural underpinnings of Hajnal's 'European' marriage pattern could not be associated with Protestantism or capitalism but must be located at least a millennium earlier in time.[41]

One might therefore suppose that certain demographic patterns to do with marriage would have crystallised after the early twelfth century (and possibly earlier) that coincided in fairly broad terms with the areas within the control of the Christian Church. Goody suggests that the increasing pressure to marry outside the kin group should have resulted in a delay in marriage in the adult life-cycle and an increase in the proportions eventually failing ever to marry. An emphasis too, on the conjugal bond and the promotion of the consensual basis of spouse choice might have served to bring about similar results through an extension of the courtship process. A reluctance to sanction, indeed a positive hostility towards remarriage, should have increased the proportion of widows in the higher age-group of Christian as opposed to pre-Christian or Islamic populations. Furthermore, the campaign against concubinage or unsolemnised marriage, if it created a stronger 'legal' sense of what constituted an illegitimate birth, should have brought about a situation in which the onset of sexual relations would have begun only after the priest's blessing and the witness of the couple's union and the nuptial mass.[42]

Mention has already been made of the Florentine *catasto* of 1427 which provides the most comprehensive body of evidence bearing upon marriage for any European area before 1550. The evidence provided by the *catasto*, relating to over 60,000 Tuscan families in town and countryside, enabled Herlihy and Klapisch-Zuber to undertake a thorough analysis of marital age and incidence.[43] Tuscan women of the early fifteenth century were young when they married; on average, they married at the age of 18 to men who were generally 10 to 12 years their senior. Very few females remained unmarried, a trait reflected in the fact that in excess of 95 per cent of women in their late twenties were recorded in the *catasto* as currently married. Women remarried relatively infrequently so that particularly large numbers of widows were encountered among females over 45 years of age. Since males married relatively late in life, their teenage brides ran high risks of being widowed at a rather early stage in their lives. The remarriage chances of these widows were considerably depressed by the preference displayed by widowers and males at their first marriage to seek spouses from among the virginal teenage female population. This constellation of marital characteristics which were displayed by the Tuscans both in the century before and in the two centuries after the Black Death can be documented to have been shared with other fourteenth and fifteenth century populations in parts of southern France and southeastern Europe.[44]

However, they were not characteristics that seem to have distinguished the populations of northwest Europe in the period after 1250, when our evidence first enables us to search for them. It is important to acknowledge that there are certain difficulties in drawing extact comparisons because evidence such as is encountered in the *catasto*, which is so rich in detail and so precise in its specification of age and marital status, is less widely available in the northwest European areas. Data from late-fourteenth century English poll tax lists purporting to record the marital status of populations of 14–16 years of age and over, and information bearing upon the marital behaviour of widowed customary tenants in the proceedings of manorial courts from 1250–1550, reveal a relatively low proportion of females currently married and a relatively high, but chronologically variable, propensity to remarry on the part of women, who in many cases took spouses who were junior to them in age.[45] Both of these characteristics suggest the presence in this region of a marital regime that was termed (perhaps unfortunately) 'European' by Hajnal when he first encountered it among early modern populations in areas to the north of the Alps.[46] In his original study Hajnal misinterpreted the evidence from the English poll taxes which has in recent years been subject to intensive scrutiny and seems to show few signs of precocious female marriage age, particularly if account is taken of the under-recording of females, many of whom would appear to have been unmarried.[47]

Yet it is another feature relating to the circumstances of females that highlights a social trait of fundamental significance in differentiating late medieval Italian society from those in northwestern Europe. This particular feature of the social structure requires us to delve into the circumstances of young persons, especially females, aged from approximately 10–25 years. In what sense and to what degree were children retained within the households of their parents until marriage in the two areas? Indeed to what extent is the actual notion of departure from the natal hearth at all relevant for children of both sexes prior to marriage? For students of family history this issue was brought to the fore in 1982 in a second essay of classic status by Hajnal in which he distinguished between rules applying to two very basic systems of household formation in pre-industrial societies. These rules are set out in Table 2.1.[48]

Table 2.1
RULES APPLYING TO HOUSEHOLD FORMATION
IN PRE-INDUSTRIAL SOCIETIES

1. Formation rules common to northwest European simple household systems.	2. Formation rules common to joint-household systems.
a. Late marriage by both sexes (mean age at first marriage are, say, over 26 for men and over 23 for women).	a. Earlier marriage for men and rather early marriage for women (mean ages at first marriage are under 26 for men and under 21 for women).
b. After marriage a couple are in charge of their household (the husband is head of household).	b. A young married couple often start life together either in the household of which an older couple is and remains in charge or in a household of which an unmarried older person (such as a widower or widow) continues to be head. Usually the young wife joins her husband in the household of which he is a member.
c. Before marriage young people often circulate between households as servants.	c. Households with several married couples may split to form two or more households, each containing one or more couples.

Hajnal focused his comparison of these two systems on marriage age and the residential rules relating to the location of the newly-married couple. It should be stressed that in Hajnal's formulation both the marital and pre-marital behaviour of women is critical in differentiating one system from the other. In what Hajnal labels a 'northwest European household formation system' the mean age at marriage for women was over 23 years, whereas in the joint-household formation system which is not allocated to a specific geographical context, women married at ages below 21 years. Marriage in the joint-household formation system involved a young couple starting life together in the household of the husband's parents (patri-virilocal). Females left their natal hearths at an early age to move from a situation in which they had been under their father's or brother's authority and protection to one in which they were very much subordinate to a husband who was likely to be significantly older and a father-in-law who in all probability would have assumed the role of patriarch. By contrast, in the northwest European system the newly-married couple established a separate (neolocal) and economically independent residence. Furthermore in the latter system it was highly likely that both bride and groom would have spent a good deal of the ten to fifteen years prior to their marriage not as residents within their parents' household, but living with persons to whom they were generally, although not invariably, *unrelated*, as servants or apprentices (rule 1c). It is important to stress that this pattern of what Laslett once termed 'extra-familial secondary socialization' applied with equal probabilities to males and females.[49] Females were as likely as males to leave home in their early teens to work under contract as live-in servants for an employer to whom they were generally unrelated by blood or marriage.

Hajnal also suggested that the northwest European household formation system possessed, as a consequence of life-cycle service, an institution that was capable of expanding to absorb those who delayed their marriage in difficult periods when the accumulation of resources by potential married couples would take longer. While Hajnal did not define this process he was suggesting that there was an inverse relationship between real incomes and the incidence of service among those in the age groups 10–30 years.[50]

* * *

Our concern in the remainder of this chapter is with the two themes of service and the retention of unmarried females in, and their departure from, households in the later Middle Ages in both northern and southern Europe. Any investigation of these issues is handicapped by the absence of evidence that lends itself to the techniques of analysis that have defined the debate on the early modern sources. To date only one, albeit brief, discussion of Hajnal's model has been made by a medievalist writing of medieval Europe and it is helpful for our purposes that the comments were directed towards fifteenth-century Tuscany. Herlihy in his interpretative synthesis of households in medieval Europe notes Hajnal's 'stimulating' study and refers, in particular, to the rule specified for the northwest European household formation system relating to young persons who 'before marriage often circulate between households as servants'. Herlihy comments with reference to Tuscany in the early fifteenth century:

the medieval household system reconstituted on the basis of the Florentine data resembles the model in that the flow of young persons in and out of households in relation to their age is crucial to it. It differs, however, in two important ways. The flow of young people among households is not, at Florence, limited to servants. And the movement is across wealth categories, up or down the social scale. Hajnal seems to assume that the transfers are predominantly horizontal, that is, between households of comparable wealth and social status. He does not explore the possibilities that the giving and receiving households differed in the resources they commanded, and that the transfers were in different directions at different ages. These issues merit further examination.[51]

It remains unclear from these comments and request for further research whether Herlihy is suggesting that the early fifteenth-century Florentine household formation system is to be seen as resembling the northwest European regime or whether it shares any common features with Hajnal's joint-household formation system. It is perhaps noteworthy that Herlihy makes no reference to the use made by Hajnal in his own study of Tuscan data from the *catasto* of 1427. In fact, Hajnal utilises data relating to all ever-married males and to those ever-married males who were specified as household heads for the countryside around Pisa.[52] In employing these data Hajnal was investigating his rule 1b, relating to household residence and headship; in the northwest European regime newly married couples proceed immediately to head their own households while in joint-household formation systems grooms who marry patrivirilocally are frequently obliged to wait for some years before they attain this position.[53] Hajnal showed that of the younger men (in their twenties and thirties) many fewer than half were heading their own household. Hajnal argues that such a pattern was indistinguishable from that to be found in the Indian state of Maharashtra between 1947-51.[54] On the basis of that society's failure to abide by rule 1b, Hajnal argues for late medieval Tuscany's membership of the joint-household formation system. He did not proceed to test the rules relating to marriage age for females although we have already noted the analysis undertaken by Herlihy and Klapisch-Zuber which shows how early females married and how few had failed to marry by their mid-late twenties. Unfortunately, Hajnal did not reflect in his consideration of data from the Tuscan *catasto* on the issue of the inter-household circulation of young adults, particularly females, in service.

In what follows an attempt will be made to show how very different were the Italian and northwest European populations of the later middle ages in relation to the circulation of young adult females between households. Furthermore, it will be argued that this contrast in social structures created divergent population trends of such an order that it would be unwise to regard post-Black Death demographic conditions in

Europe as fundamentally uniform even though mortality trends, if not levels, in the bulk of the continent may have been exogenously determined. It will be suggested that much of the divergence in experiences in these two late medieval settings could be attributed to differences in the relative importance of household formation rules 1c and 2b. In pursuing this consideration of the Hajnal 'model' it is also important to assess whether the rising real incomes that were features of both societies in the century after the Black Death led to declines in the incidence of, and the time spent in, service as the resources for marriage were more rapidly accumulated by young adults.

Our discussion is therefore focused on the issue of servants, the movement between households of young persons, and on marriage ages and proportions in both northern and southern Europe in the late Middle Ages. The review of the evidence that follows is primarily concerned with young adult females in the two regions. Despite all of its remarkable qualities the Florentine *catasto* of 1427 is a frustrating document to employ in assessing the extent to which Hajnal's rule 1c was a readily identifiable feature of that society. One obstacle confronting any attempt to quantify the incidence of service derives from the fact that adult servants, even when resident in their master's household, were to submit their own tax declarations, while young servants or apprentices would consequently be included in the households of their natural parents.[55] Sons or close kin who were living abroad were usually counted as members of their parents' or brothers' households. Klapisch-Zuber has argued that the majority of parents took care to cite those of their children put out to service, even though they were away; this implies that the overall accuracy of the total population count was not adversely affected by this rule.[56] However, the geographical distribution of the recorded tax-paying population may have been distorted by the tendencies of rural areas to appear to contain more people than they did, and urban areas to be depressed as a consequence of those servants who had moved from country to town being recorded as domiciled in the countryside. Herlihy and Klapisch-Zuber suggest that this omission from urban households served to lower urban populations by some small measure equivalent to the size of the servant population normally resident within the town.[57]

Some 736 servants (0.2 per cent of the recorded Tuscan population) were actually declared, of whom 456 were males (a servant sex ratio of 162.8). Of these almost 42 per cent of the males and slightly more than 33 per cent of the females were aged between 8 and 17 years.[58] If we assume that servants were not necessarily allowed to slip from the tax record as a consequence of wholescale under-reporting, in order to reach the minimum level (6 per cent of the population in service) needed to accord with Hajnal's rule 1c, at least 15,000 individuals who normally co-resided in the households of their employers would instead have been listed in the households of their parents; if the usual level of servant-keeping reflected in rule 1c applied, then a further 25,500 servants would have been misplaced in the record of the *catasto*.

We must recall that if these servants were as likely to be female as male and, in conformity with Hajnal's northwest European regime, were never married, given that there were 21,000 unmarried females recorded in the age group 8–18, then between 33 and 48 per cent respectively of that female age-group would have had to be in service. Such levels of female servant-keeping would hardly appear compatible with the expressed views of Herlihy and Klapisch-Zuber regarding the overall incidence of servants in early fifteenth-century Tuscany. Klapisch-Zuber writes that 'it is false to say, in effect, that medieval houses abound in domestic servants' and Herlihy comments that 'servants and slaves are few in both the city and countryside' suggesting that high wage rates made it difficult for households to hire a form of employee that had become expensive under the conditions of late medieval demographic malaise.[59] It should, in addition, be stressed that if the 'hidden' servants were present to the extent required by the northwest European rule 1c then the evidence in the *catasto* would imply an age pattern of service in Tuscany that differed fundamentally from that found in Europe north of the Alps in the early modern period when it can be unambiguously specified. In the latter region the majority of servants of both sexes were to be found in the age groups 15–25, with only a small number in those age groups within which most of the never-married Tuscan female servants would necessarily have been found, given the very high proportion of females reported as married over the age of 18 years.

Of course, Hajnal's consideration of servants in the northwest European regions is founded upon a portrayal of them as unequivocally celibate and therefore focuses upon a very concentrated age-span within the life-cycle of both sexes. Klapisch-Zuber has published two very important studies in which she considers 132 agreements reached between relatively high status heads of Florentine families and women entering their households as servants which are recorded in family account books or journals (*ricordanze*).[60] While this evidence does not yield specific information on the age of servants who hired themselves to such persons, Klapisch-Zuber convincingly employs the distinction to be drawn between the term *monna*, generally reserved, on the one hand, to wives, widows and middle-aged women and, on the other hand, those females listed under their father's name and who are never qualified as *monna*. Of the female servants she investigated on that basis, Klapisch-Zuber discovered that married women and widows outnumbered unmarried females in the ratio of 3:2.[61] Consequently, she concluded that 'domestic service drew from the stock of available women without particular preference for the unmarried'. While some older females identified as household servants can be found in populations abiding by the northwest European rule, they constitute no more than an extremely small minority of this social category.

It is perhaps revealing that the discussion of servant-keeping undertaken by Barbagli in an important overview of Italian family history in the period from 1400 to 1900, in which he presents servant age-patterns for a number of northern and central Italian communities in the early and mid-sixteenth century, shows that sizeable numbers of servants of both sexes, but especially females, were listed aged 30 years and over.[62] It is unlikely that those females in service over 30, relative to those under that age would have coexisted in a ratio of 3:2, as found in the households of relatively wealthy Florentines in the late fourteenth and fifteenth centuries. However, it appears that 15 to 25 per cent of each five-year age group in the female population over 30 years of age were listed as servants in both Parma and Verona in 1545. It is also noteworthy that in both these communities marginally more than 30 per cent of the households contained servants of both sexes who constituted just over 15 per cent of the total population.

Of course, the incidence of servant-keeping in Parma and Verona is in line with that revealed by a Florentine census of 1552 when 16.7 per cent of the population were recorded as in service, of whom 70 per cent were female.[63] Although the unsatisfactory state of our knowledge of servants in the Florentine population of 1427 makes any discussion of change over time particularly difficult, there is reason to suppose that servants as a feature of the social landscape had increased markedly over the course of the late fifteenth and sixteenth centuries. Such a trend is also detectable in Verona where it would seem that free servants were 'properly' recorded in the homes of their employers in 1425.[64] At that date 12 per cent of the households contained live-in servants who constituted just over 7 per cent of the total urban population. By 1502 servants made up 12.4 per cent of that population and grew in number, although less rapidly than in the late fifteenth century to reach 14 per cent of the population in 1545.

There is still a relative dearth of studies of service in Italy, particularly in the sixteenth and seventeenth centuries. It is necessary, therefore, to exercise caution in advocating the existence of patterns that could well turn out to be premature until much more work is completed. Mitterauer in a recent, but pioneering, consideration of service in seventeenth and eighteenth century Italy, drew the conclusion that servants in Europe north of the Alps tended to be young and unmarried, while in both urban and rural Italy they were less numerous, older and sometimes married and not infrequently widowed.[65] Barbagli in his survey of the early modern evidence for north and central Italian towns argued for a decline in the incidence of servant-keeping from a sixteenth-century high point, in part because of the disappearance of the practice of keeping *garzoni* (apprentices).[66] Notwithstanding this decline in apprenticeship, the evidence for urban populations in these areas of Italy reveals no tendency for service to become feminised. Such a development, however, was to occur in the late eighteenth and early nineteenth centuries. A wide-ranging survey by Arru of the 'distinguishing features' of domestic service in Italy places stress on two striking attributes; one concerns the tendency for relatively large proportions of servants to derive from older age groups such that in a sample of urban populations from the seventeenth and eighteenth centuries, 40–65 per cent of female servants and 50–70 per cent of male servants were over 30 years of age; the other was the high ratio of male to female servants in town when compared with north European urban communities for comparable periods in time.[67] Such a feature of urban social organisation appears to be closely connected with the relatively low rates of female migration to towns before the early nineteenth century. As Arru stresses females had 'to have legitimation to be able to move to the city, hence in the placement of women, whether young or old, moral protection, reliability and protection of honour were the elements most stressed'.[68] The attributes of those in domestic service that have recently been documented in Italian towns of the early modern period are consistent with many features that have been stressed in the studies of service in early fifteenth-century Florentine society and its growth as an institution in the late fifteenth and early sixteenth centuries.

Klapisch-Zuber provides us with the most sophisticated account of this process of growth in urban servant populations during the late fifteenth and early sixteenth centuries.[69] This explanation is directed towards developments in Florence and is concerned to establish whether the economic circumstances of the early fifteenth century (in which demographic conditions brought about an improvement in the remuneration of salaried employment) had an impact upon the work done in Florentine households by those whom she terms 'female outsiders'. Klapisch-Zuber, like Herlihy, is struck by the relative scarcity of servants in the early fifteenth century and explains their limited appearance in households as a function of their high cost in so far as she is able to demonstrate that the salaries of female servants more than doubled in the century after 1348, and actually overtook those paid to males. While total employment in service may not have grown under these circumstances the servant population came to be dominated by older married or widowed females who entered into service for brief periods as a solution to short-term economic difficulties. Indeed the noteworthy scarcity of married workers created conditions that enabled widowed females to move from service into the wider labour market and back again with relative ease. Klapisch-

Zuber also identifies a growth in the incidence of a younger category of unmarried servant, who often entered into contracts with an employer at the age of 8 or 9 years. Servants employed under these arrangements would not receive their wages until their employer judged them to be of marrying age. Indeed the employer might be responsible for the servant maid's dowry and sponsor her wedding which often occurred under his roof. In general, Klapisch-Zuber presents us with an account in which service for the unmarried female was always to be regarded, at least for females with marital aspirations, as a last resort. She even suggests that it was an institution that may actually have jeopardised the servant's marital claims as living and working in such a 'context', away from the protection of her male kin, her honour would have been endangered. Klapisch-Zuber goes so far as to argue that for the unmarried female to be paid for her services was to place herself on the very margins of respectability.[70]

However, demographic recovery in the last third of the fifteenth century began to drive down real wages. It also seems to have led to greater competition, at least before 1500, with men for work as domestic servants. As a consequence domestic service became for a while more masculinised; men began to 'crowd out' females from this sector of the labour market. Nonetheless, over the second half of the century leading up to 1552 Klapisch-Zuber sees a real growth of service as an activity for women.[71] She intriguingly relates this change to other developments occurring in Florence's marriage market. Through their use of Hajnal's method for the calculation of the singulate mean age of marriage from census data Herlihy and Klapisch-Zuber have charted the course of marriage age changes through the late fourteenth and fifteenth centuries.[72] In Florence, as in Tuscany more generally, marriage was distinguished by a large age gap between husband and wife. Throughout the fifteenth century that gap between Florentine husbands and wives almost always exceeded 10 years, with grooms of approximately 30 to 31 years of age taking brides of between 17 and 20 years. The tendency through the late fifteenth century was for male marriage age to rise and for female marriage to be drawn up in its wake. Herlihy and Klapisch-Zuber's explanation for these shifts depends in part upon treating the age gap between husband and wife as a structural constant through which other economic or demographic changes were reflected or mediated.

Much of the change, they suggest, originates from improving life expectancy that both generated demographic growth and increased competition among males for a fixed or, at best, slowly growing number of niches in the Florentine economy. The delay to male marriage age that these difficulties caused increased the likelihood that the numbers of males of 'appropriate' marriage age would shrink relative to the size of the age group from which brides were drawn. As a consequence, the age gap between bride and groom ensured that there would be an over-supply of females entering into the marriage market relative to males, notwithstanding the tendency of widowers, but not widows, to remarry. The rising male age of first marriage is, so Herlihy and Klapisch-Zuber argue, reflected in a tendency for dowries to increase in value over the course of the fifteenth century. This build-up of pressure manifests itself most strikingly in the Florentine Commune's intervention into the marriage market through the establishment of the *Monte delle doti*, which provided fathers, at least among the more substantial citizens, with a means of financing dowries that would mature at a time appropriate for the daughter's marriage. The desperate search for a means of funding dowries is also reflected in the growth of charitable donations to assist in the provisioning of girls with modest dowries. Indeed the contracts whereby young girls entered into domestic service for a long period of up to 8 years may be seen as a variant of this process whereby servant employers made arrangements for a section of the poorer female populace.[73] Likewise, the dowry-creating activities of the charitable fraternities may have served the same purpose. Perhaps the most striking accompaniment of all of these increasing difficulties that were making entry into marriage less probable or predictable was the rapid expansion of the proportion of the female population resident in convents.[74] Klapisch-Zuber, in particular, is therefore inclined to view the expansion of female domestic service in another, less elevated social echelon in the sixteenth century, as an extension of these difficulties, exacerbated by a shrinkage in access to other forms of female employment. The sixteenth century is therefore viewed as a period in which an increasing proportion of females were forced into domestic service in many cases as an alternative, rather than as a prelude, to marriage. The Florentine census of 1552 showing a very substantial presence of female servants has therefore to be understood in the context of a world where marriage was becoming increasingly difficult. A century earlier no such linkage between celibacy and domestic service appears to have existed. Indeed as Klapisch-Zuber suggests the two 'conditions' in the early fifteenth century are to be regarded as decidedly autonomous.[75]

The discussion above of both the association and the lack of relationship between live-in service and the incidence and age of marriage in Florence does not provide us with an assemblage of inter-locking parts which rests comfortably with the totality of Hajnal's northwest European household formation system. Rule 1c is largely based upon the notion that service was to function as a prelude to, rather than a substitute for, marriage, although Hajnal does not entirely rule out the latter as a possibility. Moreover, the structural underpinning of the Florentine marriage pattern in Klapisch-Zuber's account appears to be the large age gap between spouses which is a feature that is uncharacteristic of northwest European societies, in which husband and wife, at first marriage, were generally separated in age by only a few years. Indeed the northwest European system does yield a far from inconsequential proportion of marriages involving brides older than grooms. Paradoxically, the model of marriage and service in the sixteenth century, as interpreted by Klapisch-Zuber, does accord quite well with one aspect of Hajnal's argument in which in 'functionalist' terms he suggests that service 'made possible variations over time in the age at marriage and the proportions remaining never-married'. Indeed Klapisch-Zuber describes service by the mid-sixteenth century as having become a 'preconjugal purgatory' for women.[76] It remains to be seen whether that aspect of Hajnal's argument treating service as a safety-net into which young adults fell in increasing numbers during periods when marriage was perceived to be difficult to attain, and the converse in good times, as fertility adjusts in response to variations in the economic climate, is really borne out by the evidence from northwest European areas.

In pursuing this matter our attention is focused upon later medieval England as a representative area of northwest Europe, although some material from other parts of the Low Countries, Northern France, and Germany can be marshalled to broaden the discussion. It must be emphasised that no source comparable to the *catasto* of 1427 as complete in its coverage of the total population or as sophisticated in the range of information collected has survived for northwest Europe. This lacuna makes comparison with Tuscany a hazardous exercise and any conclusions therefore have to be presented most tentatively.

Some sense of the proportions of servants within various late medieval English communities can be obtained from the first Poll Tax of 1377, based on all lay persons over the age of 14. Since these data relate to the taxed population and the probability of evasion by female servants was quite high, the incidence of service revealed by these data sets has to be regarded as an underestimate. Furthermore, entry into service could have begun earlier than the age of liability for taxation which was fourteen. An investigation of the 170 places in the 1377 tax returns from the counties of Lincolnshire, Northumberland, Oxfordshire, Rutland, and Shropshire, for which nominative tax returns survive, reveals that slightly more than 8 per cent of tax-payers in those communities were servants.[77] Poll tax returns identify households and hence a calculation of the proportion of the households containing servants is possible. Once more some allowance has to be made for the fact that some households may have contained servants not recorded because the servants were under taxable age. Consequently, proportions of households containing servants must be regarded as minimal. In the urban populations for which tax data survive from 1377 and 1379 it would appear that it was normal for a fifth to one third of urban households to contain servants, whereas in the rural sample of tax-payers for 1377, servants were found in 15 per cent of households.[78] There are no English cross-sectional data that permit comparable calculations again until 1523 when 19.4 per cent of the households of Coventry are recorded as containing servants.[79] Such a figure can be compared with the Poorterie quarter of Ypres in 1506 where 30.5 per cent of households contained servants.[80] These proportions from the Flanders town are rather lower than Reims, almost a century earlier where in 1422 two of the city's wealthier parishes possessed 49 and 46 per cent respectively of their households with servants.[81] If data for the wider urban area of Reims had survived the overall proportional figure would doubtless have been lower. Comparable variations in the incidence of servants in urban households is apparent, for instance, in York in 1377 where in the wealthy parishes of St. Martin Coney Street and St. Crux 65.5 per cent and 48.3 per cent respectively of households record resident servants and where 45.5 and 35.5 per cent respectively of the tax-paying population were in service. In contrast, in the poorer extra-mural suburb of Bootham only 11.7 per cent of households were servant-keepers and 10.5 per cent of the tax-paying population were servants.[82]

Urban servant sex ratios, while volatile, were sometimes below 100.[83] Rural servant sex ratios differ significantly and could reach values as high as 190 or 200, although the excessively masculine character of these figures most likely reflects some evasion of the tax-collectors' net by female servants or their employers.[84] Such a contrast between urban and rural servant sex ratios is apparent in the English evidence of the seventeenth and eighteenth centuries which suggests that the poll taxes may well reflect a wider historical pattern (although subject to some regional variation) in which service was for the most part a more feminised activity in town than in countryside.[85]

Unlike the *catasto*, the English poll taxes do not distinguish individuals by age. In fact, the only source capable of being used systematically to recover the age of entry into service and its customary length is the evidence contained in depositions by witnesses in cases before ecclesiastical courts. Goldberg has discovered that servants form a significant proportion of deponents within the sample of surviving York cause papers.[86] The ages thereby obtained relate to the age at which the deponent testified or to the servant's age at the time of the events to which the cause related. Because of these characteristics of the evidence it is easier to obtain information on the customary age of entry into, than departure from, service.[87] It is perhaps significant that no female servant under age 12 was revealed by this evidence and no female servant is to be found who exceeded 28 years.[88] It would, however, be unwise to suppose that all young women remained in service into their early twenties before eventually departing, for the depositions also include a small but not insignificant group of unmarried women within the same age ranges who are apparently living outside of service.[89] Both these categories of unmarried females are particularly hard to detect in the late medieval Tuscan sources. In considering the period in which a servant stayed within a given position in a household the cause papers are of great value. Most likely, male and female experiences differed, at least to the extent that few girls were formally apprenticed and bound within the household of a single master for a seven-year period. It was certainly in the interests of employers of labour in the labour-starved conditions of the later fourteenth century to secure employees on annual contracts by which they were remunerated primarily in the form of bed and board, rather than hiring them for wages paid by the day. Much of the litigation surrounding infractions of the Statute of Labourers of 1351 can be interpreted to indicate such hiring preferences on the part of employers.[90] For instance, Goldberg relates the instructive case of Isabella, servant of Master John de Rissheton who was contracted for an annual term, but agreed to serve Thomas de Queldale at its expiry for a similar period. But in the aftermath of the 'Grey Death' or plague of 1361 when competition for labour was very intense Isabella had been forced to continue in service with her first master.[91] There is a certain amount of evidence indicating that some servants remained in the same household for several years but the modal pattern was one of fairly frequent, annual moves.[92]

The demand for, and the tasks performed by, urban servants were to a considerable degree sex-specific. The poll tax listings are helpful in specifying these patterns and some remarkably uniform associations emerge. Female servants were most frequently encountered in the households of persons in victualling and mercantile trades and least frequently in the metal and leather trades. The demand for women servants in the textile and clothing trades fell between these two extremes. Such patterns appear to have been related to the task performed by the servant. In contrast to the evidence we possess for Florentine households it should be noted that female servants in English towns in the late fourteenth century were not confined to non-productive households. Indeed it seems that service cannot be regarded as a purely domestic and non-economic function, or a form of disguised unemployment, or purely conspicuous consumption on the part of the employer. However, there is no doubt that the range of tasks performed by female servants in trade households tended to centre around traditional 'feminine' productive skills such as needlecraft, brewing, baking and the preparation of foods, washing clothes, and dealing in the marketplace or shops.[93]

Goldberg has delved further into the evidence left in the depositions to ascertain the extent to which a servant might have been free from formal duties and how the time was passed outside his or her employer's household. There is evidence that a considerable amount of social drinking was indulged in and there is reason to suppose that older female servants took part also. For instance, Goldberg notes the activities of Agnes Nevill, servant to a widow of Coney Street in York who visited a neighbour's house one evening and passed the hours between nine and vespers talking and drinking with the neighbour's servants.[94] As Goldberg suggests, it was probably in this informal way that servants formed their own friendship networks and exchanged information about their respective employers, and, in the case of older servants, conducted their courtships with minimal parental or employer supervision. The identification of such patterns of behaviour is of crucial importance in so far as in life-cycle terms this form of service can readily be viewed as a prelude to marriage and certainly does not seem compatible with the delimitation and policing of a social space in which sexually mature unmarried males and females were being kept apart, whether through the efforts of their kin or employers.[95]

This rather static and highly summarised account of service in English late medieval urban settlements should not be allowed to foster the impression that change over the late medieval period was minimal. The sex ratios of servants identified as beneficiaries in testamentary evidence from York (hardly ideal evidence for the purpose of delineating change in sexual composition of the urban servant labour force) seem to suggest that by the late fifteenth century female servants were being excluded from craft households.[96] This is a trend that coincided with a body of evidence indicative of economic recession in York and other English towns.[97] In the commercial sector of the urban economy, especially in mercantile households, a different trend is detectable. Here Goldberg observes sex ratios moving in favour of females and suggests that there appears to have been a polarisation of service occurring between the more prosperous mercantile households and the more masculine servant groups in the harder pressed households whose masters worked in the craft sector.[98] He has interpreted this as indicative of significant displacement of females from productive work more generally in the towns and their confinement to unskilled, non-industrial or purely domestic sectors of the economy. This may be part of a wider process associated with the feminisation of service as women's involvement in the wider labour market fell away and the status of service was undermined.[99]

What similarities and contrasts can be identified given the preliminary and rudimentary state of research into servants, very largely if not exclusively within the urban settlements of England and Tuscany? There would seem to be little reason to doubt that the proportion of households containing servants and their share in the urban populations in the period from c.1350 to c.1550 were substantially higher in the English than the Tuscan towns. A similar contrast can be drawn between the towns of northern France, the Low Countries, and Germany and those of Tuscany and some other parts of northern Italy. However, by the second quarter of the sixteenth century these contrasts, at least superficially, are rather less apparent. It remains far from clear whether the convergence that the northern urban populations of the late fourteenth and fifteenth century would appear to have made with those of north-central Italy in the overall incidence of households containing resident servants also characterises both the age and sex patterns of those who became servants, in the two regions. Prior to the early sixteenth century the evidence would seem to point to noteworthy differences. In England both males and females of approximately similar ages were drawn into service, usually between the ages of 15 and 25. The pattern of service involving older married and widowed females that Klapisch-Zuber describes for early fifteenth century Florence seems to be very largely absent from the English towns of a comparable time period. It would seem ill-advised to regard the pattern of service in the Italian urban communities prior to the late eighteenth century as unequivocally 'life-cycle' in form. The Italian behavioural patterns in the matter of servants, at least in towns for which more information has been assembled, seem to be fundamentally incompatible with Hajnal's rule 1c.

Both the surviving poll tax evidence relating to late-fourteenth century England and that from the York matrimonial litigation of the later fourteenth and early fifteenth centuries are indicative of a pattern of relatively late marriage for females which is certainly in accordance with rule 1a for Hajnal's northwest European schema. Evidence from York testamentary sources analysed by Goldberg shows that the proportion of female testators dying unmarried reached nearly 17 per cent in the years c.1426–39.[100] By contrast, in Florence, at about the same date, only some 3 per cent of women remained unmarried after their 25th birthday.[101] While a great deal of the evidence considered in this discussion suggests that later medieval English urban communities abided by all three rules that Hajnal considers to distinguish the northwest European household formation system, the issue of whether service functioned as an equilibrating force between population growth and economic opportunity remains unclear.

Perhaps we can pursue this issue in part by extending our comparison of England and Tuscany in the two centuries after 1350. A striking feature of the early modern English evidence is that notwithstanding the tremendous cyclical variations through time in fertility, mortality, and intrinsic growth rates the mean household size (M.H.S) obtained from all listings of inhabitants varied minimally between 4.75 and 4.86.[102] Furthermore, there is little evidence to suggest that over this same period the urban M.H.S. changed greatly in England, remaining throughout at close to four persons.[103] A limited comparison of late fourteenth-century England and late fourteenth- and early fifteenth-century Tuscany, which Goldberg has undertaken, suggests that urban communities in the two populations were almost identical with respect to household size.[104] In 1377 M.H.S. of tax-payers in Hull was only 3.71, in Dartmouth 3.76, and in York 4.1. In Prato in 1371 M.H.S. was as low as 3.44 and still only 3.7 in 1427.[105] In Florence and its environs M.H.S. was marginally over 3.9.[106] Goldberg's provisional analysis of late medieval and that by Wall of early modern English urban centres suggest that M.H.S remained close to four persons whenever it can be observed in census or tax evidence. By contrast, over the late fifteenth and early sixteenth centuries Herlihy and Klapisch-Zuber note that the number of households in urban communities displays very considerable intransigiency, whereas M.H.S. is far more volatile.[107] For instance, in Prato it would appear that M.H.S. rose between 1427 and 1470 from 3.73 to 4.26 and that between 1427 and 1458 in Florence it rose from 3.78 to 4.82, climbing to 5.66 in 1552. At the same time as M.H.S. expanded in the Tuscan urban settlements there would seem to have been a significant drop in the proportion of households headed by females.[108] This is a feature that mirrors developments in the urban sex ratios. Although later medieval Tuscan sex ratios seem always to have been in excess of 100, urban sex ratios were consistently higher than rural sex ratios. We have already noted that these are features which many Italian towns possessed, not only in the late medieval period but in the sixteenth, seventeenth, and early eighteenth centuries.[109] The male surplus was most apparent in the larger cities of Florence and Pisa which had sex ratios in 1427 of 117.6 and 112.3 whereas the equivalent ratios for their respective *contadi* were only 109.8 and 106.8.[110] The Tuscan towns seem to have become increasingly masculinised over the late fifteenth century and, as Goldberg notes, it would seem improbable that these sex ratios can be explained by the out-migration of females to the countryside.[111] Nor does it seem possible that the tendency to record urban-domiciled females with their rural-based parents could have occurred on a scale sufficient to produce this statistical effect.[112] It seems most likely that the *catasto* is revealing the product of in-migration of males seeking employment in the city. This represents a fundamental structural contrast with English society in the post-Black Death period where urban sex ratios (calculated for the adult population only) were in general considerably lower than those encountered in rural areas, even when allowance is made for the volatility in the data created by the failure of the poll taxes of 1379 and 1381, in particular, to record females accurately.[113]

In what sense may these contrasts be explained both by differences in the extent to which unmarried women were to be found in service and in other forms of paid employment? The relatively muted development of female service and the early age of female marriage would seem to have limited the extent to which increased recourse to female labour functioned to solve the labour shortage created by the plague. In Florence, male in-migration seems to have been one response to this problem, notwithstanding the possibility that the urban sex ratio could have been misleadingly inflated by the recording of female servants in their parent's rural households. Goldberg is justifiably impressed by evidence presented by Klapisch-Zuber who has demonstrated that Florentine multiple households responded to these conditions by failing to undergo fission when a son married and incorporated his wife in line with Hajnal's rule 2b.[114] Widows may have found the labour power of sons vital following their husband's death and the absence of fission may have led to a reduced share of all households headed by females. Such a tendency would, of course, have contributed to a growth in M.H.S. prior to that which Klapisch-Zuber has noted occurring in association with demographic growth later in the fifteenth and early sixteenth centuries. However, it would also seem that by the sixteenth century, for rather different economic reasons, sons were increasingly unable to win economic independence and consequently were unable to marry and therefore 'lingered on' in their parent's household.[115]

Labour shortages in the same period in English towns (and possibly rural areas also) seem to have been satisfied from two different sources neither of which would appear to have a significant role in the Tuscan case. On the one hand there was one source in the form of resident servant labour in which females were heavily represented, that in an era of rising wage rates and falling food prices was comparatively inexpensive for employers, and on the other hand there was frequent resort by employers to, female non-resident wage labour. Such patterns suggest that in England the family system was less retentive of female children and young adults who were freer to move out of the parental hearth and to spend an extended period prior to marriage in the households of others.[116] At no stage in the late medieval period could it be said of the English young adult female, as has been said by Herlihy of the Florentine female of the same age, that 'she was wrenched from childhood and dependency, and established as mistress of a household at the usual age of fifteen'.[117]

Of course it is apparent that by arguing for the growth of service in England and its assumed association with delayed entry into marriage along with an increasing tendency of unmarried women to be deeply implicated in the urban labour force between 1360 and 1450, we would seem to be offering an account of a trend which runs counter to Hajnal's view of service as an equilibrating force in the northwest European demographic and household system. The growing importance of service, especially in households in which women were involved in productive activities seems to have been associated with a rise in living standards of unmarried females. The growth of service seems *not* to have functioned as a safety-net into which unmarried women were drawn because material requirements needed for marriage were unobtainable. Such an argument raises the issue of the extent to which women in this situation were exercising a preference for service and/or entry into the labour market in a more general sense, not because it was a prelude to or a second-best alternative to marriage, but because it was a context which they themselves desired.[118]

It is of interest to note that with the shift of economic conditions at the end of the fifteenth century Goldberg has argued that women in English towns were becoming marginalised and their range of options was shrinking.[119] Indeed as the economic difficulties of urban economies began to manifest themselves the increasing competition amongst males for work seems to have displaced women from productive activities making marriage, as an alternative to 'independent' employment for them, more of an inevitability. It is reasonable to argue that, contrary to the views of Hajnal, service was a de-stabilising force in the English demographic regime, if it is to be assumed *a priori*, that homeostasis should prevail in the relationships between fertility, mortality, and real incomes.[120] Service appears to have increased in incidence amongst the female population when mortality-induced male labour shortages, with their high wage rates, drew young adult women into employment and away from marriage; and it seems to have contracted in its incidence for females (or became restricted to non-productive household tasks) as, in conditions of labour oversupply, women were increasingly faced with involvement in the most highly marginalised sectors of the labour market, or sought security in marriage with males who had preferential access to employment.[121] Under such deteriorating conditions, contrary to both Malthusian reasoning and the Hajnal 'service model', unmarried women chose to marry earlier, in so far as service or other forms of employment for the single woman had become an increasingly unattractive or unavailable option.[122]

Klapisch-Zuber's account of service in later fifteenth-century Florence seems to have worked much more like the institution proposed by Hajnal for northwest European areas. As population growth and reduced economic prospects led to a diminution in the marital prospects of both males and females, service, alongside the convent, grew in importance as 'slots' into which unmarried females of low and high social status respectively were pushed. Indeed it seems that by the mid-sixteenth century service and the convent were fulfilling key roles in the Florentine 'preventive' check.

These are of course contentious, theoretically unrefined arguments and to date they have been the subject of rather patchy empirical research, but the aim of this chapter has been to open up the discussion, to review and to revise certain aspects of arguments relating to systems of household formation as they were initially specified by Hajnal, and to question any attempt to treat the circumstances of unmarried women in late medieval Europe as regionally undifferentiated. The discussion has, in particular, sought to draw European attention to the neglect of servants, especially those of the female sex, as potential differentiators of European social structures and their associated demographic regimes. The tentative conclusion is that in the later Middle Ages servants differed in their incidence, age-patterns, sex ratios, and overall relationship to the household formation systems and economic trends between Tuscany and England and perhaps between other areas of northwestern and southern Europe.

It is worth recalling that Hajnal was characteristically cautious about the distinctiveness of northwest Europe and its relationship with southern Europe. He wrote 'there were in southern Europe household formation systems that did not conform to the northwest European rules, but they were probably more similar to the northwest European systems than were the joint-household systems (for example, there probably were some life cycle servants)'.[123] He felt that the way he had presented the distinctiveness of northwest European household formation systems might have 'to be modified when Southern European systems have been thoroughly studied'.[124] Hajnal's caution is fully justified although his qualifications may have more relevance to the period after 1700. However, in the later medieval period there seem to be strong reasons for allocating Tuscany, but not England, a place within that broad category of societies that are conveniently described as abiding by the rules that constitute Hajnal's 'joint-household formation system'.[125]

*   *   *

It is hoped that the argument constructed in this chapter may form a contribution to a developing discussion that moves beyond the mere establishment of regional differences in a medieval Europe that was certainly more varied than is perhaps implied by the somewhat stark concentration on two very different marital and household regimes. The discussion has been preoccupied with many of the same themes that concern Goldberg in his contributions to this volume. It endorses his claim that the social structural differences he too identifies between England and Tuscany are likely to provide an instructive framework within which to consider other major themes in European economic history.[126]

For instance, a problem that, given restrictions of space, a chapter of this kind can address only minimally has to do with chronologies of economic and cultural change which so dominate the discipline of history whether our conceptual preferences derive from liberal, neo-classical, classical or functionalist marxist theory. We are restrained to operate within well-worn periods of time or themes such as 'the twelfth century renaissance', 'the crisis of the later Middle Ages', 'the Agricultural Revolution', 'the Industrial Revolution' and so on. We allocate preferential meaning to the measures of economic well-being derived, for instance, from such sup-posedly unambiguous data as those to do with real wages, measures of occupational diversity, productivity per unit of labour input – all tending to derive from data relating, largely, if not exclusively to males. These may well provide us with levels of material well-being that could be changed in absolute terms, favourably or unfavourably for both men and women in tandem. However, it remains far from clear that in relative terms, the well-being of the sexes moved together in a synchronised fashion through all or indeed most so-called classic periods of economic and social history. Some benefits may accrue to this discussion through the incorporation of Sen's notion of 'capabilities' which entails the use of a more inclusive measure of well-being. Sen has given much thought to what he regards as the place of 'capabilities' and 'functionings' in determining living stand-ards. He distinguishes between a 'functioning' or an achievement which is evidently directly related to living conditions and a 'capability' which is a notion of freedom, an ability to choose a particular path of action which leads to an achievement.[127]

In this chapter the case of unmarried women has loomed large in an attempt to reflect upon the processes influencing the changing relative well-being of men and women and the way those changes might produce unanticipated associations between the propensity of women to enter into marriage and levels of well-being measured naively in terms of male real wages. However, the mix of capabilities and chosen achievements were in no sense fundamentally similar in all European regions. It becomes increasingly apparent that Europe lacked homogeneity with regard to its kinship patterns and family norms, which to a very considerable extent, determined whether there were large numbers of unmarried women in the age group 15–30. It was in part through these family forms that the impact of the major forces of economic change were mediated, with very different consequences for the labour force participation rates of women and total fertility.

We have considered how in the conditions of demographic malaise in the late fourteenth and early fifteenth centuries labour shortages in England gave rise to a substantial expansion of unmarried women working outside their natal households and especially in service where they were heavily involved in productive rather than domestic activities. The shift of economic conditions led to a substantial influx of unmarried women into towns and a sharp rise in the proportions of them never marrying. At the end of the fifteenth and the beginning of the sixteenth centuries a combination of urban slump and demographic growth created circumstances in which employment possibilities for females fell away. Women were displaced from productive activities both in service and as wage earners and became more strongly associated with domestic activities in service or even more marginal activities and more readily sought marriage, possibly at an earlier age and almost certainly in higher proportions.

However, in a recent work, deploying arguments which could hardly apply to late medieval England, Herlihy claims that it was in conditions of dense population and over-supplied labour markets that an increased propensity on the part of unmarried women to seek work can be most easily detected as marriage became a state that was harder to achieve.[128] Herlihy's arguments do sit comfortably with Klapisch-Zuber's account of female service in fifteenth and sixteenth-century Florence which is revealed as an institution functioning very much like a safety valve for women. There in the late fifteenth century, population growth combined with reduced economic prospects for society at large worked together to diminish the marital chances of both males and females. Work in service alongside a spinster life in the convent grew in importance as 'niches' into which unmarried girls chose to move or into which they were forced. Yet at an earlier date in the late fourteenth century, when in England girls were entering into service in such numbers that 20 to 30 per cent of urban households may have contained at least one female servant over the age of 14 or 16, this category of female employment was poorly developed in Florence. Under similar demographic conditions fewer than 4 per cent of Florentine women remained unmarried and most who did so married by the age of 18 or 19. Klapisch-Zuber presents us with an account in which service for the young unmarried Florentine female was always regarded as a last resort, for to be in service and away from the protection of male kin endangered the servant's honour and thereby reduced her 'capabilities'. On the contrary, entry into service for the female of late fourteenth and early fifteenth century English towns may have enhanced her 'capabilities', her choice-set, and her well-being in the broadest sense.

These examples should alert us to the different meanings and responses associated with the concept of 'marginalisation'. It is frequently argued that to be outside of marriage for the medieval female was to be 'marginalised'. Such may have been the case for the Florentine female in the sixteenth century but it was the increasing marginalisation of unmarried females in the urban economies of later fifteenth and early sixteenth century England that drove them into marriage. These are not just semantic matters for in the Florentine case marginalisation was the consequence of failure in the marriage market; in the English context, an increased preference for marriage was a consequence of marginalisation in the labour market.[129] Such issues only acquire meaning when their discussion is situated squarely within the contexts of specific systems of family organisation. They show how inadequate would be any simple account that attempted to propose a pan-European response of women to labour supply changes in the later Middle Ages. They also expose the distortions that can be introduced to our thinking by the approaches that were discussed in the first part of this chapter and they strengthen the case of those who would argue for comparative research and the need to jettison the idea that Europe possessed geographic integrity when attempts are made to write the marital and economic histories of women.

Notes

1 Exemplary accounts that argue in these terms are: W. Abel, *Agrarian Fluctuations in Europe from the Thirteenth to the Twentieth Centuries* (1980); R. Fossier, *Peasant Life in the Medieval West* (Oxford, 1988); T.K. Helleiner, 'The Population of Europe from the Black Death to the Eve of the Vital Revolution', in *The Cambridge Economic History of Europe* vol. IV, ed. E.E. Rich and C. Wilson (Cambridge, 1967), pp. 1–95. Brenner has initiated a debate not intended in its essentials to cast doubt on the demographic trends so much as to deny the existence of common consequences following from them. See *The Brenner Debate: Agrarian Class Structure and Economic Development in Pre-Industrial Europe*, ed. T.H. Aston and C.H.E. Philpin (Cambridge, 1985).

2 An example of an account of single-factor, trans-European demographic growth deriving from a revolution in agricultural techniques is L. White, *Mediaeval Technology and Social Change* (Oxford, 1962). For a view of European-wide demographic decline and growth as the product of epidemiological change see M. Livi-Bacci, *Population and Nutrition: An Essay on European Demographic History* (Cambridge, 1991), especially pp. 17–18.

3 E.A. Wrigley, 'Population History in the 1980s', *Journal of Interdisciplinary History* 12 (1981), p. 218; J. Hajnal, 'European Marriage Patterns in Perspective', in *Population in History*, ed. D.V. Glass and D.E.C. Eversley (1965), pp. 101–43.

4 Hajnal, 'European Marriage Patterns', pp. 101–6.

5 Wrigley, 'Population History in the 1980s', pp. 218–19; E. Gellner, as quoted by E.L. Jones, *The European Miracle: Environments, Economies and Geopolitics in the History of Europe and Asia* (Cambridge, 1981), p. 225.

6 Hajnal, 'European Marriage Patterns', pp. 118–19.

7 Following Hajnal's original inclination to treat medieval Europe as 'non-European' in its marital patterns, historians have been ready to see the European marriage pattern crystallising initially in northwest Europe (England and Normandy), before extending eastwards and southwards to encompass most of the western parts of the continent by the early seventeenth century. Explanations of this supposed process have been sought in economic and/or religious developments thought to have been peculiar to this corner of Europe. See R.M. Smith, 'Marriage Processes in the English Past: Some Continuities', in *The World We Have Gained: Histories of Population and Social Structure*, ed. L. Bonfield, R.M. Smith, and K. Wrightson (Oxford, 1986), pp. 47–8, n. 16.

8 J. Goody, *The Development of the Family and Marriages in Europe* (Cambridge, 1986).

9 *Times Literary Supplement*, October 14, 1983, p. 1107.

10 Goody, *The Development of the Family*, pp. 9–10.

11 P. Guichard, *Structures Sociales 'Orientales' et 'Occidentales' dans l'Espangne Musulmane* (Paris, 1977).

12 Goody, *The Development of the Family*, pp. 10–33.

13 Ibid., pp. 19–21.

14 Ibid., p. 20.

15 Ibid., pp. 29–30. Such a response from Goody is indeed noteworthy for Blok writes of 'the Mediterranean code of honour' as if its pan-Mediterranean diffusion can be taken for granted. A. Blok, 'Rams and Billygoats: A Key to the Mediterranean Code of Honour', *Man* 16 (1981), p. 428. While the anthropological discussion of 'honour and shame' in Mediterranean societies has failed to produce an overall argument concerning its determination, a recurrent theme in this literature concerns the fact that honour is largely defined by reference to sexuality. For an assessment of the literature that reveals this common denominator to great effect, see P. Horden and N. Purcell, *The Corrupting Sea: I: The Mediterranean World: Man and Environment in Antiquity and the Middle Ages* (Oxford, forthcoming), part 6. Case studies considered by Horden and Purcell depict how carefully female sexuality is controlled; young girls are revealed as having to be taught the values of restraint and being kept in semi-seclusion for loss of virginity means a 'failure of the family'. For an historical collection that demonstrates how vital a 'Mediterranean' concept of honour is to an understanding of behavioural patterns see, *Sex and Gender in Historical Perspective*, ed. E. Muir and G. Ruggiero (Baltimore, 1990). A particularly revealing essay in the latter collection is that by L. Ferrante, 'Honour Regained: Women in the Casa del Soccorso di San Paolo in Sixteenth-Century Bologna', pp. 46–72, which indicates how easily the perceptions of woman as independent and woman as sinner overlapped.

16 Goody, *The Development of the Family*, pp. 31–3.

17 Ibid., p. 32; Guichard, *Structures Sociales 'Orientales' et 'Occidentales'*, p. 34.

18 Goody, *The Development of the Family*, p. 33.

19 Ibid., pp. 39–47.

20 Ibid., pp. 43–4. The probabilities of dying heirless are, however, sensitive to population growth rates and fall away sharply if populations are growing. See E.A. Wrigley, 'Fertility Strategy for the Individual and the Group', in *Historical Studies in Changing Fertility*, ed. C. Tilly (Princeton, 1978), pp. 135–54 and R.M. Smith, 'Some Issues Concerning Families and Their Property in Rural England', in *Land, Kinship and Life-cycle*, ed. R.M. Smith (Cambridge, 1984), pp. 38–62.

21 Goody, *The Development of the Family*, p. 56.

22 Ibid., pp. 83–102, p. 88.

23 Goody reiterates arguments made by M. Sheehan, 'The Influence of Canon Law on the Property Rights of Married Women in England', *Mediaeval Studies* 25 (1963), pp. 109–24.

24 Goody, *The Development of the Family*, p. 155.

25 Ibid., pp. 157–82.

26 There is a large and constantly growing literature, but the following have proved to be very influential: J.T. Noonan, Jr., 'Power to Choose', *Viator* 4 (1973), pp. 419–34; C.R. Donahue, Jr., 'The Policy of Alexander the Third's Consent Theory of Marriage', in *Proceedings of the Fourth International Congress of Medieval Canon Law, Toronto 21–25 August 1972*, ed. S. Kuttner (Vatican City, 1976), pp. 251–81; C.R. Donahue, Jr., 'The Case of the Man Who Fell into The Tiber: The Roman Law of Marriage at the Time of The Glossators', *American Journal of Legal History* 12 (1978), pp. 48–53; M.M. Sheehan, 'Marriage Theory and Practice in the Conciliar Legislation

and Diocesan Statutes of Medieval England', *Medieval Studies* 40 (1978), pp. 408–60.

27   M.M. Sheehan, 'Choice of Marriage Partner in the Middle Ages: Development and Mode of Application of a Theory of Marriage', *Studies in Medieval and Renaissance History* 1 (1978), p. 5.

28   In employing the term 'triumphalist' to categorise this school I am influenced by the tone to be found in the writing of certain of its principal adherents. For instance, in writing of the Christian definition of marriage that was assuming 'a degree of completeness and consistency' by the end of the twelfth century, M. Sheehan regards it as 'the ideal [that] was to triumph', 'Theory and Practice: Marriage of the Unfree and the Poor in Mediaeval Society', *Medieval Studies* 50 (1988), pp. 458–9.

29   D. Herlihy, *Medieval Households* (Cambridge, Mass., 1985), especially chapter 4.

30   Ibid., chapter 1.

31   Ibid., pp. 38–43. Herlihy cites the work of S. Wemple, *Women in Frankish Society: Marriage and the Cloister 500 to 900* (Philadelphia, 1981), pp. 27–97.

32   D. Herlihy, 'Making Sense of Incest: Women and the Marriage Rules of the Early Middle Ages', in *Law, Custom and the Social Fabric in Medieval Europe: Essays in Honour of Bryce Lyon*, ed. B.S. Bachrach and D. Nicholas (Kalamazoo, Michigan 1990), p. 1.

33   Herlihy seems to observe a calculative strain in the Church's behaviour when he writes that 'while tying the policy closely to supposed biblical and patristic precedents, the Church seems to have been not altogether unconscious of its social consequences', Ibid., p. 13.

34   Herlihy, *Medieval Households*, pp. 74–8. In addition to Tacitus, Herlihy takes his evidence from barbarian codes and the advice of early medieval councils to suggest that age gaps between spouses narrowed. Carolingian surveys from St. Germain de Prés and St. Victor of Marseille are also used to show that the ratio of the proportion of widows to widowers was incompatible with a large age gap between spouses and that the proportions listed as bachelors and spinsters did not reflect the end product of processes associated with early marriage.

35   Ibid., pp. 73–4; For a more complex account which denies the presence of a system of marital assigns that was either dowry or brideprice in the early Middle Ages, although the argument is confined to the Mediterranean, see D.O. Hughes, 'From Brideprice to Dowry in Mediterranean Europe', *Journal of Family History* 3 (1978), pp. 262–96. C.f. Goody, *The Development of the Family*, pp. 240–61.

36   Herlihy, *Medieval Households*, pp. 79–98.

37   Under pressure to protect and develop the patrimony on the one side, and the ideas of reform on the other, Duby attempted to show how the divergence between the 'secular' and the recently reformed 'clerical ideal' of marriage was narrowed to forge a distinctive form of aristocratic familial alliance; G. Duby, *Medieval Marriage: Two Models from Twelfth-Century France* (Baltimore, 1978); G. Duby, *Le Chevalier, la Femme et le Prêtre* (Paris, 1981). If by accommodating clerical preferences for exogamy, mutual consent of bride and groom, and a clear sense of legitimacy of offspring, a means of ensuring the survival of landed dynasties was achieved, it is by no means clear what the consequences were for the status of aristocratic women. Both Duby and Herlihy believe that more intensive 'policing' of the land exchanged with women at marriage seems to have been one outcome and women within these social ranks are portrayed as having come under more intensive masculine subjection as the proportions both of their father's land which they received as dowry and of their husband's as marriage portion were reduced.

38   The evidence for an improvement of female life expectancy is far from abundant and as such can be regarded as no more than a possibility. Much of the evidence relating to the Classical period is dependent upon statements made by classical authors who note that females lived shorter lives than males. For early medieval European societies

mortality differences between the sexes are derived from the Carolingian surveys that record a high ratio of males to females, supposedly indicative of poorer survivorship among women. The fact that thirteenth-century commentators such as Albertus Magnus pointed to a substantial change in the relative survival likelihoods of the sexes and that the problems associated with a 'surplus of women' were becoming matters worthy of comment by contemporaries are thought suggestive of a shift of mortality patterns since the earlier period. The *pièce de résistance* in the evidence indicative of an amelioration of female mortality is thought to be data from fifteenth-century tax lists or censuses of town populations showing ratios of females to males that varied from 109 to 120 (e.g. Reims, Fribourg, and Nuremberg). See D. Herlihy, 'Life Expectancies for Women in Medieval Society', in *The Role of Women in the Middle Ages*, ed. R.T. Morewedge (1975), pp. 1–22. Such evidence is highly problematic, since Italian and other southern European cities were not marked by female surplus, suggesting differential migration and not differential life expectancy to have been the principal determinant of these patterns. Further efforts on the part of medievalists to account for these supposed improvements in female life expectancy in terms of dietary changes associated with agricultural innovations leading to the introduction of legumes appear to disregard the evidence that suggests a deterioration in diets in the thirteenth century. For a somewhat speculative discussion that accounts for an improvement in female life expectancy through dietary change and the technology of food preparation see V. Bullough and C. Campbell, 'Female Longevity and Diet in the Middle Ages', *Speculum* 55 (1986), pp. 317–25. It is noteworthy that this study adopts a pan-European approach both as regards dietary regimes and technological change and makes no mention of possible dietary deterioration after 1200.

39 Herlihy acknowledges that his evidence for 'female age at first marriage is most abundant and clearest from the Mediterranean lands, but there are indications that a comparable pattern was common also in the European north', *Medieval Households*, p. 113. However, the evidence from the 'north' comes exclusively from the urban patriciate, the aristocracy, and individuals who are the subject of Saints Lives.

40 For instance, Goody ponders whether 'that very critical feature of Hajnal's "European Marriage Pattern", namely late marriage, is linked to the projection of marriages outside the circles of consanguinity, affinity and even friendship . . .', *The Development of the Family*, p. 31.

41 Goody, *The Development of the Family*, p. 9. In fact in his most recently published work, *The Oriental, the Ancient and the Primitive: Systems of Marriage and the Family in the Pre-industrial Societies of Eurasia* (Cambridge, 1990), pp. 485–7, Goody is insistent that the late and low intensity marriage regime that Hajnal saw as so distinctive can have little claim to being a factor that accounts for the economic precocity of Western Europe. Indeed in listing such characteristics as the elementary nuclear family, bilateral kindreds, late marriage of males and females, living-in servants, and close relations between parents and children as those often associated with the 'Uniqueness of Europe' he claims that 'there was no question of any being peculiar to, or probably "invented" in that region'. In these comments we encounter Goody's clearest statement that none of these characteristics can be attributed to the clerical reform of marriage that he previously argued had detached Europe from Eurasia in the fourth century A.D.

42 For an attempt to relate certain of the potential demographic consequences of clerical reform to the spatial distribution of European marriage patterns which reveals nothing to suggest that the continent possessed geographical coherence, see R.M. Smith, 'Monogamy, Landed Property and Demographic Regimes in Pre-Industrial Europe', in *Fertility and Resources*, ed., J.M. Landers and V. Reynolds (Cambridge 1990),

pp. 170–8. Not all of our intellectual energy should be expended on the pursuit of regional demographic patterns relating to marriage. Biller in a paper forthcoming in *Social History of Medicine* under the title 'Questions about the history of medieval women' reminds us that Church law and liturgy were more variable and were more shaped by the societies in which they existed and functioned than is suggested by the arguments of the 'triumphalists'. He draws attention to Esmein's observations that it was in northern Europe (northern France and Paris) that a purely consensual definition of marriage was developed and that it was in Italy (Bologna) that it was opposed and where the inclusion of secular ceremony, in particular, the *deductio in domum viri* (the transmission of the girl as object into the groom's house) was given such prominence. Biller also contrasts the practices revealed in French and English liturgies discussed in depth by J.B. Molin and P. Mutembe, *Le Rituel du Mariage en France du XIIe au XVIe siècles* (Paris, 1974) in which exchange of free consent looms large, with the picture of marital ritual recreated for fifteenth-century Tuscany by C. Klapisch-Zuber, 'Zacharias, or the Ousted Father: Nuptial Rights in Tuscany between Giotto and the Council of Trent', in *Women, Family, and Ritual in Renaissance Italy* (Chicago, 1985), pp. 178–212 where the Church is marginalised almost to the point of irrelevance; the bride is often absent and males in authority transact affairs in the presence of a notary who assumes greater importance than the priest.

43   D. Herlihy and C. Klapisch-Zuber, *Tuscans and Their Families: A Study of the Florentine Catasto of 1427* (New Haven, Conn., 1985), pp. 202–31.

44   For an inventory of this evidence see R.M. Smith, 'The People of Tuscany and Their Families in the Fifteenth Century: Medieval or Mediterranean?', *Journal of Family History* 6 (1981), pp. 110–11; See too, A.E. Laiou-Thomadakis, *Peasant Society in the late Byzantine Empire: A Social and Demographic Study* (Princeton, NJ, 1977); E.A. Hammel, 'Household Structure in Fourteenth-Century Macedonia', *Journal of Family History* 5 (1980), pp. 242–73; A.M. Landes-Mallet, *La Famille en Rouergue au Moyen Age: Etude de la Pratique Notariale* (Rouen, 1985); D.B. Rheubottom, 'Sisters First': Betrothal Order and Age at Marriage in Fifteenth-Century Ragusa', *Journal of Family History* 13 (1988), pp. 359–76; J.H. Mundy, *Men and Women at Toulouse in the Age of the Cathars* (Toronto, 1990), pp. 79–87.

45   R.M. Smith, 'Some Reflections on the Evidence for the Origins of the "European Marriage Pattern" in England', in *The Sociology of the Family: Sociological Review Monograph* 28, ed. C. Harris (Keele, 1979), pp. 74–112; R.M. Smith, 'Hypothèses sur la Nuptialité en Angleterre aux XIIIe–XIVe siècles', *Annales: ESC* 38 (1983), pp. 107–36; L.R. Poos, *A Regional Society after the Black Death: Essex 1350–1525* (Cambridge, 1991); L.R. Poos, 'Reconstructing a Demographic Region in Late Medieval England: The Case of Essex after the Black Death', in *Regional and Spatial Demographic Patterns in the Past*, ed. R.M. Smith (Oxford, forthcoming); P.J.P. Goldberg, 'Urban Identity and the Poll Taxes of 1377, 1379 and 1381', *Economic History Review* 2nd ser., 43 (1990), pp. 194–216; P.J.P. Goldberg, 'Women's Work, Women's Role in the Late-Medieval North', in *Profit, Piety and the Professions in Late Medieval England*, ed. M.A. Hicks (Gloucester, 1990), pp. 34–50; P.J.P. Goldberg, 'Women and Work in two Late-Medieval English Towns: A Study of Social Topography', in *Regional and Spatial Demographic Patterns*; J.Z. Titow, 'Some Differences between Manors and their Effects on the Condition of the Peasantry in the Thirteenth Century', *Agricultural History Review* 10 (1962), pp. 113–28; R.M. Smith, 'Some Thoughts on Hereditary and Proprietary Rights in Land under Customary Law in Thirteenth and Early Fourteenth Century England', *Law and History Review* 1 (1983), pp. 95–128; J.R. Ravensdale, 'Population Changes and the Transfer of Customary Land on a Cambridgeshire Manor in the Fourteenth Century', in *Land, Kinship and Life-cycle*, ed. R.M. Smith (Cambridge, 1984), pp. 197–226; J.M.

Bennett, 'The Ties that Bind: Peasant Marriages and Families in Late Medieval England', *Journal of Interdisciplinary History* 15 (1984), pp. 111–28; H.E. Hallam, 'Age at First Marriage and Age at Death in the Lincolnshire Fenland, 1252–1478', *Population Studies* 39 (1985), pp. 55–69; Smith, 'Marriage Processes in the English Past'; R.M. Smith, 'Women's Property Rights under Customary Law: Some Developments in the Thirteenth and Fourteenth Centuries', *Transactions of the Royal Historical Society* 5th ser., 36 (1986), pp. 165–94; J.M. Bennett, *Women in the Medieval English Countryside: Gender and Household in Brigstock Before the Plague* (New York, 1987), pp. 143–76; For a study of remarriage where its incidence may have owed something to seigneurial coercion see, E. Clark, 'The Decision to Marry in Thirteenth and early Fourteenth-Century Norfolk', *Mediaeval Studies* 49 (1987), pp. 496–511; For a study of manorial court rolls that argues for a non-European marriage regime with early marriage for both males and females see Z. Razi, *Life, Marriage and Death in a Medieval Parish: Economy, Society and Demography in Halesowen, 1270–1400* (Cambridge, 1980); For a debate concerning Razi's findings see L.R. Poos and R.M. Smith, 'Legal Windows onto Historical Populations? Recent Research on Demography and the Manor Court in Medieval England', *Law and History Review* 2 (1984), pp. 128–52; Z. Razi, 'The Use of Manorial Courts in Demographic Analysis: a Reconsideration', *Law and History Review* 3 (1985), pp. 191–200; L.R. Poos and R.M. Smith, 'Shades Still on the Window: A Reply to Zvi Razi', *Law and History Review* 3 (1986), pp. 409–29; Z. Razi, 'The Demographic Transparency of Manorial Court Rolls', *Law and History Review* 5 (1987), pp. 523–5; For a recent overview of marriage in the half-century before the Black Death see R.M. Smith, 'Demographic Developments in Rural England 1300–48: A Survey', in *Before the Black Death: Studies in the 'Crisis' of the Early Fourteenth Century*, ed. B.M.S. Campbell (Manchester, 1991), pp. 61–73.

46 Hajnal, 'European Marriage Patterns', pp. 117–19.

47 Hajnal did not appreciate the extent to which the poll taxes were subject to evasion by unmarried persons, in particular females. Nor did he appreciate that in the sample he employed, those communities with exceptionally high proportions in 1377 recorded as married came almost exclusively from Northumberland. See Smith, 'Hypothèses sur la Nuptialité', pp. 112–15. A larger sample of tax-payers listed both by name and marital condition from the 1377 returns of Lincolnshire, Oxfordshire, Rutland, Shropshire, and Northumberland reveals that 67.7 per cent of tax-payers were married, although there was a striking sexual imbalance in the population over 14 years, with a sex ratio of 108.

48 J. Hajnal, 'Two Kinds of Pre-industrial Household Formation System', *Population and Development Review* 8 (1982), pp. 449–84, especially pp. 451–5.

49 For a notion of service emphasising that it was a phase of the cycle coming after primary socialisation within the elementary family and complementing the church and the school in the overall educational process see P. Laslett, *Family Life and Illicit Love in Earlier Generations* (Cambridge, 1977), p. 47 and P. Laslett, 'The Institution of Service', *Local Population Studies* 40 (1988), p. 56.

50 Hajnal, 'Two Kinds of Pre-industrial Household', pp. 478–9. Hajnal's views on the institution of service as an agent for fertility control seem to be endorsed by Laslett when he writes 'that the number of servants and their proportions in the population vary with prospects for household formation, that is with the economic outlook and with demography', 'The Institution of Service', p. 56.

51 Herlihy, *Medieval Households*, pp. 155–6.

52 Hajnal, 'Two Kinds of Pre-industrial Household Formation', pp. 464–7. Hajnal, in fact, made use of data that were originally published in C. Klapisch-Zuber and M. Demmonet, 'A uno vino e uno pane'. La Famille Rurale Toscane au Début du XVe siècle', *Annales: ESC* 27 (1972), pp. 873–901.

53 Similar tendencies on the part of newly married males can be found in the complete Tuscan data for 1427 when a distinction is drawn between rural and urban populations. In the rural areas, for example, at age 25, 50 per cent or rural males were married, but only 17 per cent headed their own household; in the towns by age 27, 50 per cent of males were married but only 25 per cent headed their own household. See Herlihy and Klapisch-Zuber, *Tuscans and Their Families*, p. 302, figure 10.6 and Smith, 'The People of Tuscany and their Families', p. 120. For the absence of 'retirement' in fifteenth-century Tuscany in contrast to late medieval England, see R.M. Smith, 'The Manorial Court and the Elderly Tenant in Late Medieval England', in *Life, Death and the Elderly: Historical Perspectives*, eds. M. Pelling and R.M. Smith (1991), pp. 40–63.

54 Hajnal, 'Two Kinds of Pre-industrial Household', p. 466, table 10.

55 Herlihy and Klapisch-Zuber, *Tuscans and Their Families*, pp. 12–13.

56 C. Klapisch-Zuber, 'Childhood in Tuscany at the Beginning of the Fifteenth Century', in *Women, Family and Ritual*, p. 106.

57 Herlihy and Klapisch-Zuber, *Tuscans and Their Families*, p. 13.

58 Ibid., p. 331.

59 C. Klapisch-Zuber, 'Women Servants in Florence during the Fourteenth and Fifteenth Centuries', in *Women and Work in Pre-industrial Europe*, ed. B.A. Hanawalt (Bloomington, Indiana, 1986), p. 61; D. Herlihy, 'Mapping Households in Medieval Italy', *The Catholic History Review* 58 (1972), p. 8.

60 C. Klapisch-Zuber, 'Female Celibacy and Service in Florence in the Fifteenth Century', in *Women, Family and Ritual*, pp. 165–77 and 'Women Servants in Florence'.

61 Klapisch-Zuber, 'Female Celibacy and Service in Florence', pp. 172–3.

62 M. Barbagli, *Sotto lo Stesso Tetto: Mutamenti della Famiglia in Italia dal XV al XX Seccolo* (Bologna, 1984), pp. 214–38.

63 D. Herlihy and C. Klapisch-Zuber, *Les Toscans et Leurs Familles: une Étude du Catasto Florentin de 1427* (Paris, 1978), p. 520.

64 D. Herlihy, 'The Population of Verona in the First Century of Venetian Rule', in *Renaissance Venice*, ed. J. Hale (1973), p. 97.

65 M. Mitterauer, 'Gesindebedienst and Jugendphase im europaeischen Vergleich', *Geschichte und Gessellschaft* 2 (1985), p. 197.

66 Barbagli, *Sotto lo Stesso Tetto*, p. 230.

67 A. Arru, 'The Distinguishing Features of Domestic Service in Italy', *Journal of Family History* 15 (1990), pp. 547–66.

68 Ibid. Evidence from early modern southern Italy reveals a society in which servants were very rare, and although predominantly female, servants were found at all ages showing no association with a specific phase in the life-cycle. See G. Da Molin, 'Family Form and Domestic Service in Southern Italy from the Seventeenth to the Nineteenth Centuries', *Journal of Family History* 15 (1990), pp. 503–27.

69 Klapisch-Zuber, 'Women Servants in Florence'.

70 Ibid., p. 74.

71 Klapisch-Zuber, 'Female Celibacy and Service in Florence', p. 177.

72 J. Hajnal, 'Age at Marriage and Proportions Marrying', *Population Studies* 2 (1953), pp. 111–36; Herlihy and Klapisch-Zuber, *Tuscans and Their Families*, pp. 86–8.

73 Ibid., pp. 322, 331, 416.

74 R.C. Trexler, 'Le Célibat à la fin du Moyen Age: Les Réligieuses de Florence', *Annales: ESC* 27 (1972), pp. 1329–50; Klapisch-Zuber, 'Female Celibacy and Service in Florence'.

75 Ibid.

76 Ibid., p. 177.

77 PRO, E179/240/308 (Lincolnshire); E179/158/29 (Northumberland); E179/161/36–44, E179/202/59 (Oxfordshire); E179/165/21–23, E179/269/51 (Rutland); E179/166/21–33 (Shropshire). In discussing servants, both those appearing in the later fourteenth-century poll taxes and those encountered in other contemporary sources, care should always be taken when considering the terminology employed and evidence relating to the specification of a clearly stated link between a servant and his or her employer. It must be acknowledged that the terminology that confronts us is more variable than to be found in early modern sources although fifteenth-century sumptuary statutes refer to 'servants in husbandry', 'common labourers' and 'servants to any artificer' in a way which might lead us to assume that clear distinctions between co-resident servants and non-resident labourers were very familiar to those responsible for this legislation, see Poos, *A Rural Society after the Black Death*, chapter 9. In treating servants in this discussion co-resident servants are assumed to be those specifically described in the poll tax as 'A *servus* of B' or those encountered in a form such as 'A and B *uxor eius et* C *serviens dicti* A'. In considering servants in the surviving nominative tax lists of 1377 servants are almost always described in one or other of these two ways. However, the lists of 1381 are less systematic in their treatment of servants and both the terminology and lay-out is potentially confusing.

78 From the surviving urban poll tax returns the following figures relating to the proportion of all tax-paying households that contained servants in 1377 can be obtained: Carlisle 23.9 per cent; Dartmouth 30.3 per cent; Hull 14.8 per cent; Oxford St. Peter 29.2 per cent; Oxford St. Mary 26.8 per cent; the high status area within Coventry-Bailey Lane 83.6 per cent; incomplete returns for Northampton and York, giving respectively 36.2 and 38.4 per cent: Goldberg, 'Urban Identity and the Poll Taxes', table 2, p. 200. Barron reports evidence for a recently identified return for Worcester in 1377, relating to the intra-mural parishes in which 19 per cent of tax-paying households possessed servants, C.M. Barron, 'The Fourteenth Century Poll tax Returns for Worcester', *Midland History* 14 (1989), pp. 1–29.

79 C. Phythian-Adams, *Desolation of a City: Coventry and the Urban Crisis of the Late Middle Ages* (Cambridge, 1979), p. 131.

80 H. Pirenne, 'Les Dénombrements de la Population d'Ypres au XVe siècle (1412–1506)', *Vierteljahrschrift für Social-und Wirtschaftsgeschichte* 1 (1903), pp. 13, 15, 19.

81 P. Desportes, 'La Population de Reims au XVe siècle', *Moyen Age* 52 (1966), p. 489.

82 Goldberg, 'Urban Identity and the Poll Taxes', p. 202, table 3 where similar intra-urban variations in servant keeping are reported for the tax-paying households of Hull in 1377, ibid., pp. 200, table 2.

83 Goldberg, ibid., reports 29 urban servant sex ratios from the taxes of 1377, 1379, and 1381, of which 8 were below 100.

84 In Rutland in 1377 the servant sex ratio for 24 vills was 195 and for the surviving returns for Oxfordshire, Lincolnshire, and Shropshire it was 162. However, more balanced sex ratios are reported from rural areas in the West Riding of Yorkshire in 1379 where rural crafts were an important feature of the local economy, see Goldberg, 'Women's Work, Women's Role', pp. 36–7.

85 For late seventeenth century contrasts between rural servant sex ratios that were as high as 227 and urban sex ratios as low as 71 and proportions of servant-keeping households in rural and urban areas of 14 and 58 per cent respectively see R. Wall, 'Regional and temporal variations in English household structure from 1650', in *Regional Demographic Development*, ed. J. Hobcraft and P. Rees (1980), p. 107, table 4.10.

86 P.J.P. Goldberg, 'Marriage, Migration, and Servanthood: The York Cause Paper Evidence', above p. 4.

87 Ibid.

88 Ibid., pp. 4–5.

89 Ibid., pp. 6–7. Evidence from the poll taxes suggests that in towns households containing and headed by unmarried females, who were not necessarily widows, not infrequently exceeded 20 or 25 per cent of all households. See Goldberg, 'Women and Work in Two Late Medieval English Towns', especially tables 4 and 5.

90 Smith, 'The People of Tuscany and Their Familes', p. 124; L.R. Poos, 'The Social Context of Statute of Labourers Enforcement', *Law and History Review* 1 (1983), p. 30. For an analysis that emphasises a 'demand side' approach to service which the evidence, particularly that relating to litigation under the Stature of Labourers, is thought to reflect, see Poos, *A Rural Society after the Black Death*, chapter 10. For a 'supply side' approach to this same evidence which interprets the litigation to indicate a disinclination on the part of servants, or potential servants, to hire themselves out for extended or annual contracts under conditions of high *per diem* wages and labour shortages see C. Dyer, *Standards of Living in the Later Middle Ages* (Cambridge, 1989), p. 213 and S.A.C. Penn and C. Dyer, 'Wages and Earnings in Late Medieval England: Evidence from the Enforcement of the Labour Laws', *Economic History Review* 2nd ser., 43 (1990), pp. 366–9, 374–5.

91 P.J.P. Goldberg, 'Female Labour, Service and Marriage in the Late Medieval Urban North', *Northern History* 22 (1986), p. 23.

92 Goldberg, 'Marriage, Migration, and Servanthood', p. 5; Poos, *A Rural Society after the Black Death*, chapter 9 suggests that most of the disputes in manorial courts concerning litigation over hiring periods and the Statute of Labourers cases indicate that it was rare for servants to stay longer than one year with an employer. See too, M. Kowaleski, 'Women's Work in a Market Town: Exeter in the Late Fourteenth Century', in *Women and Work in Pre-industrial Europe*. ed. Hanawalt, pp. 145–64.

93 P.J.P. Goldberg, 'Female Labour, Status and Marriage in Late Medieval York and Other English Towns' (unpublished Ph.D. thesis, University of Cambridge, 1987), p. 199.

94 Ibid., p. 209.

95 Ibid., pp. 212–18.

96 Ibid.

97 Goldberg is at pains to stress the employment difficulties confronting females in the late fifteenth century. It should be noted that it has been suggested that Goldberg's arguments developed in the context of the city of York are unlikely to possess 'universal applicability for not all fifteenth-century towns experienced economic recession', M. Kowaleski, 'The History of Urban Families in Medieval England', *Journal of Medieval History* 14 (1988), p. 58. There were some 'successes', largely confined to the southeast, the south and especially London, where there is reason to believe the demand for female labour may have held up even into the early sixteenth century. See C. Barron, "The Golden Age" of Women in Medieval London', *Reading Medieval Studies* 15 (1990), pp. 35–58.

98 Goldberg, 'Female Labour, Status and Marriage', p. 218.

99 The situation in the sixteenth century is most definitely in need of research and although there are no sources comparable to the poll taxes, much can be revealed by judicious use of parish registers. For instance, the London population of the late sixteenth and early seventeenth century had become highly masculinised based on the sex ratios of burials in the London parish registers. See J. Boulton, 'London Widowhood Revisited: The Decline of Female Remarriage in the Seventeenth Century and Early Eighteenth Century', *Continuity and Change* 5 (1990), p. 342; R. Finlay, *Population and Metropolis: The Demography of London 1580–1650* (Cambridge, 1981), pp. 139–42. For discussion of the restricted economic possibilities for women in sixteenth-century London see

S. Rappaport, *Worlds Within Worlds: Structures of Life in Sixteenth-Century London* (Cambridge, 1989), pp. 31–42. Further discussion of deteriorating employment prospects for females and their increasing vulnerability can be found in M. Roberts, 'Women and Work in Sixteenth-Century English Towns', in *Work in Towns 850–1850*, ed. P.J. Corfield and D. Keene (Leicester, 1990), pp. 92–4. For a valuable study showing over the course of the sixteenth century in Bristol a growth in the segregation of female apprentices from males and their confinement to the occupation of 'servant maid' along with their total elimination from trades into which males were also bound, see I.K. Ben-Amos, 'Women Apprentices in the Trades and Crafts of Early Modern Bristol', *Continuity and Change* 6 (1991), pp. 227–52, especially pp. 232–4.

100 Goldberg, 'Female Labour, Service and Marriage,' p. 35.
101 Herlihy and Klapisch-Zuber, *Les Toscans et Leurs Familles*, p. 661.
102 R.M. Smith, 'Fertility, Economy and Household Formation in England Over Three Centuries', *Population and Development Review* 7 (1981), pp. 599–600. See too, Wall, 'Regional and Temporal Variations', p. 98, table 4.5.
103 Ibid., p. 103, table 4.6; C. Phythian-Adams, *Desolation of a City*, p. 301, table 34; Goldberg, 'Female Labour, Status and Marriage', p. 308.
104 Ibid. Goldberg suggests that values for urban households were close to 4.0 in 1377. It is hard, however, to accept his view that household size in towns was likely to have been larger, because of the urban demand for servants, than that in the countryside, in so far as it is doubtful whether the same multiplier for converting tax-payers to total 'population' can be employed in both contexts. See Goldberg, 'Urban Identity and the Poll Taxes', p. 213 and n. 42.
105 Goldberg, 'Female Labour, Status and Marriage', p. 308; C. Klapisch-Zuber, 'Demographic Decline and Household Structure: The Example of Prato, late Fourteenth to Fifteenth Centuries', in *Women, Family and Ritual*, pp. 23–35.
106 Herlihy and Klapisch-Zuber, *Tuscans and Their Families*, p. 74.
107 Ibid., pp. 282–3, 308, table 10.5.
108 Klapisch-Zuber, 'Demographic Decline and Household Structure', pp. 30–1.
109 Barbagli, *Sotto lo Stesso*, pp. 216–33; Arru, 'The Distinguishing Features of Domestic Service in Italy', pp. 550–4; C. Schiavoni and E. Sonnino, 'Aspects generaux de l'evolution démographique à Rome 1598–1824', *Annales de Démographie Historique* (1982), pp. 91–109.
110 Herlihy and Klapisch-Zuber, *Tuscans and Their Families*, p. 157.
111 Goldberg, 'Female Labour, Status and Marriage', p. 310.
112 It has been noted above that the number of unmarried females over 20 years of age was insufficient, even if all those declared in the tax return of their father's household in rural areas were in reality living in Florence and other towns, to counteract the substantial male surpluses in the urban component of the Tuscan population. See above, p. 29.
113 Kowaleski, 'The History of Urban Families in Medieval England', p. 55. Goldberg has proposed that this female 'surplus' found not only in English but other northern European towns in the late fourteenth and early fifteenth centuries 'may suggest a relatively high level of female migration away from rural districts, notably areas of arable agriculture at a time of transition from arable to pasture farming, to the apparently expanding economies of later fourteenth-century towns; 'Urban identity and the Poll Taxes', p. 213. These are distinctly plausible suggestions, for he has also drawn our attention to the contrast between sex ratios in parts of the West Riding where a functionally inter-connected pastoral and craft-based rural economy may have been more retentive of female labour, producing sex ratios slightly below 100, and Rutland where in a predominantly arable economy rural sex ratios were in excess of 100. See Goldberg, 'Women's Work, Women's Role' pp. 36–8. However, rural sex

ratios in the poll taxes were generally in excess of 105 in 1377 and 120 in 1381 and the gap between them and urban sex ratios is insufficient to be primarily the product of differential mobility of the sexes. The urban share of the total population was just not large enough to have absorbed the emigration of 10 to 25 males per 100 that the recorded sex ratios in rural areas if accepted at face value would imply. Some legitimate exclusion of females on account of poverty (especially widows) is likely to have been an influence tending to masculinise populations whether in town or country. Evasion of the poll tax by females must be considered the major determinant of the rural male 'surplus', unless it is to be assumed that female neglect and infanticide or a greater feminine susceptibility to infectious disease were important influences. It can be shown, where all three tax returns survive, that as tax populations shrank through failure to capture those in theory eligible for inclusion, the resultant tax-paying populations became progressively masculinised. These issues are dealt with in greater detail in R.M. Smith, *The Poll Tax Returns and the Social Structure of Late Fourteenth-Century England* (Oxford, forthcoming).

114 Goldberg, 'Female Labour, Status and Marriage', p. 311; Klapisch-Zuber, 'Demographic Decline and Household Structure', pp. 32–3.
115 Herlihy and Klapisch-Zuber, *Tuscans and Their Families*, p. 92.
116 Developments in the late fourteenth and early fifteenth centuries have to be seen against a much longer established historical background of high mobility for both sexes, especially young adults of both sexes, that can be readily documented in England before 1350. For a survey of the evidence see Smith, 'Demographic Developments in Rural England 1300–48', pp. 73–5.
117 Herlihy, 'Mapping Households in Medieval Italy', p. 16.
118 P.J.P. Goldberg, 'Mortality and Economic Change in the Diocese of York', *Northern History* 24 (1988), p. 52; Goldberg, 'Female Labour, Status and Marriage', pp. 296–329; Goldberg, *Women, Work, and Life Cycle in a Medieval Economy* (Oxford, 1992); R.M. Smith, 'Women's Work and Marriage in Pre-industrial England: Some Speculations', in *La Donna nell'Economia Secc. XIII–XVIII* (Prato, 1990), pp. 31–55; R.M. Smith, *The Population History of England 1000–1540* (Manchester, forthcoming), chapter 10.
119 Goldberg, 'Female Labour, Service and Marriage', pp. 35–7.
120 Such a view that regards mortality as an exogenously determined demographic variable, which through its impact on *male* real wages works to determine the pace with which marriages are founded, and hence fertility levels set, is treated in its most analytically sophisticated, but gender-blinkered, fashion in R.D. Lee, 'Population Homoeostasis and English Demographic History', in *Population and Economy: Population and History from the Traditional to the Modern World*, ed. R.I. Rotberg and T.K. Rabb (Cambridge, 1986), pp. 75–100.
121 On the destabilising effects of service on the early modern English demographic regime see Smith, 'Fertility, Economy and Household Formation', pp. 602–6 and Smith, 'Women's Work and Marriage in Pre-industrial England', pp. 35–47; A. Kussmaul, *Servants in Husbandry in Early Modern England* (Cambridge, 1981), pp. 110–14. For a fuller discussion of the early modern English demographic regime with implications for approaches that might profitably be taken to the late medieval period see R.M. Smith, 'Exogenous and Endogenous Influences on "the Preventive Check" in England 1600–1750: Some Specification Problems', *Economic History Review* (forthcoming) and R.M. Smith, 'Geographical Aspects of Population Change in England 1500–1730', in *An Historical Geography of England and Wales*, ed., R.A. Dodgshon and R.A. Butlin (1991), pp. 164–75. See too a very important, highly thought-provoking paper with obvious repercussions for issues raised in this current discussion by T. Guinnane, 'Re-thinking the Western European Marriage Pattern: The Decision to Marry in

Ireland at the Turn of the Twentieth Century', *Journal of Family History* 16 (1991), pp. 47–64.

122   As we become better informed about demographic conditions in the two centuries after the Black Death we are obliged to recognise that the regional dynamics within Europe were far from being synchronised within one grand cycle of 'decline' and 'recovery'. Demographic recovery in England was apparently more sluggish than in some of her continental European neighbours. The English population in the early sixteenth century was still well below that of 1377, see Smith, 'Geographical Aspects of Population Change', pp. 153–4; Smith, 'Demographic Developments in Rural England', pp. 48–52; L.R. Poos, 'The Rural Population of Essex in the Later Middle Ages', *Economic History Review* 2nd ser., 38 (1985), pp. 522–3; E.A. Wrigley and R.S. Schofield, *The Population History of England 1541–1871* (1981), pp. 563–8. Tuscany provides us with evidence to chart the course of population change from 1427 to 1551. While in the countryside or *contado* of Prato, for instance, population had fallen perhaps to one-third of its early fourteenth century size in 1427, by 1551 the rural population had grown a further 80 per cent. Comparable population losses were encountered in the Florentine *contado* which in 1427 had a population that stood at two-thirds of its pre-Black Death size. Here too, growth was clearly apparent after 1460, with an estimated mean annual growth rate of between 0.6 and 0.8 per cent from 1469 to 1552. Tuscan growth rates have been considered relatively low when compared with those found in Sicily where the population expanded at rates closer to 1 per cent per annum over approximately the same period. See S.R. Epstein, 'Cities, Regions and the Late Medieval Crisis: Sicily and Tuscany Compared', *Past and Present* 130 (1991), pp. 17–18. Epstein remarks that high growth rates in the century after 1450 were 'not unusual for the Mediterranean regions'. His calculations for Provence suggest mean annual rates of increase of 1.74 per cent between 1471 and 1540. There is little in the evidence from England in the century after 1450 to suggest growth of the scale found in these southern French and Italian examples. The decidely 'lagged' appearance of English demographic trends is suggestive of behaviour that held back fertility, and recovery in numbers assuming that England was no more susceptible to epidemic disease at this period than most other parts of Europe. Cf. Goldberg, 'Mortality and Economic Change', pp. 49–55.

123   Hajnal, 'Two Kinds of Household Formation System', p. 476.

124   Ibid. Scholars working on north-central Italy are inclined to argue that Hajnal mis-specified the relationship between joint households, servants, and marital patterns with respect to that region. Most, if not all, of this critical comment derives from studies undertaken on data from the nineteenth century, where the evidence reveals female ages at first marriage over 21, although post-marital residence continued to be patrivirilocal. See the collection of studies edited by M. Barbagli and D. Kertzer on 'Italian Family History 1750–1950', in *Journal of Family History* 15 (1990), M. Barbagli, 'Marriage and the Family in Italy in the Early Nineteenth Century', in *Society and Politics in the Age of the Risorgimento*, ed., J.A. Davis and P. Ginsborg (Cambridge, 1991), pp. 92–127 and D. Kertzer, 'Household History and Sociological Theory', *Annual Review of Sociology* 17 (1991), pp. 155–79. Only a few of these recent studies have addressed the issue of servants in the wider context of the economics of family life. It has, however, been claimed that a 'tremendous number' of children left their natal household 'at a tender age to enter some form of service': D. Kertzer and C. Bretell, 'Advances in Italian and Iberian Family History', *Journal of Family History* 12 (1987), p. 102. Servants have certainly been found in the joint households of nineteenth-century share croppers; they were predominantly male (*garzoni*) with a sex ratio of 300 to 350. Domestic service does become a more noteworthy feature of the urban social landscape in the late eighteenth century, although it displayed char-

acteristics which distinguished it from the phenomenon documented in early modern English towns. The evidence (see the studies listed in ns. 62, 65, and 68) points to an age pattern which suggests that women above 30 were as likely to be servants as those below, and males were more prominent as servants than in the urban populations of northern European cities of a comparable period. See too A. Arru, 'Il Matrimonio Tardivo dei Servi e delle Serve', Quaderni Storici 68 (1988), pp. 469–96. Urban service did, however, become increasingly feminised later in the eighteenth and early nineteenth centuries, although the mean ages may still have differed from those displayed by unmarried female 'life-cycle' servants in northern Europe. For instance, in Perugia the mean age of female servants was 33 years, see L. Tittarelli, 'I Servi Domestici a Perugia a Meta dell'Ottocento', Quaderno dell'Istituto Interfacoltà di Statistica, Università di Perugia 10 (1985), pp. 27–88. Such features of service that have so far been brought to light in Italian research from the fifteenth to nineteenth centuries have failed to show age and sex patterns that approach those which Hajnal regards as characteristic of the northwest European household formation system. In the latter system the incidence of service for females rose from very low percentages in the age group 10–14 to between 35 to 45 per cent of all females in the age group 20–24 before falling off thereafter to minimal proportions in the age group 30–39 (less than 10 per cent), see Hajnal, 'Two Kinds of Pre-industrial Household Formation', pp. 471–3. It is also important to note that in the northwest European contexts female servants were, when the overall incidence of service was high and male labour was in short supply, i.e. c.1360–c.1450 and c.1650–c.1750, deeply implicated in productive, market-orientated, and not exclusively domestic tasks. Comparable characteristics and periodicities have yet to be revealed in the north-central Italian evidence.

125 The claims to admit Tuscany to a European or northwest European marital 'club' are made most effectively by those who have studied that region in the period after 1750. There is a growing body of evidence that suggests such a realignment in marital practices in north-central Italy as well as southern France and north-central Spain: Smith, 'Monogamy, Landed Property and Demographic Regimes', pp. 176–80; R. Rowland, 'Sistemas Matrimoniales en la Peninsula Iberica (siglos xvi–xix) Una Perspectiva Regional', in Demografia Historica en España, ed. V. Perez-Moreda and D.S. Reher (Madrid, 1988), pp. 74–137; F. Benigno, 'The Southern Italian Family in the Early Modern Period: a Discussion of Co-residence Patterns', Continuity and Change 4 (1989), pp. 165–94; L.R. Poos, 'The Historical Demography of Renaissance Europe: Recent Research and Current Issues', Renaissance Quarterly 42 (1989), pp. 794–811.

126 See pp. 12–13.

127 A. Sen, 'The Standard of Living II; Lives and Capabilities', in The Standard of Living, ed. G. Hawthorn (Cambridge, 1987), pp. 36–8.

128 These arguments are to be found in an overview of women's work in medieval Europe that treats changes through time as if they were, for the most part, universal throughout an undifferentiated medieval Europe: D. Herlihy, Opera Muliebria: Women and Work in Medieval Europe (Philadelphia, 1990) and D. Herlihy, 'Women's Work in the Towns of Traditional Europe', in La Donna Nell'Economia Secc. XIII–XVIII (Prato, 1990), pp. 103–30. An analysis of Florentine economic change in relation to the labour force participation levels of women closer in spirit to the arguments developed in this chapter is J. Brown, 'A Woman's Place Was in the Home: Women's Work in Renaissance Tuscany', in Rewriting the Renaissance: The Discourses of Sexual Differences in Early Modern Europe, ed. M.W. Ferguson, M. Quilligan, and N.J. Vickers (Chicago, 1986), pp. 206–26. Brown is impressed by the contrast between the numbers of working women mentioned in Tuscan sources of the late thirteenth and early fourteenth centuries and their relative rarity in the following two centuries. She

notes, too, the growth in female labour force participation in the late sixteenth and early seventeenth centuries. She is impressed by the *cultural* prohibition on women's activities outside the house (pp. 213–14) and reflects on the contrast with 'England and other parts of France where women married later and there was a different perception of the marketability of women's skills' (p. 366 n.4). She is alert to the realm of cultural and social values that affected the world of women's work, cf. K. Arrow, 'Economic Dimensions of Occupational Segregation: Comment', in *Women and the Workplace: The Implications of Occupational Segregation*, ed., M. Blaxall and B. Reagan (Chicago, 1976), p. 236. Such an awareness is hard to detect in an otherwise first-rate study of women in late thirteenth and early fourteenth-century England: Bennett, *Women in the Medieval English Countryside*, pp. 189–98. By giving primacy to the household as the principal context within which women functioned, she argues that periods of economic privation were those in which women's involvement in the 'public economy' was maximised so as to supplement inadequate household resources. Such an argument aligns her with Herlihy in so far as we are given an account of women entering employment outside the hearth only in times of declining living standards and quickly retiring to their domestic space as times improve. For rather different interpretations of Bennett's empirical findings see Smith, 'Women's Work and Marriage', pp. 52–3 and Graham, below pp. 136–48.

129 These distinctions are perhaps as important as the 'public/private' dichotomy that tends to dominate much of the theory encountered in writing in this field and serves to associate conjugality with female dependence. For instance, see J.M. Bennett, 'Public Power and Authority in the Medieval English Countryside', in *Women and Power in the Middle Ages*, ed., M. Erler and M. Kowaleski (Athens, Georgia, 1988), pp. 18–36. Cf. P.J.P. Goldberg, 'The Public and the Private: Women in the Pre-Plague Economy', in *Thirteenth Century England III*, ed. P.R. Coss and S.D. Lloyd (Woodbridge, 1991), pp. 75–89.

3

Marriage Patterns and Women's Lives: A Sketch of a Pastoral Geography[1]

P.P.A. Biller

University of York

Using sparse statistical material, historians have suggested long-enduring and contrasting demographic and social patterns in northwestern and southern Europe. In this chapter I am assuming their case, and turning to one type of evidence, pastoral manuals.[2] If you try to exclude what these manuals have in common, does what is left in manuals from northwestern and southern Europe correlate with these patterns? Does it suggest that there are elements in these manuals which were, once, pastoral responses to demographically and socially divergent patterns in northwestern and southern Europe?

The study of medieval pastoral manuals and the study of medieval demographic and social history have principally been separate exercises, and a sketch of the historiography of the first, at least, is a necessary introduction to the current theme. Medieval pastoral manuals – manuals of directions for parish priests instructing them generally in their duties or more narrowly on how to hear confession and impose penance – have long attracted serious study. An early landmark was Pantin's account of the fourteenth-century English priests' manuals. Boyle's Oxford doctorate was under Pantin's supervision and devoted to the same manuals, in particular the most important of them, the *Oculus Sacerdotis* of William of Pagula. Many later articles from him have illuminated the sources, writing and manuscript diffusion of the others, and also John of Freiburg's *Summa confessorum*. Pantin also supervised the research of Haren, whose doctorate dealt with another of these manuals, the *Memoriale* of 1344.[3] Outside Oxford the most notable contribution has been Michaud-Quantin's history of medieval confessors's manuals, and their use in Tentler's *Sin and Confession on the Eve of the Reformation*.[4]

Some of the underlying preoccupations of these scholars have been traditional. Michaud-Quantin was concerned with the history of a literary genre. Pantin, in a general book on the fourteenth-century Church, was using them as part of his thesis that one should approach this Church forwards from the reforming legislation and spirit of the fourth Lateran

Council of 1215, not backwards from the Reformation and later medieval 'abuses'. They helped in his more positive picture. Boyle's concern with pastoral care, and, to this end, the elementary education of the clergy is not fundamentally different from Pantin's, but it has come later, with sharper emphases. Among the latter is his concern to wrench attention away from the speculative 'scholastic' element among the Dominicans and towards their practical, concrete, and educational interests. This he has done through studying the education of the *fratres communes*, showing the significant pastoral element in St Thomas's quodlibetic questions and the way these entered pastoral manuals, and also through a revolutionary interpretation of the *Summa theologiae*, whose pastoral (not speculative) part proved to be what later medieval Dominicans found most interesting.[5] These historians have been concerned to see these texts and their authors within the context of the history of the Church's effort to instruct those who in turn instructed the faithful. Other historians have come from outside with other concerns. The theme of Tentler, for example, was 'social control': manuals as the textual survivals of a system of confession which had a social function, maintaining 'social control'.[6] A subtler and more interesting approach has come from Bossy, who has mined these texts to investigate the thesis that the Church moved in the later middle ages, in Gerson's period, from greater concern with other-affecting sins to greater concern with sins affecting the individual, internally, and God. This would be supported, for example, in sex, by a move from concern with adultery to concern with masturbation;[7] or more generally by a move from concern with the seven deadly sins towards concern with the Ten Commandments.[8] Two caveats are needed in this historiographical sketch. The picture I am giving, of 'inside' and 'outside' historians, oversimplifies. Pantin, for example, clearly indicated the interest of the texts for social history. In what follows I am offering another 'outside' approach, but I do not see it as discrepant with, nor do I dissent from, the approaches of Pantin and Boyle. The fundamental and first interpretation of these texts much be, in Boyle's terms, their authors' aim, their position in a tradition of instruction and reform, and their dissemination among friars and parish priests. In addition, further illumination of these texts will come in the first instance from more of the meticulous positive research of this school.

The authors of these manuals inhabited the Latin Church, which was both universal and local. In any particular part of the Europe which could be called Latin Christendom, this Church existed in (and in some sense was) a local community, a community which both shaped the local church and was shaped by it. Pastoral manuals express or reflect a mixture of universal and local themes, concerns, and pressures. Here earlier historians have pointed the way. In an article on synodal legislation published in 1965, Cheney dwelt on the strength of local custom in particular churches, and on diocesan and regional diversity. 'These statutes penetrate more profoundly than general laws or academic writings. They are faithful witnesses of the problems posed to the bishop of a diocese. . . .'[9] In 1968 Brentano, like Boyle a former pupil of Pantin, published a comparison of the English and Italian Churches in the thirteenth century.[10] This showed not only what the two Churches naturally shared, but the extraordinary regional contrasts, ranging from administrative structure – for example, the tiny dioceses of Italy, the large ones of England – to forms of piety, contrasts of longer roots and duration than his title indicated. His was a model of the advantage of the comparative method; to know one thing better, systematically compare it with something which has a sufficiency both of sameness and difference.

The treatises I am surveying range in date from the late twelfth to the mid-fifteenth century, and were written by authors in or from England, Germany, northwestern France, Tuscany, and northern Spain. They and their dates are detailed in a bibliographical note. Most heavily used among the manuals relating principally to England are those written by Thomas of Chobham, William of Pagula (and 'a second edition' by John de Burgh), and an anonymous, the author of the *Memoriale presbiterorum*. Peter the Chanter's *Summa* was not strictly a manual, but it has been included here because of its influence on Chobham, and through him on the whole English tradition. Representing southern Europe are, mainly, manuals from northern Spain and Tuscany, written, respectively, by Guido of Monte Roterio and St Antoninus of Florence.

The manuals have obvious variations in scope. They may just be on the administration of confession. They may deal with all the sacraments. They may go beyond, and include much general advice to the parish priest, or little. They may vary in colour, from fairly dry compendia of selections of canon law appropriate to parochial duties, to the rich, almost 'socio-satirical' material of confessors' questions to different estates in society which are listed in the *Memoriale*. Their form varies from arrangement around sacraments or sins to alphabetical arrangement by theme. Some are very long, some very short. However, these variations do not fundamentally weaken the first impression we gain, which is of sameness.

They were written by men living in the same centralised Latin Church, whose general pastoral aims were shared. The strongest expression of this was their use of the same major sources in canon law and theology, especially after the fourth Lateran Council of 1215. Most of the sources in canon law were the standard collections or decrees of general councils which were diffused throughout the Latin Church, beginning with Gratian's *Decretum*. We find Raymond of Peñafort's *Summa de Casibus* or Guillaume Durand's *Repertorium* in the manuals from fourteenth-century

England, in John of Aurbach, in Guido's *Manipulus*, or in the *Astesana*. The more concrete pastoral theology of one northwestern centre, Paris, flowed in all directions. At an earlier stage it was the problems discussed by the circle round Peter the Chanter in late twelfth-century Paris which found echoes in Thomas of Chobham. Then the row of mid-thirteenth-century commentators on Peter Lombard's *Sentences*, St Bonaventure, St Thomas, and St Albert, find their pastoral material extensively used in most of the important later manuals, either directly, or, as Boyle has demonstrated, indirectly through their heavy use in John of Freiburg's *Summa confessorum*. From early fourteenth-century Paris comes the rich moral-social material of Pierre de la Palud's commentary on the fourth book of the *Sentences*, and it is precisely this which looms large in mid-fifteenth-century Italy, in its extensive use in St Antoninus's *Theologia moralis*.[11] Boyle has also drawn attention to the interest in concrete pastoral moral problems in the 'what you will', quodlibetic disputations of thirteenth and early fourteenth-century Paris, problems, for example, concerning loans, or marriage, or doctors' consciences.[12] This Parisian material was also dispersed widely through Latin Christendom, again partly through John of Freiburg. See how the *Manipulus*, though written by a parish priest of Teruel in northern Spain, still bears heavily and precisely the imprint of theological quodlibetic debate from this northern city in 1290, and a later development of it: 'Master Godfrey of Fontaines, Master of Theology in Paris, in one of his quodlibets adds another case, that is, when someone confesses some sin but neither regrets it nor is penitent about [his other?] sins . . . is he bound to confess again? . . . Brother Ber[n]ard of Ganhac [Gannat, Auvergne], Bachelor in Theology, formerly [bishop-] elect of Clermont, says in his *Correctorium*, against what was said by Master Godfrey, that he is not bound to confess again. . . .'[13]

When we turn to the sources of differences, we have first the variation in these authors' individual experiences. Their expression is often obvious. John of Freiburg was a Dominican, the author of the *Astesana* was a Franciscan; the one included more Dominican writers, the other more Franciscan. There are particulars of careers, and specific experiences in those careers. William of Pagula, as an episcopal penitentiary appointed to Reading in 1321–2, had had the job of examining those special sins which a parish priest was required by law to remit to the penitentiary, and accordingly he introduces a detail about sexual morality by saying 'as bishops' penitentiaries know well'.[14] St Antoninus's knowledge and protection of the *Ospedale degli Innocenti* in Florence connects with whatever he may write about abandoning children.

Most important in the sources of differences in the manuals were the broader contrasts of the social and cultural milieux of different regions in which these men grew up and lived. An inner, concentric circle is formed by the character of the church of their region. They thought of these, explicitly, as regional. Guido contrasts a practice in his church with the French church, to the north, and in referring to the latter as the 'Gallican Church' implies ready common awareness of differing identities.[15] The authors – mainly after 1215 – looked to local synodal and conciliar legislation. Guido refers to the *synodale* each curate will have, his copy of his diocese's synodal statutes. St Antoninus refers to synodal constitutions. An allusion by John de Burgh, will be, for example, to the Council of Lambeth, 1281.[16] Regionalism enters strongly here, for such local re-legislation adapted the law of the universal Church. It is faster or slower in introducing law, and it adds, omits or emphasises. Synodal constitutions contain the universal flecked with the local. As Thomas of Chobham wrote, 'there are diverse canons according to diverse regions'.[17]

Beyond this circle, the law and custom of regional churches, lay an outer circle: the lay people of particular regions among whom lived the authors of pastoral manuals, and the parish priests who possessed these manuals and the texts of synodal constitutions. Something of these lay people – their languages, culture, customs, and professions, and the political communities to which they belonged – seeps into the manuals. All the more redolent because of their Latin surroundings are the infiltrations of snatches of vernaculars. Abandoned children enter the *Memoriale* as 'fundlinges'.[18] William of Pagula reflects multilingual England in his provision of both French and English forms of baptism.[19] John of Freiburg inserts a short phrase in German into his instructions to a priest about interrogating the laity about their modes of love-making.[20] Some infiltrations are fragmentary and allusive, some explicit, such as St Antoninus's references to what is customary in Italy, or in Florence, or Bologna. Places and travel enter. 'What', writes John de Burgh, 'if I have heard someone publicly excommunicated in London and later find him in York, where nothing is known about this?'[21] German city authorities and city work provide the context for John of Aurbach's allusion to city regulations for a *mechanicus*.[22] A particular southern political community fleetingly appears in Guido's citation of the current King and Queen of Aragon (Alfonso IV and Leonora of Castile) as examples of contracting marriage through procurators.[23] Any pastoral author envisages men committing the sin of pride, but the specific example which is envisaged by St Antoninus – pride in pictures on the walls of one's house – together with his references to scholars studying poetry excessively, and to the masters and scholars of Bologna, evoke the high culture and places of higher learning specific to early Renaissance Italy.[24] His definition of 'sedition', 'when one part of a city rises up against another', conjures up Dante's Florence and Martines's analysis of violence and disorder in medieval Italian cities.[25]

Against this broader background, it is proposed here to survey some themes concerning women's lives and marriage-patterns whose treatment in the manuals might, or might not, reflect such regionalism. Many caveats are needed, the first group of which concern the sureness of what follows. In the comparisons and contrasts drawn in this chapter, I lay some weight on the significance of authors' silence about a theme, or their uniquely emphasising it. Because the texts are lengthy, and most are not available in modern editions, there is a danger of my missing texts, sources of texts or parallels to texts which, if not missed, might alter the weight. Again, after the fourth Lateran Council of 1215 local, reforming, conciliar, and synodal legislation was in some areas both a heavy influence on pastoral manuals and a concurrent source of instruction of priests. I do not discuss regional variation in the use of such legislation to educate the parish clergy in this chapter; fuller examination of regional variations in the manuals would need patient establishment of this particular context. Further, there is the Ariès sin – Ariès, who built much on the lack of medieval treatises on the moral upbringing of children, not realising that literary genre was the explanation, since such material was found in medical treatises, not in autonomous treatises. Here, where the pastoral texts are deliberately paraded in isolation from other evidence, the possibility of committing this sin is evident. Brevity has meant confining this study to a small selection of manuals in Latin, a selection which under-represents parts of Europe, in particular German-speaking areas. It has entailed excluding parallel discussions in texts outside pastoral literature, and all but the briefest allusion to a few items in the vast secondary literature which now exists on the related fields of medieval social history. Caveats, secondly, need to be stated about the questions I have put to the manuals. These questions are on such themes as women, age at marriage, care of babies. Both the contents of manuals and the approaches of modern historical demographers, especially Smith, have suggested these questions. They are, however, only some of the questions which could be put. I have not taken some important areas, such as service as a life-stage or widow remarriage, and asked what could be found in the manuals. What follows is a preliminary, provisional, and rough sketch, subject to much correction, containing signposts for further questions and research.

1. Girls

The *Memoriale* has the most developed treatment of different groups in society of any manual, and it is not surprising to find it according a few lines to girls as a group: what penance to be imposed upon them? What is envisaged is their being too lascivious, during the day wandering through streets and squares, running dances, and at night-time wandering danger-ously, because unescorted, to vigils and funeral wakes.[26] Day-time wandering and dances could be found among the concerns of moralists anywhere. With more even-handedness St Antoninus, in his *Confes-sionale*, provides a section for enquiries in confession entitled 'From Boys and Girls'. The confessor asks about carnal sins committed by boys or girls or with themselves, and urges (as confessors' manuals usually did) caution in interrogation, lest they learn sins they previously did not know. This, he adds, is especially to be observed with girls.[27] It is an interesting emphasis, but the late date of the treatise may be more significant than its regional context. Bossy has adverted to growing moralists' interest, from Jean Gerson's time, in children's consciences. This chronological point may be the first theme for further investigation.[28] In an aside, when discussing choice of a girl for marriage, St Antoninus says that one can conjecture about a girl on the basis of her mother, for 'girls converse more or less continuously with their mothers, little with their fathers', an observation not matched in the English manuals.[29]

2. Prelude to Marriage

Formal social arrangements loom large in St Antoninus's *Confessionale*, beginning with the theme of formal reception of a man in the house of an unmarried girl. This occurs in questions on the sin of excess in dress or make-up. Though such excess is a mortal sin when it is done for show or vainglory, or to attract men's desire outside marriage, a careful exception is made, where it is venial, 'for receiving a man, if she is unmarried'.[30] This is expanded in his *Theologia moralis* to 'if she intends . . . to be drawn into marriage'.[31] Then there is a question in confession for the marriage-broker, and a Latinised version of his vernacular name. 'If he was an intermediary, who is called a *sensalis* in some places, especially in Italy . . . If the intermediary acting in marriages which are to be contracted employs lies and suchlike, [and does this] to the perceptible injury of those who are contracting, he sins mortally.'[32] In the *Theologia moralis* a *sensale's* payment by both parties 'according to the custom of the country' is stated to be unobjectionable, but a *sensale's* lies are exemplified: 'he must avoid lies when, for example, he tells one of the parties something else [viz. something other than the truth] – let us say, to the girl who wishes to marry or to her relatives who are negotiating, this, that [the prospective husband] is rich, when he has little or nothing, that he is decent and good, when [the *sensale*] knows he is licentious, dissolute, and a gambler. . . .'[33] Comparable provisions are absent in the northern texts.

I have not yet noticed contrasts in provisions about breaking engagements, though further enquiry might show varying emphases. Once
again, the *Confessionale* of St Antoninus stands out for the directness and
precision of its attention to sexual behaviour subsequent to engagement
(in interrogations to the married): 'One should note here that in many
places, although the fiancés [*sponsi*] do not consummate marriage with
their fiancées [*sponsis*] before nuptials, they do however perform many
shameful and corrupt things with them, visiting them etc.'[34]

3. Age at First Marriage

Unfortunately for historical demographers, the first ostensible concern of
pastoral authors in the common section or chapter 'On the age of those
contracting' was the legal boundary, which meant a quotation from canon
law on the minimum age for boys and girls. These priests and penitentiaries lived among and dealt with men and women about whose
marriage-patterns they could have ventured some comment, if there had
been an appropriate literary outlet. But there was no such outlet, and they
do not comment directly. All we can do is observe nuances in their
handling of the legal minima, and conjecture. One possible nuance is
observable when we compare John de Burgh and St Antoninus, in the
Theologia moralis. St Antoninus devotes considerable space to the question
of the validity of marriage where one party is six months under the
canonical minimum, and cites a great range of authorities on it, the
sentence commentaries of Pierre de la Palud and St Albert the Great, the
Summa confessorum of John of Freiburg, and canon law works of Geoffrey
of Trani and Hostiensis. St Albert was a compendious source for a
Guinness Book of (biological) Records for later medieval readers. St
Antoninus turns to him on the theme of precocious maturation. The case
quoted is that of a girl who, allegedly, conceived when nine and gave birth
when just ten. The text goes on, 'And the [natural] philosophers say that
some are born . . . who are apt for intercourse more quickly than others.
And I believe that these things vary accordingly to hot and cold places,
just as impregnation and bodily growth varies.'[35] There had been earlier
Tuscan moralist comment, from the Franciscan preacher Servasanta of
Faenza, on the ideal of late marriage practised by a northern people.
Implied by Servasanta is a contrast with his own Tuscan milieu and his
audience's own social practice of low age at first marriage for girls.[36] One
could conjecture that muffled reactions to a southern European marriage-
pattern are being conveyed in St Antoninus's harping on the theme of low
age, use of a text on early conception in a girl, and raising of variation
according to the climates of regions. Turning to an English source, John

de Burgh's is quite a voluminous treatment of marriage, but he despatches
this particular subject in about sixty words, simply stating the minima, and
citing canon law; low age is of no special interest to him. We could also
compare the treatment of age when contracting in William of Pagula's
Oculus sacerdotis and the Italian *Astesana*. I would suggest – but with some
hesitancy – that the nuances of their treatment fall into a similar, though
not so black and white, pattern of lesser and greater attention to the
minima.[37]

Discerning nuances here is tricky. Length of discussion one might take
as significant, but length can depend on the degree of legal knottiness of a
problem, not its extensiveness in social practice. It can also depend on a
literary-intellectual matter, the degree to which a treatise is an academi-
cally legal discussion rather than a practical compendium. One could
advance this as a reason against discerning a contrast between the *Oculus
sacerdotis* and the *Astesana*. It is a less easily sustainable objection when
applied to the other two. Both St Antoninus's and John de Burgh's were
practical works, and the interest displayed in the former's in low age is
quite remarkable.

4. Solemnisation of Marriage

'One [sort of] marriage is lawful, one clandestine. Lawful marriage is when
a wife is asked for from those who have power over the woman, when she
is espoused by [her] parents, and dowered . . .': so opens the treatment of
clandestine marriage by Raymond of Peñafort.[38] The text which Raymond
was quoting was widely found (with minor variations of wording) in the
standard collections of the twelfth century – in Gratian's *Decretum*[39] and
Peter Lombard's *Four Books of the Sentences*.[40] It was an ancient text,
attributed falsely to Pope Evaristus, and a famous one. What is significant
here is that it had a strategic place in Raymond, whose text was known
and quoted almost universally. Although the text is quoted in relation to
secrecy or openness, it has further significance. Since Peter Lombard
himself, when he was quoting it, pointed this out – that it goes against
consent – few educated theologians and lawyers could ever have ignored
this erosion of consent and 'power over the woman'.[41] It is this text which
Guido chooses for a strategic location; it introduces his short treatment of
clandestine marriage.[42] On the other hand John de Burgh chooses not
even to include it in the quite long section on clandestine marriage in his
Pupilla oculi.

After concluding his general discussion of clandestine marriage, John de
Burgh proceeds with the well-known provisions for three-fold publicity:
'Banns therefore are to be published in churches by priests before the

solemnisation of marriage.'[43] John de Burgh displays the care and precision which are a commonplace in other English manuals. This theme of publicity of forthcoming marriages through the local parish church has been studied by Sheehan on the evidence of thirteenth and early fourteenth-century conciliar and synodal legislation and within the problematic he puts forward of 'community control'.[44] The statutes from France, currently in course of publication by Pontal, show a similar spread of this legislation, through dioceses in the thirteenth century, in Paris, the west, Bordeaux, and Angers. In some southern dioceses, Albi and Sisteron, they appear similarly, but another widespread southern set, the statutes for Nîmes, which were repeated for Arles, Béziers, Lodève, and Uzès, stands out. The provision for banns is vaguer; it lacks the specifying of three-fold publicity.[45] The saturation of the English evidence, and a vagueness encountered in some of the most southern France statutes, may provide a context for the explicitly regional comment of one southern writer. In his northern Spanish setting Guido writes about banns with a hint of distance, historical, regional, and linguistic. 'It was decided in a general council [i.e. the fourth Lateran Council] . . . And this is best observed in the Gallican churches, where for three Sundays or three solemn days [three-fold publicity] . . . and in *Francia* [i.e. Ile de France or Northern France?] they call this "banna".'[46] The negative implications of this with regard to Guido's own northern Spanish setting or parts of southern France (for *Francia* may well mean northern France) are not spelled out.

The intrusive presence or interesting distance of the Church also appear in the treatments by St Antoninus and the *Memoriale* of the question of a wife's obedience to her husband, discussed in section 8 below.

5. Sentiment

Some pastoral or penitential material contains gloomy things about women or sex; these themes are not pursued here. Some also display ideals of love in marriage and concern about such love. In questions to the married in a quite widespread manual of about 1300, usually named by its incipit, *Sacerdos igitur*, the second question is, 'Whether they love each other really and with conjugal embrace'.[47] Here a manual retains an echo of another world, the legal treatment of marriage cases and a canonist's or judge's interest in the existence or non-existence of sexual relations, but it also advises a priest to show a pastor's concern with love between the married. John of Aurbach's question to the married of either sex about their treatment of each other asks whether they reside together, render the marital debt (viz. sex), show 'conjugal affection', and are faithful.[48] The words, including 'conjugal affection', are rooted in canon-legal vocabulary, but they take on a special colouring with John's emphasis on what is mutual: do they render the debt 'in mutual subvention and servitude'? There is continuous reference to a high ideal of married love in the English texts. Thomas of Chobham writes, 'In contracting marriage a man gives a woman his body, and she hers; apart from the soul, nothing under the sky is more precious.' Later, after a conventional, but to our eyes extraordinary and repellent, reference to a husband's correction of a wife, Thomas goes on to say that 'nothing should be dearer to him [the husband] than his wife'.[49] William of Pagula writes thus: 'When a priest carries out the solemnisation of marriage he should instruct the man to put the ring on the fourth finger of his wife['s hand]', and then he inserts a text quoted via Gratian, that the 'ring is a general sign of mutual love, or rather this, that by this pledge their hearts are united; and the ring is placed on the fourth finger because in that finger there is a vein which leads right up to the heart, and likewise the man and woman ought to be of one heart.'[50] John de Burgh frames his treatment of marriage with comparable statements of ideals. He concludes his introductory chapter on marriage and its definition with this vocabulary: 'the union of the sincere love of a man and his wife, between them . . . the union of charitable love of God and the faithful soul, which is represented by the consent and sincere love of the man and the woman who contract [marriage] according to law'.[51] To the end of the concluding chapter in the marriage section he tacks an addendum about wives, which begins thus: 'Note according to the Master [Peter Lombard] in the fourth [book] of the Sentences, Eve was made *from man's side*, not from another part, *for this reason*: to show that *she was created* in a society of love – lest, *if she had* by chance *been made from the man's head, she should have seemed to be brought forth for domination*, or, *if made from his feet, brought forth in order to suffer servitude*. From which it appears that a wife is not to be honoured by her husband like a lady, nor to be treated vilely like a hand-maid, but really loved as a companion.' The mixture which follows does not eradicate the initial impression made by these, strategically located, statements.[52]

In the background is the exalted language of the marriage liturgy itself, which, as Molin and Mutembe have shown, took its shape and had its most rapid early diffusion in the England and Normandy of the years after c.1100.[53] Traces of this liturgy and its sentiments are not difficult to find in the following centuries in the northern manuals, while the liturgy is absent and it is harder to find expression in the ideals in the southern manuals.

6. Avoiding Offspring: 'Contraception' and Abortion

Noonan describes two of the principal texts present in the principal theological and canon-legal textbooks of the mid-twelfth century (Gratian's and Peter Lombard's), which were common sources for the authors of the pastoral manuals. These were the text *Aliquando*, which specified avoiding conception with the words 'procure poisons of sterility', and made a clear distinction between this and extinguishing a foetus – sinners might do the latter if the former did not work. The other was the text *Adulterii malum*, which described intercourse between man and wife where the member was used for a purpose which has not been granted by God. Avoidance of conception is not spelled out as intention or motive, but clearly the text could be intended to include this, most plausibly in connection with the practice of *coitus interruptus*.[54] Not emphasised in Noonan's account is a third text, *Solet quaeri*, present in the same collections, which deals with the question of whether those who marry only for incontinence (desire) and not in order to have offspring are in fact married. Even though they have not married with the motive of generating offspring, they are married if, during their married life, 'they will have not avoided generation of offspring', this being spelled out as 'either if they do not wish children to be born or also if by some evil act they bring it about that [children] are not born'.[55] Additionally, from standard twelfth-century texts, there was the ordinary gloss on Onan, making it clear that his spilling of seed was 'in order not to fecundate Tamar'.[56] From the thirteenth century Noonan points to the inclusion in the Gregory IX's *Libri Quinque Decretalium* of 1234 (cited from here on as the *Decretales*) of *Si conditiones*, which indicated a pre-nuptial pact 'to avoid offspring' as nullifying a marriage.[57] These texts were embedded first in what were textbooks for lectures and commentaries in faculties of theology and canon-law, and in the *studia* of the mendicant orders, and through both they found immense replication and diffusion.

These texts were, further, the sources (sometimes via intermediaries) for authors of pastoral manuals. These authors found in them a vocabulary: *procure poisons of sterility; avoid generation of offspring*, or *avoid offspring; act so that children should not be born; spill seed in order not to fecundate*. Facing in two directions, both towards these texts on the one hand and their own pastoral experience on the other, these authors may reflect trends of time or area through the special emphases of their use or extension of these texts. Detecting such emphases, however, is fraught with pitfalls. One tends, for example, to encounter *poisons of sterility* very often. Could this reflect majority practice? Or could it reflect the prominence and ease of location of *Aliquando*, which eventually may have impelled some readers and writers to use the phrase as a holdall and/or euphemism, covering both (narrowly) potions and (broadly) anti-conceptional activity of any kind? I prefer this second interpretation, but my preference rests on nothing more solid than repeated reading of these texts and a sense of their prose-styles.

The theme can be and is put forward under a variety of headings, and the first significance of these is what they show about awareness of anti-conceptional behaviour. The manuals are saturated with concern about avoiding conception. It is not only that it would be difficult to find any important manual which did not contain some material on avoiding conception; in some it is the author's first concern. In the *Sacerdos igitur* manual, the very first question to be put to the married is 'whether they contracted marriage with the intention of having children.'[58] In St Antoninus's *Confessionale*, in the section on questions to the married, the part on the sexual act also starts with this, with a note that the act is a mortal sin when outside the appropriate receptacle 'in such a fashion that seed is not received in order to avoid offspring and generation'. It then proceeds to the first and second questions: 'If he/she has used marriage outside the appropriate receptacle. If he/she has done anything to avoid generation.'[59]

I outlined in an earlier article one chronological pattern, the extraordinary degree of concern about avoidance of conception expressed in a cluster of texts in the first quarter of the fourteenth century.[60] This is amplified in what follows. The background was a tradition of already considerable concern. Among the cases discussed by Peter the Chanter in late twelfth-century Paris, one concerns the procuring of poisons of sterility, in a fashion (a particular medical problem is involved) which suggests that this is readily part of one's mental world.[61] In the early thirteenth-century Robert of Flamborough's penitential uses *Si aliquis* on 'doing something to or giving something to drink to a man or a woman so that he/she cannot generate or conceive',[62] while Thomas of Chobham's penitential manual touches upon it several times: a nullifying precondition to marriage ('I take you as mine under this condition, that we procure sterility so that we never generate offspring'); under the sin of anger and the sub-sin of killing, 'to procure sterility'; under lust, and the sub-category of sin against nature, 'some abuse their wives, not in the place granted for this . . .' – and here the motive of avoiding conception is not stated.[63]

In these pastoral works of the late twelfth and early thirteenth century the theme is present, but it does not have pride of place, and there seems to have been no special development in treatment or vocabulary. The first quarter of the fourteenth century sees the appearance of a number of writings which show marked development. In both southern and northern treatises, the *Astesana* and the *Confessionale* of John of Freiburg, there is use of a different phrase, 'procuring some impediment to offspring', which is reminiscent of the phrase of an earlier southern Franciscan, Peter John Olivi, 'procuring [an?] impeditive to offspring', used in a text written before 1279.[64] *Impede* is, of course, an obvious word (see its use by Peter the Chanter, below), but *impediment* and *impeditive* seem to be additions to the conventional vocabulary of *procure poisons of sterility, act to avoid,* etc., and they seem to represent a development in conciseness. More precisely and demonstrably significant is the treatment of avoidance of conception by William of Pagula. Citing *Aliquando* and *Adulterii malum,* William wrote that the parish priest 'ought' frequently to make public [the lesson] that a man when carnally knowing his wife or another woman ought to do nothing on account of which conception of a foetus is impeded'. After some discussion of the sin and various ways of irregularly emitting seed William concludes: 'it is necessary to make this public in church; for the penitentiaries of bishops know well that there are many these days who believe that the sin against nature in many cases is not a sin, which is a matter for grief. So the parish priest can safely say among his parishioners, "You ought to know that if someone has knowingly and willfully emitted the seed of coitus in any way other than naturally with his wife, he sins gravely. . . ."[65] Elsewhere William spells out a priest's words of enquiry in confession to a penitent man: 'Brother, everyone ought to know that if he has ever emitted the semen of coitus knowingly and while awake other than naturally with his wife . . .'.[66] The formulation is a holdall, although William's introduction to what a priest ought to make public indicates that sex between man and wife or man and woman where conception is deliberately avoided loomed largest in his thoughts.

One could be misled if one over-emphasises the precise dates of composition of Astesanus's or William's works – 1317 and 1320–7. Works of comparable character were not composed in, for example, 1291. Looking backwards one might see in William's words a slightly late reaction to something which may have been accelerated by the population pressure of the mid- and late thirteenth century. Looking forward, can one see subsidence? Boyle has shown that mid- and later fourteenth-century manuals were, for the most part, reworkings of William's fundamental text. The *Speculum curatorum,* ascribed to Ranulph Higden and the year 1340, inserts under 'The things a priest ought to declare on Sundays and feast-days' what amounts to a brief version of William: 'item, he should declare that in carnal intercourse nothing should be done whereby conception [*conceptus*] can be impeded'.[67] Very near in time (1343) the anonymous *Regimen animarum* simply repeats the whole of William's treatment.[68] In stark contrast is the most influential work of later fourteenth-century England, the *Pupilla oculi* of 1384, whose author put it forward, in the introduction, as a reworking of William's treatise. It is lengthy, includes much of William, has some material on avoiding conception, but it does not include William's discussion and advice to the priest frequently to warn in public against couples having sex in ways (by context, *coitus interruptus*) which avoid conception.

Perhaps significant both to this sequence and consciousness about the relation between individual anti-conceptional behaviour and population is a text which appears in William of Pagula's treatment of *luxuria*, sexual sin, under the seven deadly sins, and, under *luxuria*, the sin against nature. Here sin against nature may include any unnatural spilling of seed, but *coitus interruptus* may predominate. The two sentences I am about to quote are immediately followed by a reference to God striking down Onan because 'when knowing his wife he deprived her of conception by spilling his seed on the ground'. 'Item', so goes the statement, 'those who labour in this vice and [form of] homicide are, spirtually, the enemies of God and the human race. For in what they do they are saying to God, "You created man and woman in order for them to multiply. We will devote care in order for them to grow less".'[69] I have not yet traced an earlier source for this text – if there is one literary source – but again there is a pattern of three stages in this text's presence in fourteenth-century England. The first is its entry into William's treatise, c.1320–7. In William's version it acts as a holdall for any sort of non-procreative spilling of seed, while at the same time through the reference to Onan's wife and depriving her of conception it suggests heterosexual *coitus interruptus*. The second stage is the 1340s, when the text has mixed fortunes. It survives in the *Regimen animarum*, where it is copied. On the other hand, in Ranulph Higden's *Speculum curatorum* it is abbreviated. This abbreviation, further, omits the reference to Onan's wife, and inserts the word *sodomite*; the sentences have been contracted to a narrow reference to the infertility of homosexual acts. The third stage is 1384; the text does not appear in John de Burgh's *Pupilla oculi*, the second edition of William.[70]

Can we discern reactions here to changing circumstances, the responses of pastors to different patterns of behaviour in their married flock, which are in turn responses of the married to the different population conditions of c.1300 and the mid- and later fourteenth century? If so, these are reactions which are detectable principally in the English manuals. Perhaps there is more responsiveness in the northern manuals? Occasionally the writings become a little more specific, whether on social category of the sinner, the motive for avoiding conception, or the method, and the first two of these are more marked in writings from the north, or, at least, are found there earlier. Northern writers paying attention to poverty as a motive range from Burchard of Worms (a woman's motive)[71] to Peter de la Palud in the early fourteenth century (a man's motive).[72] Although St Antoninus was to quote Peter de la Palud in his compendious *Theologia moralis* on poverty, he did not do so in his *Confessionale*.[73] Precise analysis had taken place in late twelfth-century Paris. Peter the Chanter's discussion of procuring sterility was of a case, which was quickly specified: 'someone's wife has been ruptured in the navel through repeated childbirth. The doctors tell her that if she gives birth again she will die. Nevertheless her husband asks for [her rendering of] the debt [sex]. Is she bound to render it, since for certain she knowns that she will die if she conceives? She knows that if she renders the debt she will conceive, because she is still young. Item, one asks if she can procure sterility for herself, not principally in order to impede childbirth, but in order not to die in childbirth.'[74] Late twelfth-century Paris had seen wider discussion of this issue, and a probable echo was found a few years later in Thomas of Chobham, who is said to have known Peter and to have been his pupil, when he was analysing a woman's motives. After specifying lust and avoiding the pregnancy which might betray a woman's indulging in lust, he proceeded to say that 'others, however, do this in order to avoid the pain of giving birth'.[75]

7. Abortion, Regime of Pregnant Women, Care of Children, Infanticide

Thomas of Chobham joins together care of pregnant women, attempts to bring about miscarriages, and the theme of maternal breast-feeding opposed to wet-nursing, while the *Decretales* juxtapose titles on infanticide and abandonment of children.[76] Both provide support for Smith's suggestion that one should examine a continuum here – attitudes to foetus and baby through from conception to early nurture.[77] Examing such a continuum, we find contrasts between the English and the southern manuals, first that the former are more attentive and detailed and the latter are more cursory.

Before a closer examination of this, one immediate contrast should be noted, in the specific medical milieux which are evoked for abortion. In the English *Memoriale* a quite extensive treatment of the sins of doctors and surgeons (*medici*) deals with such themes as practice by the untrained, negligent medical practice by the trained, excessive fees, and intervention by religious who have no knowledge based on experience (*experimentaliter*).[78] However, abortion is not mentioned here. The principal detailed treatment of abortion is in the list of questions to the married woman, where it is linked with avoidance of conception: 'if she ever drank, or gave others to drink, any potions or the juice of herb, in order not to conceive by someone, or whether she gave [to others] or drank in order to bring about abortion, that is, to kill the foetus . . .'.[79] The author discusses what is to be done with such sins elsewhere. He lists procuring abortion or sterility in oneself or another as a sin to be remitted to the bishop, and provides penance for one hitting or giving a potion to a pregnant woman.[80] There is nothing else suggesting a wider milieu of guilty parties.

When we turn to St Antoninus we also find attention to abortion in questions for the married woman. He envisages the involvement of others, more precisely than the *Memoriale*: 'this is a mortal sin in her, and in anyone else who gives advice or help in this', and he also envisages involuntary miscarriage.[81] The sharpest divergence from the *Memoriale* comes, however, with the appearance of the theme in two other sets of questions intended for two other categories of penitent. A doctor (*medicus*) is to be asked 'if he gives medicine to a pregnant [woman] to kill the foetus, even [i.e. including the case where this is] for the preservation of the mother'. Druggists [*armatarii*] are asked if they 'instruct [about the use of?] or sell those things which procure abortion'.[82] St Antoninus envisages a wider range of methods. He establishes more and precisely specified guilty co-operating parties and sinful activities – pregnant women in taking, doctors in giving medicines, druggists in instructing and selling. Further, he briefly alludes to an ethical problem of doctors which had been formulated and debated in a quodlibetic question of the Dominican John of Naples, possibly during his time as lector in Naples (from 1317): 'Whether a doctor should give medicine to a pregnant women from which the death of the child [foetus] would follow, though the death of both would follow if he did not give it?' Fuller discussion, with explicit citation of John's quodlibet, is given in the account of doctors' vices in the *Theologia moralis*.[83]

There is a broader contrast between the manuals, but the most important elements common to the manuals need first to be briefly listed. These were the texts in Gratian's *Decretum* and Gregory IX's *Decretales* relating to abortion (already mentioned in section 6, above), infanticide, and exposure. The canon *Consuluisti* in the *Decretum* was fundamental in providing the outlines of care of the babies and concern with their deaths, and a vocabulary which is repeated in most later local legislation and pastoral manuals. 'Parents are to be admonished [*monendi*] and publicly advised [*protestandi*] that they should not place beside themselves in a bed [*in uno collocent lecto*] their babies, so that they should not be suffocated or smothered [*suffocentur vel opprimantur*] through some negligence which might arise; in this case they are guilty of homicide.'[84] In Gregory's *Decretales* three texts appear under the title 'On those who have killed their children', the first two dealing with wilful killing. The first, a letter from Alexander III (possibly 1159 × 1160) to the Bishop of Tournai, deals with an unmarried woman who has wilfully killed her child: she should be induced to enter a monastery, and there do perpetual penance, unless carnal fragility suggests that she should be given licence to marry. The second, a letter of Lucius III to the Bishop of Paris (1181 × 1185) deals with the case where the wilful killer is a married woman with children: she is not to be separated from her husband, so that she can continue to bring up her other children. The third, a letter of Alexander III, deals with 'the babies who are found dead with the father and mother, [where] it is not clear whether the baby was smothered or suffocated by the father or mother, or whether it died by its own death', and adds the vocabulary of 'will' [*voluntas*] and 'event' [*eventus*] to make the distinction between willed and accidental death.[85] The texts are complementary. Prevention is prominent in Gratian, whilst Gregory IX's concern is with discriminating measures about the guilty after the event. Both collections are briefer on exposure. Gratian's *Si expositus* and Gregory IX's *Si a patre* both deal narrowly with the question of claims made over a found child, whether by finder or reclaimer.[86]

Important in the present enquiry is, first of all, the different pressures brought to bear by these collections on the compilers of pastoral manuals. Where there is weighty material (infanticide) and slight material (exposure) in the principal canon-legal collections, my initial hypothesis is that there is significance in silence on the first and almost any mention of the second. My second hypothesis is that considerable care and concern may not be a direct index of the incidence of infanticide and exposure. It is in the first instance evidence of itself – concern. Pastoral authors when expressing this concern could have been the mouthpiece of opinions shared more broadly in the communities in which they lived. Where they tended more to silence they may have been thereby showing that they were themselves members of communities which more readily accepted, and perhaps had a higher rate of, infanticide and exposure. A final pressure is one of detail, that of vocabulary. Trexler used 'suffocation' in Florentine legislation to indicate a way of killing.[87] Clearly, the vocabulary of *oppressio* and *suffocatio* is a bequest from authoritative canon-legal texts. It is the influence of this vocabulary which is, first of all, revealed in its further use, not necessarily the precise way of killing envisaged by any later author.

Guido of Monte Roterio deals with infanticide under confession and the imposition of penance. He expounds several cases concerning 'parents in whose beds children are found dead', following the three cases of Gregory IX's *Decretales*. The language of part of Gratian's *Consuluisti* is inserted into the third – 'if negligently he/she has placed the baby beside him/herself in the bed, and has found the baby dead in the morning'[88] – without, however altering its purpose, declaring what is to be done *after* the deed. While Guido's outline of different cases and penance is clear and precise, it entirely omits anything which might reflect the thrust of Gratian's *Consuluisti* – public warning, prevention. One would look for this in the third part of his treatise, 'Those things which pertain to the instruction of the people', but in vain.[89] He has nothing to say about exposure.

Under the heading of confessional questions asked about the fifth commandment, St Antoninus lists abortions and infanticides of various modes, motives, and degrees of will, in two instances with medical detail. 'If a pregnant woman has procured an abortion for herself through medicines or exertions or some other way. . . . If a woman kills her child wilfully in order to hide her crime. . . . If a mother or nurse stifles a child whom she is keeping beside her in a bed, inadvertently smothering her. . . . If a pregnant woman brings about an abortion which is contrary to her intention or plan, if she was committing obvious negligence in this, such as jumping too much, or working too much and inordinately, or through [sexual activity in order to satisfy] inordinate lust.'[90] Causes of miscarriage are expanded in the *Theologia moralis* to include '[if] a pregnant woman . . . carries a heavy weight'.[91] The question about stifling recalls the wording of *Consuluisti* (*suffocat . . . opprimens*), though the person evisaged lying beside the baby is not father and/or mother but mother or nurse. St Antoninus does not copy the precise cases of Gregory IX's *Decretales*, as does Guido, but like Guido he echoes their drift, discriminating different degrees of sinfulness and penance in events which have taken place. There is nothing explicitly directed towards prevention, although one could suggest that prevention is implied in the treatment of inadvertent abortions. As we shall see later, while St Antoninus does not mention exposure, he does envisage more formal abandonment to a *hospitale*.[92] The coverage of infanticide in the very large *Theologia moralis* is of startling brevity, mainly two references to 'when through negligence [women] smother little ones they have in bed with them' (this in a list of vices of the married), and '[when] a nurse places a little child beside her in bed, and while asleep presses it down' (this in a list under 'Anger', sub-heading 'homicide', sub-group 'cases of unintended homicide').[93] Notable is this: although a parent has to be specified when the entry is in a list of vices of the married, when St Antoninus is freed by his heading – unintended homicide by anyone – the person he envisages is a nurse.

English manuals from Thomas of Chobham's to John de Burgh's stand in stark contrast. They devote far greater attention to the theme, and they consistently show interest in prevention. There already existed a tradition in northern penitential collections of close attention to abortion and infanticide.[94] Robert of Flamborough lies in this tradition in his repetition of a discrimination about degrees of sinfulness of abortion – less penance on a 'little poor woman, if she did this because of the difficulty of feeding [the baby]' – and in his precise specification of the circumstances of negligence: 'If a mother has placed a baby by a hearth, and some man has put water in the cauldron, and the baby dies because of an overflow of boiling water . . .'.[95] Added to this tradition was the acute interest in debate of concrete moral problems shown by Peter the Chanter and his circle in Paris in the 1180s and 1190s. One question concerning *procuring sterility* to avoid death in childbirth has already been noted, but there were others on the themes of miscarriage, abortion, and exposure. 'A priest is following the hounds and smashes [*oppressit et allisit*] a pregnant woman against a wall. She falls down, wailing. Afterwards for three weeks she is at home, complaining a bit; meanwhile, she goes on carrying things to the market. However, at the end of three weeks she has an abortion.' What of the priest's guilt?[96] As Baldwin has shown with painstaking brilliance, Peter tended to discuss problems he had encountered and of which he had real knowledge. His own origin among the minor nobility of mid-twelfth-century Beauvaisis lends special significance, then, to another question he raised about noble girls. 'Some noble girls who stifle their offspring . . . are so ashamed that they in no way want to confess except to a private priest. What should happen?'[97] Another question relates to a 'certain monk whose abbot had placed him in charge of a certain house. He finds outside the house which had been entrusted to him an abandoned little baby, very recently born, and already about to die through hunger and cold. The aforesaid monk wants to take him up and look after him. The brothers forbid him, and also the abbot, for two reasons: 'to avoid evil suspicion . . . and to avoid other little women being encouraged by this example to abandon their children in the same place, were they to see the brothers taking care of this baby . . .'. Peter does not advise him to be inobedient, but 'if he did do so, nature and his piety would go far to excuse this inobedience, because of [the baby's] pressing necessity'.[98]

Baldwin has described the various links which connect Peter and his circle with reform in the thirteenth century, the fourth Lateran Council, but also through pupils' pupils, and in the first instance through men like Thomas of Chobham and Stephen Langton, with the remarkable pastoral efforts of synodal and conciliar legislation in England up to the late thirteenth century. A comparison of the legislation which is available in modern editions – Powicke and Cheney's two volumes of English legislation between 1205 and 1313, and the first three volumes of Pontal's edition of thirteenth-century legislation – suggests some contrast between England and France (or southeastern France) during this period. English legislation is saturated with provisions about child-care and infanticide: Canterbury I, Salisbury, Grosseteste's instructions to his archdeacons, Coventry, Exeter I, Lincoln, Worcester, Norwich, Winchester II, Durham II, Durham peculiars, Chichester, Ely, Wells, London, between the first of these (1213 × 1214) and the last (1245 × 1259).[99] All follow the thrust of Gratian's *Consuluisti*, that is they envisage legislation which instructs a parish priest in the way he in turn should instruct his parishioners, all directed towards *prevention* or preventive care. 'Women' or 'mothers' are to be admonished. Grosseteste adds nurses to mothers, as do Worcester, Norwich, and Ely. There is to be 'frequent preaching' (Grosseteste, Lincoln, Norwich, Winchester II, Ely), preaching every Sunday (Salisbury I, Worcester), or 'solemnly on feastdays' (Durham II). Women should 'feed [babies] with care' (Canterbury I, Salisbury I, Exeter I, London II). They should not place babies beside them in beds 'unless the baby is three or thereabouts' (Coventry), as death or stifling or danger 'often occurs' (variously expressed in Grosseteste, Durham II, Ely). Further baby-care is specified. A baby put in a cradle should not be there in such a fashion 'that it can be turned over and the baby fall on its head' (Coventry), and babies 'should lie in firmly fastened cradles' (Worcester). This extends to baby-sitting. Women should 'not leave babies alone near water without someone on the watch' (Salisbury I). There is less direct interest in abandonment, apart from much provision about the baptism of abandoned children, and one remarkable provision in London I for enquiries about 'parishioners who are suspected of stifling or exposing offspring'.

When we turn to the thirteenth-century French statutes we find one set from the southwest, Bordeaux (1234), which contains the instruction that priests should preach to the people (women are not specified) that 'babies should not be placed side by side in beds with parents or nurse, but should be carefully placed in cradles'.[100] Apart from this there is silence. One might explain this by the earliness of some of the legislation. However, the southeastern statutes, Albi (1230) and Sisteron, Nîmes, Arles, Béziers (1252), were drawn up during the full spate of English legislation on the theme.

An existing northern tradition then, viz. late twelfth-century Parisian discussions, and a background of what seems to be intense English interest in care, and preventive care, of children, is the intelligible background for the extraordinary treatment given to this theme by Thomas of Chobham, and after him, following in his path, later English manuals. Thomas raises the matter in two passages, the first, under cases reserved for a bishop: 'stifling of one's own offspring, or when a baby, through parents' negligence, falls in fire or water, through lack of someone on watch. Therefore priests ought to warn parents in church against having babies in bed with them, or careless binding them in their cradles, or leaving them without someone on the watch. . . .'[101] Thomas was active in the diocese of Salisbury as sub-dean between 1206 and 1208, and in the chapter by 1214, and there is a close connection between this passage and the similar legislation in Salisbury I.

The second, very lengthy, treatment, appears under killing, and the sub-section, 'Those who kill their own offspring'. Thomas sees five ways in which women do this: (i) 'when they procure poisons of sterility, or (ii) when after conception the foetus is forced out by violence, or (iii) when after childbirth [the baby] is separated from the [mother's] own breasts, or (iv) when it is cast out and exposed, or (v) when through negligence it is stifled in the bed of the sleeping mother'. Thomas then tracks through his five categories, devoting most attention to (ii) and (iii), having previously discussed (v). Most of his discussion relates to the care of the pregnant woman and breast-feeding. It is quoted here at length:

> Priests therefore ought to charge women who are pregnant . . . not to press on with heavy work after conception, because doctors say that [even] with light work the foetus is cast out from the womb after the beginning of pregnancy. A certain woman who wanted to cast out her foetus has been written about: she gave three jumps from a bench to the ground, and on the third jump the foetus fell out to the ground, wrapped round in a little skin. It is clear from this that the women who have not been instructed about this often eject some conceived foetus, either through work or exertion. The fact that separating a baby from the [mother's] own breasts is a matter which pertains to killing is clear from the writings of the saints [i.e. fathers], who say that no milk is so suitable for nursing a child as maternal milk. Therefore a [baby] often perishes when it is nursed with strange milk, with, so to speak, a contrary nutriment. This can happen because the complexion of the nurse is contrary to the baby's complexion, and thus the baby contracts some corruption from milk which is contrary to it. . . . A woman who disdains to nurse the offspring she conceived is crueller than any beast. She fed it in her womb with menstrual blood and now she neglects to nurse it with God-given milk. For God gave women breasts and commanded milk to grow in them so that a woman could rear her offspring thus. Now, however, there are those sorts of women who try to invalidate God's work and nullify the milk which God created for use. Priests should sharply rebuke such women, and impose heavy penance [on them] for disdaining to feed their babies according to nature's use. What if the woman is delicate and says she cannot bear such labour: was she not [already] so delicate when she underwent intercourse and the labour of giving birth? If she truly cannot bear the labour, she should at least feed and wash the baby when she can, so that she does not seem [to be trying] to overturn nature through never deigning to go near her own offspring.[102]

The precise sources of this have not been traced. The vocabulary of part – *complexio, contrarium nutrimentum*, etc, – suggests a medical textbook, and the brief but precise question about the delicate woman is similar in character and form to the questions raised in Paris by Peter the Chanter, some of which demonstrably affected other parts of Thomas's manual.[103] The passage as a whole is remarkable, both for the way in which Thomas sets care in a spectrum which runs from conception through to feeding, and for the heavy emphasis on this care, whether preventive care of a pregnant woman or of a baby which is to be breast-fed and, at the very least, washed and dealt with by its own mother. When William of Pagula came to write his *Oculus sacerdotis*, he adopted the whole of the passage translated above for insertion into his section on penance, beginning, however, with a singular ('A priest should charge a pregnant woman . . .') and omitting the story about the three leaps.[104] His equivalent of Thomas's earlier passage is, however, an interpolation of the words of *Consuluisti* under the list of 'Those things which a priest ought to preach', with an addition to the text: 'if for a little while a baby's mouth is covered by some cloth it is easily stifled'.[105] These repetitions and inclusions were enough to provide for wide diffusion of the passage in later medieval England, through the *Oculus* itself, the *Regimen animarum* of 1343 which copied these two sections, and John de Burgh's *Pupilla oculi*. John included an abbreviation and adaptation of William (or Thomas): 'A pregnant woman should be suitably charged to avoid strenuous work in case danger arises from it. After childbirth women should breast-feed their own children, unless they are excused through reasonable cause, so that they should not seem to make light of the gift of God, abundance of milk. No milk is so suitable for feeding a child as mother's milk, so the doctors say.'[106] In his section on stifling he concentrates on *post-factum* penances, recalling the wording and teaching of Gregory IX's *Decretales*. He refers to a parent's guilt in not applying due care, 'especially', he writes, 'because there is the command in the canon that no one should allow a small baby to lie beside him/herself in a bed . . .'.[107] The implication is significant – that by that date guilt is exacerbated because parents would know through their parish priests about this warning.

Standing somewhat apart from the mainstream of texts from England is the *Memoriale* of 1344. All the more significant, therefore, are its emphases which perhaps betray the influence of an English milieu in general. Its treatment of 'Penances on parents who have killed their children' is remarkable for its length and careful discriminations. The latter include a distinction between bed and cot-deaths, and this itself is followed by an unusual statement about paternal love: 'whether the child was stifled thus in bed by the sides of its parents. . . . If, however, it was found dead in a cot, a lesser penance should be imposed, because it is presumed that this did not happen through sure knowledge but rather through some lack of care. For it is not to be assumed that a mother is forgetful of a child. And it is said, no less, that paternal love conquers every other love.'[108] In questions to be put in confession there are interesting areas of overlap and contrast with St Antoninus's *Confessionale*. Both include questions to be put to a woman about abortion and stifling of babies, but the *Memoriale* alone – and alone among all such lists I have examined – goes on to include a question about abandonment: 'Item, has she ever abandoned her child. That is, when stupid women place their children in or outside a church, and leave them there without anyone in charge. Such abandoned children are called in English *fundlinges*.'[109] St Antoninus refers to a different guilty person, action, and setting in an earlier question, under the heading of 'On the government of parents concerning children and household': 'has he through some cruelty or avarice sent off his children, even the illegitimate ones, to a *hospitale*'.[110] In the manuals' concern, or lack of concern, I have not noticed distinction being made between the sexes. Evoked in England are women, local church, and 'foundlings'; and in Tuscany a father, and a more formal arrangement involving an institution.

8. Conduct in Marriage

Compared here, first, are texts on a wife's duties. The *Memoriale* and St Antoninus's *Confessionale* both underline a wife's obedience, but the words are significantly different. St Antoninus's questions is, 'If a wife was inobedient and quarrelsome and of her own mind towards her husband'.[111] The question in the English text – among various questions to be put to the married woman – is whether the wife has shown her husband due *reverenciam et subieccionem in domo in mensa et in lecto*.[112] Apart from *domo* this is a Latin version of part of the wife's vow in the marriage liturgy, which runs in the vernacular in the Sarum rite: 'to be bonere and buxum in bedde and atte borde'.[113] In the mid-fourteenth-century English text a woman is to be reminded in confession of the wording of the vow in the Church's liturgy, and of this vow in relation to her husband. In mid-fifteenth-century Tuscany, however, there is no echo of the Church or a Church liturgy, in words which do not need anything other than a source in the thought and vocabulary of the laity. St Antoninus goes on to include questions which could not be found in the English texts: 'If she was impolite and difficult towards the in-laws and kin [from the context, the *cognatos* referred to here must be husband's kin]. . . . If she does not want to follow her husband [when] he changes domicile.' 'If she was very lacking in order and negligent in the government of the house.'[114]

When one turns to the husband's duties a comparison of William of Pagula (who deals with this under 'accidie') and St Antoninus shows much expected overlap, for example: 'If a man did not maintain his wife sufficiently' (William);[115] 'If a man did not provide his wife and household with necessary things – not, however, superfluous ones' (St Antoninus). St Antoninus goes further than William, however, in asking, 'If he was jealous and excessively suspicious of her, or very remiss in custody of her'.[116]

Here in the *Confessionale* and the *Theologia moralis* there are several distinct emphases. The vocabulary of 'government of the house', 'governor of the household', 'domestic care', and repetitively, the 'house', springs partly from the peculiar importance of the 'house', *casa* in Tuscan society, which Klapisch-Zuber has discussed, and partly from the vocabulary of a tradition of thought about the household whose longer roots are apparent in the treatment in the *Theologia moralis* of Economic Prudence [viz. prudence concerning household administration].[117] This section's title recalls Aristotle's *Economics*, and its contents are related explicitly to the generalising statements about the household in Aristotle's *Politics*.[118] One notable statement comes when St Antoninus deals with women giving charity, itself a common theme, but set by St Antoninus within a briefly stated rationalisation of sexual division: set against women, who supply charity, are 'Men [who] are intent on trading activities and other great works . . . .'.[119]

When one turns to sexual behaviour by spouses (apart from contraception, discussed above), one again finds many areas of overlap, such as equality in repaying the marital debt, which need no insistence here. One peculiarity is St Antoninus's treatment of pregnancy. Here one usually finds manuals dealing with sexual relations *between* spouses during pregnancy, and in substantial agreement on the issue. St Antoninus is singular in including the question 'If [a wife] gave permission to her husband to go to other women while' she was pregnant'.[120] Of clearer significance are some divergences in the treatment of fidelity. Three things stand out in the *Memoriale*, firstly the broad social canvas within which it is set. Adultery is dealt with in lists of questions to various estates, not just to a woman: 'You ought to ask a knight . . . whether he is an adulterer';[121] 'if he [a merchant] ever travelled to another kingdom or province, and, pretending to be unmarried, contracted *de facto* marriage there, or, even though not contracting, committed adultery';[122] 'Concerning sailors . . . all are adulterers or fornicators, because in all the countries or regions they visit they either contract marriage *de facto* with various women, believing that this is lawful for them, or etc.';[123] 'Concerning married women. . . . Item, enquire about adultery . . .'. Secondly, the author is clear on his own, moralist's, ideal of a single standard here – '[a man and a woman] are not judged other than equally in a case like this' – and at the same time there is no reference in his text to the reality or consciousness of double-standards among laymen – other, that is, than that of sailors! Thirdly, the over-riding concern he displays when specifying questions to an adulterous women is the orderly transmission of property: 'Item, enquire if she as a married woman had ever conceived in adultery a boy or a girl, and if the child had been so raised that it had succeeded or was in a position to succeed to the inheritance of its father, with the resulting disinheritance of its putative father.'[124] Lack of the social canvas in St Antoninus should not be underlined – the extensiveness of this in the *Memoriale* is unique among the Latin manuals from an English milieu – but worth attention is what he chooses for special discussion in the *Theologia moralis*. 'It is extraordinary', he writes, 'that men totally want their wives to be chaste and not to look at another man, and when they do behave indecently men regard this as the greatest of injuries to themselves, and rightly so, for [such a wife] brings upon him very great shame and confusion: for an adulterous wife is a disgrace for all the kin, detestable and hateful before God and the whole world, worthy of temporal and eternal fire. But these husbands think their own practice of any sort of indecency is licit, so long as their wives are faithful.'[125] Standing out in St Anoninus, then, is a sharper profile to a double-standard described by him as a conscious outlook among laymen, the prominence of shame and honour, and, once again, also the prominence of kin – here mentioned before God!

I have left to the last here a theme treated by the *Memoriale*, that of women leaving. The text quoted earlier on obedience goes on, after the echo of the Sarum marriage vow, as follows: 'for there are women these days who hold their husbands in contempt, and leave them, living on their own, for many wish to dominate who ought to be subordinate'.[126] Should we lift off one layer of the text, the veil of the moralist's preoccupation with obedience, contempt, and subordination of wives to husbands? If we do, we seem to be left with this residue in the statement: '[there are] women [many?] . . . living on their own'.

9. Matrimonial Causes

One of the commonest of professions to receive attention was that of the advocate. St Antoninus, for example, devotes much in both the works examined here to the sins of advocates.[127] However, the English sources stand out for the strong and specific attention they devote to one particular role of an advocate, namely in marriage cases. In the *Memoriale* the question list 'Concerning advocates' asks the following: 'Item, have you informed or instructed false witnesses how to attest false things in any causes, most particularly matrimonial, or have you knowingly made use of their depositions; item, have you ever put forward or had put forward any frivolous pleas in matrimonial causes or any others in a malicious way, in

order to prevent marriages reaching their due [conclusion] or to prolong
the proceedings of such causes, againt justice'.[128] The concern is also
shown in the questions 'Concerning officials and rural deans': 'Item, have
you ever delivered an unjust or wicked sentence, which had been arrived
at in some ecclesiastical, matrimonial or other cause, perhaps because you
did not consult books or men learned in the law about it'.[129] Behind the
Memoriale stand the sources which it is, mainly, quoting: English
legislation, which showed intense concern, going back to the Council of
Oxford (1222); and beyond this legislation one can see probable roots in
Peter the Chanter's circle, one member of which, Robert de Courson,
showed concern with irregular conduct of marriage cases.[130] Parallels can
be seen in William of Pagula, who briefly recites some typical marriage
cases,[131] and his follower John de Burgh, who devotes a section to 'How
one should proceed in matrimonial causes'.[132] This attention would not be
remarkable in more purely academic canon-legal treatises, but is so when
one considers both that it was displayed in treatises which were so carefully
directed towards the daily practical and pastoral concerns of a parish
priest, and also the silence of Guido and St Antoninus.

10. Widows

'Widowhood' can be a commonplace in manuals, for example in repetitions of the topos of the spiritual fruitfulness of virginity, widowhood,
and marriage, or as a condition, along with being poor or an orphan,
deserving charity or special canon-legal provision, or as one of the
circumstances of status to be considered when imposing penance: 'what [to
impose on] widows'. Beyond such widely shared points, widowhood
attracts little attention in the English manuals.

In St Antoninus's *Theologia moralis*, however, the title 'On the
condition of the married' is paralleled by the later, though obviously
shorter, chapter entitled 'On the condition of widows'. Here, insinuating
itself into a brief spiritual treatment of widows, their three-fold division
into widow 'of the devil', 'of the world', and 'of the Lord', is the personal
and social world of the ordinary widow, under the moralist's lens:

> The widows of the world are those who live decently, intend to marry
> in their own time, or, if they do not intend to marry are not doing
> this for the Lord but for the sake of the world [viz. for worldly
> reasons], to avoid the vexations of marriage, to be mistress of their
> own things, and suchlike. These are wont to devote themselves a lot
> to looking after and improving temporal things, and they apply
> themselves little to spiritual exercises, only temporal things. Also,

many of them hand over their dowries to usury in various ways, either with their husbands' relatives, letting them go for a fixed return, or giving them to merchants under the pretext of deposit, etc. And sometimes in return for their dowries they receive more than what was owed.[133]

11. Sexual Morality Outside Marriage: Prostitution

In many manuals we are likely to find penitential concern with men's recourse to prostitutes. St Antoninus provides a question to peasants and farm-workers and a reference to prostitutes' earnings (that they should go to almsgiving), and John de Burgh a question for scholars, about frequenting prostitutes.[134] The manuals diverge, however, in the attention they pay to prostitutes themselves, and to prostitution as an institution. Apart from the references just mentioned, there is nothing in St Antoninus's *Confessionale*. In the *Manipulus curatorum*, again, apart from a glancing reference to poverty as an alleviating circumstance to be considered when dealing with a woman who has committed sexual sin, there is nothing.[135] *Ad meretrices* or *De meretricio*: a list of questions to prostitutes as penitents, or an autonomous treatment of prostitution – both are missing in these two southern authors.

When we turn to the English and Paris sources we find both, in large measure. Once again, Thomas of Chobham's treatment was fundamental. Apart from two scattered discussions – on pimping and on whether prostitutes may licitly retain their immorally gained earnings – Thomas gathers his treatment of this theme into a four-chapter separate section, 'On Prostitution'. Chapter 1 contains a definition, and chapter 2 a general discussion of why the Church tolerates prostitution, and miscellaneous provisions. Prostitutes should be excluded from communion unless they repent; they should not have access to the altar. On Saturday evenings, however, in Paris, when women offered candles, prostitutes mingled with them, and there (Nôtre-Dame) they wanted to offer a window. The theme of whether one should accept their offerings is raised; many have been accustomed to say one should not. Chapter 4 discusses price, and the question of restitution if the prostitute has deceived. If naturally she would have received half a penny, but with make-up receives a penny, she should restore the difference. Most significant is the treatment 'On the Penitence of Prostitutes' in chapter 3, beginning, 'If prostitutes or whoremongers come to penitence, priests should make their shamefulness clear to them'. A hard and long discussion of their sin leads to the statement that 'Solemn penance should be enjoined on all such [women]: just as they have sinned publicly so ought they to do penance publicly'. Thomas concludes with concern about their conversion to another form of life. 'They should be earnestly encouraged to continence, because continence is the highest medicine against sexual sin [luxuria]. If, however, they cannot be induced to continence and there is great fear of their falling back into lust, they can be admitted to marriage. However, this must specially be said to them, that they can never be admitted to [bearing] witness or [making] a will or to other acts of law, because they will always be held to be of bad repute [infames]'.[136]

There was later continuity, both in William of Pagula's use of Thomas,[137] and in John de Burgh's subsequent abbreviation of this material.[138] Meanwhile, independently, another source from or relating to an English milieu, the Memoriale, paralleled this tradition both of seeing prostitution more broadly and displaying concern for the penitent prostitute. While its author does not have an autonomous section 'On Prostitution', he does set it in a wider, and specifically urban context. His list of questions to burgesses (ad burgenses), in this case property-owning burgesses, includes the following. 'Item, if the burgess has knowingly rented out his houses to public prostitutes, for them to inhabit, or if, after he knew they were prostitutes, he did not drive them out [of his houses] but let them inhabit [them] and thus, by approving their shameful way of life, committed the [sin of] pimping'.[139] His section 'What [penance is to be imposed] on a prostitute' is, once again, long, and it distinguishes forms of repentence more finely than Thomas. There are three categories, 'the prostitute coming to confession who devoutly confesses the vileness of her form of life and declares that she wishes to abstain from her sins', the prostitue who 'declares that she cannot be continent or abstain from the sin of the flesh', and the 'prostitute, broken by age and ugly of face, who has abstained from such sins perhaps because no ribald is willing any more to desire her because of her foulness – [a prostitute] who has therefore left off sinning through a certain necessity'. Compared to the earlier Thomas, the anonymous author is distinctly soft. Concerning the first category: 'you [the confessor] should promise her mercy, and that she can gain grace from God'. After enquiring about circumstances, 'you should impose a lighter or sharper penance on her, according to whether you have found her to have sinned less or more – so long as you always incline to the gentler side, always promising her the hope of mercy'. The confessor may not impose penance on the second while she remains in the sin: 'you should counsel her to confess her sins frequently and to carry out almsgiving and other good works as much as she can, so that the Lord may enlighten her heart thus [and induce her] to do true penance'. On the third 'apart from penances laid down in the canon, you should enjoin on her some private penance to be done for all the days of her life, so that she can regret and repent the sins of her past evil life'.[140]

Thomas of Chobham's was the fullest discusion, at the root of the mainline English tradition, itself springing from intense discussions in Paris in the later twelfth and early thirteenth century. Baldwin has outlined most of these discussions. Peter the Chanter raised the questions of prostitutes restoring their gains if they had used fraud; the greater fraudulence of a private courtesan compared to a street woman; their conversion of their gains into alms (they must do this); the effect of their excommunication – they cannot be kept from church, but should be excluded from communion.[141] To be added to Baldwin's outline is Peter the Chanter's statement that public prostitutes should be denied not only communion but consecrated ground if they died impenitent, and that one may celebrate mass for them, and his asking whether they should be prayed for after death.[142] Baldwin went on to outline the range of opinion at Paris, including Robert de Courson's harsh notion that they should be expelled from a city, and the connections of these densely detailed Parisian discussions with attempts at reform, through Fulk of Neuilly's preaching campaigns, and Innocent III's concurrent letter to all the faithful, declaring the meritoriousness of rescuing women from brothels and marrying them.[143] What is present, then, in later England, is the influence of this, mediated partly through Thomas: considerable attention to prostitution, and the penitent prostitute. If we ask about development over time in England, we can point tentatively to the severity of the earlier Thomas, the discriminations and (comparative) leniency of 1344, and an abbreviation of Thomas (or Thomas in William of Pagula) in 1384 in the *Pupilla oculi*, which not only may reflect less interest but also, notably, does not include the theme of marriage for the reformed prostitute. Even with this decline, the attention to prostitution and the penitent prostitute in the English tradition remains in sharp contrast with the lack of interest in southern manuals.

12. Women's Dress

The tradition of moralists harping on women's vanity, apparel, and make-up, from the early father's onwards, marks most manuals to some degree. The degree itself may vary – ranging from John of Aurbach's brief question for women, 'Have they adorned themselves with liquid [make-up] or otherwise in order to draw men's love to them', to precise specifications of a style or mode of make-up.[144] Such are given briefly in the questions to married women in the English *Memoriale* and very extensively in the Tuscan *Confessionale*. Not only is the Tuscan work much longer, it also discriminates between various motives and degrees of sinfulness: 'if . . . for show and vain-glory'; 'if . . . to induce men to desire them outside marriage'; 'if she has plucked hair from her neck or eyebrows or beard or brow for lasciviousness or to please men looking [at her] or disdain – for this is a mortal sin unless she does it to remedy severe disfigurement or so as not to be looked down upon by her husband'; 'if she has taken excessive care, pains, and time in adorning herself, or has displayed excess in the wearing of clothes, beyond her status or condition or against the custom of the country, or has used excessively delicate and soft clothes'; 'if she has taken inordinate pleasure in such things'; 'if out of lasciviousness and vanity a woman has used man's clothes'; 'if a woman has coloured herself or used some other figment for the sake of beauty'; if she has . . . to please her husband, or to receive a man if she is unmarried, or to avoid being looked down on by others, this is not in itself a mortal sin, but rather venial'.[145] The *Confessionale* also diverges from northern manuals in the degree and specificity of its attention to men, under the heading 'On the immodesty of men'. 'If for show and greater glory he had superfluous ornamentation and apparatus in his clothes, that is, if he was dressed in linen or purple though not authorised to do so, or in clothing which was embroidered or had depicted on it falcons, or [sun-] rays, and suchlike . . . If he stood around women or visited them dressed in an indecent way, showing his thighs and other indecent things, inciting them to lust . . . .'[146]

Juxtaposition with other evidence might show how precisely pastoral manuals react to trends in fashion. The first question to married women in the *Memoriale* asks 'whether they have used superfluous, pompous, monstrous, and inordinate apparatus on their heads', and goes on to specify why: 'because they go round horned and in a monstrous way', viz. they wear flamboyantly horned head-dresses.[147] The third question is 'whether they have juiced [viz. used liquid make-up] their faces with unguent or colour in order to appear redder or whiter to men'.[148] Both overlap and contrast appear with the Tuscan *Confessionale* in 'On the immodesty of women'. Women are to be asked about 'adornment of juices [liquid make-up], hair [using a term which may mean hairdo or wig], jewels, costly clothes, and their furs, trains, and too-high and painted shoes such as Italian women frequently use, and crowns or flounces on their heads'. A longer list of fashions appears in the *Theologia moralis*.[149]

Ephemeral fashions may be of less interest to the current enquiry than deeper and longer-lasting contrasts in styles. 'Such as Italian women frequently use': St Antoninus is very conscious of variation according to region, and in the *Theologia moralis* sets one such variation into European geography: 'If it is a question of the usage of a country – so, for example, the way women wear dresses cut to the neck and open downwards, for the showing of the chest and breasts, as they do in the Rhineland. . . . If it is a question of the common usage of a country – women wearing clothes with trains which stir up the dust and clean the streets [as they draw them along] with them, as is the case in Florence . . .'.[150] Attractive is the possibility of investigating the multiform and elusive links of such variations with other cultural and social patterns. Beyond the pictorial images conjured up in the modern reader's mind by St Antoninus's Tuscan references – the flamboyant male display and female fashions of paintings surviving from early Renaissance Italian cities – there are deeper themes for speculation, one of which is suggested by St Antoninus. When addressing the question of women's greater interest in dress, he produces this rationalisation: 'Since they are not able to make an appearance or to raise themselves up in important business – for they [cannot do this] either in rule, or teaching, or conducting affairs, and suchlike – they [can] at least look to gain glory in the semblance of beauty.'[151] The interest of St Antoninus's more intense preoccupation with women's dress and his rationalisation of their preoccupation in terms of their firm exclusion from the public sphere needs no spelling out. I have not yet noticed any precise parallel in northern manuals.

*   *   *

The pastoral manuals are significant in two ways, as litmus tests of particular societies, and as archaeological survivals from those societies. As litmus tests they act by showing patterns in particular societies. In contrast with the minute particularities shown by later medieval archival research, what pastoral manuals show are simplicities and archetypes. Self-evidently these are archetypes in the minds of moralists; less self-evident is the relation of these archetypes with other contemporary ideas and realities, a relation on the one hand of opposition or contrast, on the other hand of similarity or reflection. An obvious if superficial example of 'similarity' or 'reflection' as the appropriate categories is the theme of the milieux for abortion which are evoked by St Antoninus or the English texts. St Antoninus's is one which can include doctors and medicines, and druggists supplying medicines and instruction. Elsewhere St Antoninus details the medical world of Florence – for example, doctors paid by the community, and a statute laying down that some druggists should be open on feast-days.[152] In a recent monograph Park has produced a rather modern picture of medicine in Florence in the later fourteenth and fifteenth centuries. Her prosopographical study makes familiar some of the doctors and apothecaries of the city, and shows both dense public and private provision of medicine, and considerable lay confidence in it. She portrays Italian city-states as having 'forms of medical organisation' which 'were arguably the most advanced', and England as, relatively, 'back-ward'.[153] Her contrast deserves further enquiry, but in the current state of research it clearly provides intelligible contexts for the contrasting worlds of abortion which are suggested by the fourteenth-century English and fifteenth-century Tuscan texts.

The original and fundamental outlines of the revolution which Smith brought about in demographic and social history consisted of a broad contrasting of marriage-patterns, i.e. low age at first marriage for girls in southern Europe, high age in northwestern Europe, coupled with a high proportion not marrying.[154] Many of the results of the research of other scholars, though often differing in particular theme and approach, can be set within this framework, and within the further elaboration of it by Smith himself and Goldberg. The results to which I am alluding include, on the one hand, the demonstration by such scholars as Sheehan, Molin, and Mutembe of the 'churchiness' of marriage in northwestern Europe, the creation in this area of the marriage-liturgy, and its emphasis on consent and a high ideal of married love, which could be regarded, as Smith has said, as compatible with northwestern European social structure. They include, on the other hand, many of the results of research on southern Europe, for example, Hughes's attention to long duration, the long duration of cultural aspects of marriage in the Mediterranean world, in particular the role of shame and honour,[155] and Herlihy's attention to the demographic aspects of marriage and women's lives, particularly the low age at first marriage of girls and the high proportion of widows in Florentine society.[156] They also include what has been shown by the most illuminating searchlight of scholars specialising in this area, Klapisch-Zuber's, which has played on the marginalisation of the Church from Tuscan marriages, the image of widows, the degree to which 'houses [were] made by men' and 'woman's identity [was defined] in relation to houses of men', and the prominence of their kin. For the sake of simplicity, in what follows I call this regional approach 'Smith's framework'.[157] It is not my intention either to produce a brief account of Smith's framework, nor to repeat the contrasts in pastoral literature which I have suggested in this chapter. In this conclusion I want only to suggest juxtaposition of the two.

Clearly much of the pastoral material should be set within Smith's framework, still under the categories of 'similarity' or 'reflection'. The Church – its banns, its liturgy, and its marriage vows – envelopes the contracting of marriage in the northwestern manuals. It is more easy to find a high ideal of sentiment in these works. On the other hand, southern manuals, particularly St Antoninus's, try to regulate a world which is Klapisch-Zuber's world of formal visits and marriage brokers.[158] St Antoninus's attention to lowest possible age at marriage and regional variation in coming to sexual maturity should be set beside earlier Tuscan moralising about the ideal of a high age of marriage practised by a northern people, by implication in contrast to Tuscany. Could one see them as (slightly veiled) reactions to the southern European marriage regime of low age at first marriage for girls? His writings continue to 'reflect' related themes – the importance of husband's house and kin to Tuscan women, the prominence of widows, the double-standard of sexual morality and the significance of 'honour' in the culture of the southern marriage regime, the sharpness of the notion of women's exclusion from the public sphere. His high consciousness of separateness, here, is set within a literary tradition – precocious lay interest in Aristotle's *Politics* and *Economics*, which Siraisi has shown as far back as early fourteenth-century Bologna, in the milieu of educated doctors. [159] It is inadequate to leave this as a scholarly demonstration that the vocabulary of separateness comes from Aristotelian moral works. What was it in the existing ideas about separateness held by men in these parts of southern Europe, and what was it about the society in which they lived, which made that vocabulary so attractive, and at such an early stage in the lay reception of the *Economics*? Set against this is the northwest. Here there are contrasts, implied by many areas of silence or less emphatic statements, which have been detailed in the main part of this chapter. Set against this also are the interesting implications – with regard to the demographic pattern and women's mobility and existence outside marital homes – of the allusion, in 1344, to (many?) women living on their own.

Were the study of dress further advanced, this theme might be added. Because it is more intangible my point needs exemplification. Used in order to provide it, here, is a text from outside pastoral literature, the *Itinerarium* of an early fourteenth-century Anglo-Irish friar, Symeon Symeonis. This contains an account of his journey from Ireland to the Holy Land, and it is packed with his observations of the cities and societies he encountered. Passing through London, Paris, Avignon, and Nice, Symeon described much, but women's appearance did not yet intrude. Departing from Venice he came to Zara, and here his comments on women's ornament and dress began – briefly on the women of Zara, at greater length on the wives of Latins in Crete, longer still on Muslim women in Alexandria. In Venetian-ruled Crete the wives of the Latins are adorned like those of the Genoese: 'when one of them becomes a widow, she seldom or never is married again nor is she adorned with a nuptial garment, but wears a black widow's veil; nor does she ever walk with a man, or sit upon the same seat either in church or elsewhere, but with her face veiled and heaving sighs she ever seeks solitary places.' In the account of Muslim wives in Alexandria, the description of their dress (white mantles, 'veiled and covered up to such an extent that their eyes can only be perceived with difficulty through a very narrow veil of black silk', etc.) is woven into and is part of an account of the description of their social confinement ('virtually always confined to their houses and exluded from all superfluous social intercourse'), the basis in the Koran for this, and the way splendour of clothing influenced people's assessment of women's nobility and wealth. [160] Symeon's text is very suggestive about a cluster of dense interconnections between long-lasting forms of dress on the one hand, and religious, cultural, social, and demographic patterns on the other. Symeon only addresses the starkest of contrasts: my point is that investigation of evidence about the nuances of regional differences inside Europe, including evidence in pastoral manuals, might cast further light on this suggestive cluster. It might also cast further light on the cultural and social significances of a European regionalism parts of which, at least, impressed the mind of St Antoninus, a man who was also prepared to suggest a connection between dress and women's exclusion from the public sphere.

Clearly the categories 'similar' and 'reflection' need to be applied carefully in the area of prostitution. Self-evidently attention paid to prostitution in the manuals does not correlate with the incidence of the phenomenon. What the manuals may 'reflect' are degrees of concern and interest in reform, as well as possible regional variations in the degree to which prostitution was seen to be more or less the concern of ecclesiastical or secular authorities.

The point needs greater emphasis on the question of attention to care of foetus or child, because there are two recent interpretations in this area which mislead. Boswell's description of Gratian as 'authorising the exposure of children' is part of a tendentious polemic, which does not advance understanding. [161] Legislation dealing with the consequence of sin did not imply to Gratian or Gregory IX their approval of sin. An example is Peter the Chanter's discussion, where the point – the tension between the need to help a particular child and the fact that doing so might cause more abandonment – shows more complex and idealist consciences at work. Shahar sees legislative and pastoral concern over these things as straightforward evidence for their occurrence. [162] This is over-simple. Since abortion, infanticide, and abandonment are known for much of Europe, but intense preventive concern seems to some degree regionally confined, it would seem more reasonable to see intense concern coming from those areas where standards were high, in England in particular. An example from another genre of texts can be adduced here, commentaries on that part of book VII of Aristotle's *Politics* which raises the theme of over-population and exposure of children. Although there are dangers in detecting nuances in these commentaries, it seems worth noting that one (from 1317–19) pays considerable attention to this passage in Aristotle, ventilating the themes of abortion, exposure, the notion of superfluous population, and the ways in which a person's life may be against the common good – for example, because he eats, or is deformed – before reminding the reader that these seem cruel in the Christian religion. Despite the final caveat the author seems remarkably ready to explore these harsh themes. It is a southern text, from the court of Aragon.[163] In an as yet unpublished paper Smith has suggested a broad contrast between gentler and harsher regimes of care in northwestern and southern Europe, set within a denser account of contrasting demographic regimes which cannot be summarised here.[164] Clearly the view offered here of contrasts in the pastoral manuals should be juxtaposed with this proposition.

One manual reflects a particular view in a particular place at a particular time. It is a transmission by one author of commonly shared law and theology, filtered through his view of the particular needs of instruction of the parish clergy, and through them lay people, in the region in which he lived – qualified, of course, by the fact that he is often passing on material which he has taken from earlier sources, which has already been filtered by predecessors. Manuals, however, should not only be seen in this light. The insidious effect of scholarship which is directed principally towards seeing 'reflections' in them is this: one tends to neglect the positive presence and positive force of the manuals themselves, and their readers and users.

Take the data of manuscripts and printed editions of the principal manuals surveyed in this chapter, excluding Peter the Chanter's *Summa*, which had a more academic circulation, and the *Memoriale*, which is only known in three manuscripts. The rest had massive circulation. There are still extant over 150 manuscripts of John of Freiburg's *Confessionale*,[165] over 200 of Guido's manual,[166] over 200 of St Antoninus's *Confessionale*, all of which had many printings. When one uses present location as a rough way of suggesting the probable broader lines of past locations, the divisions into northern and southern parts of Europe are not perfect – for example, many manuscripts of Guido's treatise survive north of the Alps. However, there is a general pattern of distribution. On the one hand, in the north there is Thomas of Chobham's manual, still extant in over 100 manuscripts. 'Popular in England and on the continent north of the Alps, it seems to have had its greatest success in Germany where the largest number of manuscripts is found'; and it was printed twice, in Cologne and Louvain.[167] There is William of Pagula's manual, still extant in 50 manuscripts in England, whose dissemination would have to include the manuscripts of later versions, including its second edition, the *Pupilla oculi*, which is extant in 42 manuscripts, and 'was printed at least three times between 1510 and 1518, at London, Rouen, and Paris'. After a survey of the richly varied evidence for the later medieval dissemination of the *Oculus sacerdotis* – including priests' wills and a reference to it on a Buckinghamshire brass – Boyle writes that one 'might suggest that the *Oculus* had won a place for itself as a regular item of church furniture'.[168]

Turn briefly to the south, and consider the dense presence of St Antoninus's *Confessionale* in southern Europe. Over 190 manuscripts are still extant in Italy, Spain, and southern France. In addition there are 15 manuscripts of an Italian translation, a printing of a Spanish translation, and manuscripts of a Croat translation. Of all St Antoninus's penitential works there are 119 incunabular editions.[169]

The pervasive and long-term influence of these manuals in these particular societies of northwestern and southern Europe may be impossible to grasp and delineate with any precision, but it should not therefore be ignored or underestimated. When one considers the contrasts which have been surveyed in this chapter, for example, on the theme of preventive care of babies, or contracting marriage, one should reflect further on the fact that the material on these themes was contained in – or significantly absent from – manuals which had massive presence in different parts of Europe: parts of parish furniture over several centuries. They are substantial archaeological survivals of the societies of northwestern and southern Europe.

Notes

1   Acknowledgements are due here to the stimulus of Richard Smith's work in general, and in particular his unpublished paper 'Infanticide and Female Neglect: Further Thought on the Medieval Evidence', delivered at the Wellcome Research Unit, Oxford, in December 1990: the idea which is central to this chapter occurred to me while listening to it. I am grateful to Jeremy Goldberg for encouraging me to write this chapter, to All Souls College for facilitating research with a Visiting Fellowship, and to Sue Reedie for help in obtaining material. There is a large but less precisely definable debt to my former tutor, Billy Pantin.

2   Bibliographical note.

(A) Given here are, first, abbreviations of the principal secondary works concerning medieval pastoral manuals:

Boyle, *Pastoral Care*: L.E. Boyle, *Pastoral Care, Clerical Education and Canon Law, 1200–1400* (1981); reprinted articles, cited below by Roman numeral, which indicates position in the reprint.

Bloomfield: M.W. Bloomfield, B.-G. Guyot, D.R. Howard, T.B. Kabealo, *Incipits of Latin Works on the Virtues and Vices 1100–1500 A.D., Including a Section of Incipits on the Pater Noster*, Medieval Academy of America 88 (Cambridge, Mass., 1979).

Michaud-Quantin: P. Michaud-Quantin, *Sommes de casuistique et manuels de confession au moyen âge (XII–XVI siècles)*, Analecta Mediaevalia Namurcensia 13 (Louvain, Lille, Montréal, 1962).

Pantin: W.A. Pantin, *The English Church in the Fourteenth Century* (Cambridge, 1955).

(B) The following is a list of the manuals cited here, given in chronological order, indicating the ms. or text used, and brief bibliography:

Bartholomew of Exeter: Bartholomew of Exeter, *Poenitentiale*, ed. A. Morey, *Bartholomew of Exeter, Bishop and Canonist* (Cambridge, 1937), pp. 163–300. See p. 174 on date, between 1150 and 1170.

Peter the Chanter: Peter the Chanter, *Summa de sacramentis et animae consiliis*, ed. J.-A. Dugauquier, Analecta Mediaevalia Namurcensia 4, 7, 11, 16, 21 (Louvain, Lille, 1954–67). See J.W. Baldwin, *Masters, Princes and Merchants. The Social Views of Peter the Chanter & His Circle*, 2 vols. (Princeton, NJ, 1970), vol. 1, pp. 13–14. Between 1191/2 and 1197.

Robert of Flamborough: Robert of Flamborough, *Liber Poenitentialis*, ed. J.J. Francis, Pontifical Institute of Medieval Studies, Studies and Texts 18 (Toronto, 1971). See pp. 1–52, Michaud-Quantin, pp. 21–4, Baldwin, *Masters, Princes and Merchants*, vol. 1, pp. 32–3; 'probably 1208–13', Robert of Flamborough, p. 9.

Thomas of Chobham: Thomas of Chobham, *Summa confessorum*, ed. F. Broomfield, Analecta Mediaevalia Namurcensia 25 (Louvain, Paris, 1968). See pp. xi–lxxxviii, Boyle, *Pastoral Care*, IV, pp. 86, 93–4 and n. 3, Michaud-Quantin, pp. 21–4, Baldwin, *Masters, Princes and Merchants*, pp. 34–6; 'in all likelihood completed and in circulation by c.1216', Thomas of Chobham, p. lxi.

John of Freiburg: John of Freiburg O.P., *Confessionale*, used here in Oxford Bodley Ms. Laud Misc. 278; see Michaud-Quantin, pp. 49–50, T. Kaeppeli, *Scriptores Ordinis Praedicatorum Medii Aevi*, 3 vols. published (Rome, 1970–), vol. 2, pp. 433–6 (no. 2346), Bloomfield, p. 498 (no. 5755). Date? John ob. 1304.

Sacerdos igitur: Anonymous, *Sacerdos igitur*, Vatican Ms. Pal. Lat. 719; see Michaud-Quantin, p. 85, who says it can 'remonter à la fin du XIIIème ou au début du XIVème siècle'.

Astesana: Astesanus of Asti O.F.M., *Summa de casibus conscientiae* (pre-1479, place?); copy used here is Oxford Bodley Auct. 4.Q.1.16; see Bloomfield, pp. 279–80 (no. 159), Michaud-Quantin, pp. 57–60, Boyle, *Pastoral Care*, III, pp. 261–2. c.1317.

William of Pagula: William of Pagula, *Oculus sacerdotis*, Oxford Bodley Ms. Rawlinson A 361; see Pantin, pp. 195–202, Boyle, *Pastoral Care*, III, pp. 262–3, IV, IX, p. 21, and XV, pp. 418–19 n.20, 432–4. 1320–7.

Guido: Guido of Monte Roterio, *Manipulus curatorum* (c.1475, Albi); see Bloomfield, pp. 243 (no. 2796), 326 (no. 3862), 428–30 (no. 5019), where over 200 mss. are listed, though H.S. Otero states that there are more than 180 mss., 'Guido de Monterio y el "Manipulus curatoru"', *Proceedings of the Fifth International Congress of Medieval Canon Law* (Vatican, 1980), pp. 259–65; see also P. Michaud-Quantin, 'Gui de Montrocher', *Dictionnaire de Spiritualité* 6 (Paris, 1965), cols.1303–4, and Boyle, *Pastoral Care*, III, p. 267 and n.79. 1333. The edition used here is unfoliated, and is cited here by numbers referring to its divisions and subdivisions, which are briefly outlined here to facilitate reference from my footnotes. The work has a prologue, and then three parts. (I) The first *particula* is divided into seven *tractatus*: the first two of these deal with sacraments in general, the third to the seventh with sacraments other than confession. The seventh is on marriage; this is divided into two *partes*, the first (*De sponsalibus*) with five chapters, the second (*De matrimonio*) with eight chapters – the last of which, on impediments, is divided into sixteen *particulae*. (II) The second *particula* is on confession and is divided into four *tractatus*, on penance, contrition, confession, and satisfaction; each of these is divided into chapters. (III) The third *particula*, on the instruction of the laity, is divided into four chapters, on the articles of faith, the ten commandments, and the Lord's prayer, and the endowments of the blessed.

Ranulph Higden: Ranulph Higden, *Speculum curatorum*, Oxford Balliol Ms. 77, and Cambridge University Library Ms. Mm.i.20; see Pantin, p. 203, Boyle, *Pastoral Care*, III, p. 267 and n.80, Bloomfield, pp. 103–4 (no. 1063), c.1340.

Regimen animarum: Anonymous, *Regimen animarum*, Oxford Bodley Ms. Hatton 11; see Pantin, pp. 203–5, Boyle, *Pastoral Care*, IV, pp. 95–6 and n.4, XV, pp. 429–30 and n.77, Bloomfield, p. 85 (no. 0835). 1343.

Memoriale: Anonymous, *Memoriale presbiterorum*, Cambridge Corpus Christi College Ms. 148, which has been compared with BL, Ms. Harl. 3120; this comes from Norwich Cathedral Priory, M.R. James, *A Descriptive Catalogue of the Manuscripts in the Library of Corpus Christi College Cambridge*, 2 vols. (Cambridge, 1912), vol. 1, pp. 336–7. See Pantin, pp. 205–11, and extracts edited pp. 270–4, Bloomfield, p. 230 (no. 2631), and n.3 below. 1344.

John de Burgh: John de Burgh, *Pupilla oculi* (Paris, 1510). The edition used here is Strasbourg, 1518. See Pantin, pp. 213–14, Boyle, *Pastoral Care*, III, p. 263, IV, pp. 84–5, 94–5, IX, pp. 19, 21, Bloomfield, pp. 215–16 (no. 2441). 1384.

Antoninus, *Theologia moralis*: St Antoninus O.P., Archbishop of Florence, *Summa theologica* (Venice, 1477–9); here it is used in the ed. by P. Ballerini, 4 vols. (Verona, 1740); see Michaud-Quantin, pp. 74–5 and n.3bis, Kaeppeli, *Scriptores Ordinis Praedicatorum*, vol. 1, pp. 80–2 (no. 239), Bloomfield, p. 367 (no. 4355). c.1440–54.

Antoninus, *Confessionale*: St Antoninus O.P., Archbishop of Florence, *Confessionale* (Cologne, c.1470); see Michaud-Quantin, p. 74, Kaeppeli, *Scriptores Ordinis Praedicatorum*, vol. 1, pp. 92–6 (no. 256); p. 256, part of it is before '12 VII 1440'; Bloomfield, p. 140 (nos. 1501–2). The questions are divided into three parts, each with subdivisions, as follows: (I) *Interrogacio . . . de decem preceptis*, ten divisions by commandment; (II) *Interrogacio . . . de viciis capitalibus*, seven divisions by sin, (1) *superbia*, (2) *invidia*, (3) *ira*, (4) *accidia*, (5) *avaritia*, (6) *gula*, (7) *luxuria*; (III) *Interrogaciones quoad status hominum*, questions ordered under particular estates, beginning *quoad coniugatos*. References in these notes are to parts, in the case of part 1 followed by numerical reference to commandment, in the case of part 2 followed by numerical reference to sin, in the case of part 3 followed by specification of estate.

John of Aurbach: John of Aurbach, *Summa* (Augsburg, 1469, unfoliated). See Bloomfield, pp. 115 (no. 1193), 395 (no. 4668). John is given as vicar of Bamberg. 1469?

3   M.J. Haren, 'A Study of the "*Memoriale Presbiterorum*", a 14th-century Confessional Manual for Parish Priests' (Unpublished D.Phil. thesis, University of Oxford, 1975).

4   T.N. Tentler, *Sin and Confession on the Eve of the Reformation* (Princeton, N.J., 1977).

5   Boyle, *Pastoral Care*, II, VI, pp. 263–6; L.E. Boyle, *The Setting of the "Summa theologiae" of Saint Thomas*, The Etienne Gilson Series 5 (Toronto, 1982), pp. 26–9.

6   See the comments on Tentler's earlier presentation of his approach in L.E. Boyle, 'The Summa for Confessors as a Genre', *The Pursuit of Holiness in Late Medieval and Renaissance Religion*, ed. C. Trinkaus and H.A. Oberman (Leiden, 1974), pp. 126–30.

7   J.A. Bossy, 'The Social History of Confession in the Age of the Reformation', *Transactions of the Royal Historical Society* 5th ser., 25 (1975), pp. 33–8, where the discussion is more about the second.

8   J.A. Bossy, 'Moral Arithmetic: Seven Sins into Ten Commandments', in *Conscience and Casuistry in Early Medieval Europe*, ed. E. Lites (Cambridge, Paris, 1988), pp. 214–34.

9   C.R. Cheney, 'Aspects de la l'législation diocésaine en Angleterre au XIIIe siècle', *Etudes d'histoire du droit canonique dédiées à Gabriel Le Bras*, 2 vols. (Paris, 1965), vol. 1, pp. 52–3.

10 R. Brentano, *Two Churches, England and Italy in the Thirteenth Century* (Princeton, N.J., 1968).

11 J. Dunbabin, *A Hound of God, Pierre de la Palud and the Fourteenth-Century Church* (Oxford, 1991), p. 43.

12 Boyle, *Pastoral Care*, II, and IX, p. 21.

13 Guido, 2.3.7. See Godfrey's text in *Les Quodlibet de Godefroid de Fontaines*, ed. M. de Wulf and others, Les Philosophes Belges, Textes et Etudes, vols. 2–5 and 14 (Louvain, 1904–37), vol. 4, fasc. 2, ed. J. Hoffmans, pp. 242–6, and see on it P. Glorieux, *La*

Littérature Quodlibétique, 2 vols., Bibliothèque Thomiste 5 and 21 (Paris, 1925–35), vol. 1, p. 160. On Bernard of Auvergne see Kaeppeli, *Scriptores Ordinis Praedicatorum*, vol. 1, pp. 198–210, and, on his attacks on Godfrey, M. Grabmann, *Mittelalterliches Geistesleben*, 3 vols. (Munich, 1926–56), vol. 2, pp. 548–9. In this and subsequent translations literalness has been preferred to fluency.

14 See n.65 below.

15 See the discussion of solemnisation of marriages below, and n. 46.

16 John de Burgh, fo.11vb.

17 Thomas of Chobham, p. 251; first pointed out by Boyle, *Pastoral Care*, IV, pp. 93–4 n.3.

18 Quoted in n.109 below.

19 William of Pagula, fo.105ra.

20 John of Freiburg, fo.355ra: 'Circa luxuria. . . . *Item, si modo non debito iacuit cum muliere. Sed de hoc caute inquirendum est et tantum in genere. Et si aliquod modum inordinatum expresserit confitens, queratur ulterius si aliquam aliam inordinacionem commiserit, et nichil ei specificetur ne malum discat. Potest autem circa hanc materiam in principio sic queri in genere, latine,* "Habuisti aliquos gestus inordinatos cum mulieribus?", *teutonice,* "Hetest du iede heme geb [?] geberde mit vrowen die niht zimelich waren?"' This text needs attention from a German philologist, and comparison with other mss.

21 John de Burgh, fo.77va.

22 John of Aurbach, *Pars 1, De confessione, particula 1, de actu auditionis confessionis, circumstantiae:* 'Si mechanicus . . . *secundum artem suam, utrum illum exercuerit bona fide non sophisticando vel fraudem commitendo ad preiudicium proximi, et an laboravit et fecerit secundum statuta et ordinaciones civitatis.*'

23 Guido, 1.7.2.5.

24 St Antoninus, *Confessionale*, III, *Circa magistros et doctores, Circa scolares.*

25 Ibid., II.3.

26 'Quid puellis. *Si puella fuerit sub potestate parentum vel eciam sui iuris fuerit et forsan nimis la[s]civa fuerit, discurrendo per vicos et plateas de die, choreas ducendo, et de nocte ad vigilias et exequias mortuorum periculose accedendo*', *Memoriale*, fo.53ra.

27 St Antoninus, *Confessionale*, III, *A pueris et puellis.*

28 Bossy, 'Social History of Confession', p. 36, and *Christianity in the West 1400–1700* (Oxford, 1985), p. 49.

29 Antoninus, *Theologia moralis*, vol. 3, col.20: '*Et quia filiae quasi continue conversantur cum matribus, parum cum patribus, ideo ex matrum moribus potest conjecturare de moribus filiae, quae praeponitur pro conjuge*'.

30 Antoninus, *Confessionale*, II.1: '*Si . . . ad recipiendum virum si est innupta*'.

31 Antoninus, *Theologia moralis*, vol. 2, col.596: ' . . . *aut ut conjugio trahatur*'.

32 Antoninus, *Confessionale*, III: '*Si fuit mediator, qui dicitur sensalis in aliquibus locis, precipue in Ytalia . . . Si in matrimoniis contrahendis mediator existens utitur mendaciis et huiusmodi in notabile damnum contrahentium, peccat mortaliter*'.

33 Antoninus, *Theologia moralis*, vol. 3, col.309: ' . . . *caveat a mendaciis, puta referendo uni partium aliud, puta mulieri nubere volenti, vel propinquis ejus hoc tractantibus, illum esse divitem, qui nil vel parum habet; esse modestum et bonum, quem novit esse discolum, dissolutum, & lusorem, et hujusmodi*'.

34 Antoninus, *Confessionale*, III, *ad coniugatos:* '*Et hic advertendum est quod in multis locis quamvis sponsi non consummant matrimonium cum sponsis ante nuptias, multas tamen turpitudines et corruptelas faciunt cum ipsis, eas visitando etc*'.

35 Antoninus, *Theologia moralis*, vol. 3, col.72: '*Et philosophi dicunt quod quidam nascuntur . . . qui citius aliis sunt apti ad coitum. Et puto quod variantur haec in locis calidis et frigidis, sicut & ipsa impraegnatio & corporis incrementum*'. The passage quoted from Albert's

Sentences commentary is not contained where one might expect it, that is, in his commentary on the treatment of age of marrying in Peter Lombard's fourth book, distinction 36; it is likely to occur in his *De animalibus*. If this is so, the imprecision in citing Albert would suggest St Antoninus's use of Albert through an intermediary.

36   Servasanta's text is discussed in my forthcoming article, 'Medieval "Demographic Thought" Around 1300 and Dante's Florence', which will appear in a volume of studies on Dante, edited by J.C. Barnes, in the series 'Publications of the Foundation for Italian Studies', University College, Dublin.

37   John de Burgh, fo.126vb; William of Pagula, fo.142rb; Astesana, 8.4, *In qua etate possunt contrahi sponsalia et matrimonium*.

38   Raymond of Peñafort, *Summa de poenitentia et matrimonio* [= *Summa de casibus*] (Rome, 1603), p. 520. On later use of Raymond's *Summa*, see Boyle, *Pastoral Care*, III, pp. 249–53, VI, pp. 260–6, and Boyle, *Setting of the 'Summa'*, pp. 6–7.

39   Gratian, *Decretum*, 30.50.1, *Corpus iuris canonici*, ed. E. Friedberg, 2 vols. (Leipzig, 1879), vol. 1, col.1104.

40   Peter Lombard, *Sententiae in IV Libris Distinctae*, 4.28.2.1, ed. I. Brady, 2 vols., Spicilegium Bonaventurianum 4–5 (Grottaferrata, 1971–81), vol. 2, p. 433.

41   Ibid., p. 433: '*Illi etiam sententiae, qua dictum est solum consensum facere coniugium, videtur contraire quod Evaristus Papa ait*'.

42   Guido, 1.7.2.6.

43   John de Burgh, fo.127va.

44   In various studies, for example, M.M. Sheehan, 'Marriage Theory and Practice in the Conciliar Legislation and Diocesan Statutes of Mediaeval England', *Mediaeval Studies* 40 (1978), pp. 408–60.

45   *Les Statuts Synodaux Français du XIIIe siècle*, ed. O. Pontal, 3 vols. published, Collection de Documents inédits sur l'Histoire de France, Section de Philologie et d'Histoire jusqu'à 1610, 9, 15, 19 (Paris, 1971–88), vol. 1, pp. 67, 180, 182, vol. 2, pp. 28, 66, 116, 118, 206, 378, 380, 392, vol. 3, pp. 110, 122, 261.

46   Guido, 1.7.2.8: '*Et istud optime servatur in ecclesiis gallicanis, ubi per tres dies dominicos vel per dies solennes antequam contrahitur matrimonium, indicitur in ecclesia quod, si aliquis sciat aliquod impedimentum quare matrimonium non debeat fieri, illud proponat, et istud vocant "banna" in Francia*'.

47   *Sacerdos igitur*, fo.18va: '*utrum se invicem diligant sincere et coniugali affectu*'.

48   John of Aurbach, *Pars 1, De confesione, Particula 1, de actu auditionis confessionis, circumstantiae*: '*Si penitus est in statu coniugatorum . . . Item, utrum habitet cum coniuge, et an in redditione debiti mutuis subventione et servitute ac alias se invicem affectatione coniugali se pertractent et thori fidem observent*'.

49   Thomas of Chobham, pp. 362, 375: '*Item, in matrimonio contrahendo dat vir mulieri et mulier viro corpus suum, quo nihil habet pretiosus sub celo preter animam*'; '*nihil debet ei* [viz. the husband] *esse carius uxore sua*'.

50   '*Quando sacerdos facit solempnitatem matrimonii debet informare virum ut apponat annulum in quarto digito uxoris sue . . . propter mutue dileccionis signum commune, vel propter id magis ut eodem pignore eorum corda iungantur. Et in quarto digito anulus inseritur quia in illo digito est quedam vena quod protenditur usque ad cor, et sicut debent esse unius cordis vir et mulier, xxx. q. v.*, quod in primis' (Gratian, *Decretum* xxx.v.7, ed. Friedberg, col.1106), William of Pagula, fo.70ra. To be noted here is William's use of many standard authorities via intermediaries, especially John of Freiburg, which Boyle has shown, which may explain the textual divergence of the part quoted from Gratian.

51   John de Burgh, fo.123va.

52   Ibid., fo.145ra. The reference is to Peter Lombard, *Sententiae in IV Libris distinctae* 4.28.4.1, ed. Brady, vol. 2, p. 435; the imprecision of the quotation suggests an intermediary.

53   J.-B. Molin and P. Mutembe, *Le Rituel de Mariage en France du XIIe au XVIe siècle* (Paris, 1974).

54   J.T. Noonan, Jr., *Contraception: A History of Its Treatment by the Catholic Theologians and Canonists* (Cambridge, Mass., 1965), pp. 214–16.

55   Gratian, *Decretum*, 32.2.6, ed. Friedberg, vol. 1, col. 1121; Peter Lombard, *Sententiae*, 4.31.3.5, ed. Brady, vol. 2, pp. 444–5.

56   P.P.A. Biller, 'Birth-control in the West in the Thirteenth and Early Fourteenth Centuries', *Past and Present* 94 (1982), pp. 5–6.

57   Noonan, *Contraception*, p. 220.

58   *Sacerdos igitur*, fo. 18va: 'A coniugatis matrimonio copulatis inquirendum est utrum contraxerint matrimonium intencione prolis habende ad laudem Dei educande, vel intencione libidinis faciende'. The implied reference is to *Si Conditiones*.

59   Antoninus, *Confessionale*, III, *Ad coniugatos*: 'Item, de actu coniugali nota, quod quandoque sit ubi est manifestum mortale, scilicet cum sit extra vas debitum, tamen eo modo ut non suscipiatur semen ad evitandam prolem vel generacionem . . . Circa predicta autem sic formantur interrogaciones. Si videlicet usus est matrimonio extra vas debitum. Si aliquid fecit ad evitandum generacionem'.

60   Cited in n. 56 above.

61   See discussion below, and n. 74.

62   Robert of Flamborough, p. 223; as noted there, n. 85, earlier used by Bartholomew of Exeter, p. 222.

63   Thomas of Chobham, pp. 148, 464, 398.

64   *Astesana*, 8.9: '*procurando impedimentum aliquod prolis*'; John of Freiburg, fo. 362r: '*Item, si mulier aliquod impedimentum fecit ne conciperet, et idem de viro*'. The passage from Peter John Olivi is discussed and quoted in the forthcoming article which is detailed in n. 36 above.

65   'Item, frequenter publicare debet quod vir cognoscendo uxorem suam vel aliam mulierem carnaliter nihil faciat neque uxor eius propter quod impediatur concepcio partus, quod si fecerit gravius peccat quam si cognsceret aliam mulierem carnaliter, xxxii. q. vi, Aliquando et q. vii, Adulterii [referring to Gratian, *Decretum*, xxxii.ii.7 and xxxii.vii.11, ed. Friedberg, cols. 1121–2 and 1143] . . . Et istud est necessarium in ecclesia publicare, ut bene sciunt penitentiarii episcoporum, quia multi sunt hiis diebus qui credunt in multis casibus peccatum contra naturam non esse peccatum, quod dolendum est, et ideo presbiter potest secure sic dicere inter parochianos suos, "Scire debetis quod si quis semen coitus emiserit scienter et eciam voluntarie aliter quam naturaliter cum uxore sua quocunque modo fecerit debet dicere confessori suo"', William of Pagula, fo. 50r. The passage is discussed in Biller, 'Birth-control', pp. 22–5.

66   'Et potest sacerdos dicere sic penitenti: "Frater, unsquisque debet scire, si unquam semen coytus emiserit sciens vel vigilans aliter quam naturaliter cum uxore sua quocunque modo fuerit, graviter peccat"', William of Pagula, fo. 7rb.

67   Ranulph Higden, Cambridge UL Ms. MM.i.20, fo. 118v: '*Item, proponatur quod in copula carnali nil fiat unde conceptus posset impediri, quia hic magis peccaretur quam si uxor aliena cognosceretur, 37. q. 7, Aliquando et q. vii, Adulterii*'.

68   *Regimen animarum*, fo. 57ra–b.

69   'Item, laborantes hoc vicio et homicidio spiritualiter sunt hostes Dei et generis humani. Facto enim dicunt Deo: "Masculum et feminam tu creasti ut multiplicarentur; nos operam dabimus ut minuantur". Unde legitur Gen. xxxviii Iona [better in the version in Oxford Bodley Rawlinson Ms. A370, where instead of Iona: quod Onan] in cognoscendo uxorem suam privans ea conceptu semen fundebat in terram, et ideo percussit eum Dominus et mortuus est', William of Pagula, fo. 98ra.

70   *Regimen animarum*, fo. 43ra; see Ranulph Higden's abbreviation and alteration of the text's direction, Oxford Balliol Ms. 77, fo. 46va: '. . . semper sodomite sunt hostes Dei et

generis humani. Impediunt enim multiplicacionem quam Deus providit. Unde legitur Gen. 38 quod Deus percussit Onan quia fudit semen in terram'.

71 Noonan, *Contraception*, pp. 199–200.

72 Biller, 'Birth-control', p. 25, and Dunbabin, *Hound of God*, p. 49.

73 Noonan, *Contraception*, p. 269.

74 Peter the Chanter, III (2b), p. 463.

75 Thomas of Chobham, p. 464.

76 See the further discussion of Thomas below, and n.102; Gregory IX, *Libri Quinque Decretalium*, 5.10–11, ed. E. Friedberg, *Corpus iuris canonici*, 2 vols. (Leizig, 1979), vol. 2, cols.792–3.

77 This suggestion was made in the unpublished paper cited in n.1 above.

78 '*De medicis*', *Memoriale*, fos.68va–69a.

79 'Circa mulieres coniugatas et eciam viduas necnon alias corruptas. . . . *Item, si unquam potabat, vel aliis dederit ad potandum, liquas potaciones vel succum herbarum ne possit concipere, vel dedit [sic] aut potabat ad faciendum aborsum, hoc est ad interficiendum fetum vel conceptum in utero: quia forsan latenter concepit de dampnato coitu*', ibid., fos.26ra, vb.

80 '. . . *quando quis procuraverit aborsum seu sterilitatem in se vel in alia*', ibid., fo.29rb; '*Si quis percusserit mulierem pregnantem, vel eciam si dederit aliquid ad potandum, ut puta venenum vel aliquod poculum, et sic interfecit partum in utero conceptum*', ibid., fo.36rb.

81 Antoninus, *Confessionale*, I.5, quoted in n.90 below.

82 Ibid., III, *Circa medicos*: '*si medicinam dat pregnanti ad occidendum fetum, etiam pro conservatione matris*'; *Circa armatorios*: '*si docent vel vendunt ea que procurant aborsum vel aliud ad interficiendum . . .*'.

83 Antoninus, *Theologia moralis*, III, col.283. On the quodlibet, John of Naples, X.27, see Glorieux, *Littérature quodlibétique*, vol. 2, p. 170.

84 Gratian, *Decretum*, 2.5.20, ed. Friedberg, vol. 1, cols.462–3.

85 Gregory IX, *Decretales*, 5.10.1–3, ed. Friedberg, vol. 2, cols.792–3.

86 Gratian, *Decretum*, 1.87.9, and Gregory IX, *Decretales*, 5.11, ed. Friedberg, vols. 1, col.306, and 2, col.793.

87 R.C. Trexler, *Synodal Law in Florence and Fiesole, 1306–1518*, Studi e Testi 268 (Vatican, 1971), p. 64.

88 Guido, 2.4.5.

89 Guido, 3.1–4.

90 Antoninus, *Confessionale*, III.5: '*Si mulier gravida procuravit sibi aborsum per medicinas vel labores vel alium modum, etiam si non sequatur effectus, quod mortale est in ea et in quocunque ad hoc consulente et cooperante, non tamen est casus episcopalis. . . . Si mulier occidit filium suum sponte ad occultandum crimen suum . . . Si mater vel nutrix suffocat filium quem tenet iuxta se in lecto inadvertenter opprimens eum: quod mortale est propter negligentiam, et casus episcopo reservatus. Si gravida mulier preter intencionem seu propositum aborsum facit, si comisisset in hoc notabilem negligentiam ut quia nimis saltavit vel quia nimis inordinate laboravit vel propter inordinatas lascivias: non esset absque mortali. Idem in viro vel alio percutiente eam unde hoc sequatur*'.

91 Antoninus, *Theologia moralis*, II, col.860: '. . . *vel mulier praegnans saltat, aut magnum pondus portat*'.

92 See n.110 below.

93 Antoninus, *Theologia moralis*, III, p. 116, and II, col.860: '. . . *quando ex negligentia [mulieres] opprimunt parvulos in lecto secum eos tenentes*'; '. . . *vel nutrix ponit parvulum filium iuxta se in lecto, & dormiendo calcat*'.

94 See, for example, Bartholomew of Exeter, pp. 218, 222.

95 Robert of Flamborough, p. 222 (following Bartholomew of Exeter and Ivo of Chartres).

96 Peter the Chanter, III (2b), p. 569.

97 Ibid., III (2a), p. 280.

98 Ibid., III (2b), p. 726.

99 *Councils and Synods with Other Documents Relating to the English Church II AD. 1205–1313*, ed. F.M. Powicke and C.R. Cheney, 2 vols. (Oxford, 1964), vol. 1, pp. 32, 183, 204–5, 214, 234–5, 274, 302, 351, 410, 432, 444, 457, 520, 590, 648; enquiries about stifling or abandonment, p. 632.

100 *Statuts Synodaux Français*, vol. 2, p. 46.

101 Thomas of Chobham, p. 215.

102 Ibid., pp. 464–5.

103 Thomas's editor, Broomfield, connects Thomas's mention of a woman's triple jump in order to induce miscarriage with Macrobius's *De somno Scipionis*, Thomas of Chobham, p. 465, n.44. The source is likely to be a medical treatise – in which such passages are easily found – rather than Macrobius, in whose text, as Broomfield notes, the number is seven, not three.

104 William of Pagula, fos.11vb–12ra, beginning '*Sacerdos debet iniungere mulieri pregnanti ne post conceptum partum laborioso operi insistat . . . .*'.

105 Ibid., fo.52va: '*si per modicam horam os parvuli aliquo panno fuerit velatum, de facili extinguatur*'.

106 *Regimen animarum*, fos.56va–b, 57ra.

107 John de Burgh, fos.55ra–b, 59ra.

108 '*Item, si pater vel mater occidit filium suum, quia forsan oppressit eum de nocte in lecto, tunc debes diligenter inquirere an ille qui sic occidit fuerit in culpa, quia forsan non adhibuit eam diligenciam quam adhibere debuit, et sic culpa precessit casum: quo casu . . . Item, debes diligenter inquirere an filius sic fuerit suffocatus in lecto* [BL Ms.: *lectum*] *iuxta latus parentum: quo casu maiorem et graviorem penitenciam debes inponere, quia presumitur quod culpa precessit casum. Si vero* [BL Ms. omits *vero*] *fuerit mortuus repertus in cunis: minor penitencia debet inponi, quia presumitur quod hoc non contingit ex certa sciencia,* [from *hoc* to *sciencia* BL Ms. has: *culpa non precessit, et similiter quod hoc non contingit ex certa sentencia*] *sed pocius ex quadam incuria; quia non est presumendum quod mater* [BL Ms.: *mulier*] *obliviscatur filium. Et dicitur nihilominus quod paternus affectus* [BL Ms.: *effectus*] *vincit omnem alium affectum* [BL Ms.: *effectum*]', *Memoriale*, fo.35va–b. I have not identified the precise source for the distinction between bed and cot-deaths, which is probably a legal commentary on the title cited in n.80 above; noted by Pantin, p. 205, is the possibility that the author of the *Memoriale* was a Doctor of Canon Law.

109 '*Item, an unquam exposuit filium suum, hoc est quando fatue mulieres ponunt filios suos in ecclesia vel extra et eos relinquunt sine custodia, et tales expositi in anglico vocantur "fundlinges*"', *Memoriale*, fo.26va–b.

110 Antoninus, *Confessionale*, I.3, : '*De gubernacione parentum quoad filios et familiam . . . Si propter avariciam vel crudelitatem filios suos etiam illegitimos misit ad hospitale*'.

111 Ibid., III, *Ad coniugatos*: '*Si uxor inobediens et contentiosa ac sui sensus erga virum fuit*'.

112 '*Item, si non obedierint maritis suis tamquam dominis, debitam reverenciam et subieccionem in domo, in mensa, et in lecto exhibendo* [BL Ms.: *in domo et in mensa et in loco et in lecto exhibendo*]; *quia contempnunt maritos suos et ab eis recedunt, seorsum commoranto* [sic], *et multe volunt dominari que tamen debent subesse*', *Memoriale*, fo.26ra–b.

113 *Manuale et Processionale ad usum insignis Ecclesiae Sarum*, ed. W.G. Henderson, Surtees Society, 63 (Durham, London, Edinburgh, 1875), p. 19*; see also p. 167* for a similar formula in a fifteenth century Hereford ms.

114 Antoninus, *Confessionale*, III, *Ad coniugatos*: (continuing from the part quoted in n.111) '*Si nimis inculta et negligens fuit circa gubernacionem domus. Si irreverens et discola fuit ad soceros et cognatos. . . . Si non vult sequi virum transferrentem domicilium*'.

115 '*De accidia . . . Si vir uxorem suam sufficienter non exhibuerit*', William of Pagula, fo.7ra.

In John de Burgh, fo.51rb, 'according to means' and 'as obliged' are inserted: 'Si vir uxorem suam secundum facultates suas non debite exhibuerit'.

116   Antoninus, Confessionale, III, Ad coniugatos: 'Si vir non providit uxori et familie in necessariis non tamen superfluis. . . . Si zelotipus et nimis suspiciosus fuit contra eam vel nimis remissus in custodia eius'.

117   C. Klapisch-Zuber, Women, Family, and Ritual in Renaissance Italy (Chicago, 1985), throughout; see especially pp. 117–19.

118   Antoninus, Theologia moralis, IV, cols.53–62; see the reference to the Politics, cols.53, 57. See n.151 below.

119   Ibid., IV, cols.55–6; see also III, cols.17, 19.

120   Antoninus, Confessionale, III, Ad coniugatos: 'Si dedit licentiam viro eundi ad alias cum pregnatur'.

121   Pantin, p. 270.

122   'Circa mercatores et burgenses. . . . Item, si unquam transtulerit [BL Ms.: abstulerit] se, habens uxorem in uno regno vel provincia, ad aliud regnum vel provincia, et ibi fingens [BL Ms., instead of ad aliud . . . fingens has: et in aliud regnum vel provncia fingit] se absolutum [BL Ms.: solutum] contraxerit matrimonium cum aliqua de facto, vel eciam non contrahendo adulterium comiserit [BL Ms.: comisit]', Memoriale, fo.24rb.

123   Pantin, p. 273.

124   'Et hoc quod hic dicitur de muliere adultera seu alia meretrice ex turpi causa donante seu dona recipiente debent [should be debet] intelligi et dici de quocunque adultero et fornicatore ex huius causa turpi donante seu recipiente, quia isti non iudicantur ad imparia in casu isto. Item, inquiras de adulterio . . . Item, inquiras de adulterio . . . Item, inquiras si coniugata unquam concepit [BL Ms.: conciperit] filium vel filiam in adulterio, et si filius sic susceptus successit in hereditate, vel succedere deberet patris sui putativi, et sic verus heres exheredatur', Memoriale, fo.26va.

125   Antoninus, Theologia moralis, III, col.17: 'Mirabile est, quod viri omnino volunt, uxores esse castas, nec ad alium aspicere virum, & quando inhoneste se habent, ad maximam injuriam sibi adscribunt, & merito, quia inducit sibi talis maximam verecundiam & confusionem: nam mulier adultera est opprobrium totius parentelae, detestabilis & abhominabilis coram Deo et toto mundo, digna igne temporali & aeterno. Sed ipsis maritis videtur sibi licere omnem inhonestaem exercere, nullam fidem servantes uxoribus'.

126   See n.112 above.

127   Antoninus, Confessionale, III, Circa advocatos, procuratores et notarios; Theologia moralis, III, cols.253–69.

128   'Circa advocatos . . . Item, informasti vel instruxisti falsos testes in aliquibus causis et maxime matrimonialibus ad falsa deponendum, vel eorum deposicionibus scienter usus fuisti . . . Item, proposuisti unquam vel proponi fecisti in causis matrimonialibus aliquas excepciones frivolas vel quascunque alias maliciose, ne ipsa matrimonia debitum possent sortiri effectum, vel ut processus causarum huius contra iusticiam diucius suspenderentur [BL Ms.: suspenderetur', Memoriale, fos.20vb, 21rb. The phrases come from English legislation; see n.130 below.

129   'Circa officiales et decanos rurales . . . Item, tulisti unquam iniustam vel iniquam sentenciam diffinitam in aliqua causa ecclesiastica, matrimoniali, vel alia, forsan quia prius non consuluisti libros super hoc vel iurisperitos ut debuisti', ibid., fos.19vb, 20ra.

130   Councils and Synods, ed. Powicke and Cheney, vol. 1, p. 107; for variants and repetitions, see further pp. 77 n.7, 258–9, 275, 332, 356, 387, 493, 521, and vol. 2, pp. 723, 849, 906, 999, 1057–8, 1088. For earlier French concern, by one in Peter the Chanter's Circle, see Baldwin, Masters, Princes and Merchants, vol. 1, pp. 334–5.

131   William of Pagula, fos.140rb–1rb.

132   John de Burgh, fos.112vb–3rb.

133   Antoninus, Theologia moralis, III, col.160: 'Viduae autem mundi sunt, quae quidem

honeste vivunt, intendunt tamen nubere tempore suo, vel etiamsi non i[n] tendunt nubere, non faciunt propter Deum, sed propter mundum, ut vitent molestias conjugii, vel sint Dominae rerum suarum et hujusmodi. Hae solent multum vacare temporalibus conservandis et augendis, & exercitiis spiritualibus parum insistunt, sed temporalibus. Et etiam plures dotes suas tradunt ad usuram diversis modis, vel apud consanguineos virorum, cum certa mercede dimittentes, vel mercatoribus sub nomine depositi dantes etc. Et aliquando pro dotibus suis accipiunt plus debito.'

134   Antoninus, *Confessionale*, 2.5: 'De turpi lucro . . . Si recepit pecuniam pro turpitudine ut meretrix debet illam pauperibus dare, non tamen de necessitate'; 3, 'A rusticis et agricolis: . . . si ad meretrices accessit'; John de Burgh, fos.52vb–3ra: 'Scholares iuvenes interrogentur . . . si discholi fuerunt, discurrendo per vicos et plateas, tabernas aut meretricum cellulas . . . frequentantes'.

135   Guido, 2.3.9.7: (concerning sexual sin) 'utrum peccaverit ex libedine [sic] vel ex paupertate, et istud habet locum potissime in mulieribus'.

136   Thomas of Chobham, pp. 403–4, 340 (pimping), 296 (prostitutes' earnings), pp. 346–53 (prostitution). Some of this has been discussed in Baldwin, *Masters, Princes and Merchants*, vol. 1, pp. 134–6.

137   William of Pagula, fo.11va–b.

138   John de Burgh, fo.55rb.

139   'Item, si burgensis locaverit scienter domos suas meretricibus pupplicis ad inhabitandum, vel si postquam novit ipsas esse meretrices non expulit eas sed inhabitare permisit: et sic earum turpem vitam approbando [BL Ms.: comprobando] lenocinium comisit', *Memoriale*, fo.24rb.

140   'Quid meretrici. Si meretrix ad confessionem veniens vite sui vilitatem [BL Ms.: ad utilitatem] devote confitendo fateatur se velle abstinere a suis peccatis: veniam sibi promittere debes et graciam a Deo consequi. Et diligenter inquirere debes modum et circumstanciam peccatorum suorum, [BL Ms. omits suorum] videlicet de adulteriis et incestibus, et an cum personis regularibus vel secularibus, et [BL Ms.: et per] quantum tempus sic turpem vitam duxit. Et secundum quod repperieris [BL Ms.: reperis] ipsam magis vel minus deliquisse [BL Ms.: delinquisse], penitenciam acriorem vel leviorem ei inponere debes, dummodo ad partem benigniorem semper declines [BL Ms.: declinans], spem venie semper sibi promittendo. Sed si fateatur se non posse continere, vel se [BL Ms. omits continere vel se] abstinere a peccato carnis, nullam poteris sibi dare salubrem penitenciam, nec ipsa aliquam fructuosam facere potest penitenciam [BL Ms. omits penitenciam] durante [sic] in huiusmodi peccato. Sed sibi iniungere debes quod a precepcione corporis cristi se abstineat quousque vere penituerit; quia quamdiu fuerit in tali peccato mortali non debet communicare corpus cristi. Et debes sibi consulere quod frequenter confiteatur peccata sua, et elemosinas ac alia bona opera in quantum poterit faciat, ut sic dominus cor suum illustret ad veram penitenciam peragendam. Et si talis forsan senio confracta et facie deturpata abstinuerit [BL Ms.: abstinuerit] se ab huiusmodi peccatis, forsan quia nullus ribaldus eam propter sui turpitudinem ulterius vult appetere, et sic quadam necessitate peccare desinuit: preter penitencias a canone statutas debet [BL Ms.: debes] sibi iniungere aliquam privatam penitenciam omnibus diebus vite sue peragendam, ut sic de mala vita preterita dolere valeat et penitere', ibid., fo.51ra–va.*

141   Baldwin, *Masters, Princes and Merchants*, vol. 1, pp. 134–6.

142   Peter the Chanter, III (2a), p. 278.

143   Baldwin, *Masters, Princes and Merchants*, vol. 1, pp. 136–7.

144   John of Aurbach, *Pars, 1, Particula 1, De actu auditionis confessionis, circumstantiae*: 'Et a mulieribus si . . . suco vel alias ad rapiendum viros in amore ipsarum se ornaverunt'.

145   Antoninus, *Confessionale*, II.1: 'Si usa est sucis et aliis ornatibus ad ostentacionem et inanem gloriam suam. Si usa est sucis et aliis ornatibus ad inducendum viros ad sui concupiscenciam extra matrimonium: quia est mortale indubitanter. Si ob lasciviam vel ad placendum aspectibus virorum aut ad contemptum depilavit collum aut supercilia aut barbam vel frontem: quia mortale est nisi id faceret ad vitandam nimiam deformitatem: ut non*

despiciatur a suo legitimo viro. Si adhibuit nimian diligenciam et studium et tempus ad ornandum se, vel si fecerit excessum in portatura vestium ultra suum statum vel condicionem vel non secundum morem patriae, vel usa est vestibus nimis mollibus et delicatis quia peccatum est. Et si inordinate delectatur in huiusmodi, ita quod etiam si sciret homines ex huiusmodi ornatu scandlizari id est trahi ad sui concupiscenciam: quia mortale est. Si ex lascivia et vanitate mulier est usa veste virili: mortale videtur esse. . . . Si ad complacendum viro suo vel ad accipiendum virum si est innupta vel ne despiciatur ab aliis vel ex aliqua levitate usa est suicis vel aliis ornamentis superfluis: non est de se peccatum mortale, sed potius est veniale'.

146   Ibid., III.1: 'De immodestia virorum . . . *Si ad ostentacionem et maiorem gloriam superfluum habuit ornatum et superfluum apparatum in vestibus, videlicet si vestitus est bisso vel purpura cum ad hoc non est autorizatus, vel veste racamata aut picturata a falconibus, a radiis et huiusmodi . . . Si coram mulieribus stetit aut incessit inhoneste vestitus, demonstrando femoralia et alia inhonesta incitantia ad libidinem . . .'.*

147   'Primo, si use fuerint superfluo, pomposo, monstruoso et inordinato apparatu capitum suorum, quia cornute et monstruose incedunt, quod est species superbie', Memoriale, fo.26ra.

148   'Item, si sucaverint [BL Ms.: sulcaverint] facies suas, ipsas unguendo collirio [?] vel unguento [BL Ms. omits collirio vel unguento] ita quod rubicundiores vel candidiores hominibus appareant', ibid., fo.26rb.

149   Antoninus, *Confessionale*, III.1: 'De ornatu superfluo et inhonesto etiam interrogande sunt mulieres: scilicet de ornatu sucorum, capillature, gemmarum, vestium preciosarum, et de foderaturis et caudis earum et planellis nimis altis et pictis, quibus ut frequenter utuntur mulieres ytalice, et coronis aut balsis capitum et huiusmodi'. See also *Theologia moralis*, II, col.594.

150   Ibid., II, col.591: 'Si enim de usu patriae est, ut mulieres deferant vestes versus collum scissas & apertas usque ad ostensionem pectoris et mamillarum, ut in partibus Rheni; valde turpis et impudicus est talis usus, & ideo non servandus. Si de usu communi patriae est, deferre mulieres vestes caudatas pulverem excitantes, & viam mundantes cum eis, ut fit Florentiae, hoc turpe est . . .' Note, however, Dante, in the early fourteenth century, mentioning pulpit condemnation of topless Florentine women, *Purgatorio*, 23.100–2.

151   Ibid., II, col.590: 'Et quum non valeat apparere vel exaltari in magnis negotiis, quia nec in regimine, nec in docendo, vel negotiando & huiusmodi, saltem in apparentia pulchritudinis quaerit gloriam consequi'.

152   Ibid., II, col.183: 'Aut igitur medici sunt salariati a communitate . . . '; col. 317: 'De armatariis . . . super quo [reference to feast-days] inde civitates bene ordinatae, ut Florentia, solent providere ut aliqui ex eis teneant apothecas apertas, puta unam pro quarterio, & huiusmodi'.

153   K. Park, *Doctors and Medicine in Early Renaissance Florence* (Princeton, NJ, 1985), p. 7. The massive treatment of doctors and druggists by St Antoninus, Archbishop of Florence, constitutes additional evidence about Florentine medical practice.

154   The fundamental articles were R.M. Smith's 'Some Reflections on the Evidence for the Origins of the "European Marriage Pattern" in England', *The Sociology of the Family: New Directions for Britain*, ed. C. Harris (Keele, 1979), pp. 74–112, and 'Hypothèses sur la nuptialité en Angleterre aux XIIIe–XIVe siècles', *Annales: ESC* 38 (1983), pp. 107–36.

155   D.O. Hughes, 'From Brideprice to Dowry in Mediterranean Europe', *Journal of Family History* 3 (1978), pp. 262–96.

156   Most conveniently in D. Herlihy and C. Klapisch-Zuber, *Tuscans and Their Families. A Study of the Florentine Catasto* (New Haven, 1985), pp. 210, 217.

157   See the essays translated in the book cited in n.117 above.

158   Klapisch-Zuber, *Women, Family and Ritual*, pp. 178–212.

159   N. Siraisi, *Taddeo Alderotti and His Pupils. Two Generations of Italian Medical Learning* (Princeton, NJ, 1981), chapter 3, especially pp. 73–7, 86–94. See n.118 above.

160   *Itinerarium Symonis Semeonis Ab Hybernia Ad Terram Sanctam*, ed. M. Esposito, Scriptores Latini Hiberniae 4 (Dublin, 1960), pp. 36, 42, 60, 62.

161   J. Boswell, *The Kindness of Strangers. The Abandonment of Children in Western Europe from Late Antiquity to the Renaissance* (1989), p. 277.

162   S. Shahar, *Childhood in the Middle Ages* (1990), p. 129.

163   The text is studied in P.P.A. Biller, 'Aristotle's *Politica* and "Demographic" Thought in the Kingdom of Aragon in the Early Fourteenth Century', *Annals of the Archive of "Ferran Valls I Taberner's Library"* 9/10 (1991), pp. 249–64; see p. 261.

164   See n.1 above.

165   See the list in Kaeppeli, cited in n.2 above.

166   See the list in Kaeppeli, cited in n.2 above.

167   Thomas of Chobham, p. lxxv.

168   Boyle, *Pastoral Care*, IV, p. 94.

169   Kaeppeli, *Scriptores Ordinis Praedicatorum*, vol. 1, pp. 92–6; Michaud-Quantin, p. 75, n.3bis.

4

'For Better, For Worse': Marriage and Economic Opportunity for Women in Town and Country

P.J.P. Goldberg
University of York

A number of recent individual case studies, including Graham's chapter on Alrewas, are concerned with the role played by women within the economy of later medieval England.[1] These address the issues of the sexual division of labour and of secular change, but rightly shy away from any attempt to describe or explain changing patterns of female employment between town and country. Other works, notably by Razi, Smith, and Bennett, consider the issue of marriage, though exclusively in a rural context.[2] Whereas Razi uses manor court rolls to describe a comparatively early marriage regime in pre-plague Halesowen, Smith employs poll tax evidence from late fourteenth-century Rutland to suggest a late 'north-western' marriage regime. Only Bennett, sidestepping the narrower demographic question, explores the possibility that villein women may sometimes have exercised some influence over the choice of marriage partners reflected in the purchase of their own marriage licences. Our own evidence for age at marriage suggests a more complex pattern with real differences between town and country, but the sample is too small to be sensitive to secular variation.[3] Only an analysis of the actual deposition evidence and the patterns of litigation offer the possibility of better understanding the actual circumstances that lay behind individual marriages and how this may have changed over time. This present chapter thus attempts to take scholarly research one stage further by exploring the relationship between the demand for female labour in the town and in the country, the differences in social structure as they affected women between town and country, and the possible demographic implications of these differences. Our principal concern is to establish how far there were real differences in the degree to which women were able to make heard their own voices in decisions regarding marriage over time and between town and country.

The hypothesis explored here is twofold: firstly that economic opportunities for women tended to be more developed in town than in rural society, and secondly that the greater the economic autonomy of women, the greater the control women exercised over their own marriages, the later their marriages would tend to be, and the lower the associated marriage rate. Conversely, and here the Tuscan experience is especially telling, where women enjoyed few opportunities for paid employment, and were thus more economically and emotionally tied to their parents, the less was their influence in matters relating to marriage and the earlier their marriages. The first hypothesis may immediately be explored from poll tax evidence. The poll tax returns for 1377 and 1379 provide a valuable base for comparison between town and country, and between differing agricultural economies at a single moment in time.[4] These suggest that adult women tended to outnumber men in urban society, but that the reverse tended to be true of smaller village communities. Thus there were 103.5 males over fourteen paying tax to every 100 females in Rutland (excluding Oakham), but the equivalent sex ratio was only 92.7 in Hull and 89.7 in Carlisle.[5] Servants of both sexes were likewise more commonly associated with towns than rural settlements, a significantly higher proportion and variety of urban households containing servants than was true of the countryside. Thus some 15 per cent of rural Rutland households contained servants in 1377 as against over 30 per cent in York at the same date.[6] In part this may be ascribed to the relative paucity of artisan households in rural communities compared to their urban counterparts. A relatively high proportion of such households as are found did indeed contain servants. More male than female servants are found in arable regions, whereas in pastoral districts and towns the balance seems to have been more equitable. In Rutland, for example, the service sex ratio (the number of male servants to every 100 female servants) was 161.9, but in pastoral Howdenshire it was 94.4. In Howden itself the ratio was 84.7, in Hull 119.1, and in Carlisle 113.2.[7]

Another striking feature is the comparative absence of adolescent and adult children residing with their parents within urban society when compared with country settlements. It follows that the proportion of dependent children to servants is low in towns, but relatively high in the countryside. Expressed as a child-servant ratio (the number of servants to every dependent child recorded) in respect of trade-related households, Oakham had a ratio of 0.11, Pontefract a ratio of 0.14, and Doncaster 0.18. In contrast, Rutland excluding Oakham had an equivalent ratio of 1.44, the rural districts of Strafforth wapentake a ratio of 0.86, and the equivalent parts of Tickhill wapentake 1.40. A similar pattern existed in respect of all households. Here the child-servant ratio for Pontefract was 0.22, but for most of rural Strafforth 2.09. It thus appears that within rural households as a whole young persons of both sexes were much more likely to remain at home, where their labour was exploited by their parents, than to live away from their natal home as servants working for others, and that in arable regions young women would have been especially likely to have lived at home perhaps until marriage. Rural artisans in particular seem to have relied as much on the labour of adolescent daughters as on servants, though this is again most marked in arable regions. In rural Rutland craft households drew disproportionately upon male servants and female children. Whereas the child sex ratio for all households in rural Rutland is evenly balanced at 101.0, in craft households only it is only 69.6.

Towns, in contrast, ever dependent upon migrant labour, seem to have absorbed large numbers of young males and females alike to fill positions as servants, but they also exercised a particular pull on women who are found in most areas of the urban economy. The probability is that this pull was at the expense of those arable regions that, in the context of rising labour costs and declining grain prices, are known to have been experiencing particular hardship by the time of the poll tax. Any contraction of arable farming would have seen a local shedding of labour despite the wider context of labour shortage. Women would have been especially vulnerable, but equally would have found opportunities elsewhere attractive. The limited poll tax evidence supports this hypothesis. Three communities destined to become deserted medieval villages, viz. Normanton in Rutland, Golder in Oxfordshire, and Lemmington in Northumberland, display abnormally high sex ratios of 141.7, 144.4, and 156.3 respectively.[8] Pastoral economies seem to have been better able to retain the young of both sexes since women were employed in a range of occupations including carding, spinning, and weaving, washing and shearing sheep, milking cows and sheep, making butter and cheese, which were not readily available in arable regions.

The poll tax evidence accords well with the deposition material contained within the York cause papers. Although the cause papers can offer only a tangential glimpse of the range of employment in which women were engaged, they underscore the arable – pastoral – urban division already outlined. In rural causes wives and daughters alike were part of the familial economy. Women are observed weeding crops, reaping, winnowing, milking cows, brewing, and even purchasing sheep. A mid fifteenth-century cause refers only to Alice Vasour as working in the fields, and Alice Reding is described merely as a '*mulier bone industrie*', though she may have woven cloth.[9] A cause of 1361 describes how Elena Wright served her 'husband' by winnowing and selling grain and 'in other tasks which pertain to a materfamilias'.[10] Married townswomen were similarly an integral part of the familial economy and it is apparent that the wives of artisans, like Juliana del Grene who carded wool and 'is employed in the craft of the saddler with her husband', worked alongside their partners and were thus able to continue in trade even as widows.[11] Among the independent female traders found in the urban sample were the huckster, the barber, the hosteller, the brewster, the tapster, the chandler, and the sempster or seamstress in addition to the ubiquitous spinster.[12] This list may readily be augmented from the poll tax of 1379 and 1381, but it would appear that the majority of women traders were engaged in victualling, textiles and clothing. Female servants are still more widely found, as for example the young women assisting in the shop of Robert Lascelles, a York merchant in 1429, the women servants washing cloth before it was dyed observed in a cause of 1411, or Margery Spuret whose tasks included fetching water from the river for her master, the saddler Thomas Hornby.[13] Only daughters living and working at home are inconspicuous.

It is implicit from the depositions that in rural society sons and more especially daughters frequently lived with their parents until the time of their marriage. In a cause dated 1333 the parties to a disputed marriage, viz. John, son of Ralph de Penesthorp and Elizabeth, daughter of Walter de Waldegrave, lived with their respective parents.[14] Matilda, daughter of Robert son of Richard, Joan Thorneton, Agnes, daughter of William Cosyn, and Alice Herkey were likewise all living with their fathers at the time of their contracts according to deposition evidence.[15] Urban daughters, in contrast, are rarely observed living in their natal homes once they had achieved adulthood. The daughter of William Shirwod of York, who married Walter Lemanton against her father's wishes, is a rare and late exception.[16] Servants on the other hand feature frequently both as parties and as deponents in urban matrimonial causes, but only infrequently in rural causes. Margery Spuret of York, for example, alleged that she was contracted to her fellow servant Thomas de Hornby in a cause of 1393.[17] Some of these servants appear to have been temporary migrants from the rural hinterland, as was true of Alice and Robert Dalton of Poppleton who spent time in service in York before marrying and settling in their native village, but the net flow of migrants such as Alice Spurn and Elena Blakburn, who came to York in the early years of the fifteenth century, was from country to town.[18] This pattern seems to have been especially marked in the later fourteenth and early years of the fifteenth century and can only be explained in terms of the demand for labour, including female labour, in urban society at that date.

This last may be understood in the context of demographic recession. In the decades before the Black Death the supply of labour tended to exceed demand. Unemployment and underemployment were widespread and women may well have been especially vulnerable. It has been argued on the basis of borough court roll evidence that it was precisely at this period that women migrated to towns in number, but the court rolls merely reflect the marginal economic status of women, regularly pushed the wrong side of borough trading regulations, and not their actual numbers.

The advent of plague transformed the economy by reversing the re-lationship between supply and demand for labour. Despite government legislation to the contrary, labourers were for once able to command higher wages and thus enhanced spending power.[19] This is the context for bitter contemporary comment that those at the lowest level of society had become lazy, greedy, and above their station.[20] By the 1370s the fall in population was being reflected in grain prices; spending power and the consequent demand for goods and services was further stimulated. Towns, the primary centres of manufacture and distribution, began to absorb labour to meet this demand and consequently competed with agriculture and rural industry for labour. Labour, especially of adolescents and young adults (traditionally the most mobile age groups) and of women, was thus most readily absorbed into towns from those arable regions experiencing economic dislocation. Women constituted a 'reserve army' of labour and were drawn into a variety of occupations as men began to occupy niches higher up the work hierarchy. Servants were likewise an attractive form of labour when money wages were high, but the cost of living relatively low. Continued demographic decline into the fifteenth century probably enhanced the demand for female labour, but by the middle of the century the economy was beginning to fail as markets contracted with the decline in numbers. Women appear to have been the first group to lose out as the demand for labour once more declined.

These observations provide a context for the limited, but suggestive evidence for age at first marriage derived from the deposition sample. Age data are confined to the century or more after the Black Death. As has been seen, these suggest that by this later date women in rural society often married in their late teens or early twenties, whereas in towns women married later, often after some period in service, perhaps nearer their mid twenties. Rural women appear to have married husbands some four years older than themselves, but the spouses of urban women were on average only three years older. In Tuscan society at the same period, early marriage for women, a large age gap between spouses, and the paucity of economic opportunity for women outside the natal home prior to marriage is associated with a high degree of parental control over marriage formation.[21] A simple hypothesis contrasting urban and rural experiences of marriage formation for women in English society thus follows. For urban women, notably in the labour-starved decades following the Black Death, the opportunities provided by servanthood and paid employment outside marriage, the ready availability of cheap accommodation, the relative absence of parental or wider familial constraints, and the imbalance of numbers between males and females that was a feature of English urban society at the time of the poll taxes, all tended, within the context of a late, companionate marriage regime, to enhance the degree of choice open to women. The suggestion to be tested here is that women chose marriage partners not at the behest of parents, but in their own time, opting to postpone the risky business of childbearing and limit the size of their eventual families, and on the basis of mutual attraction. Some women may have gone unwed, although it would be rash to suppose that these always chose not to marry. In contrast the possibilities for rural women to excercise choice in marriage tended to be more circumscribed. Rural women were more likely than their urban counterparts to live at home with their parents until marriage and enjoyed less scope for paid employment outside the home either as servants or otherwise. Peasant daughters may thus have been more likely to bow to parental and familial influence in respect of marriage, especially where the transmission of family land or property was tied to marriage.

Parental involvement, or the lack of it, in the process of marriage formation is reflected at a number of different levels. As has just been outlined, it may perhaps be surmised indirectly from the age and place of residence of young people at the time of their contracts. It may likewise be surmised from the type of action within the Church court. Suits for nullity, for example, on the grounds of marriage below canonical age, viz. twelve for girls and fourteen for boys, or of marriage contracted by force or under threat suggest a high degree of parental control.[22] The participation of parents in the marriage process is sometimes explicit within the deposition material itself. It is perhaps most evident, however, in the manner of contract itself. It is possible to identify three types of contract. The most complete culminated in the formal solemnisation of marriage *in facie ecclesie*, i.e. at the church door. Any form of contract that fell short of church solemnisation was branded 'clandestine'. No less valid canonically, however, was a simple, often private, and highly informal exchange of words between lovers. Agnes Kychyn, for example, contracted William Robynson in a field at Redmire in Wensleydale one winter evening using words of future consent.[23] Isabel Malt and John Hardyng contracted by a style without witnesses, but Isabel claimed her consent was conditional upon her completing her term of service and on her still liking John at that time.[24] Such contracts, however, could not be enforced through the court unless supported by at least two witnesses. In practice many contracts fell into a third category, still technically clandestine, but enjoying a real degree of publicity before a number of witnesses, including close kin or employers, gathered for the purpose of following a formalised pattern involving handfasting, a form of words that paralleled the contemporary liturgy, an exchange of marriage tokens such as rings, gloves, or coins, and the sharing of a drink.[25]

The crucial distinction thus appears not to have been between clandestine contracts and those solemnised *in facie ecclesie*, but between formal and publicised and informal and unpublicised contracts. Parental approval if not actual supervision may often be associated with the former. In the latter, as the example of Isabel Malt shows, the initiative lay entirely with the couple. Clearly some contracts began as informal and essentially private agreements to marry, 'engagements' to use modern terminology, and were repeated subsequently in a more formal and public way, though there is little to show that solemnisation in facie ecclesie was either the expected or normal conclusion to the marriage process before the end of the fifteenth century. On the other hand, some informal contracts were never intended to constitute binding marriages. Many may have been broken with impunity by mutual consent on the termination of a courtship relationship. Others, however, could be enforced by the courts against the wishes of one of the parties, even to the extent of upsetting established 'marriages'. In this respect canon law appears to have been out of tune with popular culture.

Differences in the pattern of matrimonial litigation between those causes associated with rural parties and those with essentially urban parties may help to further illuminate underlying differences in the pattern of marriage formation. Suits for divorce a vinculo, i.e. annulment, are comparatively common within the rural sample. Eight causes, of which five are located in the period 1450–99, concern forced marriages and another eight marriages within forbidden degrees of consanguinity or affinity.[26] The urban sample, however, contains only four suits alleging forced marriages and none consanguinity or affinity.[27] Whereas multi-party suits, known as causae matrimonialis et divorcii, where the court had to decide between the claims of more than one man alleged to be contracted to the same woman or vice versa, end abruptly c.1450 in the urban sample, they are found throughout the period before 1520 within the rural sample. No suits for divorce a mensa et a thoro, i.e. for legal separation on grounds of excessive cruelty or adultery, are to be found within the rural sample whereas six are found in the equivalent urban sample.[28]

Clearly a number of factors will influence these patterns and it must be taken somewhat on trust that the observed differences relate to real variations in the pattern of rural and urban litigation and are not simply the random product of a small sample. There is little to suggest that radically differing social groups are responsible for the litigation recorded in the cause papers. It would appear that the very wealthy are rarely represented and the poor not at all, except as deponents. The moderately well off, skilled artisans and traders or peasants with land to their name, are much better represented. It is thus the premise here that the differing patterns of litigation are to be understood in terms of differences in marriage formation and thus in marriage litigation between town and country.[29] A factor of crucial importance is the actual freedom afforded to young women in urban society at a time of economic opportunity to engage in and equally break off courtships compared to the relative constraint imposed upon young women from all but the least affluent families. The former could find themselves involved in disputes arising from broken courtships, a situation compounded by the ease with which a canonically valid marriage might be made. The latter had greater incentive to conceal their courtships (and possible marriages) from their parents or to attempt to break arranged marriages that proved unsatisfactory.

Multi-party matrimonial litigation would arise naturally from both milieux, but the different circumstances behind these actions is often apparent. Urban causes are almost exclusively concerned with what may be termed engagement disputes rather than established marriages. Moreover, since this litigation arose from the comparative freedom of young women and men alike both to initiate and terminate courtships, it was as often a woman whose hand was disputed between rival males as the other way around. In 1396, for example, the consistory had to decide between the rival claims of John Dyk, servant to Walter Bakster of York and William Lemyng for the hand of Joan de Markham, servant to Thomas Busse, alias Couper of York. Evidence was presented of two different informal contracts around Lent neither of which had been solemnised, the one with William Lemyng taking place in Joan's master's garden.[30] The absence of multi-party actions, or indeed suits for legal separation, after 1450 may stem both from the greater reluctance of women to break courtship relationships once their opportunities for independent employment had been seriously eroded and from an enhanced degree of parental supervision as daughters from more prosperous families increasingly remained at home until marriage. Rural multi-party causes, however, frequently concern 'marriages', usually formally contracted and sometimes solemnised *in facie ecclesie*, that were challenged by long standing pre-contracts.

Formal, solemnised contracts were made with parental consent and may, in some instances represent arranged marriages. Equally informal contracts may often have constituted love matches. Thus John Birkys of Woodhouse, observed in a cause of 1369, married one Joan at Leeds parish church, but this 'marriage' was dissolved by the court in favour of a pre-contract with Cecily Wright made five years earlier.[31] This probably represents a challenge by a jilted lover to a subsequent contract made with parental approval, but it is apparent that in some cases 'remembered' informal contracts were used cynically and even fraudulently to terminate subsequent established unions, perhaps arranged marriages that had come to grief. Alice Palmer of Folkton, in a cause of 1333, had enlisted her father's help to bribe one Ralph Fugeler to allege a pre-contract in order to effect a divorce from a husband who had proved unsatisfactory.[32] The established marriage of Joan atte Enges to John de Thetilthorpe solemnised at Kilthorpe in Lincolnshire in 1369 was likewise upset in favour of an unsolemnised pre-contract made eight years previous when Joan was a servant in York to another servant, Richard Carter. Such a contract arising out of a courtship between servants need not be doubted, but the fraudulent nature of the litigation is indicated by evidence given in the consistory that Richard's whereabouts were then unknown.[33]

Further evidence that rural parents were much more active in supervising courtships and initiating marriages is found in the number of alleged forced marriages, such as that of Alice Bellamy, threatened with being thrown down a well if she did not marry as her father directed, and in the higher instance of youthful marriages, including contracts made under canonical age.[34] Equally telling, however, is the observed instance of suits for nullity of marriage on grounds of consanguinity or affinity. The evidence for population turnover and marital exogamy suggests that these were not the simple product of a closed society.[35] Where parents were active in arranging marriages, however, it is likely that they would have looked to their social network, including kin, to discover possible marriage partners. Such contracts made within forbidden degrees were open to subsequent challenge should the marriage run into difficulties. The same was true of affinities created through sexual relations. Here arranged marriages could be upset by reference to a pre-marital liaison arising from a more informal courtship relationship. When, for example, Agnes Cosyn's parents wished to pull out of the marriage they had arranged for her with Robert Chew, they claimed that an earlier liaison between Robert and Isabella Alan created an impediment in that Agnes and Isabella were blood relations, a claim rejected by the court.[36] Causes alleging forced marriage or nullity on grounds of marriage within forbidden degrees are not found, however, in the first half of the fifteenth century. This may coincide with a period of greater autonomy for women in the countryside both through access to land and employment, and consequently to a temporary amelioration of the more negative aspects of parental control of matrimony.[37]

Though the deposition evidence in matrimonial causes necessarily focuses on the form of contract, it may also throw light on patterns of courtship and the regulations of marriage formation. Several causes show that the consent of a parent or guardian was an expected requirement for any woman contemplating matrimony. Alice Herkey is reported as having said, 'that she would never contract herself to anyone . . . unless with her parents present'. Her father elsewhere talked of having promised one John Symson to give her in marriage to his son Richard.[38] Early in the fifteenth century Agnes Fraunceys was asked by Robert de Newerk if she intended to marry his brother. She replied, 'I Will have hym in to my Husband if my Fadir will assent'.[39] In a cause of 1361 Robert Wright was asked by William de Rykall if he would give him his daughter Alice in marriage.[40] Agnes Ruke of Thorne promised to marry John Porter, but on condition that he obtained her uncle's good will. Alice Williamson of Skipsea similarly agreed to marriage provided her master, who was also a blood relative, approved.[41] In like manner, John Birkys of Woodhouse (near Leeds) asked Beatrix de Bolleton's permission to marry her niece.[42]

In practice parental of familial involvement in the process of marriage often went further. The urban evidence is slight before the end of our period, but among more substantial peasant farmers it appears to have been usual for the families to meet prior to any formal contract to discuss arrangements and dowry terms.[43] At nine on the morning of 14 February 1466, for example, Agnes Beleby together with her intended, Robert Inkersale, her parents, his widowed mother, the vicar of Rotherham and three other invited witnesses gathered at her parents' house at Greasbrough. There followed a discussion of the amount of dowry to be paid and the sum of twenty-five marks was agreed.[44] A similar gathering, also involving a clergyman, whereby a dowry of twenty marks was arranged, was held prior to the contract between Emma Corry and Thomas del Dale in 1392.[45] The fathers of Joan Serle and William Gell are reported in a case of 1428 to have agreed before the contract that each would match the other in providing livestock for the couple.[46] More substantial provision was negotiated between Cecily Fedyrston's father, the bailiff of Catton, and her prospective husband, Robert Thweng. Ralph Fedyrston promised forty marks, land at Stamford Bridge, and an office for life. Robert for his part agreed to provide Cecily with land and tenements to the annual value of ten pounds.[47]

Canon law might insist on free will as the only basis for a valid union, but where families had such a material stake in the marriage process the crucial question of choice could not be left solely to the parties contracting. The initiative in bringing young people together often lay instead with parents as is apparent in the case of Agnes Beleby and Robert Inkersale; it was only after the dowry arrangements had been agreed that Nicholas Keeton advised, 'Lat us now here or we wade any ferther what Robert and Agnes sais in this matier for in thame two lies all'.[48] Parental initiative must also have lain behind the contract between Agnes Cosyn and Robert Chew. Agnes was asked by Robert's uncle why she did not want the marriage despite her father's approval of Robert and the report that they were already contracted. She answered that she objected to being called 'lass' by Robert's family. Significantly the contract seems to have foundered subsequently as a result of a dispute between the two families.[49] The point is made most forcefully in the advice put to Margaret

Graunt when asked to contract herself to John Serle, 'Chese yow now and never say after but that it is your own dede and not oonly your freends [i.e. family]'. The full implication of these words may be appreciated from the subsequent allegation that Margaret, who was only fourteen at the time, was beaten into making the marriage with a club of hazel.[50]

Our sample is undoubtedly biased towards the contentious, but this pattern of familial direction is not found generally among equivalent urban causes where individuals seem to have had greater freedom of choice. Urban couples seem frequently to have entered into courtship and even contracted marriage of their own initiative and in full awareness of the implications of a canon law of marriage that made consent rather than publicity the basis for a valid union. It is not possible to read cause papers and still believe that marriage for love was an invention of the eighteenth century. One man remarked of Margaret Thweng and John Kirkeby who had just exchanged marriage tokens, 'By my faith, I would rather than twenty nobles that I and another woman that I know were as close as you two are'.[51] In a cause of 1392 Agnes Nevill testified how one evening the previous year when in service to a York widow she visited a group of servants in a neighbour's house. Whilst they were talking and drinking together after their day's work they were joined by John Beek, a saddler, then also apparently in service, who asked Marjory Tailiour, one of the company, to be his wife. When she agreed, he garlanded her with cowslips and maidenhair.[52] According to her uncle, when Isabel Foxhole, then his servant, contracted marriage to John Lytster of Pontefract, the latter claimed that he had never seen a woman that he was better able to love.[53]

Servants enjoyed particular freedom to conduct their own courtships and were constrained only by the need to obtain their employers' consent or wait until their term of service was completed. When John Dene asked one Roger why he was such a frequent visitor to his house, he told him that he wished to marry his servant Katherine. Asked by her master if she wanted to marry Roger, Katherine replied, 'Yes, by my faith, I wish to if you and my mistress here present will allow it'.[54] There is little to suggest that employers had the same vested interest as parents in determining choice of spouse. When John Warryngton was forced by his irate master, John Bown to marry Margaret Barker, a fellow servant whom he had seduced, it was because Warryngton's behaviour was both in breach of his contract and a threat to Bown's reputation as a paterfamilias.[55]

The initiative for making rural marriages may often have lain with parents, but this did not preclude young people in the countryside sometimes taking the initiative in much the same way as their urban cousins. At times choice may have been exercised by the couple contracting subject only to parental or familial consent. This pattern may indeed have been the norm. It was true, for example, of Alice Wright and

William de Rykall noted earlier. When William asked Alice's father if he could marry Alice, he replied, 'if it pleases Alice, I am well satisfied'.[56] At other times individuals may have feared that this consent would be difficult to obtain. When in 1454 Richard Northcroft and Margaret Atkynson of Billingley (near Barnsley) exchanged vows before just two witnesses, Margaret was concerned to keep the contract quiet for a long time as she did not wish certain of her friends (presumably family) or relatives to hear of it.[57] Alice Cure, faced with strong parental disapproval of her contract to John Acton, subsequently claimed that she had been forced by him to consent.[58] It was only the most determined who were, like Margery Paston, able to withstand the full force of parental opposition in the knowledge that canon law was on their side. The courage of Elena Couper of Welton is conspicuous among the cause papers and was perhaps as rare in her day.

We are told that one Sunday before Pentecost in 1490 Elena called her young man to a friend's house that she might have witnesses to her contract. She then prompted him with the following words:

> John, ther is two yonge men abowte me in the town to have me to wiffe. And I have lovyd the thys two yer. And yow knowest wele that yow and I be handfast bitwixt us. And bycause yow shalt not varry nor take an othir and love an othir better then me, we wilbe handfast here afore thies folkes at they may beyr record theropon.

Thus prompted, John Wystowe plighted his troth. Elena's mother responded less favourably to the news declaring:

> thow filth and harlot. Why, art thow handfast with John Wistow? When thy fadre knowys it he wylle dynge the and myschew the.

Elena chose not to await her father's return, but passed the night at the house of a friend. The next morning her father, John Couper arrived, but he was only admitted on condition that he would do Elena no harm. He furiously reproached her for contracting herself without his knowledge to the one man he most disliked.

> And she fell down upon her knees before her father and said, 'Sir, that at I have doon I will performe if the law will suffre it for I wyll have hym whosoever say nay to it. And I desire no more of your goodes but your blessyng'.

Her father conceded, 'Thow shalt have it as thow deservys it'. Elena thus got her way, but seems to have deserved better of her husband. On learning that the marriage could go ahead, he replied, 'We must tarry tyll the houce be reddy'.[59]

Elena Couper sacrificed material advantage for the right to choose her own husband. It follows that daughters of poorer families, who could contribute little in terms of land or wealth, may often have enjoyed greater freedom. This is difficult to demonstrate, however, in as much as the main evidence for the status of parties below the rank of aristocracy is in itself derived from reference to dowry provision. Alice Redyng, who successfully brought a suit to enforce a contract of marriage with John Boton, chapman, worked as a servant and could claim little weath. Significantly she alleged a future contract that had been consummated and there is no evidence of any formal family involvement.[60] Isabella Laurens was drinking with friends at the tavern within Christmas week 1471 when she turned to Thomas Gell with the words, 'Thomas, I luf you wele'. Isabella's status is not apparent, but the circumstances of her alleged contract do not suggest wealth.[61] It may be, however, that our sample is biased towards the better off and that our analysis consequently understates the relative freedom of courtship that many countryfolk may have enjoyed.

For women, however, there was a negative side to any lack of parental supervision of and restraint in courtship. The risks women faced if they entered into a sexual relationship without a properly witnessed contract are well illustrated within the cause paper evidence. Several causes concern attempts by women to enforce dubious contracts against lovers who had abandoned them. The court was obliged to reject Beatrix Pulane's claim to have contracted Thomas Newby before two witnesses in view of the number of young men who testified that Thomas was playing football at the time.[62] Still slighter is the evidence for a formal contract in the case of Agnes Vasour and William Warthyll of Newton upon Derwent. Agnes had long been William's mistress and was to have a child by him, but when Agnes' stepfather asked William why he would not marry her, he replied that he would either marry her or leave her. In the event he left Agnes in favour of another woman whom he contracted formally with her parents for witnesses.[63] In 1354 Maud Schipyn found herself being pressed to have sex with Robert Smyth. She challenged him, 'God forbid that you should have power to know me carnally unless you intend to marry me'. He replied, 'I give you my word that if I take anyone for my wife, I'll take you if you will let me have my will with you', a reply that should have warned Maud, but she responded, 'I give you my word that I will let you have your will with me'.[64] Joan de Brerelay at least had witnesses and was under less immediate threat when Thomas Bakester made a similar request. 'Not unless you marry me', she replied, to which Thomas agreed 'if she would wait for him to finish his apprenticeship'. When Joan's case was heard in 1384, Thomas had failed to honour his promise, although a child that was born to them was then seven and a half years old.[65] Still more precarious was the position of Alice de Wellewyk who likewise consented to intercourse only if she had a promise of marriage. Robert de Midelton replied, 'I do not want to marry you unless I know you are able to conceive and have a child by me'. By the time Alice had had his child, Robert was already looking to marry another.[66]

The risk young women ran by entering into a sexual relationship as part of their courtship could be a shared concern. When in 1381 Alice de Baumburght found Robert Peper in bed with Agnes Besete she insisted that he contracted marriage to her and even dictated the appropriate form of words to the reluctant Robert.[67] In two instances the woman's brother chose to force a recalcitrant lover to make a binding contract. Perhaps young women found it easier to confide in their brothers than their fathers that they were in trouble. John son of Ralph of Pennysthorpe (near Patrington) was set upon in 1332 by Richard, brother of Elizabeth de Waldegrave, and a handful of armed men whilst he awaited Elizabeth in the bakehouse of her father's home one night. He was forced at the point of a sword to be handfast with Elizabeth.[68] It was alleged in another cause dated 1431 that John Ward was likewise confronted in his master's barn by his lover, Alice Skelton, her brother, Thomas Holme and his wife, and two other men armed with axes. John threatened Thomas, his hand upon his dagger, that unless he married his sister he would lose his life, but John refused on the grounds that he was already contracted to another.[69]

Forced marriages were, however, invalid under canon law and the power families had over men who took advantage of their daughters was slight. One can sense the frustration and anger experienced by one Ydonea when she attempted to prevent the marriage of Nigel le Roser to Agnes, the daughter of Beatrix on the grounds that her own daughter, Alice Godewyn, a close relative of Agnes, was already pregnant by him.[70] Well-to-do families could not have tolerated such a situation and would thus have ensured close supervision of their daughters' courtships. Such a pattern may lie behind the higher incidence of leyrwyte levied on daughters of poorer villein families than on those of more substantial families.[71] But village women who had no land or wealth to offer may have gambled upon a sexual relationship in the hope that this would lead to a binding contract. By analogy with the early modern era, moreover, the earlier the mean age at first marriage for women, the more likely they would have been to enter into risky relationships. The impression gained from the urban cause paper sample, on the other hand, is that though contracts, which may often have been consummated, were dishonoured from time to time, these were rarely such long standing relationships. Urban women had through paid employment the luxury of exercising more mature decisions about marriage and may not have been so readily frightened into an unsatisfactory relationship lest that be their only opportunity to secure a partner.

This chapter is an attempt to make some sense of sometimes inscrutable source material. It has necessarily over-generalised and over-simplified the differences between urban and rural experiences, and may have put too great a weight upon statistical evidence based upon small samples. The hypothesis it explores, namely that there is a close relationship between economic opportunity for women and their ability to control decisions in respect of matrimony, and that the more autonomy women enjoy, the later they will tend to marry, does, however, seem to fit the evidence to a degree that is surely not the product of chance. In rural districts, where opportunities for women to find employment outside the home, in service or otherwise, tended to be relatively limited, daughters more often than not lived at home. If their parents had land or capital, they also had a vested interest in the marriages of their daughters.[72] In such situations women may have been married at an earlier age than their urban counterparts to men chosen more by their parents than themselves. Where women achieved emotional and economic independence from parents through service or other paid employment, as was more often true of urban society, they were enabled to exercise greater personal choice and to delay marriage, even to get by without marrying. Perhaps the point is obliquely illustrated by the case of one Lucy who married William Broun around 1350. William proved an unsatisfactory husband who regularly beat her. Just before autumn 1356 Lucy left William. When she returned at the end of autumn William was living with another woman and refused to be reconciled to the wife that had left him when he had most need of her labour. For William a wife was a valued source of labour. For Lucy labour was a marketable commodity that for a few brief months during the harvest of 1356 freed her from an unloving husband and allowed her control over her own affairs.[73]

Notes

1   For example J.M. Bennett, *Women in the Medieval English Countryside* (New York, 1987); P.J.P. Goldberg, 'Women's Work, Women's Role in the Late-Medieval North', in *Profit, Piety and the Professions*, ed. M.A. Hicks (Gloucester, 1990), pp. 34–50; B.A. Hanawalt, *The Ties that Bound* (New York, 1986); R.H. Hilton, *The English Peasantry in the Later Middle Ages* (Oxford, 1975), ch. 6; M. Kowaleski, 'Women's Work in a Market Town: Exeter in the Late Fourteenth Century', in *Women and Work in Preindustrial Europe*, ed. B.A. Hanawalt (Bloomington, 1986), pp. 145–64; S.A.C. Penn, 'Female Wage-earners in Late Fourteenth-century England', *Agricultural History Review* 35 (1987), pp, 1–14.

2   For a bibliography of writings in this area see Smith, above p. 50–1, n.45. See also J.M. Bennett, 'Medieval Peasant Marriage: An Examination of Marriage Licence Fines in the *Liber Gersumarum*', in *Pathways to Medieval Peasants*, ed. J.A. Raftis (Toronto, 1981), pp. 193–246.

3   See above pp. 7–9.

4   The poll tax has been a generally neglected source, but criticisms directed in effect at the controversial third tax of 1380–1 need not detract unduly from the earlier tax returns for 1377 and 1379. The returns surviving for Rutland in 1377 and those for the West Riding and Howdenshire within the East Riding for 1379 seem generally reputable even allowing for the probability of evasion. PRO, E179/165/21–3, E179/269/51 (Rutland); 'Rolls of the Collectors in the West-Riding of the Lay-Subsidy (Poll Tax) 2 Richard II', *Yorkshire Archaeological Journal* (1879–84) 5, pp. 1–51, 241–66, 417–32; 6, pp. 1–44, 129–71, 287–342; 7, pp. 6–31, 145–86; 'Assessment Roll of the Poll-Tax for Howdenshire . . . (1379)', ibid. 9 (1886), pp. 129–61.

5   P.J.P. Goldberg, 'Urban Identity and the Poll Taxes of 1377, 1379, and 1381', *Economic History Review* 2nd ser., 43 (1990), p. 200, table 2.

6   The actual York figure of 38.4 per cent is derived from a partial return that is biased towards the more prosperous areas of the city. 30 per cent or more is thus an estimate for the whole city.

7   The Howden and Howdenshire figures are derived from the 1379 returns based upon a tax population aged 16 or more rather than 14 or more as in 1377. They are thus not strictly compatible with those measures derived from the first tax.

8   PRO, E179/158/29 (Lemmington); n. 4 above. Golder (PRO, E179/161/41) is printed in M.W. Beresford, *The Lost Villages of England* (Lutterworth, 1954), p. 414.

9   BIHR, CP.E.92; CP.F.191.

10   BIHR, CP.E.84.

11   BIHR, CP.E.159.

12   Cf. BIHR, CP.E.40, 82, 89, 102; CP.F.56, 174, 182.

13   BIHR, CP.E.159; CP.F.61, 174.

14   BIHR, CP.E.26.

15   These are dated 1373, 1433, 1453, and 1507 respectively: BIHR, CP.E.113; CP.F.177, 189; CP.G.26.

16   BIHR, CP.F.244 (1467).

17   BIHR, CP.E.189.

18   BIHR, CP.F.79, 201.

19   The Ordinance of Labourers (1349) and the Statute of Labourers (1351) were intended to peg wages at pre-plague levels. The upward trend in money wages and the frequency of prosecutions under the Statute long after 1351 demonstrate the actual ineffectiveness of this legislation.

20   Cf. M. Rubin, *Charity and Community in Medieval Cambridge* (Cambridge, 1987), pp. 31–2.

21   These themes are further discussed in Smith, above.

22   For a discussion of these types of action see R.H. Helmholz, *Marriage Litigation in Medieval England* (Cambridge, 1974), p. 90–4, 98–9.

23   BIHR, CP.F.42.

24   *Visitations of Churches Belonging to St Paul's Cathedral*, ed. W.S. Simpson, Camden Society, new ser., 55 (1895) pp. 88–9.

25   Cf. D. O'Hara, 'Aspects of Marriage in Canterbury', *Continuity and Change* 6 (1991), pp. 21–6.

26   The rural sample comprises 98 matrimonial causes dated between 1306 and 1520.

27   The urban sample comprises 70 matrimonial causes dated between 1303 and 1520.

28   A number of licences for women to live apart from their husbands are also recorded in surviving court books for the period 1371–5: YML, M2/1b, fos.2v, 7v; M2/1c, fos.15v,

29, 30v. These appear to arise out of *ex officio* rather than instance actions and consequently no associated depositions are recorded. Cf. also Biller's comments about wives living apart from their spouses, above p. 85.

29 This understanding is no easy matter. The precise circumstances which led to multi-party litigation, for example, cannot be known. The court was primarily concerned to establish which union constituted a canonically binding marriage. The details deponents are asked to recall relate to dates, witnesses, and forms of words used, not to how a couple came to contract marriage in the first place, or how one alleged contract of marriage came to be set aside in favour of another. Depositions, furthermore, may only survive in incomplete form and the details may survive in respect of only one of two or more alleged contracts.

30 BIHR, CP.E.242.

31 BIHR, CP.E.103.

32 BIHR, CP.E.25.

33 BIHR, CP.E.155.

34 BIHR, CP.E.85 (1362).

35 For population turnover in the earlier fourteenth century see L. Poos, 'Population Turnover in Medieval Essex: The Evidence of Some Early Fourteenth-Century Tithing Lists', in *The World We Have Gained*, ed. L. Bonfield, R.M. Smith, and K. Wrightson (Oxford, 1986), pp. 1–22. For material exogamy see Bennett, 'Medieval Peasant Marriage', pp. 219–21; R.M. Smith, 'Hypothèses sur la Nuptialité en Angleterre aux XIIIe–XIVe siècles', *Annales: ESC* 38 (1983), pp. 128–30.

36 BIHR, CP.F.189 (1453).

37 Continued demographic recession through the first part of the fifteenth century may have enhanced demand, and hence wages, for female labour. This is suggested by the trend in wages paid for shearing sheep, for which women were frequently employed. More general economic recession from around the middle of the century coincides with an increase in matrimonial litigation alleging forced marriage.

38 BIHR, CP.G.26.

39 BIHR, CP.F.176. Agnes would appear to have been living with her father, a Newark cutler.

40 BIHR, CP.E.84.

41 BIHR, CP.F.84, 178.

42 BIHR, CP.E.103.

43 BIHR, CP.G.40, 115.

44 BIHR, CP.F.242.

45 BIHR, CP.E.215.

46 BIHR, CP.F.168.

47 BIHR, CP.F.119.

48 BIHR, CP.F.242.

49 BIHR, CP.F.189. Evidence is given of a private, informal contract, but there is also reference to negotiations for a more formal 'family' contract. It was subsequently alleged that any contract was invalid because Robert had previously had a sexual relationship with a close relative of Agnes. All marriage tokens, including a silver ring, were symbolically returned by Agnes.

50 BIHR, CP.F.308.

51 '. . . *haberemus tam invicem quantum et vos duo habetis*': BIHR, CP.F.182.

52 Noted in the vernacular as: 'cousleppis et maydengris': BIHR, CP.E.121.

53 BIHR, CP.F.81.

54 '. . . *ita per fidem meam volo si ad hoc fuit voluntas vestra et magistre mee hic presentis*': BIHR, CP.F.237.

55 BIHR, CP.F.127.

56 BIHR, CP.E.84.

57 BIHR, CP.F.194.

58 BIHR, CP.G.30A.

59 BIHR, CP.F.280.

60 BIHR, CP.E.92.

61 BIHR, CP.F.252.

62 BIHR, CP.F.137 (1423). Thomas Studdard and his son John were the only deponents who testified to Beatrix's contract. Thomas testified that he thought the couple had enjoyed a sexual relationship.

63 BIHR, CP.F.191.

64 BIHR, CP.E.70. This contract was accidentally witnessed by a woman lying sick in a neighbouring room.

65 BIHR, CP.E.255.

66 BIHR, CP.E.79.

67 YML, M2/1f fo.17v.

68 BIHR, CP.E.26. It was alleged that John was badly wounded in this ambush and stayed away from Elizabeth's house thereafter.

69 BIHR, CP.F.200. Alice's deponents claimed that John contracted willingly. The men with axes were carpenters carrying the tools of their trade who had been invited to witness the contract.

70 BIHR, CP.E.241B.

71 Z. Razi, *Life, Marriage and Death in a Medieval Parish* (Cambridge, 1980), p. 66. See also T. North, 'Legerwite in the Thirteenth and Fourteenth Centuries', *Past and Present* 111 (1986), pp. 3–16. For an alternative interpretation see L. Poos and R.M. Smith, '"Legal Windows onto Historical Populations"? Recent Research on Demography and the Manor Court in England', *Law and History Review* 2 (1984), pp. 149–50.

72 Cf. Hanawalt, *The Ties that Bound*, pp. 198–200.

73 BIHR, CP.E.77.

5

'A woman's work . . .': Labour and Gender in the Late Medieval Countryside[1]

Helena Graham
London

The importance of the contribution of women's labour to the economy of the peasant household, the village and urban centres in the late medieval ages has, until recently, been largely ignored by historians. Abrams and Power in the earlier part of this century did begin to deal with the working lives of women in the town and countryside in the late medieval period.[2] However, it has only been in the last ten years or so that the ground broken by these historians, the issue of women's work and the sexual division of labour, has become a legitimate area of historical investigation. The impetus for this renewed interest clearly comes from the growth of the women's movement in the late 1970s and the development of a feminist analysis.

Hilton has argued that a large proportion of the immigrants into the small towns of the late middle ages were women, that these women were primarily engaged in the petty retail trades of the market, and mainly sold foodstuffs.[3] Kowaleski's study of late fourteenth-century Exeter also shows the propensity of women to engage in victualling when working for wage or for profit. However, even in the selling of foodstuffs the more specialised and capital intensive trades such as butchering and baking were the preserve of men.[4]

Kowaleski goes on to point out that regardless of the type of work women performed, there were certain basic characteristics which distinguished female employment. For example, unlike men who usually specialised in one trade or craft and whose work patterns were stable, most women practised more than one trade and their employment tended to be intermittent. Only older widows and single women, with fewer family and household demands than other women, exhibited work patterns similar to those of men, that is they were more likely to work full time for wage or for profit. Kowaleski also finds that women rarely benefited from formal training in the workplace, and even when they did receive some skilled training they tended to hold low-status marginal positions within individual trades.[5]

Turning to rural areas historians have stressed the important contributions made by women to the peasant economy. Power noted that most married women were expected to share all the husband's labours on the family holding, on top of running the house, making cloth and clothes.[6] Hilton has stated that women members of peasant households would have to do manual tasks on the holding interchangeably with men, and were not confined to traditional womanly tasks such as looking after the poultry, milking the cows, and winnowing the grain.[7] In support of this, Hanawalt's use of coroners' rolls has shown the extent to which children of peasant households were often neglected because both parents were out at work.[8] Middleton has pointed out that among seasonally hired labourers women were involved in a wide range of agricultural activities.[9] Village by-laws of the late thirteenth and early fourteenth centuries reveal women not only following the harvest as gleaners, but the able-bodied amongst them were to help with the reaping if needed.[10] More recently, work by Penn on indictments brought under the Statute of Labourers of 1351 has shown that in the labour-starved period after the Black Death women were an essential part of the harvest labour force. They were not confined to secondary tasks, but were also involved in reaping the corn itself, and were highly mobile and independent labourers free from familial restrictions.[11] In short, and in the words of Power, 'In fact there was hardly any work except ploughing for which they [peasant women] were not engaged, for example, planting peas and beans, weeding, reaping, binding, threshing, winnowing, thatching. They did much of the sheep shearing.'[12]

Bennett's study of gender and household in the manor of Brigstock in the first half of the fourteenth century, has also underlined the importance of women's labour to the peasant household.[13] Bennett goes on to show how, in contrast to men, peasant women's legal, economic, and social position within their community was influenced by marital status.[14] However, women were always politically subordinate to men and excluded from the political government and decision-making processes of their communities.[15] Bennett, like Kowaleski, finds that it is only as adolescent daughters or as widows that women's legal, economic, and social position more closely matched that of men.[16] In this chapter I will attempt to test some of these observations using the data available in the excellent series of court rolls of the manor of Alrewas.

Alrewas is a small village situated in the southeastern region of Staffordshire, some seven miles from Burton-on-Trent and five miles from Lichfield. The actual manor of Alrewas was ancient demesne and, in the fourteenth century, encompassed the village of Alrewas and the hamlets of Orgreave, Fradley, and Edinghale. In the 1340s the manor had an estimated population of some 600 persons, the majority of whom were customary tenants.[17] Alrewas was at this time a forest parish of 4,300 acres typical of the central Midlands, with most of the parish held in one manor by a local gentry family, the Somervilles.

The lords of Alrewas held courts regularly every third Saturday throughout the year, giving 17–18 courts per annum with two views of frankpledge. The surviving courts start in June 1259, although from 1259–1327 only 74 courts survive for ten calendar years. From 1327–75 only the years 1330–1 and 1342–3 have substantial gaps.[18] It is in the three-weekly courts, when the ale tasters presented those who had brewed for sale, that we have record of the brewers and brewsters of the manor. It is in the frankpledge courts, when the Bailiffs of the Crown presented those who had slaughtered and sold meat, baked and sold bread, and regrators or tranters of bread and ale, that we have record of the butchers, bakers, and tranters of the manor. Furthermore, in both sets of court rolls there are occasional references, in cases such as broken contracts or pleas of debt, to other trades and crafts. Aside from the court rolls of Alrewas manor, other sources used in this chapter include a rental of 1341, the subsidies of 1327 and 1332, and the poll tax listing of 1381.

Unfortunately manorial accounts do not survive for Alrewas and, therefore, it is impossible to assess the range of agricultural occupations undertaken by hired female labourers. As for the actual content of the court rolls, the majority of the business which is recorded concerns land transfers, breaking of the Assize of Ale, trespass, debt, and heriot cases. Merchet was only paid infrequently, there being just fifty-four cases for the whole period 1327–75. On top of this there is a complete absence of leyrwyte and childwyte fines, which means that, together with the lack of merchets, it is impossible to come to any firm conclusions concerning age at marriage or illegitimacy rates in the manor. This is a major limitation of the Alrewas court rolls when studying the female peasantry, as marriage and birth were such important life experiences for the women themselves, and a record of these events is crucial for historians who wish to build up as accurate a picture as possible of peasant women's lives in the late Middle Ages. Fortunately, the lords and lady of Alrewas levied a heavy heriot on tenant peasants of the manor. Thus there is a fairly full record of deaths and postmortem transfers of land where cases of illegitimacy are brought to light.

Aside from these specific weaknesses of the Alrewas material, there are others which hold true for all manorial court rolls and add to the difficulties in studying women's history of this period. For many villagers, male and female, while they may have attended court, they never had their names recorded. This under-recording is particularly true of those, such as women and children, who were less likely to be liable to the personal and tenurial obligations which brought men into court. For example, in a ten-year period between the years 1325–35, only 8 per cent of all women recorded were in court more than ten times, while 25 per cent of the men had their names recorded ten times or more. Of the 48 per cent of women who appeared only once, one quarter appeared in a land transaction, usually either associated with their husbands in the buying or selling of land or receiving small amounts of land from male relatives. Almost 20 per cent of the women recorded appeared as victims of assault or as villagers raising the hue and cry, with just 8 per cent of women cited for committing assault. Furthermore, 16 per cent of women appeared in the court rolls only to have their deaths recorded, and a substantial 12 per cent were presented just once in the ten-year period for brewing. In fact, the only reason women appeared in the court frequently in Alrewas was for brewing.

Even though women are under-recorded in the Alrewas court rolls there is plenty of evidence to support the observations made by other historians as to the important contributions made by women to the peasant economy.[20] That women would have to do manual tasks on the peasant family holding, interchangeably and alongside men, is evidenced by such cases as that of Adam Hering and his daughter who were presented and fined for illegally mowing and reaping a neighbour's meadow.[21] A village by-law of July 1342, concerned with regulating the forthcoming harvest, reinforces the need for able-bodied women to help with the harvesting by stating that 'no man nor woman who can serve for $\frac{1}{2}d.$ a day may collect thorns and whoever does shall give 2s. to the lord and church'.[22] There are numerous other cases of women breaking village by-laws alongside men. For example in August 1345 twelve women, and thirty men, are fined for failing to fulfil their customary obligation of mowing a meadow in Edinghale.[23] Women are also presented for failing to enclose their holdings on the common field at the agreed time, for illegally trespassing with animals in the common field, and for illegally blocking the pathways and numerous waterways of the manor.[24] Furthermore, many women were fined for fishing at night and other illegal times, for fishing with illegal nets or for selling the fish they had caught without licence.[25]

Pursuing the question of women's work and the sexual division of labour within the crafts and trades of Alrewas manor, this chapter will address two main points. Firstly, does the Alrewas evidence support Hilton's and Kowaleski's findings that women were primarily engaged in the petty retail trades of the manor and mainly sold foodstuffs? In the selling of foodstuffs were the more specialised and capital-intensive trades of butchering and baking the preserve of men? Secondly, was the type and nature of women's work dictated by marital status and position within the household? Was it only widows and single women who exhibited work pattens similar to those of men? In answering these two questions the butchers, bakers, and petty retail traders will be considered first. The final section of this chapter will then concentrate on the brewing of ale and a comparative analysis will be made with Bennett's work on the ale industry of Brigstock manor.[26]

Bakers, Butchers, and Tranters

The manorial court rolls clearly show that within the peasant community of Alrewas, as in other peasant communities of the late Middle Ages, there were a number of peasants who can be identified as providing goods and services for their fellow villagers. That Alrewas had market status is evidenced from the grant of a charter in 1290 to Robert de Somerville authorising a market to be held every Tuesday in his manor of Alrewas.[27] Surviving court rolls also indicate burgage tenure within the manor, and hence borough status, though the earliest reference is in May 1328 and the last September 1369.[28] Not only did Alrewas have market and borough status by the early fourteenth century, but it was also situated in the heavily wooded area of Alrewas Hay and on the banks of the rivers Tame, Trent, and Mease. One would therefore expect that the manorial court rolls would contain many references to various marketing activities usually found in small market centres, alongside crafts and trades associated with forested and riverside areas.[29]

The manorial court rolls do indicate that brewers, bakers, butchers, and tranters were regularly selling their goods and carrying on their trades in the manor.[30] Beyond these four occupations there is little evidence of recognised crafts within the manor, though the court rolls do contain occasional references to carters, fishers, and tailors in the village.[31] This lack of data is probably due to the nature of the sources, for, as Harvey has pointed out, surnames are almost the only evidence that we have for specialised crafts in the primarily agricultural village, but these can only be taken literally until the early fourteenth century.[32]

On the other hand, the fact that there were so few specialist crafts and trades being carried on within the manor reflects the limited development of the market of Alrewas.[33] The weak nature of the market of Alrewas necessarily implies that, aside from such crafts as tailoring which were all carried on by men, most marketing activities centred around the production and retail of foodstuffs. However, analysis of the victual trade of the manor shows that even in this small village market a marked sexual division of labour existed. The more capital-intensive trades – butchering and baking – were dominated by men, while petty retail trades – such as tranters – were the province of women.

On average only one or two bakers were presented in the frankpledge court, and only five individuals – all of them men – were ever presented by the Bailiffs of the Crown for breaking the Assize of Bread in the entire forty-eight year period 1327–75. This suggests that the baking of bread for sale was a specialist activity, concentrated in the hands of a few people who could afford the necessary capital outlay in grain and equipment to bake bread beyond the needs of their households. Whether or not the peasants of Alrewas often prepared their bread at home and brought it to the baker for baking is unclear. What is certain, however, is that those individuals cited as bakers ranked among the wealthier peasants of the manor and were often also engaged in the sale of ale. Of the five bakers presented, three, Adam Baxter, John Paty, and John Baxter, were regularly amerced. The first, Adam, was the most frequently presented and the most prosperous. Holding a virgate and plot of waste by the time of his death, he was a regular brewer and cited in all the extant pannage lists for pasturing pigs in the lord's woods.[34] As for the two Johns, the precise extent of their landed wealth is more difficult to ascertain, though John Baxter was a regular brewer and frequently presented for having between two to five pigs, and John Paty was a regular buyer of land.[35] In regard to the two occasional bakers, the court rolls are totally silent on one, though the other, Richard Andreu, was a frequent brewer, held half a virgate, and regularly paid pannage for pasturing on average four pigs per annum.[36]

Several of the thirty-seven butchers – all of them men – were regularly presented and must have derived a significant part of their income from the sale of meat.[37] Some of the regular butchers can be clearly identified as virgaters, many were active in accumulating land through the peasant land market, a couple lent considerable sums of money in the form of mortgages, and one, Thomas Gyn, was also listed in the subsidies of 1327 and 1333.[38] A few of the butchers, like the bakers, were also regular brewers, which illustrates the multi-occupational nature of many households within the manor.[39] Unfortunately there is no evidence that butchers' wives made black puddings, tallow candles or other by-products from the animal carcasses as found by Goldberg in late fourteenth-century York.[40] Overall, these observations suggest that bakers and butchers tended to come from the more prosperous section of the peasant community.[41]

Turning to the petty retail trades, the tranters, who are also occasionally called regrators, presented at the frankpledge court were far more numerous than the butchers or bakers. In fact fifty-six individuals were presented on at least one occasion for selling ale, bread or both. What is significant about these tranters is that the majority of them, thirty-five or 63 per cent, were women and just twenty-one – about 37 per cent – were men. A comparison of spring and autumn presentments in the bi-annual frankpledge courts reveals no significant gender-specific pattern. What is striking, however, is the predominance of women before the Black Death. Table 5.1 shows that of the nineteen years up to 1350, where tranters were

Table 5.1

TRANTERS – TOTALS PRESENTED PER ANNUM

year	females		males		total
	number	percentage	number	percentage	
1328	1	50	1	50	2
1329	1	50	1	50	2
1330	1	100	–	–	1
1331	1	100	–	–	1
1332	2	100	–	–	2
1333	–	–	–	–	–
1334	7	63.6	4	36.4	11
1335	5	100	–	–	5
1336	3	100	–	–	3
1337	7	58.3	5	41.7	12
1338	2	100	–	–	2
1339	–	–	–	–	–
1340	–	–	–	–	–
1341	4	100	–	–	4
1342	2	100	–	–	2
1343	5	45.5	6	54.5	11
1344	4	100	–	–	4
1345	2	100	–	–	2
1346	2	40	3	60	5
1347	2	66.7	1	33.3	3
1348	5	41.7	7	58.3	12
1349	–	–	–	–	–
1350	2	66.7	1	33.3	3
1351	4	100	–	–	4
1352	–	–	2	100	2
1353	3	50	3	50	6
1354	4	80	1	20	5
1355	4	100	–	–	4
1356	2	50	2	50	4
1357	2	66.7	1	33.3	3
1358	2	33.3	4	66.7	6
1359	4	57.1	3	42.9	7
1360	1	25	3	75	4
1361	6	60	4	40	10
1362	4	80	1	20	5
1363	6	75	2	25	8
1364	2	50	2	50	4
1365	2	50	2	50	4
1366	2	33.3	4	66.7	6
1367	2	100	–	–	2
1368	2	50	2	50	4
1369	–	–	–	–	–
1370	2	50	2	50	4
1371	2	100	–	–	2
1372	–	–	–	–	–
1373	–	–	–	–	–
1374	1	100	–	–	1
1375	–	–	–	–	–

presented, ten saw only women amerced and in a further four women outnumbered the number of men cited. In marked contrast to this in the twenty-one years after 1350 where tranters were presented, only five years saw a female monopoly on presentment, and in only a further six did women outnumber men. In short, in the pre-plague period women were predominantly tranters in just under three-quarters of the years. In the post-plague period women appear to have lost their semi-monopoly position to the increasing annual presentment of men acting as tranters and were only predominant in just under half of the years.

In some respects the figures given in Table 5.1 are slightly misleading, although a more detailed analysis of those individuals amerced does show the predominance of women. Table 5.2a, on the distribution of tranter fines 1328–50, reveals that thirteen women, 54 per cent, were presented in these years and accounted for just under 70 per cent of all amercements.

Table 5.2
DISTRIBUTION OF TRANTERS' FINES

a. 1328–50

category	persons		fines	
	no.	per cent	no.	per cent
regular female tranters (11 or more fines each)	3	12	29*	36
minor female tranters (1–10 fines each)	10	42	27	33
regular male tranters (11 or more fines each)	–	–	–	–
minor male tranters (1–10 fines each)	11	46	25	31
all tranters	24*	100	81	100

b. 1351–75

regular female tranters (11 or more fines each)	3	9	28*	27.7
minor female tranters (1–10 fines each)	21	62	33	32.7
regular male tranters (11 or more fines each)	1	3	24	23.8
minor male tranters (1–10 fines each)	9	26	16	15.8
all tranters	34*	100	101	100

* Two regular tranters were fined over both periods and have been included in both tables. The combined total of tranters for both periods is thus 58 rather than 56 and the number of fines in each is smaller than expected.

A total of three women were regularly amerced, whereas no male was ever regularly cited as a tranter. In the later period, shown in Table 5.2b, twenty-four women, 71 per cent, were presented and they accounted for just over 60 per cent of all amercements. These figures suggest that in the earlier part of the fourteenth century, although the actual numbers of men and women presented was roughly equal, women were far more likely to be regularly amerced. After the Black Death a far greater number of women were amerced in comparison to men, but the female share of amercements had fallen by just under 9 per cent. An explanation for the differences between the pre- and post-plague situation seems to lie in an increasing specialisation in the petty retail trade of tranters. In the earlier period three women were regular tranters whose fines accounted for 36 per cent of the total number of fines levied. In the later period four people, three women and one man, were regular tranters whose fines accounted for 51.5 per cent of the total. In other words, there was a rise of 15.5 per cent in the regular tranters' share of amercements in the years after the Black Death. The most striking indicator of this growing specialisation is the case of the regular male tranter, William Heuster, of whom more will be said later, who was amerced on twenty-four occasions and thus accounts for 23.8 per cent of all fines in the years 1351–75.

Overall, however, tranters were predominantly women. Furthermore, forty-four (79 per cent) of the fifty-six identified tranters were amerced on less than four occasions. We can infer from this that the occupation of the tranter was conditional upon the availability of surplus food or ale in the household, and supports Kowaleski's thesis as to the part-time, occasional, and non-specialist nature of women's labour.[42]

Analysis of the marital status of the thirty-one occasional female tranters reveals that the majority, whose status it was possible positively to identify, were married, retailing food as a sideline to their husbands' work and thereby supplementing their husbands' income. In fact only eight of these married occasional tranters were ever cited as 'wife of N'. Only one woman was a widow at the time she was amerced for being a tranter, and a further eight female tranters were single.[43] As for the economic status of these minor female tranters nearly all were cottagers or small-holders, and three were said to be landless at the time of their death; only two were virgaters.[44] Just under half, thirteen, of these thirty-one minor female tranters numbered among the occasional brewers of the manor. A few also regularly paid pannage for having usually just one pig.[45] All this evidence suggests that the minor tranters came from the poorer section of the peasant community of Alrewas and is in marked contrast to the economic status of the bakers and butchers.

Five peasants were amerced regularly over a decade or more, on eleven or more occasions. Of these, four were women, though the man, William

Heuster, a tranter of bread, was amerced twenty-four times and is the most frequently cited. As for the marital status of these regular tranters one, Rosa Kempe, was married to the aforementioned William. This couple also number among the regular brewers of the manor.[46] Whether or not William was representing and answering for Rosa's actions in the market place, or whether he himself was acting as a tranter and seller of ale is a matter of speculation. Amongst the minor tranters, husbands are occasionally presented in one court as a tranter of ale, but in another their wives.[47] If these husbands were answering for their wives' actions it emphasises the female-centred nature of the tranters' occupation. In the case of William and Rosa, however, the evidence suggests that the individual presented and amerced was the one active in the market place. William is listed in the 1381 Poll Tax return for Alrewas as a husbandman – *cultore* – but it is clear from the court rolls that William and Rosa made their living as petty traders and not as agriculturalists.[48] This couple were not well-endowed with land and did not enlarge their landholding beyond the cottage and burgage which they held through the *intervivos* peasant land market.[49] William and Rosa also never owed pannage for pasturing their pigs in the lord's woods. However, both were extremely active in selling bread as tranters and retailing ale; Rosa was the fifth most frequently amerced brewer of the manor. Obviously the selling of bread and ale for this couple was their major source of income.

As for the other three regular female tranters, two, Matilda Molet and Lettice Souter, were single, and the third's marital status is impossible to assess as she was only presented in court to pay her fines for being a tranter.[50] Matilda and Lettice both paid pannage at least once and Lettice was also a regular brewer.[51] The landed wealth of these three regular tranters is not possible to assess, though they all share surnames which can be identified with the non-office-holding and small-holding section of the peasant community of Alrewas. Like William and Rosa, these three women relied heavily upon the income derived from this petty retail trade.

Though the numbers are small these data concur with and support Bennett's and Kowaleski's arguments that it is only as widows and single women that women's work patterns more closely match those of men in being more full time and less intermittent.[52] Married women predominated amongst the occasional tranters and single women predominated amongst the regular tranters. In other words, the women who are conspicuous in the market place cannot be assumed to be married and have any household affiliations. Hilton has written that where men's work was centred primarily on the fields, it would be the women of the household who would be left to sell surplus food in the market place.[53] This would certainly explain the large numbers of women cited as tranters. However, this analysis does indicate that a marked sexual division of labour existed within the market place. Even though the market of Alrewas was weak and atrophied fairly quickly, and although it was primarily concerned with the production and sale of foodstuffs, the more specialised trades – butchering and baking – were the preserve of men. To what degree the women in the households of the bakers and butchers helped in the production and sale of bread and meat is impossible to tell. However, the fact that none of these women, not even as widows, were ever cited as butchers or bakers underlines that these trades were the preserve of men.

The Ale Industry

Having dealt with the butchers, bakers, and tranters of Alrewas the rest of this chapter will concentrate on the brewers and brewsters, for the only well-established industry of the manor was the brewing of ale, and it was also the most common reason for women appearing in court. There has been much debate about the brewing and retail of ale and whether it was an activity solely in the hands of women. Hilton has found in his study of women traders in small towns that the brewing of ale was by no means a female monopoly. The fact that numerous ordinances specified women, or ale-wives, as the sellers and brewers of ale leads Hilton to suggest that those males cited as breaking the Assize of Ale were in reality answering for their wives.[54]

Bennett's work on the ale industry of Brigstock manor in the pre-Black Death period has shown that in this one manor the retail of ale was indeed dominated by women and mainly wives, thus representing one of the few known public arenas that was actually opened up to women by marriage.[55] Bennett notes that the ale-wives of Brigstock were unusual in facing no significant male competition, for in the two other manors with which she is concerned, Houghton-cum-Wyton (Huntingdonshire) and Iver (Buckinghamshire), men were primarily cited as brewers.[56] The explanation for these different levels of female and male brewers is located, by Bennett, in the internal dynamics of the family economy and the flexibility of working wives. For example, Iver's villagers supported themselves primarily through stock-raising and fishing. Because these activities were not particularly intensive, Iver's males became involved in brewing and dominated this industry. In the forest village of Brigstock males not only worked in the village's open fields, but were also diverted from brewing by their activities, such as assarting, in the surrounding woodlands. In short, wives only dominated the brewing industries of their villages when the economic energies of their husbands were diverted elsewhere. Bennett supports her argument by showing how in the

Table 5.3
TOTAL NUMBER OF BREWERS AND BREWSTERS 1327–75

year	total no. female	brewers male	total courts	mean no. brewers per court	total brewers
1327	8	17	5	8.4	25
1328	16	41	20	11.3	57
1329	21	46	19	13.6	67
1330	13	36	15	14.7	49
1331	8	27	3	17.6	35
1332	21	39	18	13.8	60
1333	16	30	17	12.6	46
1334	17	36	21	12.0	53
1335	22	45	20	13.5	67
1336	22	43	20	16.2	75
1337	14	56	20	15.4	70
1338	17	56	20	21.0	73
1339	18	56	17	13.4	74
1340	21	70	19	17.3	91
1341	17	57	19	17.4	74
1342	11	42	14	12.0	53
1343	11	43	14	12.2	54
1344	12	52	20	15.3	64
1345	10	59	19	12.7	69
1346	12	51	20	13.5	63
1347	13	49	20	10.4	62
1348	12	43	19	10.0	55
1349	14	49	20	8.8	63
1350	14	18	19	7.0	32
1351	4	15	20	5.0	19
1352	5	15	19	6.0	20
1353	3	26	20	6.0	29
1354	3	20	20	7.7	23
1355	2	18	19	5.8	20
1356	3	24	19	8.5	27
1357	4	25	14	7.7	29
1358	5	18	19	7.0	23
1359	5	18	20	7.3	23
1360	6	20	16	7.8	26
1361	5	17	19	5.7	22
1362	4	12	17	5.0	16
1363	8	12	21	5.0	20
1364	7	23	18	7.0	30
1365	2	18	19	6.0	20
1366	2	22	16	7.0	24
1367	4	20	21	6.6	24
1368	6	19	19	4.7	25
1369	3	12	15	3.9	15
1370	10	9	17	4.0	19
1371	6	18	13	5.0	24
1372	3	14	11	5.0	17
1373	5	14	18	5.0	19
1374	1	13	20	4.0	14
1375	3	14	17	4.7	17

worsening economic climate of the 1340s women became more prominent
in the brewing of ale in all three communities, than in earlier decades of
the fourteenth century and this was primarily because their husbands were
forced, by economic necessity, to divert their energies away from the
household.[57]

For Bennett's thesis to be true one would expect that the forest village of
Alrewas, which, like Brigstock, was also an openfield village and continued to assart land right up into the late 1340s, would show a similar
dominance of women in the ale trade. However, analysis of all peasants
presented by the ale tasters in the three-weekly courts of the manor reveals
that this was by no means the case. Women are not apparently dominant
as brewers in Alrewas. Table 5.3, which lists the total number of male and
female brewers amerced per annum for the period 1327–75, shows that
brewers were numerous and that a very high number of individuals were
recorded as brewing each year. For example, in 1328 there are a total of
twenty extant court rolls, including frankpledge courts, and some fifty-
seven brewers and brewsters amerced, giving an average of 11.3 brewers
being fined per court. However, in this one year only sixteen, that is 28
per cent, of the total number of peasants presented by the ale tasters were
female.

Throughout the whole second quarter of the fourteenth century the
numbers of brewers and brewsters presented per annum remained high,
with the late 1330s and early 1340s appearing to have been a peak period
for brewing, reaching a total of ninety-one brewers in 1340. Once again,
though, even in this year of high activity women only account for
twenty-one that is 23 per cent, of the total number of brewers amerced. As
the 1340s progressed the numbers of brewers gradually began to fall. But it
is not until the outbreak of the Black Death in 1349 and its consequent
effects upon the population of the manor that the number of brewers
amerced each year falls dramatically. Aside from the decrease in population, this fall in numbers presented for breaking the Assize of Ale can
also be accounted for by an increased professionalisation and specialisation
by certain individuals in the brewing and retailing of ale.

Figure 5.1 shows diagramatically this fall off in the numbers of brewers
and brewsters amerced per annum over the course of the fourteenth
century. This same figure also clearly shows that the brewing of ale does
not appear to have been predominantly in the hands of women. Table 5.4
gives a breakdown of the years 1331–75 into five-year periods, along with
the average number of male and female brewers that were amerced per
annum. This table reveals that at no point did the percentage of brewsters,
as opposed to brewers, ever rise above the 33 per cent level. Does this
dominance of men in the brewing of ale imply that, as in the case of Iver,
the economic energies of Alrewas's males were not being diverted

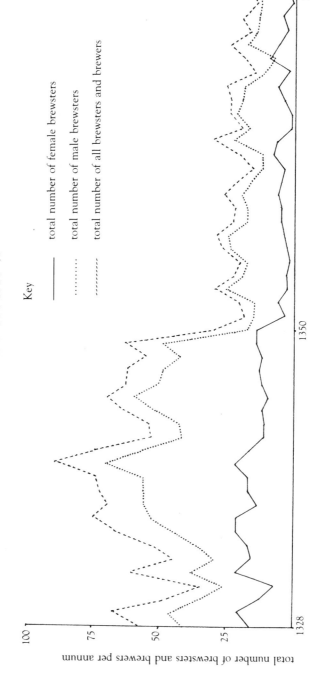

Figure 5.1

TOTAL NUMBER OF BREWSTERS AND BREWERS AMERCED
PER ANNUM 1328–75

Key

total number of female brewsters

total number of male brewsters

total number of all brewsters and brewers

total number of brewsters and brewers per annum

1328   1350   1375

100   75   50   25

elsewhere and consequently they became involved in brewing? Or could it have been the case, in line with Hilton's explanation, that those men cited as brewers were in fact paying for the fines incurred by their wives or other female members of their households?[58]

Table 5.4

PROPORTION OF FEMALE BREWERS 1331–75

period	mean number of brewers per annum			percentage female
	male	female	total	female
1331–5	35.4	16.8	52.2	32.6
1336–40	58.2	18.4	76.6	24.0
1341–5	50.6	12.2	62.8	19.4
1346–50	42.0	13.0	55.0	23.6
1351–5	18.8	3.4	22.2	15.3
1356–60	21.0	4.6	25.6	18.0
1361–5	16.4	5.2	21.6	24.0
1366–70	16.4	5.0	21.4	23.4
1371–5	14.6	3.6	18.2	19.8

There does seem to be some direct evidence in support of the latter argument from the court rolls, for there are cases where husbands are explicitly stated to be standing in for their wives' misdemeanours. For example, in the court held on 17 October 1332, William Warde is amerced 12d. for his wife who had prevented her ale from going to the lord 'when the reeve was paying for her ale'.[59] Again, in 1335, Robert Swan is fined 2s. for his wife, who 'kept her ale from the lord'.[60] Nine years later, in 1344, William and Matilda Shepherd, who were husband and wife, are attached to answer the lord for concealment. The court roll entry goes on to explain why they are to be attached: 'because when the ale tasters came to taste Matilda's ale they took her ale for selling it at three farthings a gallon, but after the ale tasters had gone she sold it at a penny a gallon to the deceit of the lord and the people's damage.'[61]

Although two of these cases do not directly relate to the Assize of Ale, they do indicate that husbands appear to have been representatives for their wives' actions when they are amerced for brewing. This hypothesis is supported by the fact that William Warde, Robert Swan, and William Shepherd all numbered among the manor's sixty-seven regular brewers. In fact Robert Swan, a half-virgater, was the 13th most regularly amerced brewer of the manor, being amerced on a total of 146 occasions between the years 1328 and 1350.[62] William Warde, a virgater, was the 22nd most regularly amerced brewer of the manor, as he was amerced 98 times in the fifteen year period 1327–42.[63] However, even though in these cases the ale kept from the reeve and lord is specified as being the ale of the wives of Robert and William, these two wives are never themselves presented by the ale tasters for breaking the Assize of Ale. More striking and revealing still is the case of William and Matilda Shepherd. William and Matilda, as noted above, were attached to answer the lord for concealment and it is explicitly stated that the ale tasters went to taste Matilda's ale and check on the price that *she* was retailing it at, but that when the ale tasters had gone she sold her ale at a higher price. However, in all of the three-weekly presentments by the ale tasters Matilda is never brought before the court and amerced for brewing. It is Matilda's husband, William, who is regularly presented.[64]

The evidence considered so far indicates that if one takes those amerced for brewing and retailing ale as those who actually brewed, the ale industry of Alrewas was not predominantly in the hands of women. However, the cases of William Warde, Robert Swan, and William Shepherd indicate that husbands may often have been answering for their wives' brewing and retailing of ale. This would suggest that the local custom of Alrewas mirrored customary law, where male heads of households were responsible for most of the fines, debts, and misdemeanours incurred by wives and other members of their households.[65] This does not invalidate Bennett's argument that who actually brewed ale was influenced by the internal dynamics of the family economy and the flexibility of working wives.[66] The local economy of Alrewas may have led to the diversion of men's economic energies elsewhere and left the brewing of ale in the hands of the women of their households, and perhaps primarily their wives. However, the above cases do seriously undermine Bennett's argument and strongly suggest that women were dominant in brewing but partly hidden in record. Perhaps even the choice of which goods were to be taken as heriot, following the death of a regular brewer and his wife, could indicate which of the two was primarily responsible for brewing. During the Black Death, Thomas and Alice Gyn, a half-virgater household, died and heriot of one heifer was claimed from Thomas and half a brewing vat from Alice.[67] Once again it is Thomas who was always presented for breaking the Assize of Ale, but Alice is never cited and only appears in the court rolls on record of her death.[68]

The Alrewas evidence thus suggests that in dealing with the ale industry one has to be aware of the vagaries of local custom in who was seen as legally answerable for the brewing carried on within a given peasant household. For this hypothesis to be true one would expect those women who were presented by the ale tasters to be widows and single women. In looking at the marital status of women amerced for brewing, I shall first deal very briefly with those who can be classified as occasional brewers and then turn to those who were regularly presented for breaking the Assize of Ale.[69]

Table 5.5 shows that for the period 1327–75 a total of 411 individuals were amerced for brewing in the court of Alrewas. Of these 411 individuals, 152 (37 per cent) were women and 259 (63 per cent) were men. The fact that such a high number of individuals paid ale fines indicates that selling ale must have been a characteristic of many households of the manor. In fact approximately just under half of all peasant households are associated with brewing in the 1330s and 1340s, though this proportion fell by just under 10 per cent in the 1370s.[70] However, Table 5.5 also shows that although participation in the ale trade was widespread, it varied greatly. Some individuals sold ale infrequently and sporadically and were probably just making an occasional profit from surplus ale which had been brewed for domestic consumption by selling the excess to their neighbours.

Table 5.5
DISTRIBUTION OF BREWERS' FINES 1327–75

category	persons		fines	
	no.	per cent	no.	per cent
regular female brewers (30 or more fines each)	11	3.0	960	11.7
minor female brewers (1–29 fines each)	141	34.0	647	8.0
regular male brewers (30 or more fines each)	56	13.6	5322	65.0
minor male brewers (1–29 fines each)	203	49.4	1261	15.3
all brewers	411	100	8190	100

In fact, these occasional or 'minor' brewers and brewsters were numerous, accounting for just over four-fifths (344) of the total number of individuals who were amerced for brewing in the years 1327–75. However, they collectively accounted for only one-fifth of the manor's ale trade; their market activity on an individual level was fairly insignificant. On average, each paid only about five fines during his or her career. Furthermore, many of these brewers and brewsters paid their ale fines over the course of many years. Table 5.5 shows that of these 344 minor brewers 203 (59 per cent) were men and 141 (41 per cent) were women. The fact that the highest number of female brewers occurs amongst this 'minor' or 'occasional' group once again underlines the part-time, occasional and non-specialist nature of women's work. It also reflects their legal position, for analysis of a sample of thirty minor female brewers shows that two-thirds appear to have been single or widows and the other third were married.

Table 5.6
FEMALE MARRIED FULL-TIME BREWSTERS AND THEIR SPOUSES

name	no. fines	rank	period	husband	no. fines	rank	period	holding
Rosa Kempe	216	5	1348-75	William Heuster	86	26	1346-73	cottage and plot
Isabella Bassett	66	35	1358-70	William Bassett	74	31	1357-68	cottage
Margery Averil	33	53	1339-47	Richard Averil	157	11	1328-42	cottage
Matilda de Catton	33	53	1368-73	John de Catton	169	8	1350-62	cottage and plot

Turning to the regular brewers of the manor, Table 5.5 shows that fifty-six (84 per cent) were men and just eleven (16 per cent) were women. Analysis of the economic status of these eleven women reveals that, as is the case for the male brewers, the ale industry was neither the preserve of the poor cottager or the more well-endowed virgater.[71] Of these eleven women six were single, four were married, and just one was a widow, i.e. just over half of the regular female brewers were unmarried.[72] As for the four married women, all had husbands who also numbered among the regular brewers of the manor. For example, as Table 5.6 shows, the previously mentioned Rosa Kempe was the fifth most frequently amerced brewer of the manor, being amerced on a total of 216 times between the years 1348 and 1375. Rosa's husband was also frequently amerced, being cited on a total of eighty-six occasions in the same twenty-seven year period. The fact that some husbands and wives were both regularly presented for breaking the Assize of Ale appears to refute the argument that the husbands of Alrewas always answered for their wives' brewing. However, analysis of the landed wealth of those couples where both man and wife were amerced shows that all of these couples were cottagers or small-holders. For example, Margery and Richard Averil were amerced on 33 and 157 occasions respectively for breaking the Assize of Ale. Both had appeared in court together on four occasions for buying and selling land. However, these land transactions involved the permanent alienation of small plots of land which were immediately bought back in the form of leases.[73] On Richard's death, in the summer of 1342, and seven years later when Margery died in the Black Death, it is recorded that Margery and her husband had merely held a lifelease in a cottage from a more wealthy peasant of the manor.[74]

In contrast to these small-holder couples, the three aforementioned husbands, who were amerced in connection with ale their wives had brewed and who were also regular brewers, were all virgaters or half-virgaters.[75] This discrepancy in who was actually amerced for brewing could therefore depend on the landed wealth of the household. A virgater came from the more wealthy section of peasant society, for 37 per cent of the peasants held less than 5 acres and 63 per cent held, at the time of their death, 15 to 30 acres, that is half to one virgate.[76] It was from this more land-wealthy group of peasants that office-holders were drawn and thus accrued to themselves power and status within their community. It is these virgaters who are more prominent in the records for buying and selling of land, bringing disputes before the court in terms of broken contract, trespass, and other such cases. A virgater would thus be more likely to be in court and engaged in court business and therefore would have also answered for his wife's brewing. On the other hand, a cottager would be less likely to have other business to transact in the court, so the person who was presented by the ale tasters was more likely to be the person actually selling the ale.

Conclusion

Analysis of the crafts and trades of Alrewas manor in the fourteenth century does show that a marked sexual division of labour existed within the market place. The market of Alrewas was primarily concerned with the retail of foodstuffs, but the more specialised and capital-intensive trades of butchering and baking were the preserve of men, while the less specialised trades – like those of tranters and brewsters – were female dominated. Men were mainly amerced for the brewing and retailing of ale which their wives had brewed, though wives of cottagers were more likely to answer personally for their own ale-selling. That husbands often answered for their wives' brewing activities, especially if they were virgaters, underlines the legal subordination of married women. Consequently, it is primarily as single women, widows or the wives of small-holders that women's work patterns are represented in the court rolls as being more similar to those of men, that is more full time, more stable, and less intermittent. However, even here these women were confined to being tranters or brewsters. Finally, and most importantly, although a clear sexual division of labour existed in the market place, the landed wealth, and thus economic status, of the households to which women belonged is significant and reveals how, even at the level of peasant society, the more wealthy married woman's identity was subsumed into that of her husband's. Perhaps the 'rough and ready equality', espoused by Power and Hilton as a characteristic of relations between peasant men and women in the late Middle Ages, is more likely to have existed, if it existed at all, at the lower level of peasant society – that of the small-holders and cottagers.[77]

Notes

1 I would like to thank Z. Razi, N. Hayward, and J. Goldberg for comments on earlier drafts of this chapter. Special thanks to Miri Krasin and Sarah Graham.

2 E. Power, *Medieval Women* (Cambridge, 1975), pp. 53–74; A. Abrams, 'Women Traders in Medieval London', *Economic Journal* 26 (1916), pp. 276–85.

3 R.H. Hilton, 'Women Traders in Medieval England', *Women's Studies* 11 (1984), p. 149.

4 M. Kowaleski, 'Women's Work in a Medieval Town: Exeter in the Late Fourteenth Century', in *Women and Work in Preindustrial Europe*, ed. B.A. Hanawalt (Bloomington, 1986), pp. 147–8.

5 Ibid, pp. 155–8; Power also makes this point concerning female work identity: *Medieval Women*, pp. 53–74.

6 Power, *Medieval Women*, p. 71.

7 R.H. Hilton, *The English Peasantry in the Later Middle Ages* (Oxford, 1975), p. 101.

8 B.A. Hanawalt, 'Childrearing among the Lower Classes of Late Medieval England', *Journal of Interdisciplinary History* 8 (1977–8), pp. 1–22.

9 C. Middleton, 'The Sexual Division of Labour in Feudal England', *New Left Review* 113–14 (1979), pp. 160–61.

10 W.O. Ault, 'By-laws of Gleaning and the Problems of Harvest', *Economic History Review* 2nd ser. 14 (1961), p. 211; *Open-field Farming in Medieval England: A Study of Village By-laws* (1972), pp. 82, 84, 92–3, 110, 120–1.

11 S.A.C. Penn, 'Female Wage-earners in Late Fourteenth-century England', *Agricultural History Review* 35 (1987), pp. 13–14.

12 Power, *Medieval Women*, p. 71.

13 J.M. Bennett, *Women in the Medieval English Countryside: Gender and Household in Brigstock before the Plague* (New York, 1987), p. 36.

14 Ibid., pp. 5–9, 128.

15 Ibid., pp. 22–7.

16 Ibid., pp. 66, 99–100, 104–5, 144, 176.

17 This figure is arrived at by multiplying the number of tenants listed in the 1342 rental by five: personal communication from C.C. Dyer.

18 Alrewas Court Rolls: CROS, D(W)0/3/1 (1259) to D(W)0/3/71 (1375).

19 1342 rental: BL, Honour of Tutbury, Selected Folios; 'The Exchequer Subsidy Roll of A.D. 1327', ed. G. Wrottesley *SRS* 7 (1886), p. 235; 'The Subsidy Roll of 6 Edward III, A.D. 1332–33', ed. G. Wrottesley *SRS* 10 (1889), pp. 84–5; 'The Poll Tax of A.D. 1379–81 for the Hundreds of Offlow and Cuttlestone', ed. W. Boyd *SRS* 17 (1895), pp. 169–71.

20 See above.

21 CROS, ROD(W)0/3/32.

22 CROS, ROD(W)0/3/27.

23 CROS, ROD(W)0/3/31, 57.

24 Failing to enclose holdings: CROS, ROD(W)0/3/18, 62. Illegal trespass: ROD(W)0/3/8, 12, 16, 33, 64. Illegal blocking of pathways: ROD(W)0/3/19. Illegal blocking of waterways: ROD(W)0/3/18.

25 CROS, ROD(W)0/3/34, 41, 51, 53, 60, 63.

26 J.M. Bennett, 'The Village Ale-Wife: Women and Brewing in Fourteenth Century England', in *Women and Work in Preindustrial Europe*, ed. Hanawalt, pp. 20–36; J.M. Bennett, *Women in the Medieval English Countryside*, pp. 120–8.

27 *Calendar of Charter Rolls, 1257–1300*, p. 342; D.M. Palliser and A.C. Pinnock, 'The Markets of Medieval Staffordshire', *North Staffordshire Journal of Field Studies* 11 (1971) pp. 50–1.

28   D.M. Palliser, 'The Boroughs of Medieval Staffordshire', ibid. 12 (1972), p. 68; CROS, D(W)0/3/9, 5. 1328; D(W)0/3/57, 9. 1365. Although Alrewas had borough and market status by 1328 it never acquired other urban characteristics, such as municipal self-government. It remained primarily an agricultural village and by 1500 was a lapsed borough and its market no longer held. Other local markets which had also fallen into disuse by 1500 include Yoxall, some four kilometres northwest of Alrewas, whose market was held on a Saturday, and Elford, five kilometres southeast of Alrewas, whose market day was Friday. The more significant urban centres close to Alrewas were Lichfield and Burton-on-Trent. The latter two also appear to be the limits of Alrewas's trading hinterland, as evidenced through broken contracts between peasants of Alrewas and residents of Burton and Lichfield. However, there is evidence that a few trading links extended beyond this boundary. For example in November 1346 Henry Ward of Alrewas was presented in a contract case over the carting of dry fish from Boston to Ruggeley, Staffs.: CROS, D(W)0/3/32.

29   J. Birrell, 'Peasant Craftsmen in the Medieval Forest', *Agricultural History Review* 17 (1969), pp. 91–106.

30   The term tranter is taken to mean a petty trader mainly concerned with the sale of small quantities of food and drink on the street or in their own homes. The term 'huckster', more usually associated with petty retailers, is never used in the Alrewas court rolls, though on a few rare occasions the term 'regrator' is found. Thus, the terms tranter and regrator are understood as local equivalents of huckster.

31   For reference to carters see note 15 above. The lord of the manor pre-1348 regularly leased sections of the surrounding waterways to a total of eleven peasants – all men – for terms of one to nine years. Fishing was a major source of income for these individuals, and their respective households; all were cottagers and yet could still afford to pay heavy water rents, on average 12s. per annum, in comparison to the land rents of 2s. per virgate. There were two tailors, both men, in the manor in the 1340s who were sufficiently well-established to take in apprentices, again both male. CROS, D(W)0/3/27, 23.3.1342; D(W)0/3/31, 23.9.1345.

32   P.D.A. Harvey, 'Non-Agrarian Activities in the Rural Communities of Late Medieval England', Istituto Internazionale di Storia Economica 'Francesco Datini' (Prato, 1982), p. 7.

33   See note 15 above.

34   Adam Baxter was presented 28 times for breaking the Assize of Bread in the period 1334–68, and 256 times for breaking the Assize of Ale in the same period. Adam is listed in the 1342 rental for holding half a virgate in Alrewas: BL, Honour of Tutbury, Selected Folios. By his death in 1369 he held a messuage, half a virgate, two cottages, a plot of waste, and another tenement for which his daughter, as heiress, owed 6s. 8d., the standard entry fine for a virgate: CROS, D(W)0/3/63, 2.6.1369.

35   John Baxter was presented fifteen times for breaking the Assize of Bread in the period 1334–49, and sixty-one times for breaking the Assize of Ale in the same period. John Paty was presented sixteen times for breaking the Assize of Bread in the period 1365–75, and at the same time bought several plots of land, waste, and a cottage paying a total of 3s. 6d. in entry fines.

36   Richard Andreu was only amerced once for breaking the Assize of Bread, but was one of the most frequently amerced brewers of the manor, being presented on 210 occasions in the years 1327–48.

37   A 'regular' butcher is defined as one who was presented on four or more occasions for 'killing and selling meat'. Most notable amongst the regularly presented butchers, who numbered fifteen, are Thomas Alcock, John Edemon, and Richard de London who were each presented on twenty-one to twenty-five occasions over twelve to sixteen years.

38   Four of the regular butchers can be positively identified as holding between half to one virgate, six were active in the land market, and two, John Edemon and John Averil,

lent fellow villagers 15s and 10 marks respectively in the form of mortgages: John Edemon CROS, D(W)0/3/52, 1361; John Averil D(W)0/3/71, 1375; Subsidies and Thomas Gyn: 'Subsidy Roll of A.D. 1327', ed. Wrottesley, p. 235; 'Subsidy Roll of A.D. 1332–33', ed. Wrottesley, pp. 84–5.

39 Of the fifteen regular butchers, four also numbered amongst those regularly amerced for breaking the Assize of Ale.

40 P.J.P. Goldberg, 'Female Labour, Service and Marriage in the Late Medieval Urban North', *Northern History* 22 (1986), p. 30.

41 Only three of the regular butchers were small-holders, holding just one cottage and a few acres of land, and not engaging in the regular sale of ale. However, all these three were each only presented on between four to six occasions over periods of two to four years.

42 Kowaleski, 'Women's Work in a Medieval Town', pp. 155–8.

43 Of the thirty-one occasional tranters, twelve were only ever cited once in all the extant records for Alrewas as tranters and are, therefore, impossible to positively identify; ten were definitely married at the time that they were amerced; and eight have been assumed to be single through analysis of their other court appearances. The husband of the widow, Mariota la Ridere, died in 1356 (CROS, ROD(W)0/3/44, 2.4.1356) and she is cited in the following year as a tranter (ROD(W)0/3/48, 21.10.1357) and pays her own pannage (ROD(W)0/3/48).

44 Landless tranters: CROS, ROD(W)0/3/36, 11.7.1349 for Alice la Bonde and Elena Gadeling; ROD(W)0/3/36, 9.5.1349 for Alice Kempe. One of the virgaters is Alice Owyn who at the time of being amerced as a tranter was married to Henry Owyn, but had previously been married to another virgater, Thomas Bernard, who died in the Black Death: ROD(W)0/3/41. Of the other virgater, Mariota la Ridere a widow, her husband had died a cottager, but seven years later Mariota bought two messuages and a virgate from a young heiress whose uncle had died in the Black Death: ROD(W)0/3/55, 25.11.1363.

45 Pannage lists where occasional female tranters pay their own pannage: CROS, ROD(W)0/3/16 and ROD(W)0/3/20 for Elena Kempe; ROD(W)0/3/21 for Lettice Annot and Elena Kempe; ROD(W)0/3/22 for Margery Dobbe and Elena Kempe; ROD(W)0/3/23 for Lettice Annot, Elena Gadeling, and Alice Ysot; ROD(W)0/3/25 for Lettice Annot; ROD(W)0/3/37 for Alice Ysot; ROD(W)0/3/48 for Mariota la Ridere.

46 Rosa Kempe was amerced 216 times and William Heuster 75 times for breaking the Assize of Ale.

47 Four couples, i.e. eight of the fifty-four tranters, were amerced in this way.

48 'Poll Tax of A.D. 1379–81', ed. Boyd, p. 169.

49 William and Rosa were both cited together as husband and wife in the *intervivos* transference of land on four occasions. William was cited alone on a further three occasions. All these land transactions involved small plots of land and by 1373, the last recorded transfer involving this couple, William and Rosa's net gain through the peasant land market was just one cottage and one plot of land: CROS, ROD(W)0/3/38, 4.6.1351; ROD(W)0/3/51, 19.1.1360; ROD(W)0/3/51, 8.2.1360; ROD(W)0/3/54, 12.8.1363; ROD(W)0/3/56, 9.3.1364; ROD(W)0/3/69, 15.10.1373.

50 Matilda and Lettice have been taken to be single from analysis of all their other court appearances where no kin, spouse or household affiliations are apparent. A third woman who is only ever cited in the court rolls as a tranter of bread and ale is Hawis de Rideware.

51 Matilda and pannage: CROS, ROD(W)0/3/43 for one pig; Lettice and pannage: ROD(W)0/3/20 for one hog. Lettice was amerced 208 times for breaking the Assize of Ale and, overall, was the seventh most frequently amerced person for this offence within the manor in the period 1328–75.

52 Kowaleski, 'Women's Work in a Medieval Town', pp. 155–8; Bennett, *Women in the Medieval English Countryside*, pp. 66, 176.

53 Hilton, 'Women Traders in Medieval England', p. 143.

54 Ibid., p. 149; Goldberg, 'Female Labour, Service and Marriage', p. 30.

55 Bennett, 'The Village Ale-Wife', p. 22.

56 Ibid., p. 26.

57 Ibid., pp. 26–7.

58 Hilton, 'Women Traders in Medieval England', p. 149.

59 CROS, ROD(W)0/3/15, 17.10.1332.

60 CROS, ROD(W)0/3/19, 1335.

61 CROS, ROD(W)0/3/30, 1344.

62 Robert Swan as a half-virgater from record of his death: CROS, ROD(W)0/3/53, 12.2.1362.

63 William Warde as a virgater from 1342 rental: BL, Honour of Tutbury, Selected Folios.

64 William Shepherd was amerced thirty-nine times in the years 1340–9.

65 F. Pollock and F.W. Maitland, *The History of English Law* (Cambridge, 1898), ii, pp. 399–436. There are a couple of cases in the Alrewas court rolls which support this view: CROS, ROD(W)0/3/33 and ROD(W)0/3/43.

66 Bennett, 'The Village Ale-Wife', pp. 26–7.

67 CROS, ROD(W)0/3/36, Thomas and Alice Gyn 20.6.1349.

68 Thomas Gyn was amerced sixty-three times in the years 1329–47 for breaking the Assize of Ale, and was also one of the regular butchers of the manor.

69 An 'occasional' brewer is defined as one who was amerced on less than thirty occasions, and a 'regular' brewer was one who was amerced on thirty or more occasions.

70 The figure for the 1330s and 1340s is calculated by comparing the households listed in the 1342 rental with those individuals amerced for brewing: BL, Honour of Tutbury, Selected Folios. The figure for the 1370s is more unreliable as the 1381 Poll Tax listing has been used: 'Poll Tax of A.D. 1379–81', ed. Boyd, pp. 169–71.

71 Of these eleven women it has only been possible to assess the landed wealth of seven, of which one was a virgater (CROS, ROD(W)0/3/13 – Alice Fox), one a half virgater (ROD(W)0/3/36 – Elena widow of Henry son of Geoffrey), and the rest cottagers.

72 Six single women: Lettice Souter, Alice Fox, Isabel Ysot, Matilda Edemon, Margery Gyn, and Elena Gadeling. Their single status has been assumed from analysis of all their court appearances and family reconstitution.

73 CROS, ROD(W)0/3/8; ROD(W)0/3/18.

74 Richard's death: CROS, ROD(W)0/3/27; Margery's death: ROD(W)0/3/35.

75 See above on William Warde, Robert Swan, William Shepherd, and Thomas Gyn.

76 The percentage of virgaters as opposed to small-holders is based on analysis of the landed wealth of peasants whose deaths are recorded in the court rolls.

77 Power, *Medieval Women*, p. 74; Hilton, *The English Peasantry*, p. 105.

6

'How ladies . . . who live on their manors ought to manage their households and estates': Women as Landholders and Administrators in the Later Middle Ages[*]

Rowena E. Archer
Manchester College, Oxford

A presumed fundamental aridity may render administrative history unattractive to many as an area of research. The process of institutions expanding and fragmenting into smaller and yet more bureaucratic units seems a guarantee of dullness, not to say tedium. Such a view is too narrow and surely ill-judged. In a recent paper to the Royal Historical Society, Professor R.A. Griffiths took pains to stress the humanity of the subject through the careers of highly professional bureaucrats, and perhaps this examination of the role of some of their employers will further ameliorate the concept of dryness.[1]

The centrality of administration to daily life is probably its first claim to historical importance. The structures and systems of organisation adopted by the landowning classes of the later middle ages were absolutely essential to the proper management of the property upon which all other aspects of their lives depended. The largest proportion of a landowner's time was, therefore, taken up with the exercise of multifarious responsibilities and the fulfilment of commitments arising from the need to administer and nurture the acres which formed the chief determinant of his worldly status. Such matters can hardly ever have been far from his mind. The greater the estate the greater the burden that had to be borne and the greater the risks to personal prestige and family fortune when failure to carry that load engulfed a particular generation. All who had a direct concern in the land had a contribution to make and nowhere can the partnership between

* Christine de Pisan, *The Treasure of the City of Ladies or the Book of the Three Virtues*, ed. S. Lawson (Harmondsworth, 1985), p. 130. I am deeply indebted to Jeremy Goldberg for his help and great patience and also to Michael K. Jones and Margaret Condon who commented on earlier drafts of this chapter.

men and women be more consistently viewed than in the preservation of the landed inheritance which had been created by the union of husband and wife and bonded by the birth of an heir. A common interest in expanding and maintaining the property in their charge promoted a sense of common purpose in which both parties played complementary and overlapping roles. Virtually all women of property could expect to exercise a measure of administrative responsibility wherever and whenever the need arose, circumstances alone determining the range of their activities.

For the fourteenth and fifteenth centuries the extant evidence, although scattered and often fragmentary, survives in sufficient quantity to allow some assessment of the collective expertise of aristocratic women and of their success rate in estate management. It points strongly to a contemporary supposition that no undertaking that might normally be deemed the responsibility of men should lie outside the purview of wives, sisters or mothers. Regardless of sex, competence in this field was not much commented upon though failure in the form of mounting debts, extravagance or negligence might lead to contemporary condemnation.[2] If husbands have left little record of their gratitude to their partners in the administrative enterprise it is perhaps because co-operation was too commonplace to elicit particular comment. Their wives were their 'adjutants' and their expectations of them were consequently high.[3]

The scale of the burden of administrative accountability was clearly immense. The lady as landholder was just as important as her male counterpart. F.W. Maitland has described her parity at law with men: 'The woman can hold land, even by military tenure, can own chattels, make a will, make a contract, can sue and be sued.'[4] It was marriage which changed the nature of her status, but Eileen Power's warnings against exaggeration of the penalties or disadvantages of the feudal landownership of women must be heeded.[5] Moreover, whatever the law might dictate in terms of the subordination of a wife and her property to her husband and whatever the theoretical implications that carried so far as management or alienation were concerned, circumstances frequently left wives as the sole representatives of their spouses. In the normal course of their lives noblemen spent a good proportion of their time engaged upon the king's service, frequently necessitating long spells overseas. This was the common lot of many during the period of the Hundred Years War. Katherine Neville, married in 1412, had charge of the vast Mowbray estates from 1417 to 1422 when her husband, John, served an unbroken period in France for Henry V. A nobleman's own business often carried him away from the *caput* of his patrimony, as often as not to London. Imprisonment as a result of war brought wives the extra burden of raising a ransom,[6] while incarceration for crime or political miscalculation brought, in addition to administrative pressure, an immeasurable degree of painful ignominy and uncertainty.[7] Several wives, like those of Richard II's judges, bore the anxieties and insecurities of being the dependant of disgraced exiles;[8] and for all the glory attached to crusading, such ventures threw all the business of management on spouses for indeterminate but usually protracted periods.[9] Christine de Pisan, whose own experience was of the Franco–English hostilities, perhaps went too far in saying that barons who sought honour should spend the least possible time on their property, but she was demonstrably on safe ground in describing the ultimate effect:

> Because barons and still more commonly knights and squires and gentlemen travel and go off to the wars, their wives should be wise and sound administrators and manage their affairs well, because most of the time they stay at home without their husbands, who are at court or abroad.[10]

The immensity of the managerial task is also made plain through consideration of a woman's education in this period. Evidence of any kind of training in basic administration is hard to find. Education of women was essentially informal, the product of upbringing by other women. This much can be universally agreed, but a clear idea of what was deemed appropriate in the education of women is harder to establish partly because here, as in so many respects, ambivalence of attitude has left a trail of confusion. Selective reading may suggest that formal education of women was generally condemned. It was not much discussed by educationalists and writers like Philip of Novarre, Robert of Blois, and Giles of Rome. The views these did offer concentrated upon seclusion of women and good character formation. Sewing, spinning, and silk work were advocated chiefly as a remedy for idleness; reading, regarded with deep suspicion, was grudgingly conceded as a requirement strictly for the high born lady; and writing was censured as subversion.[11] Such opinions were at best a reflection upon their authors' prejudices and can hardly be said to have borne much relation to reality. A more positive and certainly more realistic note is struck by St. Jerome in his letter to Laeta urging that her daughter Paula should have her own set of boxwood or ivory letters and should be taught to read and write.[12] Vincent de Beauvais, though he placed great emphasis on inculcating in girls virtue and good behaviour, followed Jerome's views and his contemporary, Peter Dubois, advocated Latin and one other language, grammar, logic, religion, and medical skills for boys and girls.[13] In the early fourteenth century Francesco di Barberino had a clear reason for female education: 'If it happens that she inherits lands she will be better able to rule them and the acquired wisdom will help her natural wisdom.'[14] Christine de Pisan's contribution is disappointing. The main thrust of her views on education is the familiar one, directing attention to moral excellence and propriety. Her chapter on upbringing of children which does advocate reading and writing has less practical instruction than might reasonably be hoped for in so avowedly practical a manual. The only hint of something relevant to preparation for administrative duties is the broad comment 'she ought not to be educated entirely indoors, nor in only the great feminine virtues'.[15]

It would be unwise to assume from these gleanings that women were totally unprepared for the many and varied demands that came with great estates. The evidence of book ownership suggests that probably most of them did learn to read, particularly in the later middle ages. An increasingly favoured illustration in books was of women reading, especially in depictions of the Virgin, and the illustrations in general had immense educational and practical value. The Hours of Catherine of Cleves carried powerful reminders to the owner of her duties in estate management in the illustrations of the lady supervising her workers and their products.[16] Writing was a less vital skill since it could always be done by a scribe. The least traceable but probably the most important single preparation for the future was the expertise acquired through parental example and by simply being, in early life, in the midst of routine estate management. The hurly-burly of such a life surely taught its own invaluable and enduring lessons. An early sixteenth century household like that of the duchess of Norfolk could offer the opportunity to learn to audit all manner of accounts and fulfil all manner of duties so that Cardinal Wolsey's nephew could present on his *curriculum vitae*, 'Item he has thexperiens in dyverse offices and Roomes abought a gret estate, as well consernyng the Chambre, as otherwyse. These he had thexperiens with the seid duchess'. Such households also provided an endless training ground for the next generation of masters and mistresses. John Fairechild may have been formally educated as a lawyer but then, as now, there was nothing quite like experience to prepare one for work.[17] Success must at all stages have depended in some measure upon trial and error and many lessons must have been learned through direct experience.

Perhaps because a greater interest attaches to the actions of the absentee husbands – compounded by the fact that the accounts and estate documents were prepared in his name as though he were indeed present – and because of the rather ambiguous picture painted by contemporary educationalists, the tenure of estates by women has rather tended to be viewed as some kind of *inter-regnum* falling between two more important periods of male tenure. Yet it can hardly be presumed that contemporaries necessarily took such a view. In such a hierarchical society as that of later medieval England servants normally obeyed the commands of their superiors, lord or lady. Certainly a problem exists in assessing the power of landowners to direct and control their property. Their ultimate accountability is accepted but actual proof of direct action by lords can be difficult to pinpoint. Vital questions endlessly intrude themselves. Where did initiative for a particular action originate? How directly should the lord be accredited as a successful manager? Much spade work was done by officials and servants and though some of these come across as characters and individuals many remain obscure, and the historian's capacity to judge the true source of power can too easily depend upon chance details of close supervision by, or specific orders from, the lord. Determining the level of action is just as difficult for the lord as it is for the lady, but if it is presumed that good stewardship reflects the firm hand of a committed lord of the manor, then the same presumption must be allowed for the lady. It may well be that being, for the most part, less distracted by political or military concerns, women in charge of estates devoted more of their available time to the property than men. There is no fundamental reason for concluding that maladministration will be the inevitable consequence of female tenure of land. When John Mowbray ordered an eyre in his lordship of Chepstow in 1415 his justices dealt with offences and venialities committed by his own servants since his succession to his estates two years earlier. Although the property had long been administered by the widow and then the daughter of Thomas of Brotherton, there was nothing to suggest that the lordship had been poorly governed in the last years of the fourteenth century, even though Margaret of Brotherton was nearly eighty when her tenure came to a close.[18] In evaluating the capacity of women to administer their estates the burden of proof must surely lie with those who believe, or suspect, that lands which were for long periods in the hands of women were liable to suffer neglect. It cannot be right to presume that most women were disinterested in the fate of lands and family or that they had so little regard for their sons or absentee husbands that they usually abrogated their responsibilities.

If it is difficult to be certain of the level of direct action by landholders it is even harder to measure levels of influence. This, however, is particularly important with regard to wives who were subordinated by the law to their husbands. Their power of influence day to day may have been considerable and in purely practical terms probably overrode matters of mere legality. Here the historian is helped by suggestions of a high degree of confidence and trust on the part of men and by signs of genuine devotion by competent wives and mothers. It is time to consider some examples.

On the last day of April 1450 William de la Pole, duke of Suffolk, penned a final letter to his son and heir. The essence of his advice to the boy was fear God, fear the King, fear his mother, and shun bad company. Of these three the most immediate was clearly mother.

> I charge you, my dere sone, alwey, as ye be bounden by the
> commaundement of God to do, to love, to worshepe youre lady and

moder, and also that ye obey alwey hyr commaundements, and to beleve hyr councelles and advises in alle youre werks, the which dredeth not, but shall be best and trewest to you. And yef any other body wold stere you to the contrarie, to flee the councell in any wyse, for ye shall fynde it nought and evyll.[19]

Such sentiments were wholly consistent with those expressed the previous year in his will in which he named his duchess as his sole executrix 'for above al the erthe my singuler trust is moost in her'.[20] This daughter of Thomas Chaucer, then about forty-five years old, already twice widowed and enjoying a jointure in all the de la Pole estates, in accordance with their marriage settlement of 1430, thereafter more than fulfilled the expectations of father and son in her powerful maintenance of the estate.[21]

She seems always to have had a powerful influence on Suffolk although, equally, to have been strongly attached to him.[22] Many grants to William also included Alice, their greatest joint venture surely relating to the foundation of the almshouses at Ewelme (Oxon).[23] In the sixteenth century John Leland remarked that Suffolk 'for love of her and the commodite of her landes fell much to dwelle in Oxfordshir and Barkshir wher his wife's landes lay.'[24] The marriage would seem to have constrained her little. Two episodes which reveal an unsuppressed spirit during her marriage may be cited. James Gresham writing to Judge William Paston in 1444 about land in Paston recorded an exchange with Dru Barentyn. The latter had taken the Judge's bill to Alice whom he said remembered the matter well and insisted that there was no cause for concern therein. Barentyn, though impressed by the interview, advised Gresham to go and see Alice and press more firmly for clarification. The two men had argued. Gresham said he would never be admitted to her presence and Barentyn told him he must find a way. Gresham informed the Judge that he did not dare because he would have to do so *via* her men and since he knew not which of them would be favourably disposed he did not want to risk explaining, 'to hym yat wolde yow not weel in yis matier'. He awaited further instructions. Clearly Gresham and Barentyn found her both important and formidable long before she had sole charge of any property.[25]

Much more startling and colourful is the story of Alice's activities in the company of Sir Thomas Tuddenham and John Heydon contained in the complaints of the city of Norwich about their oppressions and extortions in the 1440s. There it was stated how Alice, while countess of Suffolk, 'cam to the said cite disguised lyke an huswyf of the countre and the said Sir Thomas Tudenham and two other person wt her also disguysed'.[26] The party adjourned to Lakenham woods, 'to tak the ayr and disport theymself'. Unfortunately for all, one of the keepers of the city ditches, not recognising the party, issued a challenge. A fight ensued between Sir

Thomas and the keeper 'wher by the seyd Duchesse was sore afrayd'. Tuddenham was arrested and imprisoned. Just exactly what Alice was up to or what her husband thought of such disporting is unclear although evidently the countess was capable of considerable mischief and, certainly, to this event in the woods, the city of Norwich ascribed the displeasure of wife, husband, and affinity which led to a royal seizure of its franchise.[27]

Alice was quick to recover from the murder of Suffolk. Nothing came of the Commons' Bill for her removal from the King's presence and as Colin Richmond so graphically put it. 'like a lioness she scattered the vultures and had her pick of the carcass'.[28] Margaret Paston declared in 1462 that the people 'love not in no wyse the Dwke of Sowthfolk nor hys modyr'.[29] Seven years later she voiced strong suspicions to her son of rather underhand behaviour by the duchess pending a royal visit to Norfolk to investigate Paston claims:

> The Duchesse of Suffolk is at Ewhelm, in Oxford shir, and it is thought be your frends her that it is do that she myght be ferr and ought of the wey, and the rather feyne excuse be cause of age or sikenesse, and if the Kyng wold send for her for your maters.[30]

To that equally wily Norfolk gentlewoman, Alice de la Pole's sixty-four years did not constitute a credible reason for her absence: Alice was fit and menacing. The Paston accounts of the assaults on Hellesden, Drayton, and Cotton point to that at least. In 1472 Margaret Paston put it to her son bluntly: 'the Duchess of Suffolkes men sey that she wull not departe from Heylesdon ner Drayton, – she wuld rather departe from money.'[31] Long experience in East Anglia may account for Alice's toughness. After Suffolk's death in 1450 she had faced the aggression of the duke of Norfolk who seized her manor of Stockton and refused to relinquish it even after Alice had demonstrated her rights there. In 1454 her receiver-general, Andrew Grigges, listed the manor on his accounts but recorded only its occupation by Norfolk and a warrant from his mistress for payments for relevant legal advice. Twice in the 1450s she petitioned chancery for the restoration of Stockton but unfortunately the outcome of her suit is unknown.[32]

Although hers may not always have been a harassing and vexatious administration, it was generally stern and exacting, for only thus could she preserve it and only thus did she command. She had moved swiftly in May 1450 to secure the keeping of the de la Pole lands and was already appointing officials by early June. She had been promised the wardship of her son in 1444 and certainly held it by 1453, arranging the latter's marriage to a daughter of the duke of York in 1458.[33] The 1453–4 accounts of Andrew Grigges capture a strong sense of Alice's control over the administration by reference to her personal receipt of revenues, her authorising of disbursements, appointing officials, seeing to a perpetual memorial for her late husband, and consulting her council in a year in which she divided her time between her Suffolk home at Wingfield and the capital.[34] She had both that capacity for detail and a long memory that were essential for firm administration. Work was certainly delegated but not without proper account being kept. When Sir John Boteler complained in 1465 that a servant of Alice's had taken 'the stonys of a grete walle' from his property in Berrick Salome over twenty years before and used them to repair the manor house at nearby Ewelme, Alice ordered her council to hold an inquiry. The investigation, duly recorded in a written memorandum, revealed that Alice's father, Thomas Chaucer, had bought the stones and that they had been used to repair Ewelme church. To her servant William Bilton she wrote about her books in her 'closette by grounde', which were to be put somewhere else in case of harm; about 'my litill cofre of gould', that he was to send to London, 'by some sure felyship . . . y^t it be surely sent'; and about money. Of this last 'xx^{li} in grotis oute of a bagge leeing upon the coffre in my closet', she wanted the remainder after certain named persons had received small sums with a list of precisely who had had what and she warned Bilton, 'take good hyde about you for sherewes ben nyghe'.[35]

Perhaps the experience of trouble in East Anglia bred a particularly hardened type, for, as de la Pole political ascendency was eclipsed in the 1450s and 1460s, there emerged from the opposing Mowbray camp a woman of comparable influence and ability. The name of Elizabeth Talbot, duchess of Norfolk, was to be invoked more often than any other by Sir John Paston and his brother during the long years in which they sought the recovery of Caister. Sir John never ceased to ask his brother's help in importuning the duchess nor, in spite of delays and negative replies, in believing that ultimately she would be his salvation. Throughout 1472 he wrote extensively of her influence as an intercessor with her husband and with some confidence since, 'every man tellyth me that my Lady seyth passyngly well of me allweys notwithstandyng'.[36] He worried late in the year at possible misinterpretation of his remarks to Elizabeth on her pregnancy when he told her directly, 'my Lady was large and grete, and that itt [the child], sholde have rome inow to goo owt att'.[37] He worried too that no messages would reach Elizabeth as she withdrew for the birth and so he sought and acknowledged another telling influence: 'that my moodre, iff she weer at Norwyche, she myght speke with hyr, for that she is a woman and off worshyppe. I thynke that my moodre sholde meve my Lady moche.'[38] From 1473–5 inquiries touching Elizabeth's support continued to pour from Paston pens. John assured his brother in October 1475, 'My lady sweryth . . . that she wold as fayne ye had it as eny body', but as progress was negligible he wrote that he was leaving Norfolk's service.[39] The suddenness of Norfolk's death on 17 January 1476 took everyone by surprise. Sir John lost no time in sending his own man to Caister and he parried criticisms of unseemly behaviour and warnings of Elizabeth's displeasure. There was a new danger now, for the duchess was pregnant again: 'lat us alle prey God sende my Lady of Norffolk a soone, for uppon that restythe moche mater; ffor if the Kyngys soone mary my lords dowghtr, the Kynge wolde that hys soone sholde have a ffayr place in Norffolk.'[40] In February the young John informed his brother that he had reassured the duchess about rumours that Sir John purposed to take advantage of the frozen moat to force an entry. Within five months Caister had been recovered.[41] Just how much was due to Elizabeth Talbot must remain beyond certainty, but the Paston letters are a rich source for that intangible element of female influence which was a power at work in fifteenth-century East Anglia.[42]

Though Christine de Pisan gave little attention to educating women in the business of administration she had plenty to say about their actual participation in estate management. It formed the substance of the seventh teaching of Prudence as well as two other chapters of the manual.[43] As such the work bears close comparison with the thirteenth century rules for the widowed countess of Lincoln known as *Saint Robert's Rules*.[44] Four treatises belong to this era, all of a distinctly practical nature, of which only the *Rules* were specifically intended for a manorial lord, though it is not now known whether they were requested by or offered to Countess Margaret. It is futile to argue either that this reflects upon the lady's greater need for guidance or, conversely, that it demonstrates her greater assiduousness in administration, since proof of both is wanting. It does, however, seem rather extraordinary that with a work of the popularity of Walter of Henley's *Husbandry* no copies are known to have belonged to a manorial lord although one turned up in the commonplace book of a seigneurial lady. Walter's modern editor suggests, however, that it was being read by lords in the later middle ages and was popular with monastic communities even though it was more applicable to lay estates.[45] The anonymous *Seneschaucy* did not fare much better though the placing of a chapter on the lord's duties ahead of that on the duties of his staff suggests that some copyists believed lords would profit from a perusal of its contents.[46]

The *Rules*, containing some thirty clauses based entirely on good administrative practice, pre-supposed a fundamental ability to supervise officials and the workings of the household. They left nothing to chance, no place for shirking responsibility. An intimate knowledge of each property, its customs, and services was deemed essential. 'If plaintiffs come to you about injuries done them or demands made on them', he advised, 'you yourself ought to study your rolls concerning that manor.'[47] The *Rules* covered everything from budgeting to administration of escheats and wardships. The burden which they represented may have seemed altogether too demanding for the countess for she remarried very soon after her first husband's death. Over the ensuing centuries similar works intended for the guidance of women appeared. *The Book of the Knight of La Tour-Landry* contained a knight's instructions for his three daughters. The knight's other book of his instructions for his son is only known by his passing references to it in the former.[48] The *Menagier de Paris*, described by its editor as 'by far the most exhaustive treatise on household management which has come down to us from the middle ages', was the work of an elderly Parisian for a young wife whom he expected would remarry when he died, and, for a non-aristocratic audience, the English poem *How the Good Wijf taughte Hir Doughter* addressed many issues basic to sound governance.[49]

Christine de Pisan's manual, however, broke new ground for it was the first piece to be written by a woman for other women and its comprehensive nature is striking. Revenues and expenditure; appointment and dismissal of servants; sound knowledge of the law and local customs; competence in the field of war and defence; a grasp of seasonal work, including ploughing and sowing; and all aspects of husbandry, including care of stock, were part and parcel of the daily grind on a large estate. It remained for Christine, in many ways, man's work which had to be performed according to the habits and practices of dead or absent lords and at several points she urged her readers to adopt the 'heart', or the 'spirit', of a man. In legal matters she wrote plainly, 'if she wants to win, she must adopt a man's heart (in other words, constant, strong, and wise)'. She knew well the weaknesses and the reputation of her own kind for she went on to warn, 'she must not collapse like a simple woman into tears and sobs'.[50] In practice surviving evidence points to a considerable toughness and tenacity by women who found themselves in charge, many displaying a more exacting rule than their partners.

Once married, women are notoriously difficult to trace at work. Surviving estate documents seldom refer to a wife's participation even during prolonged periods of her husband's absence. The warrant of Katherine Neville, duchess of Norfolk, to her husband's receiver-general, ordering him to pay John Home, while the duke was in London for Henry VI's coronation, is a rare survival in terms of this type of document, although there must have been many similar ones. None of the surviving receiver-general's accounts for the duke gives any hint of Katherine's activities although all three relate to years during which John Mowbray was absent, in one instance for the entire twelve months.[51] In spite of this it is not difficult to support the contention that it was not some effacing law which determined the course of personal relationships between husband and wife – theirs was a partnership. Legal dependence of wives on husbands looks far more like inter-dependency when examined closely.

Here, of course, the historian is helped by the letter collections of the fifteenth century. These are too well known to need much discussion here, save only to recall that the concerns are not simply those of household organisation, food or clothing. In September 1465 John Paston wrote exactingly to his wife although he had seen her in London shortly before.

> Item, I pray yow remembir and rede often my bille of erandes, and this letter, till it be don; and all such maters or articles as ye spede herof, crosse hem yat ye may knowe hem from tho yat be not sped; and send me answere of your good speed. . . . Though I write certeynly, if ye loke hem lightly and see hem seld thei shall sone be forgete.[52]

On that occasion he addressed her as 'myn owne dere sovereyn lady' and she could justifiably describe herself as his 'captainess', she who routinely undertook rent collecting, bargaining, counselling, accounting, and the endless defence of Paston property.

Another sign of this mutual respect and co-operative effort can be detected in a couple's attitude to their holdings. The law dictated that upon marriage a woman's property passed under the control of her husband, but it is evident that, in practice, a clear distinction was often made between their respective lands. This might on occasion enable wives to dispose of their own property. Joan de Geneville, countess of March, used part of her inheritance in favour of younger sons.[53] More commonly wives were specifically involved in matters directly concerning their lands. This was particularly likely where the wife was wealthier or of higher rank than her husband. Henry, Lord Stafford was largely dependent upon the income of his wife Lady Margaret Beaufort and she was with Stafford when they toured her estates in the West Country in 1467.[54] Sometimes the distinction was maintained for practical reasons. Jasper, duke of Bedford treated the estates of Katherine, dowager duchess of Buckingham as a separate unit after their marriage, partly out of administrative convenience.[55] A hint of some kind of distinction lies behind James Arblaster's direction to the bailiff of Maldon in 1472 that he be 'redy with all the accomptanttys belongyng to my lady'. Elizabeth, duchess of Norfolk's interests were to be dealt with separately even in her husband's lifetime.[56] Elizabeth Stonor, whose London connections from her first husband were so useful to her second, spent a good deal of time among mercers in the city, writing to William Stonor about their business affairs.[57] Records of legal proceedings show women joining forces with their husbands in matters concerning their own estates and, in many instances, their dower from previous marriages. Just such a case was brought by John and Margaret Elys against John Welles of Cambridge who 'by cunning and sotell imagination', as minister of the ordinary, had tampered with the will of Margaret's father Robert Couper. They complained that 'he hath overdrawed with ynke repelled and annulled', the clause in Robert's will leaving his property to Margaret.[58]

The joint venture was perhaps most seriously tested in practice in times of stress. Medieval women took their fair share of assault and battery in the name of family property. Sometimes the most ordinary administrative tasks could lead to disaster. J.C. de Croidoun complained in the early fifteenth century that a bailiff of the archbishop of Canterbury had attacked and 'defoilla carnelement' his wife Margery who was simply 'passant a surveier ses servantz overantz en le champe'.[59] On a larger scale defence of home and castle was a sufficiently regular occurrence for Christine de Pisan to include advice in her manual on weapons, how to attack or defend and how best to command men-at-arms.[60] The experiences of Margaret Paston do not by any means stand alone here. In the thirteenth century Nichola de la Hay earned the gratitude of King John for her defence of Lincoln Castle.[61] In 1338 William Montague, earl of Salisbury, found himself unable to make any headway against Agnes, countess of Dunbar who defended Dunbar castle for nineteen weeks, forcing the English to abandon their attempted assault.[62] Three years later while the same earl was a prisoner in France his own wife successfully resisted the efforts of King David of Scotland to take Wark-on-Tweed. Jean Le Bel describing Katherine de Grandison as 'une des belles et des vaillans dames d'Angleterre', recorded how she held the town on the first day and how 'la vaillant dame reconfortoit tousjours ceulx du chastel, et vrayement, au confort et au regard de telle dame, ung homme en debvoit valoir deux au besoing'. Overnight the countess despatched her husband's nephew to Edward III who at once repaired to her rescue and it was because of her stout defence of his interests, according to Le Bel, that the King subsequently sought her favours.[63] The wives of lesser landholders were no less adept, some displaying a *sangfroid* which is more arresting than the story of the attack itself. There is an extraordinary calm in the now lost letter which Joan Pelham addressed to her husband at the end of the fourteenth century. She began in due humility expressing affection and thanks for his letter. She wished him success over his enemies and stated her desire for further news. Then she wrote,

> iff it lyke zow for to know off my ffare, I am here by layd in manner of
> a sege with the counte of Sussex, Sudray and a great parcyll off Kente,
> so that I ne may noght out nor none vitayles gette me.

She suggested he consult his council if he thought fit to send some aid and after a comment redolent of fairly dire straits – 'this cuntree have yai wastede' – she closed with the blessing, 'the Holy Trinyte zow kepe fro zour ennemys'.[64] Sometimes the exchanges between the lady and her assailant were exceedingly blunt and defiant, as in the case of Jane Prince in the 1470s or Alice Knivet in 1461 who shouted at the King's commissioners that if they attempted to enter Buckenham Castle (Norf.) she would defend it 'for lever I had in suche wyse to dye than to be slayne when my husband cometh home, for he charget me to kepe it'.[65]

For both men and women recourse to the law for matters relating to property was common place and the latter displayed a shrewd grasp of the system and an ability to pursue their interests through its various channels. The surviving accounts of Elizabeth Berkeley, countess of Warwick, cover a period when she, at the centre of the Great Berkeley Lawsuit, was alone for several months while the earl was in France. The suit concerned her claims to the Berkeley inheritance and she appeared in person before the king's council at Westminster to plead her case against James Berkeley.[66] The same James could evidently boast a wife of equal calibre. Smith's *Lives* describes Lady Isabel as 'principal stay and follower of their suits and business'. The lady herself had no doubts about her abilities when she wrote to Lord James, 'keep well about you 'till I come home and treat not without me and then all things shall be well.'[67]

Christine de Pisan was a little ambiguous about women and the law. At heart she apparently felt that it should be avoided but could see that women should defend their rights 'boldly by law and reason'.[68] In practice many women brought law suits particularly as widows, these last often doing so in order to secure their dower or bequests made by their husbands which were being retained by feoffees and executors. Margaret de la Pole, countess of Lincoln, brought suits against the prior of Bromholme who owed her £20 granted to her out of one of her husband's manors and against John Dryland for detinue of deeds.[69] Margaret, Lady Powis sued her half brother John, Lord Audley and the bishop of Hereford who refused to deliver an obligation given as security for the performance of her marriage.[70] Between 1473 and 1476 Anne Neville, dowager duchess of Buckingham had suits pending against twenty-three people for recovery of debts and Lady Margaret Beaufort, as guardian of Edward, duke of Buckingham, brought twenty-eight suits for debt on her ward's estates in 1497–8, just before he came of age. Of Margaret Beaufort it can fairly be said that an acute sense of her legal rights and pursuit of her dues by legal means was one of the keys to her highly successful administration.[71]

Equally, many women were impleaded for all manner of misdemeanours from assaults, false actions of debt, detine of goods, chattels or muniments and even to murder. A group of Welshmen appealed to Henry Beaufort, bishop of Winchester, about the oppressions and trespasses of Joan, Lady Abergavenny, and her steward in the duchy of Lancaster lordship of

Monmouth which had resulted in the death of one poor individual who 'because yat he compleyned hym they hanged hym withoute any processe'.[72] The blatant aggression of some wives was patently a great headache on occasions. John de Bradbourne found himself accused by John Doune esquire of Utkinton, the master forester of Delamere, not on account of his own behaviour, but rather that of his wife. Doune appealed to chancery that Cecily, blaming him for the death of a son by a previous marriage, sent her servants daily to murder him and her servants.[73] Litigiousness in the fifteenth century was not by any means a characteristic limited to landed men.

It is primarily among archival material relating to widows that the most copious evidence for women in charge of property is to be found. With their common law dower of one-third of their dead husband's estates, often swollen by substantial jointures and, in some cases, by bequests of life interest in an inheritance made by their dying lords, they could exercise exclusive control over and full responsibility for land. Legally recognised as *femme sole*, the widow who chose to remain *in pura vidua etate sua* finally received positive acknowledgement and outward acceptance as master of her due portion.[74] Accounts, valors, deeds, acquittances, letters, and legal documents at last reflected absolutely what, in many cases, she had probably had a considerable role in during her marriage, and it is these that stand as judge and jury of her administrative acumen.

A precise quantitative evaluation of instances of land in the hands of women presents some tough challenges but, although an accurate figure of the proportion of estates so administered is not possible, something less impressionistic than the simple statement that dowagers were common in the later middle ages may be achieved. Cokayne's *Complete Peerage* describes 151 titles which, according to modern doctrine, were held by various families in the course of the fifteenth century in England.[75] Between 1400 and 1500, 495 individuals lived and died as holders of these titles.[76] Of these, 120 were either widowers, unmarried or cannot be certainly said to have left a widow. It is, of course, difficult to quantify the impact of the 375 widows. Their survival meant that 76 per cent of noble estates were reduced by at least one third for, on average, a period of seventeen years.[77] Jointures and gifts *in extremis* would tend to increase this fraction. While forfeiture resulting from treason and attainder worked in the opposite direction, it is not likely to reduce the overall minimum fraction of one-third. Certainly the case of Elizabeth, countess of Oxford, shows how women could suffer, but most enjoyed the legal protection for their jointures and most saw attainders reversed.[78]

The income tax returns for 1436, for all their limitations, contain data of unique value. The English higher nobility then comprised three dukedoms and eleven earldoms.[79] Of these, the dukedom of Norfolk and the earldom of Arundel were held by minors and the total value declared for the rest was £13,108.[80] The twelve adult peers were barely half the story of aristocratic wealth in 1436, for three duchesses and ten countesses controlled a significant proportion of the estates being administered by the greatest English landowners. Margaret Holland, duchess of Clarence and Katherine Neville, duchess of Norfolk, with six countesses[81] declared net incomes totalling £4,802 – a 27 per cent share of the value of aristocratic estates. In 1953 Ross and Pugh, reassessing the returns, identified as 'a substantial omission', dower incomes not included in the baronial schedule.[82] Firstly, the earls of Warwick and Huntingdon were married to the dowager countesses of Worcester and Arundel respectively.[83] Secondly, Margaret, duchess of Clarence, was also dowager countess of Somerset.[84] More substantial than these, however, were the properties held by Jacquetta, duchess of Bedford, Constance Holland, countess Marshal, Anne Talbot, countess of Devon, Alice Sergeaux, countess of Oxford and Isabel Russell, countess of Wiltshire for whom no declarations were made.

Ross and Pugh suggested that the duke of Bedford's assessment would have equalled that of Gloucester so, by allowing Jacquetta one-third of that figure, she would have had a minimum income of £525.[85] Of the four 'hidden' countesses, all had remarried, thereby in theory surrendering full authority to their new husbands. It has already been suggested that a distinction was maintained between the lands of husband and wife and that this may have been especially so where second or third husbands were of lower social status. In 1436 this may have been no more than a convenient excuse to avoid tax, but the countesses Devon, Oxford and Marshal had all disparaged themselves on remarrying. Anne Talbot had administered her large share of the Devon estates for some ten years before her second marriage, while Alice Sergeaux had spent four years in charge of her dower before marrying her esquire Nicholas Thorley. It is not known exactly when Constance Holland remarried, but she was an experienced administrator. It was to her, not to her husband, that Henry IV had pointedly granted Mowbray property as gradually he made restoration to the family of his old adversary, Thomas, duke of Norfolk (d. 1399).[86] John Lewys, the couple's receiver, was Constance's man, his early career having been in the service of the Hollands, and his appointment on 1 October 1401 was as receiver of *her* lands which he was to administer to *her* best advantage.[87] As widow of a condemned traitor after 1405, Constance faced exclusion from her dower but persuaded her royal uncle to override the law. Having struggled thus, and with her brother-in-law the Mowbray heir, she received a substantial livelihood and was probably celibate until 1413 when she married Sir John Grey.[88] The last 'hidden' countess, Isabel Russell, is of little relevance so far as administration is concerned as her petition for dower in the lands of her traitorous husband had not been granted. The three countesses between them probably commanded estates worth £1,883.[89]

Conclusions based upon the 1436 figures must, of course, be tentative. Firstly, the two excluded earls need to be added, bringing the total assessed wealth of the upper ranks of peers to some £14,458.[90] The proportion of this held by all their female counterparts amounted to one-third. It is impossible to know how accurate or how typical such a figure may be, but there is surely enough evidence to substantiate the simple statement that dowagers were common in the later middle ages and that they could marshal between them an extensive administrative expertise. What did it all involve in practice and how well did such landowners fare?

Christine de Pisan was well placed to give practical advice to widows. She acknowledged the need for mourning deceased husbands, but urged the noblewoman not to over-indulge her sorrow, rather to ply her mind and action to the understanding and fulfilment of her husband's will and the pursuit of her dower rights.[91] The first of these was often onerous, complex, and fraught with practical difficulties and delays.[92] Equally entangled was the assignment and securing of dower. Of the logistics of this there are but passing glimpses, but it raises again difficult questions about consultation and influence on escheators, jurors, feoffees, and heirs. One tiny example provided by the circumstances surrounding the sudden death of John, duke of Norfolk, in January 1476 suggests that lobbying in the right quarter could be important. Sir John Paston, still chasing the elusive restoration of Caister, was warned by his brother that the duchess might occupy the place herself. In spite of an advanced pregnancy and, doubtless, shock and grief, Elizabeth Talbot had seen her danger. On 3 February John Paston reported, 'it is promysyd my lady by my Lord Chamberleyn that the *diem clausit extremum* for my lord shall not be delyverd tyll she be of power to labore hyr sylff her most avauntage in that mater'.[93] There was evidently scope for a widow to play an active role in the settlement of the deceased's estate though how many did and to what effect must remain at best speculative.

In the actual assignment of dower the award of whole manors was presumably fairly straightforward. The property simply passed intact, often with the same officials in charge, to the dowager, though it was not uncommon for the heir's receiver-general to continue to enter the name of the estate on his lord's annual account with an appropriate explanation regarding its revenue. Actual thirds left two administrative choices – either receipt by the widow of one-third of the clear value from the heir's officials or some scheme for sharing the administration. Both arrangements had their problems. In 1403 the receiver of Elizabeth Fitzalan, duchess of Norfolk, accounted for thirds of several small Suffolk estates, noting that his lady's son, the earl Marshal, had received the profits and that nothing had come to him.[94] The earl's accounts do not record payment being made for these although they do show payment of shares in the profits of three larger East Anglian manors.[95] A different arrangement pertained in South Wales where Elizabeth's dower assignment complicated the accounts of Sir Hugh Waterton, the custodian of the lordship of Gower during the earl Marshal's nonage. He made constant reference to receipts being reduced owing to the duchess's third, but recorded that the wages of local officials were sometimes being paid, two-thirds by him and one-third by Elizabeth.[96] Some divisions of property were nothing short of tortuous. Elizabeth, Lady Zouche's dower included an assignment of five parts of a messuage, seven shops, and 27s. 8d. in London, divided into twelve, while that of her mother, Elizabeth, Lady Despenser, could not be precisely divided to the last penny and so contained a proviso for the rendering of an excess of 10s 4d to her son.[97]

Such administrative nightmares and the letter of the duke of Suffolk of 1450 present a need to assess the attitudes of heirs to surviving mothers, grandmothers or sisters-in-law. It is tempting to move to the conclusion that the late middle ages was peopled with disgruntled heirs much preoccupied with ill-wishing their mothers to an early grave. Certainly in many instances sons stood to gain materially from their mother's death, but much evidence suggests that they generally set a high premium on the experience and expertise of a mother's lifetime sharing in estate administration. This more positive view may perhaps be explained by the simple fact that widows were sufficiently numerous in the period to be regarded as a perfectly normal feature of life and provision for them to be only proper and fitting.[98] The Paston boys did not dwell on the longevity of the matriarchs of the family nor on the resulting diminution of their own holdings. John Paston's last surviving letter to his mother is a fine tribute from a son to one whom he regarded with immense respect.

Modyr, savyng your pleasure, ther nedyth non enbasatours nor meanys betwyx yow and me; for ther is neyther wyff nor other frend shall make me to do that that your comandment shall make me to do, if I may have knowlage of it.

He went on to promise her total commitment as executor of her will for he said:

I wot well non oo man a lyve hathe callyd so oft upon yow as I. . . . Also at the makyng of your wylle. . . . I nevyr contraryed thyng that ye wold have don and performed, but alweyso ffyrd my sylff to be bownde to the same.[99]

Throughout the Paston correspondence there are innumerable tributes, comments and acknowledgements regarding the advice and help of Margaret.

Such declarations were, moreover, not merely the product of a healthy respect engendered by strict upbringing. Active co-operation in a society that did not regard dependence as something regrettable was entirely normal. Maud, Lady Grey of Rotherfield was widowed in June 1375 and on 8 August wrote to the chancellor saying that she had agreed with her son about what precisely she should have in dower.[100] Similar arrangements for the widow of Thomas of Brotherton and Elizabeth, Lady Zouche, noted that assignments had been made with the assent of the heirs.[101] Self-interest must have encouraged co-operation for it was clearly not in the interest of the heir to see any diminution of what at some point, however distant, would fall to him. This applied even to the most minor aspects of inheritance. Agnes Paston held the advowson of Oxnead as part of her dower and presented to the living in 1475. In 1478 her rights there were threatened by the duke of Suffolk who had already made a false presentation at Drayton. Sir John Paston's intervention on her behalf was the product of genuine concern for her rights, but tinged with that element of self-interest. He wrote to his brother:

> Item, bothe ye and I most neds take thys mater as owr owne, and it weer ffor noon other cawse butt ffor owr goode grawnt dames sake; neverthelesse ye woote well thatt ther is an other entresse longyng to usse afftr her dyscease.

In the following year Agnes's son William wrote to her servant Richard Lee when his mother's rights there were again under threat.[102]

It would be false to suggest that women could always manage on their own without the help or advice of male members of the family – Agnes Paston's problems over her advowson show that just like lords, ladies did not find administration always ran smoothly – nor would it be correct to pass over serious friction between relatives over the assignment to, or holding of property by, surviving mothers. Relations between Agnes Paston and John Paston I were poor and between Sir John and his mother Margaret they were also sometimes very strained. But so too were such relations between the menfolk of that family who clashed for reasons of inheritance, wills, and landed divisions.[103] From the time of Glanvill a need had been recognised for provision of a remedy at law in instances of unfair measurement of thirds.[104] Problems over waste were a genuine cause of concern although where widows were guardians of their sons' property they took great care of the estates in their charge. Just as heirs had good reason to protect a mother's dower, so too did widows have a certain self-interest to encourage the maintenance of the land which sustained them. Elizabeth, Lady Clifford (d. 1424), brought two cases in chancery during her widowhood, one against some Hartlepool ruffians detaining rents and services due to her as guardian of her son and another against an individual committing waste in one of her parks.[105] It might be supposed that her own income was her primary concern on both occasions, but whatever combination of interests was involved, it is quite clear that motivation pointed broadly in the direction of the integrity of the estates and the receipt of revenues.

It has already been shown how widows sometimes had to use the law against their husband's feoffees, executors or third parties and occasionally these actions were directed at sons or daughters. Joan Wyte of Cranbrook and Mary Stapledon both used the law against their children in pursuit of dower claims, but such cases are not common.[106] It was in cases concerning stepsons and stepmothers that the greatest friction seems to have occurred. There was a strong temptation for those who were only life tenants to extract what they could from property, especially if these subsequent unions produced no children. Such seems to have been the experience of Elizabeth, Lady Zouche. The daughter of Edward Despenser, she married and produced a son by Sir John D'Arundel. Widowed in 1391, she was for a brief and childless period married to William, Lord Zouche. At his death in 1396 she was duly assigned dower in Zouche property with, as has been shown, the assent of her stepson and she seems to have resided at the Zouche manor at Eaton Bray in Bedfordshire. It was from there in 1402 that she wrote a number of letters to her receiver, John Bore, which suggest a continuing need for care and tenacity on her part regarding her Zouche estates.[107] She informed Bore that her stepson William had visited her at Eaton where she had evidently raised some contentious issues concerning firstly her servant Broke and a tenant. She described how Zouche 'hath rejagged broke ryght foule for hys doyng', which, judging from Elizabeth's subsequent comment, 'I wolde not fayle Mr. Brook at this tyme for more than hit is x tyme worth', was not quite what she wanted. There was also some business outstanding regarding her Zouche manor of Calston in Wiltshire and Lord William had bid her send her council to speak with him in London and show him the 'evedences' concerning the property. Elizabeth was firm with Bore, 'wanne ye hand all i-do with the Endentours that ye wole late putte hem alle to gader in the grete Coffyn and sende hem hom to Eytoun'. She ordered Bore to buy a piece of cheap cloth for Lord Zouche and ask him for 'the reles of Chychyly and Skot' as he had promised. Here too was sign of tension for the letter was endorsed by Bore to the effect that he procured the cloth and had secured Scot who was Zouche's prisoner, delivering him to his lady at Eaton on 29 April, six weeks after receiving his instructions.[108]

Securing dower could also be affected by the particular circumstances surrounding bereavement. Even at the best of times the death of a lord brought an unavoidable break in continuity and a degree of instability while, at the worst of times, usually in some political crisis, a widow might face an uphill struggle to secure her share. An example may easily be found in the person of Elizabeth Fitzalan. Her first marriage to William Montague had ended dramatically with his death in a tournament in 1382. A childless widow, she then married Thomas Mowbray, earl of Notting-ham, to whom she carried a number of Fitzalan estates as dowry. The association eventually brought her the dignity of duchess, but in the wake of Mowbray's disgrace by Richard II her position became precarious. As the duke was still alive in 1398, though in exile, Elizabeth could make no claim for dower, but confiscation of Mowbray estates by Richard had been done without regard for the duchess. Her father, brother, and husband had all been victims of the king and the passing references to her in this period suggest she was in dire straits, heavily dependent on the charity of one of her lord's servants.[109] The death of the duke of Norfolk in September 1399 did not really augur for better prospects since widows of traitors were barred from dower, but Henry IV, either because he had planned to re-instate the duke, or out of a sense of propriety, heard Elizabeth's plea for dower. A privy seal warrant of 6 November 1399 made a grant to her as countess of Norfolk 'en aide de sa vivre et de son etat plus honnour-ablement maintenir et sustener' and in the following months she received *ad hoc* grants as she 'is not yet dowered . . . neither has she any lands for her abode as she ought'.[110] It was not until the end of May that a proper order to the escheators was dispatched to assign formal dower and it took until 1402 to complete the settlement.[111] Elizabeth solidly kept a wary eye on the whole business. Receiving a substantial assignment of Suffolk property on 10 July 1400, she made a suit in chancery that she should be dowered in future in any lands that her husband had held, but which might not have appeared in his inquisition *post-mortem*.[112]

Scarcely less fraught were the circumstances faced by Joan, countess of March. Following the execution of her faithless husband, Roger Mor-timer, notorious lover of Edward II's queen, Edward III took steps to protect her interests in spite of the law on widows of traitors.[113] Attention, however, came to focus on Joan's own estates, notably the lordship and liberty of Trim, in Ireland. The Irish government, fully aware of its considerable value and taking advantage of its proximity and Joan's absence, seized the lordship in 1331. Joan's absence proved no stumbling block. She obtained from the king an exemplification of Henry II's grant to her forbears on the grounds that her own copy was rather aged and worn; appointed her own attorneys to take seisin of her lands; and appealed for justice.[114] In 1336, 1341, and 1347 the lordship was seized on various occasions, the last being in spite of a royal assurance that the liberty would not be taken again without prior reference to the king and council in England.[115] Joan petitioned in 1347 saying she was 'of such age that she cannot go to Ireland without the greatest peril of her body',[116] but few of her peers, men or women, visited their Irish estates and certainly in Joan's case, helped by her regular appointment of attorneys, many of whom served on more than one occasion, it was possible to keep control and she passed her Irish lands intact to her grandson, Roger Mortimer, second earl of March before she died in 1355.[117]

Dower settlement completed, administration was fundamentally conducted along the same lines as it had been during the husband's lifetime. Maintaining the familiar system, providing it worked, was the obvious line of least resistance and one of the best tools was to be found in using, where possible, the same officials, particularly in the upper ranks of the administrative heirarchy.[118] At the hub of the administration lay the widow's council upon which she, like her deceased husband, relied for advice. The importance of this body is not to be measured by the extant evidence of its activities. It was as indispensable to the widow as it had been to the lord and is just as elusive to the historian of either. Contemporaries fully recognised the threat that a well co-ordinated council could present. Margaret Paston warned her son in 1466 not to tackle Alice de la Pole without taking some of his own councillors with him for she said, 'she is sotill and hath sotill councell with here'.[119] The long absences of lords had given wives an opportunity to establish a rapport with the councillors and probably to preside over meetings. Elizabeth Talbot, duchess of Norfolk, was well accustomed to working with her husband's council and its members paid due regard to her. On more than one occasion reference was made to 'ther concell' and indeed there is some evidence that Elizabeth had her own distinct council during Norfolk's lifetime.[120] Many were happy to remain in the widow's service, especially if the heir was a minor, an indicator that service was, at least in some measure, to the family and for the future preservation of the inheritance. Examples of such loyalty may be observed in the cases of de Vere councillors, John Josselyn and James Arblaster.[121]

Elizabeth Fitzalan's reliance upon her husband's servants in 1398–9 has already been cited and it is known that the duchess had as her receiver Edward Rongton who had been in Norfolk's service since 1390 and enjoyed an annuity charged upon Mowbray estates.[122] Of even greater importance to Elizabeth was her husband's annuitant and attorney, Sir Robert Goushill. He petitioned on the duke's behalf for the office of marshal at Henry IV's coronation in 1399 apparently unaware that his lord was already dead. The following year he was with the duchess when she received the duke's remaining goods and by 1401 the pair had married without the king's licence.[123] Examples of marriages between widowed countesses and duchesses and the servants of their deceased husbands are common.[124] These unions may suggest a propensity among aristocratic women for conducting affairs, perhaps in the long absence of their lords, but they may be the quite natural end to a long and close relationship between a mistress and a faithful servant in their administration of the estates, one which had grown into a genuine affection over the years. It is also possible that such liaisons represent some kind of move on the part of widows to guarantee the integrity of the inheritance, for such a servant, familiar with the workings and extent of the inheritance, could certainly be a valuable asset at a time of uncertainty. The former relationship between the two, of servant and mistress, might possibly have assured the widow of a greater degree of control over her estates than marriage to a new outside lord might allow.

Women were, of course, perfectly capable of appointing or dismissing servants of their own choosing. Selection was a skill much commented upon by the authors of treatises on estate management. If it is true that the success of an administration resulted substantially from the sum of the services of receivers, councillors, stewards, clerks, bailiffs, and reeves then it may also be true that sound judgement of character and shrewdness in choice of such persons was one of the most important attributes needed by a landlord. Second husbands and sons often showed their appreciation of the maternal choice by later taking into their own service individuals appointed by widows. Several of the servants of Anne, duchess of Buckingham served her grandson, Henry Stafford and Reginald Bray, devoted servant of Lady Margaret Beaufort survived all her marriages and widowhoods to be acknowledged in his last years by Margaret's royal son as a man of immense soundness and managerial skill.[125] Fair and proper dealing was vital to the maintenance of good relations between the servant and the mistress. A certain degree of harshness also had its place in any such relationship. Joan Beauchamp, Lady Abergavenny took recognis-ances from her officials in order to guarantee levels of revenue in 1427–8 and when a valor for Anne, countess of Stafford was made in 1436 it was noted that a roll of arrears was delivered to her for her own reference.[126] On the other hand women were often prepared to leap to the defence of servants and tenants. Margaret of Brotherton, whose treatment of her servants appears at times to have been rather dismal,[127] presents a wholly different approach in two surviving letters, one on behalf of 'our dear and beloved Thomas de Battiford' for whom she sought a protection in the king's service and the other for Oliver de Stratton, who had been wounded in France, for whom she requested exemption from collecting an aid.[128] Some women were put to considerable trouble on account of their servants. The fate of John Prince of Essex in the 1470s offers much insight into both the attitudes of servants and their treatment, and incidentally, the power of one woman's influence.

John Prince was a servant of Cecily Neville, duchess of York and became involved in a dispute over the manor of Theydon which he claimed as his rightful property. His claims were challenged by Thomas Wethiale who resorted to violent means to secure his ends. A group of his associates wearing the livery of Cecily's son, Richard, duke of Gloucester, attacked the manor while Prince was at home. Fearful, John retreated to a safe distance in nearby woods. Not so his wife Lucy who stood her ground. The dispute became heated, Lucy's antagonist suggesting that if her husband were 'bereked' she could marry Wethiale and have the land in peace. Lucy indignantly retorted that Wethiale was 'an unthrifty and lewde symple felawe' and said she would sooner see them all hanged. Both sides invoked their respective patrons before the interview came to a close. Prince appealed to the duchess who wrote to her son 'that no man intromitt wt oure said servaunts matier savyng onely oure counsel lerned and youres.' She wrote in similar vein to Gloucester's servant Sir Robert Chamberlain telling him that the matter would be decided by their councillors. In the end Cecily prevailed over the duke. Later, however, when Prince failed to reward an adviser in the dispute, the latter turned to Cecily who appointed her council to hear the complainant's case. Prince was charged with making proper restoration.[129] In the end a combination of respect, firmness, and protection characterised the relationship between lady and servant. Elizabeth, Lady Zouche began all surviving letters to John Bore with the words 'Ryght wel by loue frend', often adding solicitously, 'I grete you wel and desyre to here of youre wel fare'. Her dependence upon him was expressed when she wrote 'and alwey I pray you that ye wolen holde on' and her trust when she assured him regarding a deal made on her behalf 'wat hende that ye make with hym in any degre I a-sente fullych ther to'. Nevertheless the letters contained a flood of requests and orders which Bore was careful to fulfil with all due speed.[130]

If successful administration must ultimately be measured in financial terms, then some assessment must be made of a landlady's management of her income. It has already been seen how Alice de la Pole, Joan Beauchamp, Elizabeth, Lady Clifford and others, in their different ways, sought to secure their revenues. For ladies, as for lords, the randomness with which accounts have survived, imposes its own severe limits upon knowledge of baronial incomes. It is, however, a fortunate accident that the extant sources for the revenues of dowagers are among the best of their kind for the English nobility of the middle ages. Thus, those of Elizabeth de Burgh, Lady of Clare (d. 1360), comprise the most complete series for any individual of the period, with just over one hundred accounts remaining for the years 1325–60.[131] Lesser quantities survive for such figures as Anne of Woodstock, countess of Stafford, Anne Neville, duchess of Buckingham, Isabel, Lady Morley, Katherine Neville, duchess of Norfolk and Lady Margaret Beaufort. Broadly speaking, the format of these accounts is no different from that of accounts prepared for noblemen. It follows the well established practices of charge and discharge accounting. The heirarchy of officials reveals a similar adherence to normal practice with receivers-general, receivers, bailiffs, and reeves remaining largely unchanged. Innovation on a large scale was rare but some changes could be introduced by widows. Anne, countess of Stafford, placed greater power in the hands of the treasurer of her household than her husband had and Anne, duchess of Buckingham's successful experiment combining the post of treasurer and receiver-general was apparently followed by her grandson.[132] Whilst changes may not have been common there was certainly little indication of creeping decay or fossilisation. Elizabeth de Burgh's system of organisation seems to have been very up to date and, in spite of annual expenditure on her establishment of around £2,000, she was never apparently short of money. She had a number of treasuries conveniently set up in various lordships as well as her own coffer for private needs and she was in the habit of making regular loans to friends.[133] New accounting procedures were readily adopted by widows. Valors, intended as a guide to future income were regularly and effectively used by them. Although this development has been traced to 'the skilled officials' of the Duchy of Lancaster late in the fourteenth century, two very fine valors prepared for Elizabeth de Burgh in 1330 and 1339 suggest an earlier and different origin. Both valors are in French, perhaps to be more accessible to the lady herself. The earliest comprises nine membranes recording, in a neat hand, the clear values, after the allowances for fees, in each balliwick or receivership. Similarly that for 1339 records the values and remaining livestock and grains, noting in places that the revenues were lower than in previous years.[134] Falls in income were common occurrences in the later middle ages, not necessarily resulting from bad management and it is not to be expected that widows could escape the real difficulties involved in preserving the highest levels of revenue. Lady Elizabeth's accounts show individual manors reaching levels comfortably in excess of those in the earlier valor, even in post-plague periods.[135] Equally impressive are the valors for Anne, countess of Stafford for 1435–6 and for Joan, Lady Abergavenny for 1427–8.[136] The latter's valor as well as recording the values of her property includes a list of her retainers and their annuities.

'There is absolutely no shame', Christine de Pisan advised widows, 'in living within your income, however small it may be, but there is shame if creditors are always coming to your door'.[137] A certain amount of economising, strict control of expenditure, and a preoccupation with debts, owing and owed, are features common to a number of dowagers. The less politically oriented administrations of widows perhaps found it easier to reduce expenditure. The need for display was not quite so pressing as it was for their husbands. Anne Neville, dowager duchess of Buckingham, faced considerable debts on the Stafford estates but, by reducing her household and hence her expenditure and by controlling local expenditure, she brought a significant improvement to the family's finances.[138] Well ordered debt settlement can be seen in the cases of both Elizabeth, Lady Zouche and her mother, Elizabeth, Lady Despenser. The latter had perhaps taught her daughter a stout lesson in such matters for certainly a small bundle of receipts and acquittances show her, after some twenty years of widowhood, still regularly paying her deceased husband's annuitants and her farm of the Despenser lands in the minority of the heir.[139] A larger collection of Lady Zouche's acknowledgements of debts to London and alien merchants, together with the latter's acquittances, reveal an orderly and proper system for the settlement of bills.[140] Alice Fitzalan, countess of Kent (d. 1416), who remained in close touch with her son, Thomas, after he succeeded his father in the earldom, urged him to see that the family receiver in Lincoln who had served without a fee or allowances for expenses for eighteen years, was paid speedily, without further delay. The young earl was perhaps not as good at paying his debts to his servants as he ought, for his widow, in 1402, had a grant from the crown to pay her husband's followers.[141] Collecting outstanding debts was a common problem in the period. Women had no magic remedy for this ill but, as Joan Beauchamp's treatment of her officers has shown, a hard line could be pursued in the effort to reduce such sums to a minimum. Lady Margaret Beaufort's pursuit of her debtors has led her most recent biographers to accuse her of avarice and, indeed, it was a case of theft which apparently caused her to build a prison for malefactors. Nevertheless, she, like many others, could not always be sure of success, and Lady Margaret was forced in the 1490s to write off over £2,000 in unrecoverable monies.[142] Even the best run administrations had their weaker sides, especially where income was at stake.

It has not been the objective here to present some feminist viewpoints of women in the later middle ages, but rather, by perusal of some of the surviving contemporary evidence, to discover something of what it was really like to be a woman of property at that time. There are, firstly, several reminders of that gap between theory and practice, between what the law dictated and what individuals did, between what a didactic treatise advised and what form a particular action took, which must make the historian of medieval women keep a firm grasp upon reality and a constant eye upon the ladies themselves. Secondly, there are clear warnings about the distortion that can easily be created by trying to isolate women from their menfolk, in some futile effort to see if they were, or even could be 'free' or 'independent'. Such notions were not characteristics of their society. There were far more important considerations, like expanding and defending the mutual interests of the couple, contributing at every level to the preservation of the 'worship' of their husbands and sons; and ultimately, adapting effectively to that mutability of the human predicament which was the reality of their crowded existence. Finally, the challenge which life on a great estate presented is etched upon the evidence. It was tough. It was demanding. It was often lonely. Above all, it was endless. There was no simple formula for success, no way of avoiding the pitfalls. Their achievements, however, were real. They rested by and large upon the structures created by their own fathers or husbands, but modified by characteristics that, for all the imperfections, were innately their own. Such tenacity and resilience as they displayed was worthy of praise. 'Any man is extremely foolish', wrote Christine de Pisan, 'of whatever class he may happen to be, if he sees that he has a good and wise wife yet does not give her authority to govern.'[143] Very few, it would seem, were that foolish.

Notes

1. R.A. Griffiths, 'Public and Private Bureaucracies in England and Wales in the Fifteenth Century', *Transactions of the Royal Historical Society* 5th ser., 30 (1980), pp. 109–30.
2. See J.R. Lander, *Conflict and Stability in Fifteenth Century England* (1969), pp. 30–4, especially regarding the incompetence of Richard duke of York. J.M.W. Bean, *The Estates of the Percy Family 1416–1537* (Oxford, 1958), pp. 144–5 notes derogatory remarks made about the sixth Percy earl. See the letter of William Harleston to Sir William Stonor warning him after his wife's death to 'kepe yow with ynne yowr lyvelode': *The Stonor Letters and Papers*, ed. C.L. Kingsford, Camden Society, 3rd Series, 30 (1919), p. 98.
3. B.A. Holderness, 'Widows in Pre-industrial Society: An Essay upon their Economic Functions' in *Land Kinship and Life-Cycle*, ed. R.M. Smith (Cambridge, 1984), p. 425.
4. F. Pollock and F.W. Maitland, *The History of English Law Before the Time of Edward I* 2nd edition, 2 vols. (Cambridge, 1968), i, p. 482.
5. E. Power, *Medieval Women*, ed. M.M. Postan (Cambridge, 1975), pp. 38, 40.
6. K.B. McFarlane, *The Nobility of Later Medieval England* (Oxford, 1973), pp. 27–33, where particular reference is made to the wives of Sir John Bourgchier and Robert, Lord Hungerford. See also M.A. Hicks, 'Counting the Cost of War: the Moleyns Ransom and the Hungerford Land Sales 1453–87', *Southern History* 8 (1986), pp. 11–31. An excellent account of how complicated and protracted ransom proceedings could be is given by M.K. Jones, 'Henry VII, Lady Margaret Beaufort and the Orleans Ransom's in *Kings and Nobles in the Later Middle Ages*, ed. R.A. Griffiths and J. Sherborne (Gloucester, 1986), pp. 254–73. Jones discusses in detail the efforts of women on both sides to settle the Orleans ransom dispute.

7   M.A. Hicks, 'The Last Days of Elizabeth Countess of Oxford', *English Historical Review* 103 (1988), pp. 76–95, describes the great difficulties faced by Elizabeth de Vere following the imprisonment of her husband John. Elizabeth Howard, wife of the imprisoned earl of Surrey, provides a further example of women left alone trying to cope with the consequences of a husband's disgrace and endeavouring to secure the good lordship of those who had become powerful in the area: *The Paston Letters 1422–1504*, ed. J. Gairdner, 6 vols. (1904), vi, p. 87.

8   C.D. Ross, 'Forfeiture for Treason in the Reign of Richard II', *English Historical Review* 71 (1956), pp. 560–75, in which Ross examines in detail the fates of widows and wives of traitors, especially those in exile. See below p. 168 the fate of Elizabeth Fitzalan as wife of the exiled duke of Norfolk between 1398 and 1399.

9   Since crusading tended to become something of a family tradition some English families faced the absences of the lords on a number of occasions. See S. Lloyd, *English Society and the Crusade 1216–1307* (Oxford, 1988), pp. 102–3 and his remarks on how few women went themselves, pp. 77–8. C. Tyerman, *England and The Crusades 1095–1588* (Chicago, 1988), pp. 208–17 considers some of the risks to wives and property while husbands were on crusade. He discusses the continuing traditions of crusading and the hazards to wives, notably the case of Thomas of Burton imprisoned by the Mamluks and ransomed by his wife who, as a result of her efforts, was herself arrested, chapter 10, especially p. 284. M.H. Keen, 'Chaucer's Knight, the English Aristocracy and the Crusade', *English Court Culture in the Later Middle Ages*, ed. V.J. Scattergood and J.W. Sherborne (1983), pp. 50–8.

10   Pisan, *The Treasure*, p. 130.

11   M. Wade Labarge, *Women in Medieval Life* (1986), pp. 38–9; N. Orme, *From Childhood to Chivalry* (1984), pp. 31–2, 176, 212.

12   *Select Letters of Saint Jerome*, ed. F.A. Wright (1934), pp. 345–7.

13   A.L. Gabriel, 'The Educational Ideas of Vincent de Beauvais', in *Texts and Studies in the History of Medieval Education*, ed. A.L. Gabriel and J.N. Garvin, 4 (1956), pp. 38–40.

14   S.G. Bell, 'Medieval Women Bookowners: Arbiters of Lay Piety and Ambassadors of Culture', in *Women and Power in the Middle Ages*, ed. M. Erler and M. Kowaleski (Athens, Georgia, 1988), p. 162.

15   Pisan, *The Treasure*, pp. 66–8, 128.

16   Bell, 'Medieval Women Bookowners', pp. 160–1. See also McFarlane, *Nobility*, pp. 41–8 on preparedness of noblemen for estate management and pp. 228–47 on education of the nobility.

17   E.W. Ives, 'The Common Lawyers in Pre-Reformation England', *Transactions of the Royal Historical Society* 5th Ser., 18 (1968), quoted on p. 152.

18   Rowena E. Archer, 'The Estates and Finances of Margaret of Brotherton c.1322–1390', *Bulletin of the Institute of Historical Research* 60 (1987) pp. 268–9; see the unfavourable comments on her administration of Chepstow in *The Marcher Lordships of South Wales 1415–1536*, ed. T.B. Pugh (Cardiff, 1963), pp. 9–10.

19   *Paston Letters*, ii, pp. 142–3.

20   *North Country Wills*, ed. J.W. Clay, Surtees Society, 116 (1908), p. 51.

21   G.E. Cokayne, *The Complete Peerage*, ed. Vicary Gibbs *et al.*, 13 vols. (1910–59), xii, pt. i, p. 434; BL, Harleian Charter, 54.1.9.

22   C. Richmond, *The Paston Family in the Fifteenth Century: The First Phase* (Cambridge, 1990), pp. 53n, 146n. I am very grateful to Prof. Richmond for his advice and his help regarding Duchess Alice. C.A. Metcalfe, 'Alice Chaucer, Duchess of Suffolk c.1404–75' (unpublished dissertation, University of Keele, 1970).

23   CPR, 1429–36, pp. 298, 508; 1436–41, pp. 80, 306, 309, 310, 366, 426; 1441–46, pp. 63, 74, 90, 198, 218.

24 *The Itinerary of John Leland In or About the Years 1535–1543*, ed. L. Toulmin Smith, 6 vols. (1906), i, p. 112.
25 *Paston Letters and Papers of the Fifteenth Century*, ed. N. Davis, 2 vols. (Oxford, 1971), ii, p. 13; Richmond, *The Pastons*, p. 5.
26 Before 2 June 1448.
27 *The Records of the City of Norwich*, ed. W. Hudson and J.C. Tingey, 2 vols. (1906), i, p. 344. My thanks to Prof. Richmond for this reference. F. Blomefield, *An Essay Towards a Topographical History of the County of Norfolk*, 11 vols. (1805–10), iii, p. 154. R.L. Storey, *The End of the House of Lancaster* (1966), pp. 217–25, describes the troubles of Norwich though makes no mention of Alice's escapade and the consequences.
28 *Rotuli Parliamentorum*, ed. J. Strachey, 6 vols. (1767–77), v, pp. 216–17; Richmond, *The Pastons*, p. 214.
29 *Paston Letters*, iv, p. 25.
30 Ibid., v, p. 15.
31 Ibid., v, p. 155; and see, iv, p. 205; v, pp. 5, 11, 12–13. Another correspondent warned with regard to Cotton that when Alice seized it she would do so without warning: ibid., iv, p. 304.
32 BL, Egerton Roll, 8779; PRO, Early Chancery Proceedings, C1/25/77; 26/164; Court of King's Bench, Ancient Indictments, KB9/918, no. 22; CCR, *1447–54*, p. 476.
33 CFR, *1445–52*, p. 154: CPR, *1452–61*, p. 69; *1441–46*, p. 319; J.A.F. Thomson, 'John de la Pole, Duke of Suffolk', *Speculum* 56 (1979), p. 529. Thomson suggests that Alice was anxious to establish some link with York 'to have a foot in each camp'. Her life annuity to William Lord Hastings may have been granted at about this time for similar reasons. Hastings was certainly party to the marriage arrangements. For his annuity see Bodleian Library, Oxford (hereafter Bodl.) Ms. DD Ewelme, a.7, A44, 1–2 (dated 1462 and 1475); *CAD*, iv, p. 26–7.
34 BL, Egerton Roll, 8779.
35 Bodl., Ms. DD Ewelme, a.7, A46, A48, 1–3: undated letters, signed Alice.
36 *Paston Letters*, v, p. 133.
37 Ibid., v, pp. 156–7.
38 Ibid., p. 162.
39 Ibid., pp. 238, 240.
40 Ibid., pp. 249–50. There is no further mention of a child born to Elizabeth Talbot.
41 Ibid., pp. 251–2, 262.
42 For a further example of female influence see below p. 171 the case of Cecily Neville, duchess of York. See also Joan of Arc who recalled the kindnesses of two women during her captivity one of whom, the 'lady of Luxembourg', had pleaded with her nephew, John of Luxembourg, that Joan should not be handed over to the English. Pernoud suggests that the death of John's aunt cleared the way for him to deliver his captive: R. Pernoud, *Joan of Arc by Herself and Her Witnesses* (1964), pp. 156, 160. My thanks to Jeremy Goldberg for this reference.
43 Pisan, *The Treasure*, pp. 76, 128, 130. The seventh teaching is devoted to keeping a careful eye on revenues and finances.
44 *Walter of Henley's Husbandry*, ed. E. Lamont (1890), pp. 124–45; D. Oschinsky, *Walter of Henley and other Treatises on Estate Management and Accounting* (Oxford, 1971), pp. 288–407.
45 Ibid., pp. 7–11, 60. There are 35 extant copies of Walter of Henley. The copy in the commonplace book is in Bibliothèque Nationale, Paris, Ms. Francais, 400. There are 14 copies of the *Rules*. I have not come across reference to any treatises on estate management in surviving inventories of books belonging to the landowning classes. Among the 21 volumes brought from Wingfield to Ewelme, in 1466, there was a copy

of 'a frensh boke of la Citee de Dames', probably Christine de Pisan's *Book of the City of Ladies*: Bodl., Ms. DD Ewelme, a.7, A47.

46   Oschinsky, *Walter of Henley*, pp. 86, 87, 98. On the whole Princes were well catered for in terms of treatises designed to instruct them on behaviour essential to good government. Such treatises did also find their way into noble collections Among the de la Pole books at Ewelme was, 'a boke of Latyn of ye Moral Instruction of a Prince': Bodl., Ms. DD Ewelme, a.7, A47. See V.J. Scattergood, 'Literary Culture at the Court of Richard II', in *English Court Culture*, ed. Scattergood and Sherborne, pp. 34–41 for cases of noblemen and women owning such books.

47   Oschinsky, *Walter of Henley*, p. 389.

48   *The Book of the Knight of La Tour-Landry*, ed. T. Wright, EETS, 33 (1868), pp. 4, 115, 205.

49   *The Goodman of Paris*, ed. E. Power (1928), p. 7; 'How the Good Wijf Taughte Hir Doughter', in F.J. Furnivall, *Manners and Meals in Olden Time: The Babees Book*, EETS, 32 (1868).

50   Pisan, *The Treasure*, pp. 128, 129, 158.

51   Berkeley Castle, Muniments, Berkeley, Gloucestershire, General Charter 4164; Accompt Rolls, Box 19, No. 9 (accounts for 1414–15); Arundel Castle Archives, Ms. A1642 (accounts for 1420–1); BL, Additional Charter, 16555, 17209 (accounts for 1422–3). References to Katherine merely concern her journeys in these years.

52   *Paston Letters and Papers*, ed. Davis, i, pp. 144–5. For a letter in similar vein, ibid., p. 129.

53   *CPR, 1327–30*, p. 317. See below p. 168 for an account of her administration.

54   M.K. Jones and M.G. Underwood, *The King's Mother, Lady Margaret Beaufort Countess of Richmond and Derby* (Cambridge, 1992). I am grateful to Dr Jones for the opportunity to consult his chapters on Lady Margaret's lands and household.

55   C. Rawcliffe, *The Staffords, Earls of Stafford and Dukes of Buckingham 1394–1521* (Cambridge, 1978), pp. 55, 127.

56   *Paston Letters*, v, p. 149.

57   *Stonor Letters*, i, pp. xxvii–viii; ii, pp. 9–11, 13–19, 22. Elizabeth spent the latter part of 1476 in London partly for pleasure but also for business. Both activities suggest a certain freedom to do as she wished.

58   PRO, C1/13/64–74; 14/13. As so often the exact date of the suit and the incidents described are unknown, as is the outcome. For cases of wives joining husbands in suits concerning the wife's property – see C1/3/40; 14/12; 5/78; 4/151; 7/46, 171, 286; 8/15, 25; 9/56, 68, 110; 10/228, 295.

59   *Anglo-Norman Letters*, ed. M.D. Legge, Anglo-Norman Texts, iii (Oxford, 1941), p. 27.

60   Pisan, *The Treasure*, p. 129.

61   D.M. Stenton, *The English Woman in History* (1957), p. 37 gives a number of examples including Nichola, of women defending property.

62   *Complete Peerage*, iv, p. 507–8 and for a poem in celebration of 'Black Agnes' see *The Buik of the Croniclis of Scotland*, ed. W.B. Turnbull, 3 vols. Rolls Series, iii (1858), pp. 341–2.

63   *Chronique de Jean Le Bel*, ed. J. Viard and E. Deprez, Societé de l'Histoire de France, 2 vols. (Paris, 1904–5), i, pp. 284–90; *Complete Peerage*, vi, p. 388.

64   M.A. Lower, *Historical and Genealogical Notices of the Pelham Family* (n.p., 1873), p. 11.

65   For Jane Prince, see below; *CPR, 1461–67*, p. 67. By the end of the year John Knivet had received a licence to enter Bokenham and he and Alice had been pardoned all debts, ibid., p. 83.

66 C.D. Ross, 'The Household Accounts of Elizabeth Berkeley, Countess of Warwick', *Transactions of the Bristol and Gloucestershire Archaeological Society* 70 (1951). For a recent assessment of the lawsuit and Elizabeth's role see Alexandra Sinclair, 'The Great Berkeley Lawsuit Revisited 1417–39', *Southern History* 9 (1987), pp. 34–50.

67 *Smyth's Lives of the Berkeleys*, ed. J. Maclean, 3 vols. (Gloucester, 1883), ii, p. 62.

68 Pisan, *The Treasure*, pp. 157–8, 82.

69 PRO, C1/212/18, 19, *post* 1487.

70 Ibid. C1/43/28, c.1466–74.

71 Rawcliffe, *The Staffords*, pp. 179–80; Jones and Underwood, *The King's Mother*, ch. 4.

72 PRO, C1/26/616.

73 Ibid., C1/6/173. Other suits against women in Early Chancery Proceedings are common. See C1/5/69, 78; 6/79, 177, 234; 9/64, 220, 221, 431; 11/429; 12/57, 64, 188, 209.

74 R.E. Archer, 'Rich Old Ladies: the Problem of Late Medieval Dowagers' in *Politics and Property: Essays in Later Medieval English History*, ed. A.J. Pollard (Gloucester, 1984), pp. 16–19 on the development of the law on dower. PRO, Chancery Inquisitions *Post Mortem*, C139/146 for Margaret, Lady Grey of Wilton, making a grant '*in pura vidua etate sua*'. Bodl., Ms. DD Ewelme, a.6. A36, a grant of a Lady Clemence begins '*in libera viduitate mea et in legia potestatie mea*'.

75 This gives a broad sample though it includes such titles as Benhale, Heron, Hilton, and others which contemporaries would hardly have recognised. It, therefore, comprises the most aristocratic of English families. Scottish and Irish titles have not been included.

76 This comprises all those married or survived by a widow during these dates excluding those who eventually ascended the throne.

77 My mean length of widowhood is probably an underestimate. For 22 women known to have survived their husbands but whose date of death is unknown, I have allowed only one year of widowhood. Where a widow's death is given as between two dates the earliest year has been chosen. For example, Elizabeth, Lady Botreaux between 1405 and 1458.

78 Hicks, 'Last days of Elizabeth', pp. 76–95; J.R. Lander, *Crown and Nobility 1450–1509* (1976), pp. 127–58.

79 Gloucester, York, and Norfolk; Arundel, Devon, Huntingdon, Northumberland, Oxford, Salisbury, Somerset, Stafford, Suffolk, Warwick, and Westmorland.

80 No figures were given for Oxford or Westmorland.

81 Eleanor Berkeley (Arundel), Maud Lovell (Arundel), Maud Clifford (Cambridge), Joan Stafford (Kent), Anne of Woodstock (Stafford), Joan Beaufort (Westmorland).

82 H.L. Gray, 'Incomes from Land in England in 1436', *English Historical Review* 49 (1934), pp. 607–39; C.D. Ross and T.B. Pugh, 'The English Baronage and the Income Tax of 1436', *Bulletin of the Institute of Historical Research* 26 (1953), pp. 1–28, quote on p. 20.

83 Isabel, widow of Richard Beauchamp, earl of Worcester and Beatrice, widow of Thomas Fitzalan, earl of Arundel. Of these only Beatrice is named and only as wife of Huntingdon.

84 It is impossible to know if the valuation of £717 given for her estate allowed anything for her comital dower.

85 Ross and Pugh argued that Jacquetta's dower was not assigned until 1437. This is certainly the year of the enrolment of the assignment but a grant of 6 February 1436 suggests she may indeed have been dowered by the date of the tax. Ross and Pugh 'Income Tax' pp. 21, 26; Westminster Abbey Muniments, London, 12164.

86 The dispute between Bolingbroke and Mowbray had ended in a duel, terminated by Richard II and a sentence of exile. Constance enjoyed favour as Henry IV's niece. *CPR*, *1405–09*, pp. 331, 402.

87 Ibid., *1388–92*, p.1; *1396–99*, p. 267; *CCR*, *1405–09*, p. 301. Lewys was subsequently kept on as property was granted directly to Thomas Mowbray. BL, Add. Ch. 16556.

88 R.E. Archer, 'The Mowbrays, Earls of Nottingham and Dukes of Norfolk, to 1432' (unpublished D.Phil. thesis, University of Oxford, 1984), pp. 142–5. In 1413 Constance and Sir John quitclaimed their rights to any additional Mowbray property, for 5000 marks.

89 Constance's dower was probably worth £900 *p.a.*: Archer, 'The Mowbrays,' p. 144; Ross and Pugh suggest at least £133 for Anne Countess of Devon; and £250 can be allowed for the countess of Oxford based on her son's petition in 1437 that his lands (two thirds of the earldom) were worth £500: Ross and Pugh, 'Income Tax', p. 23; *CPR*, *1436–41*, p. 71, for Oxford's petition.

90 Oxford's petition allows a figure of £500: see above, note 89; and Westmorland's income was probably about £850: Ross and Pugh, 'Income Tax', p. 18.

91 Pisan, *The Treasure*, p. 81.

92 R.E. Archer and B.E. Ferme, 'Testamentary Procedure with Special Reference to the Executrix', *Reading Medieval Studies* 15 (1989), pp. 3–34.

93 *Paston Letters*, v, p. 251.

94 Norfolk Record Office, Norwich, uncatalogued Phillipps Ms. 33156, referring to Cratfield, Stowpark, and Berwick.

95 BL, Add. Ch. 16556 m.23: cash livery to John Lound, receiver-general of Duchess Elizabeth, for the manors of Walton, Dovercourt and Harwich.

96 PRO, Special Collections, Ministers' Accounts, SC6/1202/15, 16.

97 *CCR*, *1396–99*, p. 3; *1374–77*, p. 306.

98 C.F. Richmond, 'Landlord and Tenant: the Paston Evidence', in *Enterprise and Individuals in Fifteenth Century England*, ed. J. Kermode (Gloucester, 1991), p. 28. Richmond comments that the Paston boys 'did not rail against their mothers for living too long'.

99 *Paston Letters*, vi, p. 54.

100 PRO, Special Collections, Ancient Correspondence, SC1/40/197.

101 *CCR*, *1337–39*, p. 582; *1396–99*, p. 3. Like agreements were made by Edmund Ferrers of Chartley: BL, Add. Ms. 24481, fo. 20; *CCR*, *1413–19*, p. 101; and Robert, Lord Morley: ibid., *1435–41*, p. 435.

102 *Paston Letters*, vi, pp. 2, 9.

103 Richmond, *The Pastons*, p. 133n; chapter six.

104 J. Beames, *A Translation of Glanvill* (1812), Book VI, p. 113.

105 PRO, C1/4/161; 16/81. The first of these is endorsed with the date 28 October 1418 and a comment that several writs had been addressed to the mob ordering them to appear before the council.

106 Ibid., C1/3/145; 9/68, 307: 12/220.

107 Ibid., Exchequer KR, Accounts Various, E101/512/10. The file contains five of Lady Zouche's letters to her receiver; a bundle of thirteen acknowledgements of debts owing with the receipts of payments made; and a bond concerning Arundel property in Sussex.

108 The endorsement records that the delivery was made to Elizabeth 'en le batailled chambre'.

109 For Elizabeth's fortunes see Archer, 'The Mowbrays', pp. 14–15. In the late summer of 1399 Elizabeth was staying in the Isle of Axholme, the duke of Norfolk's chief lordship but was residing in the home of Norfolk's councillor Thomas Brunham: PRO, SC6/909/20.

110 PRO, Exchequer TR, Ancient Deeds, series AS, E42/536. Elizabeth argued that although judgement had been made against Norfolk by authority of Richard's last parliament, Henry IV's first parliament had overturned the late King's actions therein and therefore she was entitled. PRO, Exchequer TR, Issue Rolls, E403/564, m. 4; CCR, 1399–1402, p. 67.

111 PRO, Exchequer TR, Warrants for Issue, E401/617: 23 February; CPR, 1399–1401, p. 207; CCR, 1399–1402, p. 142. To begin with Elizabeth was denied dower in the estates of Norfolk's grandmother who had died during his exile. PRO, SC6/1202/15; Archer, 'The Mowbrays', pp. 92–4.

112 CCR, 1399–1402, p. 165: CPR, 1399–1401, p. 339. In 1401 one third of the rents in Cratfield, Stowpark, and Berwick were delivered to her because they had been omitted from the assignment: CCR, 1399–1402, p. 441.

113 Joan de Geneville was a considerable heiress in her own right. In 1331 she had an allowance for household expenses and was permitted to receive her dead husband's body for burial: CCR, 1330–33, pp. 65, 403, 497; CPR, 1330–34, pp. 13, 213. She was also promised sufficient lands for her sustenance: CCR, 1330–33, pp. 99, 105, 110, 269, 311, 489, 503; CPR, 1330–34, p. 265.

114 H. Wood, 'The Muniments of Edmund de Mortimer, 3rd earl of March concerning his Liberty of Trim', Proceedings of the Royal Irish Academy 40 (1940), p. 317; CCR, 1330–33, p. 489; R. Frame, English Lordship in Ireland 1318–1361 (Oxford, 1982), pp. 73, 205.

115 CCR, 1337–39, p. 157: CCR, 1341–43, pp. 292–3, 349; CFR, 1337–47, p. 290; CPR, 1350–54, p. 178.

116 CCR, 1346–49, p. 314.

117 CPR, 1330–34, pp. 85, 248, 380; 1334–38, pp. 21, 157, 220, 516; 1348–40, pp. 460, 464; 1340–43, p. 488; 1343–45, p. 155; 1345–48, pp. 22, 349; 1348–50, p. 106; 1354–58, p. 105. Though Joan had licence to grant her Irish lands to her grandson as early as 1348, she continued to appoint her attorneys: Wood, 'Muniments', pp. 331, 353–4. The grant to Roger contained a clause allowing Joan the right to re-enter in case of default by her grandson. She seems to have kept an active interest in the lordship and in 1351 it was agreed that, although Roger legally held the lordship, it would not be seized so long as Joan lived: CPR, 1350–54, p. 178.

118 Richmond, The Pastons, p. 240n gives an example of continuity on the de la Pole lands where business begun in Duke William's lifetime was completed after his death and accounted for to his widow.

119 Paston Letters, iv, p. 221.

120 Ibid., v, pp. 150, 161, 224. In 1472 Sir John Paston was described as 'one of my Ladys consayll' and her preferred parliamentary representative for Maldon: ibid., pp. 148–9.

121 C. Rawcliffe and S. Flower, 'English Noblemen and their Advisers: Consultation and Collaboration in the Later Middle Ages', Journal of British Studies 25 (1986), p. 160.

122 See above; PRO, E101/41/17; CPR, 1399–1401, p. 91; Norfolk Record Office, Phillipps Ms. 33156.

123 Goushill had been in Norfolk's service probably from 1390 if not before: CPR, 1383–92, p. 31. Bodl., Ms. Ashmole, 863, fos. 24–5; CPR, 1399–1401, p. 207; CFR, 1399–1405, p. 130.

124 For a further example consider Katherine Neville, duchess of Norfolk who married her servant Sir Thomas Strangeways, or Alice St. Aubyn, countess of Oxford who married her servant Nicholas Thorley. See the comments of a foreign observer in, A Relation or rather a true account of the Island of England, ed. C.A. Sneyd, Camden Society, 27 (1847) pp. 26–7.

125 Rawcliffe, The Staffords, pp. 71, 153, 226; Jones and Underwood, The King's Mother.

126 R.R. Davies, 'Baronial Accounts, Incomes and Arrears in the Later Middle Ages', *Economic History Review* 2nd ser., 21 (1968), pp. 227–8n. PRO, Special Collections, Rentals and Surveys, SC11/816.

127 *CPR, 1399–1401*, p. 30 referring to her 'poor servants who have served her long without reward'.

128 PRO, SC1/40/21, 22.

129 W.C. Waller, 'An Old Church Chest, Being Notes of the Contents of that at Theydon Garnon, Essex', *Transactions of the Essex Archaeological Society* new ser., 5 (1895), pp. 12–14.

130 PRO, E101/512/10. Alice de la Pole in her exacting letters to William Bilton called him, apparently as a form of endearment 'my good cok of Bylton' and 'Cok of Bilton'. Bodl., Ms. DD Ewelme, a.7, A48, 1–3.

131 C.A. Musgrave, 'Household Administration in the Fourteenth Century with special Reference to the Household of Elizabeth de Burgh, Lady of Clare' (unpublished M.A. thesis, University of London, 1923), lists the accounts in her appendix. G.A. Holmes, *The Estates of the Higher Nobility in Fourteenth Century England* (Cambridge, 1957), pp. 35–8, 86, 109–11.

132 Rawcliffe, *The Staffords*, pp. 70, 92.

133 Musgrave, 'Household of Elizabeth de Burgh', pp. 34, 41–2.

134 C.D. Ross and T.B. Pugh, 'Materials for the Study of Baronial Incomes in Fifteenth Century England', *Economic History Review* 2nd ser., 6 (1953–4), p. 192. PRO, SC11/799, 801.

135 Holmes, *Estates of the Higher Nobility*, pp. 150–7. A.J. Pollard, 'Estate Management in the Later Middle Ages: The Talbots and Whitchurch, 1383–1525', *Economic History Review* 2nd ser., 25 (1972), pp. 555, 561–2, shows how vigorous estate management by Ankaret Talbot could not compensate for innately disastrous years in the economy.

136 PRO, SC11/816, 25.

137 Pisan, *The Treasure*, p. 130.

138 Rawcliffe, *The Staffords*, pp. 122–4.

139 PRO, E101/511/12.

140 Ibid., E101/512/10. There are 13 such documents in this file.

141 *Anglo Norman Letters*, ed. Legge, pp. 260, 268, 274; *CPR, 1401–05*, p. 30.

142 Jones and Underwood, *The King's Mother*, ch. 4. Note also Anne Neville's strictness about debt collecting: Rawcliffe, *The Staffords*, p. 147.

143 Pisan, *The Treasure*, p. 80.

7

'And Hir Name was Charite': Charitable Giving by and for Women in Late Medieval Yorkshire

P.H. Cullum
University of Huddersfield

The title of this chapter is taken from a fifteenth-century English poem called *The Pilgrim*.[1] In that work Charity is personified as a female figure providing food and shelter for the archetypal pauper, the pilgrim, or in this case pilgrims. However in preparing this chapter another woman called Charity appeared. A real woman this time, one who lived in York and was mentioned in the will of Avice de Pontefract who died in 1404. Avice left a number of bequests to very standard charitable purposes, viz. to the repair of roads and a bridge, to prisoners, to poor in and out of the maisonsdieu, and 4d. to Isabel Charyte.[2] Whether Isabel Charyte was a poor woman in need of assistance is not clear; Avice de Pontefract does not describe her in any way. Nevertheless it is likely – as it is likely that her surname is indicative of her means of livelihood – because the sum given her is in line with Avice's other charitable gifts. Room does however remain for uncertainty, and this illustrates a problem, that of exploring women's history when so much about them as individuals is uncertain. It is the intention of this chapter to examine whether charity was identified as a female activity or virtue, whether or not there is a specific pattern of female charity, and the degree to which there was a feminisation of poverty in the fifteenth century.

The main basis for this study is an examination of about 1500 wills from various Yorkshire probate collections. Wills are a valuable source for our understanding of the lives and interests of those below the level of the nobility. Nevertheless they have their limitations. In the case of married men Canon law provided for the division of the testator's property into three parts, viz. one for the heirs, one for the widow, and one at the testator's discretion for his soul. It is not always clear whether wills covered all three of these, or only the last. It is likely that practice varied. Wills contain the final disposition of property and pious intentions. They are therefore not necessarily absolutely comprehensive, for where property had already been settled, or chantries or almshouses established, these would not generally be recorded in the will.[3]

Two main samples were used in the study, viz. 242 wills from Exchequer Court Probate Register 1 and the early part of Probate Register 2 containing wills proved between 1389 and 1398, and 962 wills from Probate Register 2, containing wills covering the period 1440–59. Additional material was extracted from approximately 300 further wills taken at random from the period 1326–1530. Both wills of male and female testators and lay and clerical wills have been examined as part of a larger study on the practice of charity in the diocese of York in the later Middle Ages.[4] This allows a comparison to be made between lay male, female, and clerical wills, as well as over time between the two periods to see if there are any differences or changes in charitable practice.

A comparison of these two samples shows that by the latter period many more people were having their wills registered than in the earlier. The popularity of will-making was thus diffusing down the social scale, a process which was to continue and to accelerate after c.1500. The testators in sample 1 tend then to come from a narrower and more wealthy section of society than those in sample 2, a difference which may have been exacerbated by the changing economic climate, particularly in York, which brought economic decline from the middle of the fifteenth century. These two groups are thus not entirely comparable in social terms, so that tendencies rather than direct comparisons should be noted. No absolute measures of the amounts given has been attempted as this is problematic given the uncertainty of the relationship between lifetime and postmortem provision. Nor can we be certain that the will is comprehensive of perimortem provision. Instead the numbers of individuals providing particular forms of charity has been analysed to discover their relative popularity.

The two samples were analysed to discover the relative proportions of female, lay male, clerical, and urban and rural wills, and how far these changed over time. The proportions of each of these groups giving to charity was also discovered in order to investigate which groups were most likely to make charitable bequests.[5] The tables reveal some changes between the two samples. The proportion of lay males remains much the same, at 66.5 and 70.1 per cent, whereas those of women and clerics change noticeably. Female testators decline from 23.1 per cent of the total to 13.7 per cent, whereas clerical testators increase from 10.3 to 16.2 per cent. The decline in the proportion of female testators is largely due to a decline in the number of married female testators. This would support the hypothesis that women were becoming less financially independent from the second third of the fifteenth century.[6] In both samples women were more likely to give charitably than men. In the earlier sample 64.3 per cent of women made charitable bequests, compared to 57.8 per cent of

Table 7.1
COMPOSITION OF THE WILL SAMPLES

Sample 1 (1389–98)

	Female	Lay Male	Clerical	Urban	Rural	Total
no. wills	56	161	25	180	62	242
no. charitable	36	93	18	114	33	147
% charitable	64.3	57.8	72	63.3	53.2	60.7
% group	23.1	66.5	10.3	74.4	25.6	100

Sample 2 (1440–59)

	Female	Lay Male	Clerical	Urban	Rural	Total
no. wills	132	674	156	554	408	962
no. charitable	60	261	70	281	110	391
% charitable	45.5	38.7	44.9	50.7	27	40.6
% group	13.7	70.1	16.2	71.9	28.1	100

men. In the later sample the percentage had declined for both sexes: 45.5 per cent of women gave to charity but only 38.7 per cent of men.

This decline can be attributed to the greater social range of the testators in the latter sample, which would include more people not able to make such bequests. The decline in male charity was marginally greater than that in female charity, but the difference is too small to be significant. The difference between the two sexes is fairly stable at 6.5 and 6.8 per cent. It is probable that women as the household providers were more involved during their lives in the giving of charity at the kitchen door and continued this in their testamentary behaviour. This conclusion was also reached by Jordan who commented that sixteenth-century London 'women donors . . . were particularly concerned with the plight of the poor'. Moreover the London women donors were also 6 per cent more charitable than Londoners as a whole. Mertes too has noted that widows were the most generous donors of charity amongst noble householders.[7] Comparison with the London material suggests that women were indeed more likely to give to charity than men. It may also be significant that one of the chief activities of the beguines, that quintessentially female religious movement, was charitable work such as hospital nursing. It was a commonplace that women were more devout than men, spending more time in their devotions. It would also appear that more women were willing to spend financial as well as temporal resources. Bynum has also recently pointed to the centrality of the giving away (and giving up) of food in medieval women's piety.[8]

There is a problem concerning the differing nature of the wills which men and women were likely to make. As we have seen the number of women making wills compared with the number of men was always relatively small and declined as a proportion of the will-making population during the period in question due to the virtual disappearance of wills made by married women during the fifteenth century. In the first sample 40 per cent of the female testators were married, but in the second sample less than 15 per cent. Married women were allowed to make a will provided that they had their husbands' permission and a phrase to the effect that they had this is often included in the preamble to married women's wills. Nevertheless it seems to have ceased to be customary or at least common for married women to make a will during the later fifteenth century. Given that this was so, it raises problems about how representative the female wills in sample 2 are both in terms of comparison with male wills and also in terms of the charitable concerns and interests of late medieval Yorkshire women as a whole.

The form of female wills also appears to be somewhat different from that of male wills. They are particularly characterised by large numbers of small bequests, often of household goods, to a wide circle of friends, neighbours, and relations, by whom they would thus hope to be remembered. This is in contrast to male wills which tend to concentrate on the issues of funeral and estate, with legacies to friends and neighbours more often couched in terms of money or the personal effects of the testator. This reflects the rather different worlds that men and women operated in. Bynum points to the hagiographical cliche of the saint's father who gave alms and the mother who gave food.[9] One might then expect to find women more rarely having access to money and property to bequeath than men and thus more rarely giving these to charitable purposes. Most women gave on a small and local level. It is extremely rare to find women giving to charity in locations other than in their places of birth and residence. The impression gained, however, is that although no women could match the magnificence of the great merchants of York and Beverley such as the Holmes and the Rillestons, or the Charterhouse hospital in Hull founded by William and Michael de la Pole, where they did have access to money and property, particularly as widows, they were willing to use it for charitable purposes.

It is perhaps also true that female charity, even more than male charitable activity, is likely to be underestimated because it is invisible to the modern eye. Both male and female wills were prone to make charitable bequests to individuals without indicating that the recipient was a pauper. John Preston, bucklemaker, and John Burdon, both dying in 1400 in St Michael le Belfrey parish, York, each left small bequests to Marjory Heslington. Preston's will alone reveals that Marjory was an inmate of the Thomas de Howme hospital.

Burdon did not need to describe her as she would have been known to the executors. When female wills were concerned with a geographically and possibly socially more restricted world, this was even more likely to happen. Alice Rawdon, widow, of York (d. 1444) left 6d. to a certain poor woman, Agnes Askham, and to a certain pauper called Henry.[10] She described these two recipients as poor but did not qualify the next legatee in her will, Ellen Morpath, who received only 4d. Was she also a pauper? It is impossible to tell. It is perhaps likely that a large proportion of small monetary bequests in female wills are charitably inspired. Moreover the nature of female wills also tends to blur the dividing line between charity and all the other motives for bequests. How is the modern researcher to tell why Agnes Bedford left a green coverlet, two brass pots and an old coffer to Isabella Halytreholme?[11] Was Isabella rewarded for faithful service, or charitably endowed towards a future, or even recent marriage, or a mixture of both? Or was she a poor neighbour given some useful furnishings in memory of a friendship?

Many, perhaps most, testators made their charitable bequests through the residue of the will. Cecily Giry of York (d. 1388) wished that the residue of her goods be sold and the money to be distributed to the poor, spent on masses, and 'other pious alms where most necessity appears'.[12] William and Alice Durem made identical and reciprocal wills in 1390 before they set out on a pilgrimage to Rome, from which neither of them was to return, in which each left the residue of their goods to the other and, in the event of neither of them surviving, in alms and the use of the poor.[13] Another form which is regularly met with is the direction that the residue is to be used in masses and 'distribution of alms to the poor'. This formula is used, for example, in the will of Alice Chaffer of York (d. 1444).[14] These are not the only wills where the residue is devoted exclusively to charity to the poor. Another example is to be found in the will of Elizabeth Bristall of York (d. 1442) who left her residue 'in pure works of charity'.[15]

When people wrote that they wanted the residue of their goods used for the health of their souls, or for pious uses they were clearly not thinking exclusively in terms of sacred or ecclesiastical provision. As far as they were concerned charity was an integral part of their understanding of their devotional lives. It is only because the modern definition of the word 'pious' is so narrow that we fail to fully understand what fourteenth and fifteenth-century writers meant when they used this formula. The point is forcibly made by the will of Agnes Constantyne of York (d. 1447) who left the residue of her goods 'for the health of her soul in the repair of roads and *other acts of piety*'.[16] She clearly regarded the repair of roads, a common feature of medieval Yorkshire wills, as a charitable act of benefit both to the community and her own soul on a par with masses and money gifts to the poor.

Though the mending of roads was valuable to all travellers, from wealthy merchants to beggarly vagrants, the image of the wanderer, the pilgrim was of a poor person (cf. Charity's pilgrims already noted), and the act of assisting his or her passage was perceived as charitable. John Shadworth of London left the residue of his estate to 'pious uses and charitable works such as poor maids' marriages, the repair of bad roads, freeing of prisoners and in the help and relief of poor men and women burdened with children and ashamed to beg, and in other pious works'.[17] Thomson uses this will to illustrate the difficulty of distinguishing pious from charitable bequests 'because no such differentiation existed in the mind of the donor'.[18] Any act which improved the lot of one's less fortunate neighbour (Biblically defined) was charitable. Medieval religion, as opposed to post-Reformation religion, made the relationship between the individual and his or her neighbour an integral part of the relationship with Christ. As Christ in the York Judgement play said:

> To lest or moste when ye it did,
> To me ye did the selve and the same.[19]

Or as the book of *James* put it more succinctly 'faith without works is dead'.[20]

If to those wills which make specific charitable provision, we add those which implicitly provided for the poor through the residue of the will we can gain some estimate of the proportion of testators who expected to make some form of charitable bequest. Samples 1 and 2 show that the figures were very consistent, in the earlier period some 78.9 per cent of wills were potentially charitable, rising only slightly to 79.7 per cent in the later period. These figures can only be described as 'potentially charitable' because it is quite possible that the charitable intentions of the testator were not carried out, either because there was no residue to give away, or because the executors chose to interpret their instructions in such a way as to provide only masses, a perfectly legitimate though probably uncommon discharge of their duties. A number of female testators with surviving husbands, such as Agnes Elvelay of York (d. 1395), left the residue of their goods to their spouses to be used for alms, with consequent uncertainty as to how the husband interpreted this.[21] Such problems as the adequacy of the estate or of the executors also apply to the body of the will, but on the whole it is assumed that where these problems did not occur then specific bequests were fulfilled.

It is highly significant that whereas specific bequests to the poor were fewer in the later sample, bequests through the residue show no falling away. This is probably due to the wider social and economic spread of the later sample in which there is a higher percentage of people with limited amounts of capital and property for whom provision for the family was the major concern, but who wished to make provision for their souls in the usual way. They did so by using the residue for this purpose, hoping that there would be enough left over for something, but unable to make specific charitable bequests. It is equally significant, and indicative of the importance of the poor in the scheme of salvation that such an overwhelming proportion of the will-making population made bequests to the poor. Peter Heath similarly concluded from his study of Hull wills that among the priorities of testators 'the poor must have stood very near the top of the list'.[22]

One of the ways in which testators tried to provide for both family needs and charitable inclinations was by imposing reversions on bequests, so that if the inheritor ceased to need the gift because of death, it could then be devoted to charitable causes. Daughters' dowries not uncommonly had reversionary conditions of this kind. John Bilburgh of Wressle (d. 1456) left his daughter a dowry of ten marks, but if she died it was to be 'charitably disposed' to the poor and needy.[23] John Haynson, alderman of Hull (d. 1459) directed that if any of his daughters died their portions were to be given to the poor in alms and for their souls.[24] John Patryngton of Paull Fleet in Holderness left all his tenements and rents to his daughter, but if she died they were to go to the parish church of Paull and be divided into three: one third to be used for a chantry, one third for the fabric of the church, and one third to the poor in works of mercy.[25]

Charity could be spiritual as well as material and devoted to the souls as well as the bodies of the poor and indeed 'all the faithful dead' as so many bequests for masses and chantries had it. Isabella Barry of York (d. 1391) left twelve marks 'ad necessitatem pauperum christi', viz. six marks to a priest to celebrate for herself and all faithful Christian dead, and six marks to be distributed to the poor where most need was.[26] The organising principle of much charitable activity was the Seven Works of Corporal Mercy, that is giving food to the hungry, drink to the thirsty, shelter to the stranger, clothing to the naked, visiting the sick, comforting prisoners, and burying the dead. Joan Johnson of York (d. 1474), a widow, directed that the residue of her goods be sold and the money distributed in the name of the Seven Works.[27] That the concept of the Seven Works of

Table 7.2
MONEY DOLES

a. (1389–98)

	Female	Lay Male	Clerical	Urban	Rural	Total
no. wills	17	55	10	60	22	82
% charitable	47.2	59.1	55.6	52.6	66.7	55.8
% group	20.7	67.1	12.2	73.2	26.8	100

b. (1440–59)

	Female	Lay Male	Clerical	Urban	Rural	Total
no. wills	11	98	28	92	45	137
% charitable	18.3	37.6	40	32.7	40.9	35
% group	8.0	71.5	20.4	67.2	32.8	100

Mercy was deeply rooted is illustrated by its survival into the Reformation era. As late as 1542 the will of Jane Huntingdon of Hull left the reversion of her house to this purpose.[28] This concept will be used as the framework for looking at the practice of female charity.

Bequests of money were the most common form of charitable provision because of its flexibility. Such bequests were largely, but far from exclusively, associated with money doles at funerals. The pattern of giving is shown in Table 7.2. The wealthy Dame Joan Thurscrosse of Hull (d. 1524) directed that on the day of her burial, its octave, and on the twelve-month day 'ther be delte for my saull and al Cristen saulles peny dole to the poore people'.[29] Marion Marton of York (d. 1441) left 30s. to be distributed at the rate of ½d. per person, an amount that would have provided for 720 people.[30] This represents some five per cent of York's population in her day. Nicola de Irby (d. 1395) of York left ten marks for distribution to the poor 'and a feast for my friends'.[31] Joan Erscot (d. 1395) of York was also very generous, leaving ten marks of which all but 40s. was to go to the priests and poor of her parish of All Saints, Pavement.[32] Sometimes such bequests reveal life-time charity. Joan Bradbury of London, for example, left a bequest to each bedeman and woman 'to whom I geve every Sonday'.[33] In Bristol Alice Chestre left a tenement to her son and his heirs who were to distribute the rent from it to the poor in perpetuity, according to Burgess, 'probably continuing Alice's practice'.[34]

Not all gave money, but instead gave their goods directly to the poor. Marion Barnard of Hull (d. 1458) directed that her best household utensils be sold to pay her debts, but that the rest be distributed to the poor.[35] Isabella Barry of York (d. 1391) gave 26lb. of wool to the poor 'pro nomine christi'.[36] It is likely that Isabella was a spinster or otherwise involved in the woollen business and that this constituted her stock in trade. The choice of particular forms of charity was probably frequently decided by the trade of the testator and hence their goods. Isabella's gift is interesting also in that it was not just a simple bequest of consumables, but a way for the recipient to make more money than the value of the wool, because by carding or spinning value would be added. The poor who received this gift might have to work for the full value of the bequest to be won but it would be worth it. It might even have been a way of assisting someone in trade in a small way. Isabella may well have intended that the bequest specifically benefit women, as spinning and carding was women's work.

Twenty per cent of those giving food did so by inviting the poor, either along with friends and neighbours or separately, to a 'convocation' or wake. The more common form was to have one large wake. Isabella Barry left 20s. for her poor neighbours to be so entertained.[37] What she might have provided is illustrated by the will of Isabel Wele of York (d. 1398) who left two marks for a wake for poor men and women at which they were to be served bread, meat or fish, and drink.[38] Although the provision of a meal was in some senses simply the elaboration of the more common distribution of food and drink, it may also have had it's root in the parable of the king who gave a great feast. When those he had invited refused to come he sent his servants to collect the people in the streets, both the bad and the good, and to bring them to his feast.[39] This parable is explicitly referred to in the *Lay Folks' Catechism*, and may lie behind the bequest of Cecily, wife of John de Knaresburgh, cordwainer, (d. 1403) who left six shillings for twenty-four poor '*ad comedendum mecum*.'[40] Others provided bread and ale at the funeral feast or after, such as Agnes Elvelay of York (d. 1395) who left four quarters of malt to be brewed and one quarter of wheat to be made into bread, to be distributed to the poor on the octave of her funeral. Agnes may well have been a brewster.[41] Alice Shirwod, dying in midwinter, left all her salted meat to the poor.[42] Some made more lengthy provision. Alice Brereton of York (d. 1441), wished her sister Cecily Steatour to have sufficient victuals for the rest of her life.[43]

Receiving the stranger was rarely performed at first hand in the wills, being usually done through almshouses or maisonsdieu, but there are a few instances.[44] Indeed the distinction between receiving individual beggars or strangers into one's home and the establishment of a maisondieu may have been less clear cut than might otherwise be supposed. John de Craven's maisondieu near Layerthorpe in York may well have been in his own home and Agnes Brome of Scarborough (d. 1400) built one at the bottom of her garden![45] Agnes de Whitflete of Hedon (d. 1396) left a tenement to a couple for their lifetime, afterwards to be demised to the poor who were to pay an annual rent of 15d. to the mayor and council.[46] There was no clear dividing line between personal charity and institutional care. The one elided into the other. For most, of course, receiving of the stranger was done at one remove by giving to the hospitals and maisonsdieu which took in the poor, the sick, and the homeless, but there is no escaping the conclusion that for some it was an intensely personal responsibility.[47]

One case shows just how literally 'receiving the stranger' was taken. In 1388 Cecily Giry, a York widow, left three feather beds with their bedclothes 'in le Gestchaumbre' to remain there to serve for hospitality to the indigent poor.[48] No time limit was set on the bequest. Here was no escaping from close contact with the needs of the poor. It seems likely that Cecily's household had been used during her lifetime to her taking in beggars off the street. Nor was this just an English custom. Margery Kempe travelling between Constance and Bologna, found 'the good wives where they were housed, laid her in their own beds for God's love'. In 1393 Margherita and Francesco Datini were supporting a blind and paralysed old woman in their house in Prato 'for the love of God'.[49] Alice Claver, a widowed London silkwoman, similarly took in two children out of charity.[50]

A custom which can be found among the wills of a few lay males but rarely among those of women from c.1450 was the reception of poor men and women into the house on stated days to be given food. Richard Carlell, butcher, of York (d. 1453), directed that his wife Agnes was to take into his house five poor men or women every Sunday from the time of his death for a year, where they were to be given good food and drink. In return they were to pray for the souls of himself, his parents, his benefactors, and all the faithful dead.[51] The reason that it was a male custom was that only men had wives to survive them and make this kind of domestic provision. The wife as manager of the household was responsible for the provision of food and drink and the care of guests. A wife would not expect her husband to do this. Moreover this would have been the kind of charitable activity she would have been most likely to perform in life. Agnes Carlell was clearly performing this function as wife or household manager rather than as executor. This is emphasised by the case of Thomas Kokson of Wakefield (d. 1500), who directed not that his executor, but 'my servant Margaret Poll kepe my hous iij weiks after my buriall and to gyff and distribut evere Sonday and every Fryday xiij penyworth of whit bred to pore folks duryng iij weiks'.[52] Kokson had no widow or daughter to perform this function so he left it to his female servant to supervise. Here we can see most clearly the female responsibility for charitable provision made on a domestic basis. A similar in vivos arrangement can be seen in the letter of Francesco Datini to his wife, accompanying a 'bale of herrings and about a thousand oranges'. Margherita was to sell half and give the other half away, 'or, if you please you may give away all the herrings and oranges – the greater part to God (ie to charity) and the rest to friends and kinsfolk'.[53] While the husband made the food available, it was the wife's responsibility to dispose of it properly, as she did with other domestic provisions.

Table 7.3
FOOD AND DRINK

a. (1389–98)

	Female	Lay Male	Clerical	Urban	Rural	Total
no. wills	4	8	7	10	9	19
% charitable	11.1	8.6	38.9	8.8	27.3	12.9
% group	21.1	42.1	36.8	52.6	47.4	100

b. (1440–59)

	Female	Lay Male	Clerical	Urban	Rural	Total
no. wills	5	35	7	32	15	47
% charitable	8.3	13.4	10	11.4	13.6	12
% group	10.6	74.5	14.9	68.1	31.9	100

We must now turn from hospitality to the provision of clothing. It was a common custom, especially among the wealthier, to have a number of poor men at the funeral to act as torchbearers. These men were usually provided with clothing. It was usually men who performed this function, so they benefited disproportionately from this form of charity. However women might receive clothing for keeping a vigil over the body before the funeral. Robert de Crosse of Hull (d. 1395) left £4 for fifteen poor men and fifteen poor women to be dressed 'in northern russet or other suitable cloth', for which they were to watch around his body praying earnestly day and night, and fourteen of the men were to carry torches in his funeral procession.[54] Marion Marton of York (d. 1441) left six black gowns for six poor men.[55] Dame Joan Thurscrosse of Hull, a vowess, wished thirteen beadsmen each to have a white gown and thirteen poor women to have cloth to make each of them a white kirtle.[56] Clothing might also be distributed at some time after the funeral. Elena Milys of York (d. 1387) left her best garment for a mortuary and all her other clothing to the poor.[57] Joan More of Pontefract (d. 1448) left thirty-six ells of russet to be distributed among the poor.[58] Katherine Pacok of York (d. 1466), widow, left to a blind widow living in the cemetery of her parish church of St Mary, Castlegate, her black gown with black fur.[59] Margery Dogett of Norwich likewise left her second-best kirtle to 'blind Margaret'.[60]

It appears to have been slightly more common for women to give away their own clothing than for men to do so. Agnes Meke of York willed that her green cloak with the fur should be sold and the money given to the poor.[61] The sale of clothing rather than the donation of the garment itself occurred when the gown was a valuable one and of use to more people if converted into cash than if simply given. Such garments moreover would have been unsuitable as gifts to the poor as indicating an inappropriate social status. Most of the cloth specified for making up or immediate gift to the poor is russet, blanket, and frieze – cheap but serviceable. In this context it is worth noting that Rubin's suggestion that the poor were given grand clothes which they then sold for food, drink, and clothes, is not borne out by the evidence.[62] Her view is based upon a mistaken belief that the Irish cloth specified in one Cambridge will was of fine quality, whereas in fact Irish cloth was of a poor standard.[63] It seems somewhat curious that the poor, having been given clothing, should be expected to sell this in order to buy other clothes. The evidence that the cloth or clothes that they were given were of cheap stuff appropriate to their status suggests that these were garments which the poor would continue to wear as a permanent reminder to them and those around them of the charity of their benefactor.

Throughout the wills the emphasis is on providing gowns, but other garments also appear. Agnes de Sutton of Bootham (d. 1333) left her jewelry to be sold to buy shoes for the poor, a relatively common concern before about 1400, but rare afterwards, perhaps an indicator of a rising

Table 7.4
CLOTHING

a. (1389–98)

	Female	Lay Male	Clerical	Urban	Rural	Total
no. wills	2	11	2	11	4	15
% charitable	5.6	11.8	11.1	9.6	12.1	10.2
% group	13.3	73.3	13.3	73.3	26.7	100

b. (1440–59)

	Female	Lay Male	Clerical	Urban	Rural	Total
no. wills	6	20	2	26	2	28
% charitable	10	7.7	2.9	9.3	1.8	7.2
% group	21.4	71.4	7.1	92.9	7.1	100

standard of living even among the poor in the years after the Black Death.[64] Thomas Bracebrig (d. 1436), a former Mayor of York, left 20s. for forty pairs of shoes for poor men and 10s. for twenty pairs of shoes for poor women.[65] Hose and linen can also be found.[66]

Giving to the sick was an important charitable activity for women in the earlier period, though less obviously so in the later sample. In 1398 Agnes de Worsop of York left 20s. to the sick poor of the city.[67] In Cambridge, Katherine Cook (d. 1496) left bread and money to be distributed 'among poor people dwelling in the said parish most feable in nature'.[68] Nevertheless this apparent fall-off in interest is balanced out if one examines charity given to the maisonsdieu and almshouses. Anabilla de Holm (d. 1391) left two marks to the poor men and women in the maisonsdieu of York. Margaret Kirkham (d. 1443) left 20d. to each maisondieu in the city.[69] There seems to have been a consensus that donations to the maisonsdieu were a high priority. In sample 1 nearly three-quarters of charitable women and over half of charitable lay men gave to this particular end. Even in sample 2, of the charitable, 43.3 per cent of women and 46 per cent of lay men gave to this end. The high priority which women gave to this form of charity, especially in sample 1 is what one would expect, given the role women had as healers and carers (reflected in a number of bequests to women for nursing care during illness) both in lay society and in the hospitals. Margery Kempe seems to have spent quite a lot of time in the care of sick people, both in nursing, as with her senile husband, and also in prayer and conversation, as with her care of the woman suffering from post-partum psychosis.[70] Like her, other women probably tended to give to individual sick people known to them and thus women's giving is probably underestimated, perhaps particularly

Table 7.5
VISITING THE SICK

a. (1389–98)

	Female	Lay Male	Clerical	Urban	Rural	Total
no. wills	4	14	1	17	2	19
% charitable	11.1	15.1	5.6	14.9	6.1	12.9
% group	21.1	73.7	5.3	89.5	10.5	100

b. (1440–59)

	Female	Lay Male	Clerical	Urban	Rural	Total
no. wills	–	12	2	12	2	14
% charitable	–	4.6	2.9	4.3	1.8	3.6
% group	–	85.7	14.3	85.7	14.3	100

Table 7.6
MAISONSDIEU AND HOSPITALS

a. (1389–98)

	Female	Lay Male	Clerical	Urban	Rural	Total
no. wills	26	49	3	77	1	78
% charitable	72.2	52.7	16.7	67.5	3	53.1
% group	33.3	62.8	3.9	98.7	1.3	100

b. (1440–59)

	Female	Lay Male	Clerical	Urban	Rural	Total
no. wills	26	120	22	148	20	168
% charitable	43.3	46	31.4	52.7	18.2	43
% group	15.5	71.4	13.1	88.1	11.9	100

in sample 2. An interesting example of laywomen's collective activity on behalf of the sick poor can be found in thirteenth-century Montpellier where every Wednesday certain women from a mercantile and artisan background made a door-to-door collection of alms on behalf of the various hospitals and charities of the town.[71]

Although in the earlier period women seem to have been proportionately much more interested than men in giving to the prisons, by the later period it was not disproportionate to their numbers. All the donations were to the York prisons, as were most of the bequests by men. Most gave between 1s. and 3s. 4d. to each prison, though some specified only certain prisons, and some preferred to give to each prisoner, usually 2–4d. each. Margaret de Knaresburgh gave food to the prisoners in the Castle, St Peter's prison, and the archbishop's prison.[72] In 1474 Joan, widow of Sir John Warde left 6s. 8d. to prisoners in York.[73] None of the female testators singled out the Woman kidcote in York, part of the civic prison on Ousebridge, unlike John Newton (d. 1442) who left 3d. to each woman there, and 3s. between the prisoners in each of the Castle and archbishop's prisons.[74] Perhaps this suggests a rather small number of prisoners in the Woman kidcote.

Women's concern for the prisons must banish any suggestion that women's wills tended to concentrate solely on the private and domestic sphere. Indeed Agnes Foster the widow of a former lord mayor of London enlarged Ludgate prison in 1463. According to Stow she 'procured in a common Counsell of this Citie, certayn Articles to be established, for the ease, comforte and reliefe of poore Prisoners there'.[75] If Stow is correct, it would appear that she was able to influence the City council to make certain rules concerning the administration of the prison. These ordered that both the old and new parts of the prison should be treated as one and that prisoners should have free lodging and water. It may be significant that Ludgate was a debtors' prison, unlike nearby Newgate which housed felons and suspected traitors.[76] Debt was the result of poverty rather than criminal intentions, and its forgiveness was enjoined in the Lord's Prayer.

If women's wills tended to reflect a narrower parochial focus and more limited range of charitable concerns than men's, this was an effect of their generally lower levels of wealth and less mobile lifestyle (after marriage, if not before). It certainly did not preclude women from interest in the wider aspects of their community. Around fifteen per cent of women in both samples left bequests to the upkeep of roads, another very 'public' form of charity.[77] Christine de Pisan advocated that her princess visit hospitals in person, if not prisons: 'the good princess will never be ashamed to visit hospitals and the poor in all her grandeur . . . she will visit their bedsides and will comfort them sweetly, making her excellent and welcome gifts of alms.' Nevertheless she suggested, ladies should and indeed did, help prisoners: 'God knows how many prisoners, even in the lands of the Saracens . . . have been and are every day, in this world here below, comforted and helped by women and their property.'[78] Participation in public acts of charity was not only usual, it was positively enjoined upon women. Even in Italy the relief of prisoners (though not necessarily at first-hand) was thought suitable for a woman. The fifteenth-century Florentine Lucrezia Tornabuoni thought there was 'no better kind of charity than providing for the marriage of young women and releasing prisoners from gaol, especially poor men cast into prison for debt'.[79] And Margherita Datini was the recipient of begging letters from a prisoner, independently of her husband.[80]

No will in either of the samples mentioned the burial of any but the testator. This seems to have been the one of the Seven Works of Mercy which was regularly omitted, partly perhaps because it was the one non-gospel based Work, partly because the poor did not necessarily die at convenient times. Marion Marton (d. 1444) did, however, leave a banquer to her parish church to stand before poor widows at the funerals of their husbands.[81] The Corpus Christi guild of Walden in Essex which paid for the burial of poor strangers is a rare example in England of a confraternity dedicated to this end.[82] Guilds not infrequently performed this function in Italy, as did the Company of S. Frediano of Florence.[83] This may suggest that this was a problem more readily dealt with by other means in England, perhaps by the parish, perhaps by the hospitals and maisonsdieu. Although the wills are silent on this subject it may be that this was also a female concern. In the one surviving representation of the Seven Works in a wall-painting where the acts appear to be arranged in a gender-specific fashion, burial of the dead, or rather payment for the burial, is performed by a female figure.[84]

We will now proceed to a particular form of charitable activity not specified as one of the Seven Works, but one which seems to have been favoured by wealthier urban women, namely the provision of fuel for the poor. Only one will makes this provision in sample 1, that of Joan Stalby of Scarborough (d. 1393), who left ten cauldrons of coal for the poor.[85] In two of the cases in sample 2 the fuel to be distributed was clearly the woman's household stock: Alice Chaffer of York (d. 1444), widow, left 'all my fuel to be distributed to the poor for my soul where most need is', and in 1452 Alice Shirwod directed that all the fuel which remained after payment of her funeral expenses was to go to the poor.[86] Joan Johnson (d. 1474) left 'all [her] kindling to be distributed among the poor of Christ with the firewood and turves'. Agnes Grantham, a York widow, distributed fuel to the needy during

Table 7.7
PRISONERS

a. (1389–98)

	Female	Lay Male	Clerical	Urban	Rural	Total
no. wills	6	9	1	16	–	16
% charitable	16.7	9.7	5.6	14	–	10.9
% group	37.5	56.3	6.3	100	–	100

b. (1440–59)

	Female	Lay Male	Clerical	Urban	Rural	Total
no. wills	3	21	7	31	–	31
% charitable	5	8.1	10	11	–	7.9
% group	9.7	67.7	22.6	100	–	100

Table 7.8
FUEL

a. (1389–98)

	Female	Lay Male	Clerical	Urban	Rural	Total
no. wills	1	–	–	1	–	1
% charitable	2.8	–	–	0.9	–	0.1
% group	100	–	–	100	–	100

b. (1440–59)

	Female	Lay Male	Clerical	Urban	Rural	Total
no. wills	3	4	1	7	1	8
% charitable	5.0	1.5	1.4	2.5	0.1	2.1
% group	37.5	50	12.5	87.5	12.5	100

her lifetime.[87] Margery Dogett of Norwich (d. 1516) left one mark for wood for poor people in winter.[88] Katherine Radclyf of York (d. 1458) was even more generous leaving 40s. to buy a boatload of turves for the poor in the time of winter following her decease.[89] Agnes Brome endowed her maisondieu with six quarters of sea-coal annually.[90] On the whole these women made provision from their household stock, and showed a real concern for the household needs of the poor.

Charity towards Women

Let us now to turn to provision made specifically for women.[91] This generally fell into two distinct groups, that is for widows and poor young women on the threshold of marriage. A rare exception is the bequest by John Fitlyng of Hull (d. 1434) of 5d. to five poor women every Saturday for a year in honour of the Blessed Virgin.[92] There was also a third category of poor women, those working for their living, usually as spinsters, who were barely able to support themselves by this work. These women were left bequests only by their employers. William Shiplay of York, draper (d. 1435), left to 'each poor woman who works and spins for me, 6d'.[93] Thomas Clynt of York, (d. 1439) left 4d. to each of his woollen spinsters.[94] William Crosseby, dyer, (d. 1466) left 30s. to 'the poor women working at carding and spinning for me'.[95] In the same year Alice Chellow of York left 4d. to each poor woman who had worked at spinning for her.[96] These women, although living and working independently, were in need of charitable support due to the low level of their wages. There is also evidence that some women householders were concerned for their female domestic servants. In some cases these were probably elderly servants with long service to the houehold. Juetta de Burton left five marks to her servant Agnes and Cecily de Yharom left 20s. to her servant Margaret Akum and, if her goods sufficed, 4d. a week for life.[97]

Charitable bequests to widows were often partnered with bequests to clerks, and represent the role women, particularly widows, played in keeping vigil over the dead, and probably also in laying out the body. Margery Kempe was regularly called in to pray beside the dying, even though, as she tartly pointed out, they had often not liked her weeping during their lives. In 1332 Joan de Lepyngton left 3s. 4d. to poor clerks and widows, and in the following year Agnes de Sutton of Bootham left 20s. for the same.[98] John de Popelton (d. 1362) left 2s. to poor clerks and widows saying psalters and prayers.[99] But widows might also receive bequests independently of this function. In 1392 Nicholas de Shirburn, chaplain, left 3s. to be divided amongst six widows.[100] Roger de Burton (d. 1392) left 40s. to the poor and widows bedridden in York.[101] Thomas Bracebrig (d. 1436) left to each of five poor widows 1d. per week so long as they should live.[102] In 1346 Emma, wife of William Paynot of Easingwold, left 3d. to each widow of Easingwold, by estimation 10s. 9d. – which represents forty-three widows in a not particularly large community.[103] Richard Wartre of York (d. 1458) left 12d. to each poor woman or widow with a child or children in the parish of St Saviour.[104] This was preferential treatment as other paupers in the parish only received 4d. In 1453 Thomas Wombewell of Wombwell gave to each of five poor widows living by the chapel, 6s. 8d.[105] These widows may in fact have been living in a small hospital.[106]

Provision for the marriages of young women, particularly poor young women, tended to become more common from the middle of the fifteenth century. Of the four bequests to poor maids' marriages in sample 2, all were given by men in the 1450s. While men were willing to give to this end in the abstract, women generally gave money to young women of their acquaintance. An example of this personal approach is Juetta de Burton who in 1395 gave to 'a young woman, Isabella, £20 for her marriage or what she wants, provided it is honest'.[107] Poor maids' dowries were implicitly, and sometimes explicitly, intended to preserve young women from descent into prostitution. Three of the wills in sample 2 are from Hull and one from York, an unusual distribution given the preponderance of York wills, perhaps reflecting the prominence of prostitution as a female occupation in a port community. Two of these are portmanteau bequests: Francis Buke of Hull, (d. 1453), left £10 to prisoners and other needy poor, mending of defective roads, and the marrying of poor virgins; in 1455 Robert Belton of York gave a mere two marks to be divided among priests, friars, poor scholars, and virgins.[108] Robert Goldyng of Hull (d. 1453), left five nobles (33s. 4d.) to five poor virgins to buy five cows to furnish their marriages in honour of the

Blessed Virgin Mary.[109] More prosaically John Garton of Hull (d. 1455), left £20 to the marriage of poor girls.[110] In 1437 Thomas Kyrkeham of York left £20 to the marriage of poor maids and virgins in the city of York.[111] John Carre of York (d. 1488) left 'to xv pore madyns well disposed to mariage' £26, at 40s. each, a curious piece of accountancy which must have left two of the poor maidens well disappointed.[112] Like Margaret Bramhowe (d. 1471) who left her household utensils to be distributed among newly-married men and women in need, he was also concerned that the new marriages of the poor should not be put under an added burden of poverty and also left £20 to 'pore men and pure women wedded keepyng houshold togeder where most nede is'.[113] In 1530 Robert Jannys, a former mayor of Norwich left £20 for the marriage of twenty maidens.[114] About 10 per cent of London wills registered in the Prerogative Court of Canterbury from the fifteenth and early sixteenth centuries left bequests for marriage portions.[115]

Some women lived alone and in marginal locations. Avice de Pontefract left 4d. to a woman living in the cemetery of her parish church of All Saints, Pavement.[116] Churchyards were not an unusual place for poor individuals, particularly women, to live, probably because it was a good place to beg from the pious as they came and went from church, but also because it gave them some nominal protection by the parish priest, and possibly first call on his charity. This last might take the form of a room or dwelling in one of the rows of cottages often erected on the edge of churchyards whose rents paid for the upkeep of chantries, and whose letting was often in the hands of the parish or chantry priest.[117] Such individuals would thus be familiar to the church-going testator, who might well have given to them in the past. It may well have been that older women, in particular, were more likely to be living alone and without the economic resources to maintain a home.[118]

Women not able to live independently and living in an institution can be found throughout the period. A number of them received individual support such as Magota de la maisondieu, who received a tunic from Alice de Bridford in 1390, Dulcia Setter in Ousebridge maisondieu, who received 12d. from Alan de Alnewyk in 1374, and Joan Day, the poor little woman in a certain maisondieu to whom Joan Cottyngham (d. 1459) gave her lined russet gown and linen chemise.[119] All of the York maisonsdieu took in women, and one in St Andrewgate took only women.[120] Indeed it is quite possible that a large part of St Andrewgate was inhabited by poor women. In 1407 Joan Spenser left 'to the poor widows and my tenants in St Andrewgate 13s. 4d. between them'.[121]

Two other York hospitals came to be inhabited only by women during this period. Sometime probably in the 1380s St Nicholas, which had formerly been a leperhospital, ceased to have male brothers and held only sisters thereafter. During the 1390s the sisters received gifts from eleven of the eighteen individuals who gave to female charitable needs. Somewhere between 1433 and 1445 the inhabitants of the city maisondieu on Ousebridge ceased to be described as the 'poor of the maisondieu' and were described as the 'poor women of the maisondieu'.[122] It may also be significant that in 1461–2 St Leonard's hospital consistently supported more women than men in the infirmary even though the actual numbers fluctuated through the year.[123]

These indications of an increasingly female population in the maisonsdieu and hospitals can be paralleled elsewhere and at a slightly later date. In Norwich, St Paul's or Norman's Hospital took men and women until the late fourteenth or early fifteenth century, but only women thereafter.[124] By 1545 the maisondieu of Northallerton was housing thirteen widows, although when it was founded sometime in the mid-fifteenth century it was not then intended to be specifically for women.[125] In 1506 Alice Neville of Leeds reminded her son that he had sworn that he would 'trewly whilst he lives gyff those ij howses in Holbek that I bygged to ij pore women in his primary gyfft to charge thame that they pray duly for me and all my good doars and when on Woman dyes to put in an othr Woman *but put in no man.*' Each woman was to receive 13s. 4d. annually.[126] Alice clearly believed that women specifically had a need for charity. There does appear to be a pattern of feminisation of the inhabitants of a significant number of maisonsdieu during the fifteenth and sixteenth centuries which almost certainly reflects a feminisation of poverty during the period as economic depression and increasing guild regulation to protect male jobs restricted the kind of work available to women.[127]

For only one Yorkshire house is it possible to look with any clarity at the internal provision of charity. This is St Leonard's, York which is far from representative in that it was much larger than any other Yorkshire hospital. Moreover the only records relate to people taken in for money payments rather than out of charity, although for most of its history the majority of inhabitants were probably admitted without payment. This means that any women of whom there are records were likely to be better off than most.

The poor inmates of the hospital, who were known as cremetts, were probably usually admitted without payment, but sometimes as here, for a small fee. Sacerdotal liveries were originally intended for old and infirm priests, but even by the late thirteenth century a few of them were held by women. Cremettal and sacerdotal liveries were relatively cheap to buy: cremettal liveries cost up to £10 and sacerdotal liveries usually from £10–20.[128] The usual price appears to have been twenty marks for a sacerdotal livery and ten marks for a cremettal livery. This was considerably cheaper than a corrody, none of which was less than £20 and most were over £40. Women slightly outnumbered men in the holding of cremettal and minor liveries, the cheapest kind of purchase. With both corrodies and sacerdotal liveries they held just half the number of places held by single men.

Corrodies were principally held by married couples, and the figures in Table 7.9 are likely to be an underestimate due to what may be called the 'invisible wife syndrome'. In at least one case it only becomes clear that what had apparently been a corrody held by a single man was in fact jointly held by a couple when the man's name ceased to appear on the role of payments and was succeeded in the following year by that of his widow, who had not previously been mentioned.[129] Single women thus appear on the whole not to have been able to afford the more expensive corrodies, but married women were more likely to be able to afford these with their husbands.

Table 7.9
ST LEONARD'S HOSPITAL, YORK: LIVERIES AND CORRODIES
1392–1409

	lib. sac.	lib. cremett	corrody	habit of sister	other	total
Women	11	4	10	2	5	32
Men	19	2	18	–	3	42
Married	2	2	38	–	–	42
Total	32	8	66	2	8	116

Corrodies were probably generally drawn up for the period of the husband's life, as in the case of John and Beatrice de Cundall of Huby who bought the most expensive of all the corrodies at £81 in 1394. If Beatrice survived her husband she was to receive half the food, candles, and fuel stipulated in the agreement but not the livery suit of a yeoman of the hospital which was given to John annually.[130] In addition a few women were also appointed to the hospital as royal corrodians. Isabella de la Helde, granted the allowance of a brother in 1312, was a lady in waiting to Queen Isabella. She kept it until she died c.1342, when she was replaced by Joan Gambon as a reward for her service to Queen Philippa and princess Isabella.[131] While these two were relatively comfortable, another royal pensioner was in genuine need of charity: Matilda de Weston of Wanberge's husband had been captured by the Scots and killed 'so that his wife is reduced to beggary, being unable to work on account of age'.[132]

Maisonsdieu and hospitals may also have acted on occasion as refuges for women fleeing male violence. In an ecclesiastical cause heard in 1349 Margaret Denome was said to have fled her violent husband in the middle of the night and taken refuge in a Newcastle hospital.[133] In London in 1300 Johanna de Cherringe of Canterbury drowned between the Tower of London and the hospital of St Katherine, a hospital for women under the patronage of the queen. According to the coroner's jury she was pursued out of the gate of

Billingsgate by Laurence le Poleter who forced her to drown herself in the ditch, but it is possible that she was seeking refuge in the hospital.[134]

Charity and the Female Role

We started with the female figure of Charity leading pilgrims into her home, but this only takes us so far, as most allegorical figures of virtues were female. Of perhaps greater significance is that it is Charity's female servant who places bread on the table. A useful way into the problem is by looking at contemporary expectations through a didactic work 'How the Good Wijf taughte Hir Doughtir'.[135] The earliest version of this poem dates to about 1350, though the majority of the manuscripts which contain it date to the fifteenth century. The first stanza concerns devotion to God and attendance at church. The second instructs:

> Blethely geve thi tithys and thin offerynges bothe.
> The pore men at thi dore, be thou hem noght lothe.
> Geve hem blethely of thi good, and be thou nogth to harde:
> Seldam is the house pore ther God is stywarde.
> Tresour he hath that pouere fedith
> My leve childe.[136]

In some versions the poor are twinned with the bedridden as being deserving.[137] Another version prescribes giving clothing as well as food.[138] In all versions this order and the prominent placing of almsgiving is preserved. 'The Thewis off Gud Women' a similar didactic work of the late fifteenth century, urges:

> Be evir of pur folke petousable,
> Do Almous-deid, be cherytable[139]

but does not place this so prominently.

By contrast 'How the Wise Man Taught His Son', also of fifteenth-century date, places almsgiving relatively low on the scale of priorities – after relations with God, business, social behaviour, and the choice and treatment of a wife.[140] Christine de Pisan discusses whether in religion ladies should pursue the active or the contemplative life and concludes that they should attempt both. Her understanding of the active life is couched entirely in terms of the performance of acts of charity. The Knight of La Tour-Landry made the performance of charitable acts by noblewomen the subject of eleven of the 144 chapters of the instructional work which he wrote for his daughters.[141]

The Seven Works of Mercy were a fairly common subject for wall-paintings in churches and Tristram commented that 'it is noticeable that in almost all representations the Works are performed by a woman'. At Potter Heigham, Norfolk, for example, where only the Clothing scene is missing, the surviving Works are all performed by a female figure. At Trotton, Sussex, where the Works are represented in roundels surrounding the figure of the Good Man, receiving the stranger and visiting the prisoner are carried out by a male figure, but all the other five Works are performed by a woman.[142]

These Works thus clearly indicate that almsgiving and charitable behaviour was regarded as an important part of the female role in a way that it was not of the male role. The practice of charity was enjoined upon women as part of their domestic role and household duties. The spiritual work *Ancrene Wisse* of c.1200 distinguishes the contemplative life of Mary from the practical life of Martha, as 'Martha's role is to feed and clothe the poor, as the lady of the house does'.[143] Jacques de Vitry was not alone as a preacher in using an *exemplum* in which a merchant gave his savings to his wife, instructing her to give alms freely, but discovering on her death that she had hoarded them. The point of this story was both to encourage the giving of alms, and to suggest that it was the wife's duty to distribute the money provided by her husband. Theologians discussed the issue of whether a wife, as a subordinate to her husband, could give alms without his knowledge or permission. Aquinas came to the conclusion that she could, provided she did not beggar him in the process.[144] When a witness in a York lawsuit wanted to emphasise the good character of one of the protagonists, Agnes Grantham, a widow, she pointed to her works of charity and almsgiving. Le Blevec emphasises that it was in the daily giving at the door that the majority of female charitable activity took place.[145] From providing the household with food, drink, and clothing it was but a step to providing these to beggars at the door. Bynum has emphasised the way in which food preparation and distribution was a female activity, that food 'is *the* resource that women control'. Hence this type of giving was a 'culturally acceptable form of asceticism'.[146]

In the context of the idea that charity was a specifically female activity, it may be worth noting the foundation of an almshouse in Pontefract by Constance and Robert Knollys. Leland records a tradition that this location was chosen because it was Constance's home.[147] There is certainly no evidence that Knollys, a wealthy man with property in several parts of the country, held land in Pontefract before the decision was made to found the almshouse there. This suggests that the leading part in the foundation of Knollys' Almshouse was played by Constance rather than Robert. Constance predeceased Robert so there is no evidence of her independent interest in the hospital, but she may not be the only example of a wife who played a leading role in the foundation of an almshouse more generally associated with her husband.[148] It was not just part of the wifely role either; John Thornbury of Kent (d. 1473) asked that 'dame Philippa my doughter have an oversight that myn almesfolke in Faversham have their almes'.[149] Women were moreover capable of founding almshouses independently. We are reminded of Agnes Brome and the maisondieu at the bottom of her garden, the poor women lying in the house of Cecily Plater in St Andrewgate, York, and Joan Gregg of Hull, founder of Gregg's hospital.[150]

Charity was also a prominent part of the sanctity of a number of popular female saints of the later Middle Ages. Among these may be numbered St Bridget of Sweden, who though better known for her mystical visions and advice to the pope, spent much of her last years caring for the poor and sick in Rome. St Anne, the mother of Mary, was thought to have devoted a third of her income to widows, orphans and the poor.[151] St Elizabeth of Hungary was the queen who fed the poor, and in her widowhood retired to serve the poor and sick in the hospital of Marburg, feeding and clothing them. She is depicted engaged in distributing food and clothing to the poor from the door of her house, or possibly a hospital in a book of hours which may have belonged to William, Lord Hastings.[152] Zita (Sith or Sitha in England) of Lucca was a maidservant who regularly gave her employer's food to the poor. Both of these saints may be depicted with a loaf turning into roses or other flowers. This represents a story that despite being forbidden to give bread to the poor they did so. When challenged about bread hidden in an apron or basket, they claimed it was flowers, which indeed it was miraculously revealed to be.[153] This is an apocryphal story not attested in early versions of the lives of these saints, but indicating the expectation that female saints should be heroically charitable. These stories were intended to encourage charitable activity on the part of women, both householders and servants, even in the face of worldly discouragement.[154]

In conclusion, almsgiving was particularly enjoined upon women as part of their household duties, and this is reflected in the kind of wills which women made. Women were more likely to be charitable than men although the resources at their disposal were fewer and thus they may have given less in absolute terms. They were more likely to make charitable bequests but often on a small scale and to individuals known to them. As much of their giving was on a neighbourhood basis, it is probable that much of their charitable giving is disguised from us because they were more likely to simply name the beneficiary without describing them in such terms as 'pauper' or 'widow'. Moreover the motivation behind the giving of many bequests in female wills is lost to us and may represent charitable activity which we cannot know about. It is likely that many of the small money gifts represent very personal acts of charity. Nevertheless women did not confine themselves to private and personal acts of charity. They were also involved in acts of public charity, operating at the level of the community as a whole, giving to such ends as prisons, roads, and hospitals. In no area of public charitable activity were women noticeably under-represented, and they can be discovered as founders and patrons of maisonsdieu. Indeed they took at least an equal role with husbands in such foundations and certainly can be discovered as independent founders. There is thus no evidence of a public/private split between the charitable activities of men and women.

However women's charitable activity did grow out of their role as household managers, providers of food, clothing, fuel, and shelter to their own households and to the poor and pilgrims. It is these areas where female charitable activity was enjoined by contemporary didactic literature, and it is largely, though not exclusively, within the domestic sphere that the exemplary stories of saints such as Sitha and Anne are contained. It is precisely in these areas of domestic management and responsibility, particularly in the provision of food and drink, clothing and fuel, where women were most prominent as charitable providers.

As recipients of charity, provision was generally directed at women on the threshold of marriage or as widows, and there is some evidence of a feminisation of poverty, or at least of larger numbers of women in maisonsdieu, through the fifteenth century. This was due to developing economic depression from the second third of the century leading to a tendency for guilds to preserve male jobs at the expense of women, excluding them from secure and well-paid employment. Here the increasing emphasis on poor maids' dowries from about the middle of the century probably reflects the increased difficulty for such young women of finding employment in which they could save towards a marriage. The evidence from the purchase of liveries and corrodies at St Leonard's suggests that single women could usually only afford the cheaper places, but that marriage brought economic advantages to both men and women.

Notes

1   BL, Ms. Cotton Tiberius A VII, fo. 90; R.M. Clay, *The Medieval Hospitals of England* (1909), pp. 5–6, plate 1.
2   BIHR, Prob. Reg. 3 fo.111.
3   M.M. Sheehan, *The Will in Medieval England* (Toronto, 1963); C. Burgess, '"By Quick and By Dead": Wills and Pious Provision in late Medieval Bristol', *English Historical Review* 102 (1987), pp. 837–58.
4   BIHR, Prob. Reg. 1–13; BIHR, Archbishop's Registers, Reg. 10–24; York Merchant Adventurers' Cartulary and Deeds, D19 and D43/7; YML Dean and Chapter Probate Registers, D/C Reg. 1; P.H. Cullum, 'Hospitals and Charitable Provision in Medieval

Yorkshire, 936–1547' (unpublished D.Phil thesis, University of York, 1989), ch. 5; P.H. Cullum, *Hospitals and Charitable Care in Medieval England* (Manchester, forthcoming).

5   Each group was counted to find the total number of wills in that group, for example 132 female wills in sample 2. These were then re-counted for the number of wills which contained specific charitable bequests, in this case 60. This was then expressed as a percentage so that groups could be compared, e.g. 45.5 per cent of female wills as opposed to 38.7 per cent of lay male wills contained charitable bequests in sample 2. The number of wills in a particular group was then expressed as a percentage of the total sample, thus female testators were 15.3 per cent of the total.

6   P.J.P. Goldberg, 'Female labour, Service and Marriage in the late Medieval Urban North', *Northern History* 22 (1986), p. 37.

7   W.K. Jordan, *The Charities of London, 1480–1600* (New York, 1960), p. 30. K. Mertes, *The English Noble Household, 1250–1600* (Oxford, 1988), p. 158.

8   'L' action principale des beguines dans le siècle [thirteenth century] était la pratique des oeuvres de miséricorde': D. Le Blevec, 'Le role des femmes dans l'assistance et la charité', *Cahiers de Fanjeaux* 23 (1988), p. 175. I. Maclean, *The Renaissance Notion of Woman: A Study in the Fortunes of Scholasticism and Medical Science in European Intellectual Life* (Cambridge, 1980), pp. 20–1 and n.; C.W. Bynum, *Holy Feast and Holy Fast: The Religious Significance of Food to Medieval Women* (Berkeley, 1987), pp. 4, 88. For a consideration of charity as an aspect of the female role in the modern era see F.K. Prochaska, *Women and Philanthropy in Nineteenth Century England* (Oxford, 1980).

9   Bynum, *Holy Feast and Holy Fast*, p. 88.

10 YML, D/C Reg. 1 fos.122v, 127v. BIHR, Prob. Reg. 2 fo. 93.

11 BIHR, Prob. Reg. 2 fo.418.

12 BIHR, Prob. Reg. 1 fo. 5v.

13 BIHR, Prob. Reg. 1 fo.20. Both these wills were made on the nativity of St John the Baptist. Alice subsequently made another will on 25 October in Rome in which she is described as a widow. This was presumably a deathbed will as probate was granted on both her and William's wills on 10 February 1390–1, after the party with which they were travelling returned to York.

14 BIHR, Prob. Reg. 2 fo.91: 'elemosinis largicione pauperibus'.

15 BIHR, Prob. Reg. 2 fo.52: 'in puris operibus caritatis'.

16 BIHR, Prob. Reg. 2 fo.161.

17 J.A.F. Thomson, 'Piety and Charity in Late Medieval London', *Journal of Ecclesiastical History* 16 (1965), p. 180.

18 Ibid. Unfortunately he then went on to try to make precisely this distinction.

19 *English Mystery Plays*, ed. P. Happé (Harmondsworth, 1975), p. 645.

20 *James* 2:20.

21 BIHR, Prob. Reg. 1 fo.79v.

22 P. Heath, 'Urban Piety in the Later Middle Ages: the Evidence of Hull Wills' in *The Church, Politics and Patronage in the Fifteenth Century*, ed. R.B. Dobson (Gloucester, 1984), p. 224.

23 BIHR, Prob. Reg. 2 fo.340v: 'caritative disponantur'.

24 BIHR, Prob. Reg. 2 fo.393.

25 BIHR, Prob. Reg. 2 fo.300v.

26 BIHR, Prob. Reg. 1 fo.24.

27 BIHR, Prob. Reg. 4 fo.221.

28 M.C. Cross, 'Northern Women in the Early Modern Period: the Female Testators of Hull and Leeds, 1520–1650', *Yorkshire Archaeological Journal* 59 (1987), p. 92.

29 BIHR, Prob. Reg. 9 fo.272.

30 BIHR, Prob. Reg. 2 fos.27–8.

31 BIHR, Prob. Reg. 1 fo.89: 'et convocationem amicorum'.

32   BIHR, Prob. Reg. 1 fo.83.
33   Thomson, 'Piety and Charity', p. 181.
34   Burgess, '"By Quick and by Dead"', p. 845.
35   BIHR, Prob. Reg. 2 fo.385v.
36   BIHR, Prob. Reg. 1 fo.24.
37   BIHR, Prob. Reg. 1 fo.23v.
38   BIHR, Prob. Reg. 2 fo.13v.
39   *Luke* 14:16–24.
40   *Lay Folks' Catechism*, ed. T.P. Simmons and H.E. Nolloth, EETS 118 (1901), p. 72; BIHR, Prob. Reg. 3 fo.96.
41   BIHR, Prob. Reg. 1 fo.79v.
42   BIHR, Prob. Reg. 2 fo.238.
43   BIHR, Prob. Reg. 2 fos.35v–36.
44   'Maisondieu' was the usual term in this northern region for an almshouse.
45   BIHR, Prob. Reg. 3 fo.606; BIHR, Reg. 16 (Scrope) fo.173–v.
46   BIHR, Prob. Reg. 2 fo.2v.
47   Charitable giving to the maisonsdieu is discussed below under visiting the sick, but the maisonsdieu fulfilled a number of functions, of which care of the homeless and the sick were the principal ones, and gifts to the maisonsdieu could fulfil both works of mercy.
48   *The Book of Margery Kempe*, ed. W. Butler-Bowdon (1936), p. 103. BIHR, Prob. Reg. 1 fo. 5: *remaneant ibidem ad deserviendum pauperibus indigentibus hospitalitatis*.
49   I. Origo, *The Merchant of Prato* (Oxford, 1957), p. 192.
50   C.M. Barron, 'The "Golden Age" of Women in Medieval London', *Reading Medieval Studies* 25 (1989), p. 47.
51   BIHR, Prob. Reg. 2 fo.284v.
52   BIHR, Prob. Reg. 6 fo.96.
53   Origo, *Merchant of Prato* pp. 274–5.
54   BIHR, Prob. Reg. 1 fo.83v: 'in panno vocatur northerynrussett ut alio panno eis decent'.
55   BIHR, Prob. Reg. 1 fos.27–8.
56   BIHR, Prob. Reg. 9 fo.272v.
57   York Merchant Adventurers' Cartulary, D19 fo.122.
58   BIHR, Prob. Reg. 2 fo.169v.
59   YML, D/C Reg. 1 fo.318.
60   N.P. Tanner, *The Church in Late Medieval Norwich* (Toronto, 1984), p. 231.
61   York Merchant Adventurers' Deeds, D43/7.
62   M. Rubin, *Charity and Community in Medieval Cambridge* (Cambridge, 1987), p. 262.
63   Ibid.; E. Power, *The Medieval English Wool Trade* (Oxford, 1941), p. 15.
64   YML, D/C Reg. 1 fo.15.
65   BIHR, Prob. Reg. 3 fo.487v.
66   BIHR, Prob. Reg. 2 fo.83v (Girlyngton).
67   BIHR, Prob. Reg. 2 fo.8v.
68   Rubin, *Charity and Community*, p. 261.
69   BIHR, Prob. Reg. 1 fo.31; 2 fo.61.
70   Robert Hunter directed his executors to reward Katherine More from his goods 'pro suo assiduo labore tempore infirmitate mee': BIHR, Prob. Reg. 2 fo.159v. *Book of Margery Kempe*, pp. 260–6, 367.
71   Le Blevec, 'Le role des femmes', pp. 177–8.
72   BIHR, Prob. Reg. 2 fo.14.
73   M.G.A. Vale, *Piety, Charity and Literacy among the Yorkshire Gentry, 1370–1480*, Borthwick Paper 50 (York, 1976), p. 26.
74   BIHR, Prob. Reg. 2 fo.71v.
75   J. Stow, *A Survey of London* i (Oxford, 1908), p. 116.

76 Ibid., pp. 37–40.

77 See Agnes Constantyne above.

78 Christine de Pisan, *The Treasure of the City of Ladies*, trans. S. Lawson (Harmondsworth, 1985), p. 53; Christine de Pisan, *The Book of the City of Ladies*, trans. E.J. Richards (1983), p. 210.

79 B. Pullan, 'Support and Redeem: Charity and Poor Relief in Italian Cities from the Fourteenth to the Seventeenth Century', *Continuity and Change* 3 (1988), p. 177.

80 Origo, *Merchant of Prato*, pp. 278–9.

81 BIHR, Prob. Reg. 2 fo.93v.

82 E. Rickert, *Chaucer's World* (1948), p. 351.

83 J. Henderson, 'The Parish and the Poor in Florence at the Time of the Black Death: The case of S. Frediano', *Continuity and Change* 3 (1988), pp. 252–9.

84 E.W. Tristram, *English Wall-Painting of the Fourteenth Century* (1955), p. 260. See below for further discussion.

85 The collection of firewood was a specifically female task among the peasantry: B.A. Hanawalt, *The Ties that Bound: Peasant Families in Medieval England* (New York, 1986), p. 50. BIHR, Prob. Reg. 1 fo.59v.

86 BIHR, Prob. Reg. 2 fos.92, 238.

87 BIHR, Prob. Reg. 4 fo.221: '*omnes fasticulos ad distribuendum inter pauperes christi cum le Astilwod et terre sodijs*'. BIHR, CP.F.36.

88 Tanner, *Medieval Norwich*, p. 230.

89 Pullan, 'Support and redeem', p. 177.

90 BIHR, Reg. 16 (Scrope) fo. 173. A related concern is expressed by Margaret Paston in a letter to her husband about the tenants of Mautby, the manor which she inherited from her father: 'Item, ther be dyvers of your tenauntrys at Mauteby that had gret ned for to be reparyd, but the tenauntys be so por that they are not a power to repare hem: wherfor . . . I wold that the marche . . . be kept in your owne hand this yer, that the tenaunts myght have ruschys to repare with her howsys. And also, there is wyndfall wod at the maner that is of noo gret valewe, that myght helpe hem wyth toward the reparacion, yf it leke you to late hem have it that hathe most need therof.' *Paston Letters and Papers of the Fifteenth Century* i, ed. N. Davis (Oxford, 1971), no. 178, pp. 292–3.

91 Although provision was regularly made for women, gender does not seem to have been the usual basis for allocating donations as it was in Florence where female recipients were particularly favoured. This is because in Yorkshire women were generally regarded as being capable of earning their own living whereas this was not true in Florence. Moreover Italian widows were heavily dependent upon the return of their dowries and faced corresponding difficulties in regaining them, whereas in England it was usual for the widow to act as executor among the will-making groups: I. Chabot, 'Poverty and the Widow in Later Medieval Florence', *Continuity and Change* 3 (1988), pp. 291–3, pp. 296–301. Charity in Spain, particularly directed towards widows and poor maids, as a form of social reintegration of marginal groups, is discussed by C.L. Alonso, 'Mujer medieval y pobreza', in *La Condicion de la Mujer en la Edad Media*, ed. Y.-R. Fonquerne and A. Esteban (Madrid, 1986), pp. 261–72.

92 Heath, 'Urban Piety', p.218.

93 BIHR, Prob. Reg. 3 fo.437: '*cuilibet pauperi mulieri que michi operari et filare consuevit vjd*'.

94 BIHR, Prob. Reg. 3 fo.567.

95 BIHR, Prob. Reg. 4 fo.70: '*pauperibus mulieribus laborantibus et operantibus ex consuetudine nemdo et carpendo lanas meas*'.

96 BIHR, Prob. Reg. 4 fo.72.

97 BIHR, Prob. Reg. 1 fos.88, 93.

98 YML, D/C Reg. 1 fos.11, 15. *Book of Margery Kempe*, pp. 254–5.

99 YML, D/C Reg. 1 fo.37.

100 BIHR, Prob. Reg. 1 fo.49v.

101 BIHR, Prob. Reg. 1 fo.55v.

102 BIHR, Prob. Reg. 3 fo.487v.

103 In 1377 the population of Easingwold liable for the Poll Tax was 206. This figure is no doubt smaller than that of the pre-Black Death community, but 43 widows must still have been a high proportion of the population. B.J.D. Harrison, 'The 1377 Poll Tax Returns for the North Riding', *Cleveland and Teesside Local History Society Bulletin* 10 (1970), p. 6.

104 BIHR, Prob. Reg. 4 fo.115v.

105 BIHR, Prob. Reg. 2 fo.266.

106 Lady Joan Wombwell (d. 1454), almost certainly Thomas' widow, left money to 'le beydhous': BIHR, Prob. Reg. 2 fo.304.

107 BIHR, Prob. Reg. 1 fo.88. Lucrezia Tornabuoni of Florence financed the marriage of a poor hosier's daughter. The provision of dowries for poor young Italian women was particularly important because without one they could not marry, and it was very difficult for them to earn sufficient to save a dowry. Dowry provision was often made by Italian confraternities: Pullan, 'Support and Redeem', pp. 177, 185.

108 BIHR, Prob. Reg. 2 fos.276, 315v.

109 BIHR, Prob. Reg. 2 fo.286.

110 BIHR, Prob. Reg. 2 fo.327v.

111 BIHR, Prob. Reg. 3 fo.487.

112 BIHR, Prob. Reg. 5 fo.327v.

113 BIHR, Prob. Reg. 4 fo.34v; 5 fo.327v.

114 Tanner, *Medieval Norwich*, p. 135.

115 Thomson, 'Piety and Charity', p. 186.

116 BIHR, Prob. Reg. 3 fo.111.

117 I am grateful to Derek Keene for this suggestion. One such row survives at Holy Trinity, Goodramgate, York, but they were clearly very common.

118 Evidence from the early modern period suggests that widows, especially poorer and older widows, were less likely to remarry than comparable widowers, and their frequent lack of access to skilled work reduced them to dependency on unskilled, intermittent and low-paid work: V. Brodsky, 'Widows in Late Elizabethan London: Remarriage, Economic Opportunity and Family Orientations', in *The World We Have Gained; Histories of Population and Social Structure*, ed. L. Bonfield, R.M. Smith, and K. Wrightson (Oxford, 1986), pp. 122–4; B.J. Todd, 'The Remarrying Widow: a Stereotype Reconsidered', in *Women in English Society, 1500–1800*, ed. M. Prior (1985), pp. 65–72.

119 BIHR, Prob. Reg. 1 fo.13v; YML, D/C Reg. 1 fos.59, 290v.

120 In 1397 Thomas de Kent left 6s. 8d. to the poor women in the house of Cecily Plater in St Andrewgate, suggesting a female founder of this maisondieu specifically for women: BIHR, Prob. Reg. 2 fo.4. The maisondieu was unusually long-lived, receiving a bequest from Leonard Shaw in 1532 who left 3s. to the poor women in the 'beadehowse in Sancte Andrewgate': BIHR, Prob. Reg. 11A fo.10v.

121 BIHR, Prob. Reg. 3 fo.275v. St Andrewgate seems to have been part of the 'red-light district' of medieval York and therefore more likely to have had a relatively high population of impoverished women: P.J.P. Goldberg, 'Women in Fifteenth-Century Town Life', in *Towns and Townspeople in the Fifteenth Century*, ed. J.A.F. Thomson (Gloucester, 1988), p. 119.

122 *York City Chamberlains' Account Rolls, 1396–1500*, ed. R.B. Dobson, Surtees Society, 192, (1979), pp. 14, 30. The dates are of the two nearest surviving Chamberlains' Accounts.

123 YML, M2(6)d, fos.38–38v. Unfortunately this is the only surviving document which records the infirmary population according to gender. It is therefore impossible to tell whether this represented a change from an earlier period.

124 Tanner, *Medieval Norwich*, pp. 133–4.

125 BIHR, Prob. Reg. 13 fo. 60v. (John Cape); C.J.D. Ingledew, *The History and Antiquities of North Allerton* (1885), pp. 260–8.

126 BIHR, Prob. Reg. 5 fo. 106.

127 Goldberg, 'Female Labour, Service and Marriage', p. 35; H. Scott, *Working Your Way to the Bottom: The Feminization of Poverty* (1984) explores this concept in the modern context. The foundation of hospitals for widows and poor women and the concentration of fraternities upon the relief of women in Florence and Venice in the aftermath of the Black Death probably reflects the rather different structure of the Italian economy and society, and the very limited opportunities for women to support themselves independently in it: Henderson, 'The Parish and the Poor', pp. 259–60; Pullan, 'Support and Redeem', p. 189. By the seventeenth century women comprised the majority of the inhabitants of the beggars' hospitals of Florence and the longest stayers: ibid., p. 199. Todd, 'The Remarrying Widow', pp. 72, 79 also sees increased institutional provision for poor women and widows from the late sixteenth century in Abingdon.

128 PRO, C 270.21 no. 3.

129 PRO, C 270.21 no. 4.

130 *CPR, 1396–99*, p. 383.

131 *CCR, 1307–12*, p. 454; *CCR 1341–43*, p. 656.

132 *CCR, 1313–18*, p. 198.

133 Goldberg, 'Female Labour, Service and Marriage', p. 28.

134 *Calendar of Coroners' Rolls of the City of London, 1300–78*, ed. R.R. Sharpe (1913), p. 13.

135 *The Good Wife Taught Her Daughter*, ed. T.-F. Mustanoja (Helsinki, 1948).

136 *The Good Wife*, p. 159. Huntingdon Library, Ms. HM 128. This may in part be based upon *Proverbs* 31:20 which describes the model wife: 'She opens her hand to the poor, and reaches out her hand to the needy.'

137 Ibid., pp. 197, 203.

138 Ibid., Bodleian Ms. Ashmole 61, p. 217.

139 Ibid., p. 182.

140 Ibid., pp. 63–4.

141 Pisan, *Treasure of the City of Ladies*, pp. 43–6; *The Book of the Knight of the Tour-Landry*, ed. T. Wright, EETS 33 (1906). Geoffroy de la Tour wrote the book in 1371–2, and it was translated into English in the mid-fifteenth century, and again by Caxton who printed it in 1484: ibid. pp. xii, xv–xvi.

142 Tristram, *English Wall Painting*, pp. 101, 237, 260.

143 'Marthe meoster is to feden poure ant schruden as hus-leafdi': *Medieval English Prose for Women*, ed. B. Millett and J. Wogan-Browne (Oxford, 1990), pp. 132–3.

144 F.C. Tubach, *Index Exemplorum: A Handbook of Medieval Religious Tales* (Helsinki, 1969), p. 260. Thomas Aquinas, *Summa Theologiae*, 2a2ae, 32, 8–9. I am grateful to P.P.A. Biller for these references.

145 BIHR, CP.F.36: '*opera caritatis et elemosine pauperibus largienda*'. I am grateful to P.J.P. Goldberg for bringing this to my attention. Le Blevec, 'Le role des femmes', p. 178.

146 Bynum, *Holy Feast and Holy Fast*, p. 191.

147 J. Leland, *The Itinerary* i (London, 1964), p. 39.

148 P.S. Gold, *The Lady and the Virgin: Image, Attitude and Experience in Twelfth–Century France* (Chicago, 1985), p. 130 suggests that where charters transfer land in the name of husband and wife, this represented a secondary role for the women as 'co-alienor' or 'consenter' and that in such cases she merely assented to an act decided by the husband. However, contemporary English evidence must throw some doubt on this conclusion, at least as it applies to England. A grant by Alan son of Roger to the hospital of St Peter, York, was made at the instance and petition of his wife Ellen (*ad instanciam et peticionem*) and a gift by Ralph Buscel to the nuns of St Mary of Wykeham referred to land given both by himself and one Anketinus Norrais, in both cases by the advice and consent (*consilio et*

consensu) of their respective wives; *Early Yorkshire Charters*, ed. W. Farrar (Edinburgh, 1914), no. 308, p. 237; no. 382, p. 299. In both cases the strong implication is that although the legal title to the property was transferred primarily by the husband, the initiative for the donation lay with the wife and she can thus be seen to have had a good deal of practical influence over the disposition of property.

149   P.W. Fleming, 'Charity, Faith and the Gentry of Kent, 1422–1529' in *Property and Politics: Essays in Later Medieval English History*, ed. A.J. Pollard (Gloucester, 1984), p. 45.

150   BIHR, Reg. 16 (Scrope) fo.173; Prob. Reg. 2 fo.4; 3 fo.555v. Joan Gregg's charitable bequests are discussed by P. Heath, 'Urban Piety', pp. 224–5.

151   T. Brandenbarg, 'St Anne and her Family' in *Saints and She-Devils: Images of Women in the 15th and 16th Centuries*, ed. L. Dresen-Coenders (1987), p. 104.

152   BL Ms. Add. 54782 fo.64v. Probably made in Ghent c.1480, it contains the arms of William, Lord Hastings (d. 1483).

153   This motif is a common feature of the legends of other female saints: Le Blevec, 'Le role des femmes', p. 176. The basket of flowers and fruit which is the symbol of St Dorothy represents the fruits of faith rather than charity.

154   See M. Goodich, '*Ancilla Dei*: The Servant as Saint in the Later Middle Ages', in *Women of the Medieval World*, ed. J. Kirshner and S.F. Wemple (Oxford, 1985), pp. 119–36.

8

'Blessed Art Thou Among Women': The Archaeology of Female Piety

Roberta Gilchrist
University of Reading

This chapter presents aspects of research on the gender archaeology of late medieval England.[1] Archaeology embraces all aspects of the material past, including buildings, artefacts, and plastic media, in addition to archaeo-logical deposits buried below the surface of the ground. Gender archaeo-logy is the study of distinctions between femininity and masculinity which are socially created. These distinctions may be approached through the symbolic expression of gender identities. Medieval gender roles – the culturally accepted expectations of men and women – were intrinsic to religious belief and were played out with reference to the material world. Here the general aim is to explore the ways in which material culture reflects, and actively constructs, attitudes toward religious women.

Material culture creates and renegotiates social structures through the medium of individual human action, or agency. Thus, female agency is made visible to the enquiry, in contrast to previous archaeological approaches which have considered women in past societies merely as objects to 'be controlled and exchanged. An approach to medieval gender relations can be made by studying religious institutions and, more particularly, their relationships to medieval women. Female piety might be considered in its passive sense, through the theological construction of socially sanctioned roles for religious women. More active forms of female piety were demonstrated through women's participation in ecclesiastical institutions, principally nunneries and hospitals, and through charitable activities, religious benefaction and the commissioning of commemorative chantries and funerary art. Archaeologically these aspects of female piety translate into material forms which were either to instruct religious women (passive) or reflect beliefs held by the women themselves (active).

This approach to the study of religious women is multi-disciplinary. It not only integrates an array of medieval material culture which cuts across the boundaries of academic disciplines, but examines the inter-relationships between religious architecture and other cultural products, in particular manuscript illumination, sculpture, hagiography, liturgy and written records. The starting point for the enquiry, however, varies from a deductive to an inductive method.

The traditional role of medieval archaeology has been to test the hypotheses of historians, working deductively from written records to archaeological evidence. In contrast the intention of this paper is to elucidate an archaeological pattern – one which has been recognised inductively – with reference to historical and iconographic sources. Archaeological study of the medieval nunneries of England has suggested a high incidence of unorthodox cloister orientation.[2] The significance of the cloister orientation will be explored in terms of the motives affecting monastic patrons, planners and inmates. Particular regard is given to the role of female agency in nunnery planning, and the impact of architectural form on active and passive female piety. Nunneries were affiliated to monastic orders on a fairly casual basis, so that patrons may have influenced the location and architectural form of the house. Women were often prominent in the foundation of nunneries, acting as sole patron or jointly with husbands or other male relatives. The extent to which female interest is hidden behind the actions of male patrons cannot be gauged precisely, but is sometimes apparent. Chatteris (Cambs), for example, was established before 1016 by Bishop Ednoth of Dorchester (former Abbot of Ramsey) at the request of his sister, Aelfwen.

Of the approximately 150 nunneries known to have existed, it has been possible to compile a sample of 58 nunneries for which the cloister orientation can be identified. Of these, 29.3 per cent (N = 17) were planned with their cloister to the liturgical north of the church. North cloisters were not exclusive to nunneries; they are known to have existed at monasteries for men. No percentage is available at present, but north cloisters appear relatively infrequently within the approximate total of 900 monasteries. For the purposes of comparison, each known nunnery cloister orientation has been checked against the nearest male house of similar endowment in order to determine cloister orientation and site restrictions on planning.

Ideally cloisters would have been placed to the south of a church in order to achieve maximum light and warmth. The most significant factor in monastic planning, however, was adequate water supply and drainage. Flowing water was required behind the dormitory to flush the latrine drains; often a second source provided fresh drinking water. The water source could determine the location of the dormitory, and thus the orientation of the cloister. Where resources were available watercourses could be diverted, but poorer communities were obliged to accept the natural limitations of a site. Where north cloisters have previously been commented upon, they are assumed to be the result of topographical restrictions. While this explanation is appropriate for certain male houses, for example Rochester, Waltham, Tintern, and Buildwas, north cloister orientation may have a specific meaning within the architecture of religious women.

The lower social and economic level of nunneries may have reduced opportunities for altering unsuitable sites, so that north cloisters would reflect lack of economic power. This may be tested by mapping the water sources of the north and south cloister nunneries. If a nunnery's water source was located to the north of the site, its cloister was more likely to have been positioned to the north of the church. Where several water sources were apparent the major source for drainage has been considered. Arthington (W. Yorks), for example, has the River Wharfe to the north of the site (resulting in a north cloister), and a fresh water spring running from the ridge to the south which would have supplied drinking water. Results of the mapping are somewhat surprising: a higher proportion of north cloister nunneries (N = 7) than south cloister ones actually had water sources to the south of the site (N = 17). North cloisters were not a product of functional restrictions on planning. When the female houses are compared to the nearest male house of similar economic level, it seems that cloister orientation does not follow regional preference and is not a direct result of available financial resources. For the north cloister group 82.4 per cent (N = 14) of the nearest male houses have south cloisters; 87.8 per cent of the nearest male monasteries to the cloister group have south cloisters.

The significance of the 29.3 per cent figure for north cloisters is clearly dependent on the representativity of the sample. A similar proportion of north cloisters can be suggested through dissolution surveys of the Yorkshire nunneries.[3] When the total sample of 58 is mapped (Fig. 8.1) a distinctive pattern can be observed. The south cloisters are evenly distributed across England, whereas the north cloister type cluster into regional groups. Three discrete clusters can be identified in:

1. the southeast (Barking, Bishopsgate, Burnham, Clerkenwell, Minster in Sheppey)

2. Cambridgeshire (Cambridge, Chatteris, Denny, Hinchingbrooke, Ickleton)

3. Yorkshire and Humberside (Arthington, Thicket, Watton, Wilberfoss)

Pinley and Brewood (Shrops) may form an associated midlands pattern. Lacock, however, is geographically isolated from other north cloister nunneries. It falls within a group of north cloister monasteries in the Avon Valley of Wiltshire, which includes the male monasteries of Malmesbury, Stanley and Bradenstoke. The clusters correspond with the distribution of Saxon double houses, sited in areas of Merovingian contact (Kent, East Anglia and Northumbria). In each of the three clusters there is at least

Figure 8.1
DISTRIBUTION OF NORTH AND SOUTH CLOISTERS

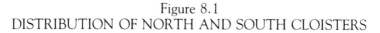

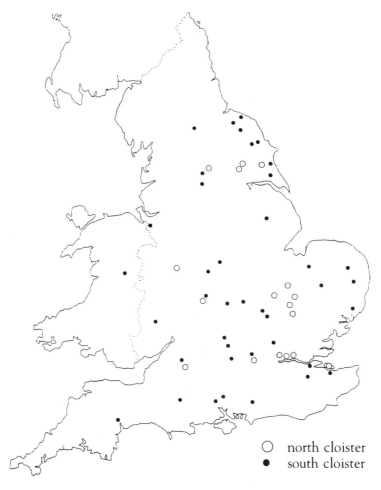

○   north cloister
●   south cloister

one nunnery refounded on the site of a Saxon house. These include Barking, Minster in Sheppey, Chatteris, Hinchingbrooke (the refoundation of Saxon Eltisley was moved here by the thirteenth century), and Watton. To some extent, north cloisters may have been nostalgic foundations recalling traditions of Saxon royal female piety.

Consideration of the foundation date, or refoundations in certain cases, reveals that the north cloister pattern does not correspond with a fixed temporal preference: they span the eleventh to fourteenth centuries. Figure 8.2 illustrates their chronological distribution. Half of the sample cluster between 1133 and 1155 but this corresponds with the densest

Figure 8.2
CHRONOLOGY OF CLOISTER ORIENTATION

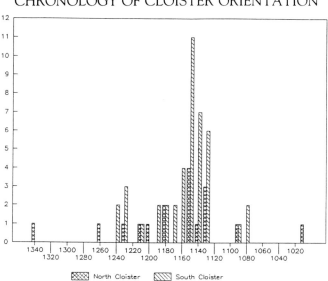

period of monastic foundation in general. The north cloisters do not reflect a centrally planned filial trait – although it may be suggested that Augustinian nunneries showed a taste for north cloisters (4N:3S) and Cistercian nunneries chose against them (1N:8S). The tendency for regional clustering lends support to the argument that the north cloister feature was a deliberate choice on the part of planner or patrons. The clusters represent the process of adopting or copying fashions in architecture which conveyed a specific social or iconographic message.

Structural Oppositions: North/South

Is the north cloister nunnery a mirror image of the south cloister male monastery? While the southern aisle of Gilbertine nunnery churches was set aside for the canons, their cloister was not placed directly to the south of the church. In contrast to certain French double monasteries, for example Marcigny, English double houses were not planned with mirror cloisters. A structuralist interpretation would assign meaning through the spatial opposites observed within the code of monastic architecture. Deep level structure is assumed to be bound together by binary oppositions, such as north/south, which are thought to comprise the underlying schemes for the organisation of material culture. Archaeologists and anthropologists have frequently identified structural dichotomies as representative of a male/female contradiction. This application divorces material from its cultural context, and assumes universal gender relations. It is well established, however, that a male/female duality was intrinsic to medieval Christian philosophy in which man represented the spiritual soul and woman represented the corporeal body.[4]

Christian symbolism recognised certain opposites in the attributes of north and south. Generally the north of a church was associated with the characteristics of night and cold, whereas the south of a church was viewed as the region of warmth and light.[5] In its liturgical associations, wall paintings and stained glass, the north part of a church was often given over to symbolism of the Old Testament, in contrast to the New Testament association of the south.[6] The observation of opposite attributes included a symbolism of the sun and moon, based on classical representations of pagan sun gods and personified as male and female respectively.[7] Augustine formed the view that the sun and moon symbolised the prefigurative relationship between the Old Testament (moon) and New Testament (sun).

A correlation appears to have developed for north/moon/female/Old Testament and south/sun/male/New Testament. It may be significant that the Old Testament abounds with female metaphors, such as God the mother and the Wisdom of God as a feminine principle, whereas female imagery is absent from the New Testament.[8] Could this symbolism of opposites and philosophy of duality have been reflected through a monastic architecture of mirror imagery? The inconsistency of the north cloister orientation, representing only 29 per cent of the total sample, suggests that a more subtle and specific meaning may have been intended.

Iconographic Architecture: The Passion of Mary and the Queen of Heaven

In the context of ecclesiastical building the north cloister nunnery may have had a special religious significance. As an architectural image the north cloister symbolised an idea. The iconographic analysis of religious architecture deals with the message contained within a structure's design. It presupposes a contemporary familiarity with specific themes or concepts as transmitted through written sources or oral tradition. The cloister orientation may be studied according to Krautheimer's approach to the iconography of medieval architecture.[9] This method is based on the premise that geometrical forms were reproduced in order to signal a particular conceptual content. The symbolic subject matter of medieval religious architecture is understood to have operated at two distinct levels. Original construction of a building would be influenced by the symbolic content intended by the designer – as something which accompanied the particular form chosen for the structure. After its construction, a level of symbolism would be imposed on the building by its observers.

To the medieval mind the dedication of a religious building was of paramount significance. The dedications of the churches associated with the north and south cloister groups can be divided into three groups: single dedications to Mary, single or joint dedications to female saints and single or joint dedications in honour of male saints. A larger percentage of the north cloister group were dedicated to female saints (29.4 per cent) than to male saints (23.5 per cent), whereas a larger proportion of the south cloister churches were dedicated to male saints (28 per cent) than to female saints (18.2 per cent).

There is some evidence to indicate that the north/south: female/male association was present in early medieval communal church worship. From Cogitosus' account of the church at Kildare, which describes a nave bisected into a northern half for the women, and a southern half for the men, and Alcuin's instructions for the proper positioning for the reception of the Eucharist, 'men in the Southern part, women in the Northern part',[10] it seems that the distinction may have been related to Eucharistic liturgy. The developing late medieval connotations of female/north can be examined in terms of Eucharistic imagery.

Bynum has noted the iconographic association of female saints with the Eucharist. A particular correlation has been observed between Eucharistic iconography and St. Barbara, between fasting and Mary Magdalene and between the Virgin Mary and tabernacles associated with consecration and incarnation. Cistercian monastic tradition associated Mary with the sacrament through a superimposition of the moment of consecration and the Annunciation.[11] Park has commented on the Eucharist significance of certain thematic wall paintings, especially of the Crucifixion.[12] Elsewhere he has noted the relevance of the Crucifixion and Resurrection for thematic iconography associated with the north transept area of churches.[13] Easter liturgy, sepulchres, and Holy Sepulchre chapels received an appropriate northern location.

The writings of medieval religious men and women have been studied by Bynum in order to assess the nature of Eucharistic piety. She has identified a particular Eucharistic emphasis in thirteenth century female devotion and provided two possible interpretations.[14] Bynum's earlier work defines women's eucharistic concern as an aspect of active female agency in which women emphasise the reception and adoration of the eucharist as a 'substitute for clerical experience'. In this scenario female religious compensate for their clerical impotency by savouring the Eucharist as the only repeatable and controllable moment of union with God. In her later interpretation, Bynum concentrates on a medieval female understanding of the Eucharist as food.[15] She argues that medieval cultural stereotyping linked women with food – as a resource controlled by women through food asceticism, charitable distribution, and food-related miracles. In the Mass a symbolic reversal was achieved whereby the male priest prepared and presented Christ as food to the female recipients.

It is important to determine whether the correlation of female worship with the Eucharist and the northern regions of churches was a product of passive or active female piety. Bynum's interpretations place emphasis on female action in constructing alternative strategies of belief. The very fact that the correlation can be detected in nunnery planning, however, suggests that it was to some extent a mainstream interpretation verified by patrons and designers. Whether the cloister iconography represented passive or active female piety, that is whether it was instructive or reflective of belief, can be tested across the spectrum of contemporary ecclesiastical imagery. The surviving liturgical evidence for English nunneries is a processional associated with the Benedictine nunnery at Chester.[16] This fifteenth-century text gives an account of the nuns' service for Palm Sunday. The priest and chanters begin while the nuns exit the quire. An anthem is said from outside the church door. They proceed singing, with the 'prestes before theym' to the high cross in the churchyard. A deacon reads a gospel while they stand 'on the northe halff' of the high cross. At this south cloister nunnery the Easter liturgy incorporated a location described as north of the crucifixional symbol. The suggested correlation of north/Easter/female saints was also expressed outside of specifically female architectural milieux. The twelfth and thirteenth century wall paintings in Winchester's Holy Sepulchre Chapel, for example, devote great prominence to the crowned Virgin in scenes appropriate to Easter/north contexts.[17]

The possible Eucharistic and Crucifixional association of the northern areas of churches may relate directly to the most basic level of the iconography of church architecture. The cruciform, or cross-shaped, ground plan was the image of Christ crucified. His head was represented by the chancel and the transepts were his hands. The Crucifixion image was the principal theme in Christian art from the ninth century.[18] Western monumental art and manuscript illuminations portrayed the Virgin Mary and John the Evangelist flanking the cross in reference to a passage from John (19:26–27), 'Jesus saw his mother, with the disciple whom he loved standing beside her.'

When translated to the format of the cruciform church building, the traditional position of the figure of the Virgin Mary was at Christ's right hand, i.e. the northern region of the church. It has been suggested that the figures beneath the cross were part of an artistic tradition of right/left symbolism of the sun and moon.[19] In this sense the iconography of the

Crucifixion corresponds with the opposition north/moon/female/Old Testament and south/sun/male/New Testament. English manuscript illuminations respected these oppositions from as early as the eleventh century. This is demonstrated by the Crucifixion illumination in the Judith of Flanders Gospels, dated to the second quarter of the eleventh century, which depicts the veiled face of the moon and the Virgin to Christ's right and the veiled sun and John the Evangelist to his left.[20] Further insight is given by the Virgin's gesture in the scene. She is shown wiping the wound in Christ's right side (the northern region of a cruciform building). The wound was said to have issued blood and water, so that it came to represent the Eucharist and Baptism.[21]

According to the iconography of the cruciform building, therefore, the association of the north transept area with the Crucifixion and Eucharist must relate to the wound. In the iconography of the Passion Cycle the Virgin Mary was portrayed tending the wound, which itself came to symbolise the birth of the Church, the 'Bride of Christ', from the wounded side of the dying Christ.[22] In late medieval imagery the Virgin came to represent both the Bride of Christ and the personification of the Church.[23] Is it possible, then, that the northern parts of churches were associated not only with female saints and female worship in general, but more specifically with the Virgin Mary at Christ's right hand?

The New Testament yielded little evidence for the life of the Virgin. Old Testament themes were borrowed instead for Marian devotion as early as the fourth century.[24] Israel's personification as the Bride of Yahweh in the Covenant, for example, could be taken to refer to Mary as the Bride of Christ. Equally the image of Sophia was pertinent to Mary (Sir. 14:20–15:8; Wis. 8:2): 'She is the Wisdom of God, the daughter of Yahweh, who sits at his right hand is is the mediatrix of all redeeming knowledge.' The iconography associated with the Marian cycle was derived either from the apocryphal texts of pseudo-Melito and pseudo-Matthew, or from Old Testament events which were thought to foreshadow Mary's life. This juxtaposition of Old and New Testament, or 'type' and 'antitype', is particularly relevant to the last scene in the cycle of the Virgin – her coronation. The Old Testament type for the episode refers to Solomon (1 Kings 2:19): 'And the king rose up to meet her, and bowed himself unto her, and sat down on his throne, and caused a seat to be set for the king's mother, and she sat on his right hand.' These types are in keeping with the Old Testament associations of the northern parts of the churches in general. The image of Mary on Christ's right hand is consistent with her positioning in Crucifixion and Coronation scenes contemporary to the north cloister constructions. Her association with the north transept area, therefore, might have accompanied the basic iconography of the cruciform plan.

It would be difficult to estimate which aspect of Marian symbolism, either the Passion or the Coronation, was most significant to the designers and observers of the north cloister nunneries. It is certain, however, that Marian symbolism was prevalent in English monastic contexts long before the cult's explosion of popularity in the thirteenth century. A nimbed, seated Mary and Child were engraved on the late seventh-century coffin of St. Cuthbert.[25] An Annunciation scene is clearly depicted in the first two panels of the mid-ninth-century Hovingham slab. Tenth-century Winchester manuscripts, benedictionals associated with Bishop Aethelwold (971–984) and Robert of Jumieges c.980, portray the Assumption of the crowned Virgin.[26] In late Anglo-Saxon England the cult of the Virgin may thus have been principally monastic and high status, but not necessarily linked to female piety.

The Coronation of the Virgin made an early appearance in English iconographic media. It predated the French 'Triumph' of the Virgin on the Senlis Tympanum (c.1170) and is said to portray Mary in a more passive posture in which she is crowned by Christ instead of being seated in equal majesty.[27] Zarnecki identified the origins of the Coronation in English art to the Winchester illuminations of the Assumption.[28] Our earliest surviving representation in plastic media is the Coronation on a capital from Reading Abbey of c.1130. Its inspirational source was perhaps shared by the first parochial rendering of the theme in the Coronation Tympanum at Quenington Church, Glos., c.1150. The appearance of the Coronation of the Virgin in monumental art certainly coincides with the densest chronological group of north cloister nunneries, c.1130–55, representing half of the sample.

The iconographic and liturgical implications of the Crucifixion and the popularity and chronological suitability of the Coronation suggest that the patrons and designers of the north cloister nunneries may have been alluding to either theme. The first level of the iconography of medieval nunneries, that of the symbolism intended in their construction, may have referred to a collage of female worship and Marian devotion. The second level of symbolic subject matter, that imposed on the building by its observers, may be examined through contemporary iconography and mystic literature.

From the north cloister nunnery of Barking, a Rood screen of the late twelfth to early thirteenth century survives.[29] The scene depicted on the screen is still clear and consists of the Crucifixion flanked by the figures of the Virgin to Christ's right and John the Evangelist to his left. Details of the internal fittings of a north cloister church can be extrapolated from the surviving Dissolution inventory of Minster in Sheppey.[30] In the upper part of the quire 'a cross of silver and gilt with the Crucifix, Mary and John' was recorded. Before the Rood over the high altar was a painted cloth of the

Resurrection, and in the 'nether part of the quire' were alabaster and painted 'images of our Ladye'. From both surviving and recorded icono-graphy it is possible to recognise the north-centred themes of the Crucifixion/Ressurection and Marian devotion.

Petroff has noted a consistency in the writings of twelfth-century female mystics (including the English Christina of Markyate) to visualise Mary in her role as queen of heaven,[31] 'they now see the whole of heaven, all neatly and hierarchically arranged, with two equal thrones in the most important position and they witness the crowning of the Virgin over her triple kingdom of heaven, hell, and earth.' We have no evidence for the imagery prevalent in the liturgy of twelfth- and thirteenth-century English nunneries. From the sixteenth-century Bridgettine text 'The Myroure of Our Ladye', however, we find a woodcut of the Coronation of the Virgin accompanies the Masses.[32] Phrases in praise of the Virgin refer to her as 'Thou that syttest at the righte syde of the fader', 'the meke mother whose trone is in heuen' and 'quienne of heuen'.

Royal foundations account for 23.5 per cent of the north cloister nunneries (4:17) in contrast to 12 per cent of the south cloister type (5:41). Warner has suggested that the image of a crowned Mary as queen of heaven would assist in ratifying the secular hierarchical order.[33] This imagery justified medieval kingship as divinely approved and 'the honour payed Mary as queen redounded to the honour of queens'. Coronation imagery may indeed have appealed to royal patrons of nunneries and a crowned Mary on Christ's right hand may have provided an appropriate scene for royal or highly born novices and nuns to contemplate. It may not be possible to recover the specific symbolism intended by patrons and designers. The imagery prevalent during the life of a nunnery, however, may have been reflected in the iconography of its seal.

Nunnery Seals: 'Blessed Art Thou Among Women'

Monastic seals were distinctive marks used by a house in closing and authenticating agreements. Seals in general were never an innovative medium since the image had to be immediately understandable within a pre-existing vocabulary.[34] During the twelfth century, historical and allegorical narratives became popular topics for iconographic seals.[35] The topic chosen for representation reflected the dedication of the church and the image of authority chosen to represent the house. It has been possible to tabulate the iconography of 135 nunnery seals spanning the twelfth to sixteenth centuries. There is some evidence to suggest that the nunneries formed a distinct group, outside of filial unities, in their usage of seals. In their choice of iconographic themes the nunneries can be understood in terms of chronology and status.

Relatively few of the seals are devoted to the imagery of Christ (N = 14 or 10.3 per cent). Houses dedicated to patron saints, rather than to the Virgin, frequently depicted the patron on the conventual seal. These are mainly Benedictine houses and make up 18.5 per cent of the sample (N = 25). Over half of the seals relate to the life of the Virgin. To some extent their imagery follows general chronological patterns in the iconography of Mary. Some of the twelfth-century seals depict the Virgin alone, either enthroned (N = 5) or standing (N = 3). By far the largest group (N = 48) display the crowned Virgin enthroned with the child resting on her left knee. This particular image, the 'Throne of Wisdom', was the most familiar twelfth-century portrayal of the Virgin. Her Romanesque treatment was as an hieratic icon – to inspire worship and awe.[36] From the thirteenth century the Gothic images which dominate Marian iconography were of the Virgin standing with the Child in her arms or the Coronation of the Virgin. The nunnery seals responded to the transition from Romanesque to Gothic to a small degree. Six seals, dating from the thirteenth to fifteenth centuries, portray the standing Virgin with Child. The eight Coronation seals all date from the thirteenth to sixteenth centuries. The popularity of the 'Throne of Wisdom', however, never waned. It was maintained as the major symbol of conventual and prioress' seals right up to the sixteenth century. Its usage spanned filiation, status, geographical and temporal space.

Gold interprets the 'Throne of Wisdom' as a statement of Christ's humanity and divinity through the Incarnation.[37] Mary's role in the scene is as a mother within the context of the Infancy cycle – not within the Marian cycle. Similarly the five seals depicting the Annunciation illustrate Mary in reference to Christ's birth. Only the Coronation seals indicate devotion to Mary in her own right. Only two of the sample of eight Coronation seals came from north cloister houses. But all of these houses did indeed have royal affiliations, thus confirming the significance of the Coronation image to royal patrons, abbesses and prioresses. The imagery pertinent to this group of houses can be explored further through surviving manuscript illuminations. The Shaftesbury Psalter (c.1130–40) and the Amesbury Psalter (c.1250–5) derive from houses which adopted Coronation seals.[38] They contain eight and four full page miniatures, respectively, in which the imagery of the Virgin can be examined. The earlier of the two Psalters, from Shaftesbury, exhibits the familiar Romanesque image of the enthroned Virgin and Child with an abbess kneeling at her feet. The Gothic Amesbury Psalter depicts the seated Virgin suckling the Child with a nun kneeling to her right. In both Psalters Marian imagery of motherhood predominates. Coronation imagery is absent.

In considering the role of female agency in the symbolism of nunnery seals it is necessary to ask how medieval nuns would have related to the various images of Mary. Gold has suggested that the Gothic images of the Coronation and standing Virgin with Child acted as models for female virtue.[39] Religious women would have identified with the attributes of humility and submission embodied by the Coronation and the aspects of tender motherhood demonstrated in the standing figures. The Romanesque seated Virgin and Child was a portrayal of Mary's singularity – her perfection that set her apart from all other women. This hieratic image recalled Elizabeth's words to Mary: 'Blessed art thou among women and blessed is the fruit of thy womb' (Luke 1:42).

The consistent popularity of this image on the nunnery seals, in addition to the maternal imagery of the illuminations, may suggest that it was in her unique position as Virgin mother that the nuns celebrated Mary. The seals from north cloister nunneries show no awareness of a Marian iconography linked to the Crucifixion or Coronation. If this symbolism was intended it was by the patrons or designers of nunnery architecture. Its connotations were not maintained throughout the 300–400 years of a nunnery's occupation. It has been suggested elsewhere that female and Marian imagery was actually more attractive to religious men than women.[40] It seems that Marian iconography was chosen as a suitable theme by those who commissioned nunnery architecture. The north cloister nunneries had a higher proportion of male founders (70.6 per cent) than the south cloisters (63.4 per cent) and a considerably lower proportion of female founders (11.8 per cent) than the south cloisters (21.9 per cent); the remainder were houses founded jointly by men and women. The iconography of the north cloister nunnery was a product of passive, instructive piety, not of active, reflective piety.

North Transept Imagery – the Web of Meanings

The association of female symbolism with the northern regions of churches could be a product of the following factors:

1. A series of structural oppositions intrinsic to Christian art which followed Classical traditions and maintained a duality between north/south, female/male, moon/sun, and Old Testament/New Testament.

2. An early medieval practice, perhaps originating in Judaism, for the segregation of men and women during communal church worship in which women receive the Eucharist in the north of the church.

3. A by-product of the iconography of the cruciform church building in which the Virgin Mary was associated with the north transept due to her

position flanking the cross, her tending of the Eucharistic wound and her personification as the Church and Bride of Christ.

4. An architectural rendering of the Coronation of the Virgin contemporary to the theme's appearance in other media and particularly appropriate to the higher proportion of royal houses in the north cloister sample.

In conclusion, the north cloister orientation may reflect an imprecise web of meanings which linked female worship, symbolism, and Mariology and signalled female piety to certain social groups, in particular high status or royal males. As a form of passive female piety, nunnery architecture simultaneously reflected belief and actively constructed and renegotiated belief. The nunneries themselves retained maternal imagery in their seals and illuminations alternative to the Marian architecture commissioned for them.

Notes

1   An extended version of this paper forms a chapter in my 'The Archaeology of Female Piety' (unpublished D.Phil. thesis, University of York, 1990).
2   R. Gilchrist, 'The Spatial Archaeology of Gender domains: A Case Study of Medieval English Nunneries', *Archaeological Review from Cambridge* 7 (1988), pp. 21–8; R. Gilchrist, 'The Archaeology of Medieval English Nunneries: a Research Design', *The Archaeology of Rural Monasteries* (British Archaeological Report 203, Oxford, 1989), pp. 251–60.
3   W. Brown, 'Descriptions of the Buildings of Twelve Small Yorkshire Priories at the Reformation', *Yorkshire Archaeological Journal* 9 (1886), pp. 197–215.
4   R.R. Ruether, 'Misogynism and Virginal Feminism in the Fathers of the Church', *Images of Women in the Jewish and Christian Traditions*, ed. R.R. Ruether (New York, 1976), p. 156.
5   G. Ferguson, *Signs and Symbols in Christian Art* (Oxford, 1966), pp. 43–4.
6   P.A. Bucknell, *Entertainment and Ritual* (1979), p. 29; Ferguson, *Signs and Symbols*, p. 44.
7   J. Hall, *A Dictionary of Subjects and Symbols in Christian Art* (1974), p. 86.
8   C.W. Bynum, *Jesus as Mother, Studies in the Spirituality of the High Middle Ages* (Berkeley, 1982), p. 125.
9   R. Krautheimer, 'Introduction to an Iconography of Medieval Architecture', *Journal of the Warbourg and Courtauld Institutes* 5 (1942), pp. 1–33.
10 Alcuin, *De Offic. lib.* iii, cii.
11 C.W. Bynum, *Holy Feast and Holy Fast: The Religious Significance of Food to Medieval Women* (Berkeley, 1987), p. 81.
12 D. Park, 'Wall Painting', in *Age of Chivalry, Art in Plantagenet England, 1200–1400*, ed. J. Alexander and P. Binski (1987), p. 313.
13 D. Park. 'The Wall Paintings of the Holy Sepulchre Chapel', *Medieval Art and Architecture at Winchester Cathedral*, The British Architectural Association Conference Proceedings 6 (1983), p. 50, n.105.
14 Bynum, *Jesus as Mother*, p. 256.
15 Bynum, *Holy Feast and Holy Fast*, p. 277.

16 J.W. Legg, 'The Processional of the Nuns of Chester', *Henry Bradshaw Society* 18 (1899).
17 Park, 'Holy Sepulchre Chapel', p. 45.
18 G. Schiller, *The Iconography of Christian Art ii. The Passion of Christ* (1972), p. 99.
19 Ibid., p. 109.
20 T.H. Ohlgren, *Insular and Anglo-Saxon Illustrated Manuscripts* (1986), pp. 257–8.
21 Hall, *Dictionary of Subjects and Symbols*, p. 85.
22 A.M. Lucas, *Women in the Middle Ages* (1983), p. 7.
23 Hall, *Dictionary of Subjects and Symbols*, p. 75.
24 Ruether, 'Misogynism and Virginal Feminism', p. 178.
25 H. Mayr-Harting, *The Coming of Christianity to Anglo-Saxon England* (1972), pl. 14.
26 M. Clayton, 'Aspects of the Cult of the Virgin in Late Anglo-Saxon England', (unpublished paper presented to the *Fontes Anglo-Saxonici*, Leeds, 1988), pp. 13–14.
27 P.S. Gold, *The Lady and the Virgin: Image, Attitude and Experience in Twelfth Century France* (Chicago, 1985), p. 53.
28 G. Zarnecki, 'The Coronation of the Virgin on a Capital from Reading Abbey', *Journal of the Warbourg and Courtauld Institutes* 13 (1950), p. 12.
29 *Royal Commission on Historical Monuments: Essex ii* (1921), p. 9.
30 E.C. Walcott, 'The Priory of Minster in Sheppey', *Archaeologia Cantiana* 7 (1868), pp. 287–306.
31 E.A. Petroff, *Medieval Women's Visionary Literature* (1986), p. 19.
32 *The Myroure of Oure Ladye*, ed., J. Blunt, EETS, extra ser., 19 (1873), pp. 293, 297, 308.
33 M. Warner, *Alone of all Her Sex* (1976), p. 104.
34 T.A. Heslop, 'English Seals in the Thirteenth and Fourteenth Centuries', in *Age of Chivalry*, ed. Alexander and Binski, p. 116.
35 T.A. Heslop, 'Seals', in *English Romanesque Art 1066–1200*, ed. G. Zarnecki, J. Holt and T. Holland (1984), p. 299.
36 Gold, *Lady and the Virgin*, p. 67.
37 Ibid., p. 49.
38 C.M. Kauffmann, *Romanesque Manuscripts 1066–1200* (1975), p. 82; N. Morgan, *Early Gothic Manuscripts 2 1250–85* (1988), p. 59.
39 Gold, *Lady and the Virgin*, p. 72.
40 Bynum, *Jesus as Mother*, p. 141.

Index